RAISED BED
FOR BEGINNERS

THE ULTIMATE STEP BY STEP GUIDE.
HOMEGROWN HERBS- VEGETABLES-
PLANTS. SUSTAINABLE, HEALTHY AND
ORGANIC TECHNIQUES

MICHAEL SQUARE

TABLE OF CONTENTS

Introduction

Raised beds can be best described as a form of a garden, constructed above the natural terrain. In raised bed gardening, the soil is usually formed in 3 to 4 feet wide beds bearing any size or shape. The ground is generally enclosed within a frame, typically made of rock, wood, or blocks of concrete.

Raised-bed gardening is a type of gardening on which the soil is fashioned in three to four-foot-wide (1.0-1.2 m) beds. These beds are constructed above the natural terrain. The beds can be of any shape or length. The formed soil is raised on top of the surrounding soil (about six inches to waist-high), and sometimes, it is enclosed by a frame usually made of rock, wood, or concrete blocks, and may be enhanced with compost.

You don't have to worry about your raised beds being infiltrated by certain "obnoxious" grass or tree roots (an aspect not typically seen in your average vegetable gardens) - this because the soil used in raised bed gardening warms up faster during spring. In addition, the elevated position of raised beds prevents weed seeds from blowing into the garden soil.

Basically, raised beds have some distinctive advantages over other forms of gardening:

- Less digging is required.

- Raised beds are heated better by the sun.

- Much easier weeding.

- Much easier to provide root crops such as potatoes, with the necessary room to grow.

- Better drainage, which means you don't have to worry about the plants being damaged due to residual water. This is the reason why plants grown in raised bed gardens suffer less from root rot diseases.

- Replenishing soil in raised bed gardening is comparatively much easier, you don't have to worry about nematodes and diseases. Any depleted soil can be promptly removed and replaced.

- It helps you save on resources. For example, you don't have to use fertilizer throughout the entire garden. Instead you apply them to the beds only.

- Foot traffic won't do any harm to the plants.

- Raised bed gardening is easy to learn - even if you are just getting started.

A raised bed garden is essential for anyone who wants to create a more complex agricultural system designed to be more space efficient and to produce the most yields. It is a proven, tried and tested method for raising production level and quality, allow gardening efficiency in small spaces; and it even saves time and money. It even allows itself to be more efficient for using soil known for being difficult to work with, such as clay.

Like its name suggests, raised-bed gardening implies that the structure where you are planting your garden in is raised off ground level. The structure, typically made of 2x4' box crates without bottoms which are filled with mounded soil and walled around with the structure. The great thing about it is that you can easily grow any vegetable on raised garden beds, as well herbs or annual or perennial blooms and shrubs.

Typically, experienced gardeners use this gardening method to avoid the numerous challenges surrounding seasonal gardening. But this doesn't mean novice gardeners should not attempt to employ this gardening technique as they make their way into the wonderful world of gardening.

The key to raised bed gardening is to ensure that you use good soil. So much so that you need to use customized soil and compost blend to ensure the success of your garden. Drainage is also an important part of gardening on raised beds and should be built into your bed structure or walls, ensuring that the soil is in place despite being able to easily drain it of excess water. Plants can be spaced closer together to make sure your production of harvests go up, and this also means efficiency when it comes to watering your garden.

Because raised bed gardening is usually used to grow edible plants, be very careful of the kind of materials you use. For instance, if you use wood that has been treated with toxins or railroad ties, this might seep its way into your vegetables and herbs. Instead, experienced gardeners use cedar wood or eco-friendly lumber.

So, we are here to tackle the most effective way to succeed in raised bed gardening. Let's start!

Chapter 1- Overview of Raised Bed Gardening

Veggies give crucial nourishment into your body and are a portion of the healthy diet plan and way of life. Specific veggies might be eaten uncooked -- just as salads whereas some others will need to get cooked. Any way we have veggies, they are all very yummy and offer enormous health advantages.

It is far more satisfying to raise your veggies and use them in your ordinary cooking! Homegrown veggies maybe not just taste delicious but are even fitter compared to the crops that are commercially grown. If you are health-conscious, absolutely nothing works a lot better than the usual full bowl of freshly prepared salad out of homegrown plants and herbs.

Plants could be Perennial, Annual, or Biennial. Perennial crops endure for at least a couple of decades ago. Annual vegetation germinate blossom and perish within a season or two over this entire year.

Biennial vegetation requires a long time to finish their entire life span.

Listing of Vegetables Can Be Grown Indoors Productively

Salad greens

Spinach -- germination period is just 6 to 12 times; is now just a winter season annual harvest water-cress -- seed germination does occur in seven to fourteen times; is now really a continuing harvest Arugula -- germinates per week; is the two continuing and yearly Mustard -- germinates in 5 to ten times; special seed species predominate every day! Lettuce -- requires 2 weeks to germinate; is still a temperate yearly or biennial.

Herbs

Dill -- germinates at per week period; is still a Yearly pill Coriander -- germination period is generally ten times; is now a Yearly herb Basil -- germinates in 6 to Ten times; is still a Yearly herb Chamomile -- seed germination period is 7 to 14 times; is continuing but increased since yearly Steak -- needs Fortnight or longer to its first g to seem; is continuing Mint -- germination period 7 to Fortnight; is continuing Tarragon -- germinates in 7 to 14 times; you Are Unable to increase French Tarragon out of seeds Sage -- germinates at a Couple of months; backyard blossom or common blossom is continuing Thyme -- may endure 3 to 4 months and occasionally over per month; will be continuing.

Plant mixtures

If you intend to cultivate more than one harvest at one moment, then there are distinct mixes you may like to abide by along with Distinct plants possess similar demands nutrient conditions, germination period, progress phases, etc. Growing this sort of plant together might assist you to produce plants of far better quality and amount.

Here's a list of plants which possess similar demands:

Tomatoes

Tomatoes are the absolute most widely used vegetable in this type of gardening. Most commercially developed berries belong to the indeterminate type. In the event you would like to cultivate smaller berries to fit your area needs, then decide on seeds so.

Tomatoes ripen in just about any type of Raised Bed technique; however, a Drip process would be your very best. Seed germination period is just 3 to 6 weeks; also, it'll simply take one hundred days until you may realize your tomato crops endure veggies; however, they often persist in creating veggies for your year. Similar plants: Peppers and Cucumbers.

Lettuce

An All-Time favored amongst Raised Bed farmers. Leaf lettuce can be a far greater choice compared to thoughts carrot.

Nutrient Film process might be your optimal/optimally strategy to cultivate Lettuce; otherwise, you might even increase it into an Ebb and circulation or trickle system.

Lettuce seeds germinate in 4 weeks to 2 days also certainly will be chosen at 3-5 to 4-5 times, so to keep up a constant source of seed, lettuce them just about every day or two.

Similar plants: Spinach, Basil, and foliage plants.

Carrots

Carrot can be an origin crop that grows nicely in Perlite; thus, will almost any additional origin harvest such as radish and beets.

Roots crops take a huge expansion mattress to raise and acquire totally. It requires about 6 to ten weeks to allow its seeds germinate and 2.5 to a couple of weeks to crop. Other similar plants: Beets, Leeks, Radish.

Cucumber

Cucumbers are long-lasting plants and keep steadily to give up fruits to a few weeks. European cinema types are simpler to cultivate in raised beds. Cucumbers need to have considerable distance and encouragement to cultivate.

Basil

Basil is an herb that develops involving 12 to 18 inches tall. Buds and blossoms must be pruned frequently to motivate continuing development.

It requires about 6 to ten weeks to its Basil seeds to germinate and certainly will create refreshing leaves for three weeks to 4 weeks. After three weeks to 4 weeks, the older chamomile plant must have been substituted using a fresh 1.

Similar plants: Spinach and Lettuce

Beans

You can harvest substantial returns from bean blossoms. An Ebb and Flow process works nicely with Perlite or expanded clay pellets. Seed germination normally takes about 3 to 2 days; also, you may begin harvesting within six weeks to fourteen days. You may keep on opting for three days to 4 weeks.

Peppers

Peppers can be found in the number of colors and tastes. You may grow both equally sweet and hot peppers. Use a trickle machine or an Ebb and Flow process to cultivate those veggies. Pepper vegetation expands tall -- with an increasing content that gives the essential service is necessary; you may use rock-wool for seed germination and after use Perlite blended with Vermiculite and nice gravel.

It requires 10 to fourteen weeks for seed germination, and you'll be able to harvest from the 4th calendar month.

Other similar plants: Tomatoes and Cucumbers.

Spinach

Spinach develops nicely within an NFT Process or an Ebb and Flow Technique. You may use rock-wool for seed germination; maintenance must be chosen to present enough escalating distance for all these plants differently you hazard racking them. The common space enabled between 2 vegetation is 20 sq. Inches.

Seed germination takes 6 to 1-2 weeks, and the very first crop begins just from the conclusion of 2nd calendar month (approx. fifty to sixty times).

Other similar plants: Basil, Lettuce.

Why choosing raised bed

1.   Easy to assemble. Building a raised bed garden isn't hard to do and it is even easier if you buy it in a kit form because it involves the sourcing of materials, measuring and cutting to size out of the equation; therefore, the kit saves time and limits

waste. The raised beds can be built out of wooden, sleepers or corrugated sheeting. The steel raised beds come in a flat package and they don't take long to assemble. They are also long-lasting, durable, strong, and termite resistant.

2. Making use of raised beds saves you the stress of having to till up your soil from year to year to get fertilizer added. The raised beds can easily be maintained by adding materials such as mulches, manures, compost and other soil materials from the top. The raised beds have a way of getting their tilling done themselves since roots and worms can easily push their way through the soil themselves.

3. The pathways created by the raised beds make it easier to maintain because of the definitive line between the path and the bed.

4. Weeding a large area of land can lead to knee and back strain as well as exhausting a large amount of your time. Making use of the raised beds saves you a lot of stress and the back pain that might come up from bending to weed.

5. Due to the smaller amount of space with which the raised bed garden is built, they are more easily nurtured. This will in turn help with good aeration, reduced soil compaction as well as fewer weeds and pests. Once you have all these, you can be sure of having more vegetation being produced from the raised garden.

6. The raised beds can be created with wire mesh below them so that they can be easily moved around for sunlight. This is also beneficial to crop rotation practice.

7. With less compaction of dirt, your soil will get drained easily. Using the raised beds enables moisture to move around and get drained when the needs arise. This will, in turn, provide healthier plants and better production.

8. The problem of pests is something that cannot be entirely avoided when it comes to gardening. Making use of the raised garden hinders pests from getting through to your plants because the beds are positioned above the ground and pests can't jump from plant to plant like they do in a traditional garden. The box helps in creating a barrier, thereby making it difficult for the pests to operate.

9. The use of the raised beds garden protects bulb plants from being feasted upon by squirrels or birds and even from bugs and larger pests.

10. The better aeration and non-compaction of the soil provided by the raised beds help the roots in spreading out more easily.

11. The raised beds work fine for an area where there is a limited growing season. This is because the soil used for raised beds is not part of the ground which enables them to thaw

faster when compared to a traditional garden. This allows you to plant earlier compared to planting into the ground directly.

12.   The raised beds make your garden neater and visibly appealing. They can be made with sitting areas on the sides as well to make it easy to perform most of your farming activity.

13.   The use of a raised bed garden provides you with more options in terms of how large or small you want them to be. This is not possible with traditional gardens because creating the desired plot size can be quite difficult. As for the raised bed garden, you have more flexibility to build your garden based on your taste.

14.   The raised beds are comfortable physically and logistically. There is less room for weeds to grow and less time required to protect your garden from unwanted weeds.

Chapter 2: Planning and Building Your Garden

Basic designs of raised garden beds

1.   Built-In Raised Beds

2. Sheet Metal Raised Beds

3. Square Foot Raised Beds

4.   An Herb Spiral

5.   Hoop House Raised Bed

6.   Raised Bed Border

7.   Trough Gardens

8.   Tiered Raised Bed

9.   Show Off Your Container Collection

10. Custom Design Raised Beds for Your Space

Best materials for your raised beds

Choose a material that is durable and resistant to rotting. Cedar planks would be your best option, as well as your most common, but Vermont white cedar, yellow cedar, Juniper and Redwood are also great options.

What size to make it

It really depends on how big or small you want it to be. Typically, raised garden beds are built around a foot tall to up to around three feet. If you want to go taller, note that the weight of the soil will add pressure to your entire structure. As such, you should make sure that the entire structure supports the weight of the soil via cross-supports.

Generally, however, beds should not be made wider than four feet across, so that you can easily access each side of the garden.

How deep should the soil be? —

Depending on the kind of plants that you want to grow in your garden, you must determine how deep your soil should be to ensure that the roots will have enough room to grow.

What tools you will need

1.   Wood

•   Use 2x2' boards or planks for the sides

•   Use 4x4' corner posts for support

2.   Fastenings

•   You will need 3.5 inch #10 coated screws—6 screws for each corner and two for each mid-span post.

3.   Cross supports

•   Use ½ inch aluminum flat stock

4.   Tools

•   Hand saw

- Square

- Carpenter's level

- Mallet

- Screwdriver

- Hacksaw

- Drill

Putting it all together

Step 1:

Using your square, mark the ends and saw the boards according to your desired length. Place a couple of screws in each corner to keep the boards in place temporarily. Place it on a flat or level surface and do this for both the ends and the sides.

Step 2:

Cut the post pieces a little longer than your intended size. Set the first post into the corner and drive the post into the ground until it is anchored and steady. Screw the frame into the post using around two screws per side to secure. Set the other posts in place using the same procedure.

Step 3:

Secure the bottom row of the boards—this will be almost at ground level—by screwing the boards into the posts. Use the hand saw to remove any wood that is sticking out.

Step 4:

If your raised garden bed is higher than 8 feet, be sure to attach cross bracing to secure your raised bed. Drill a hole on each end of the wood and use a 1" screw to attach it to the posts on each side of the span.

Big Garden Bed or Small Garden Bed: Which is Better?

When it comes to size, we need to consider width and height primarily. Length is going to be determined by how much space is available in the garden. You could have a raised garden bed that goes on forever (if you had the space). This infinite bed could produce quite well if it had enough height for the roots of the plants and small enough width for you to be able to check and tend to each plant. Length doesn't need to factor into considerations of size and so we can toss any concerns about that variable out the window.

Left with width and height, we can start to address the question of whether it is better to be big or small. The best answer to this question is: "either." The real problem in size doesn't come from being big or being small but from being too big or too small. With size, the problem areas are on either end of the size chart (tiny or huge) but the middle part of that chart (small or big) is a perfect fit for your raised garden bed. Let's start with width.

If your raised garden bed isn't wide enough then you may not have any space to grow your plants. It is easy to look at a garden bed with a tiny width and know that your plants won't fit and so this isn't a problem that most gardeners run into. The more common issue is to have too wide of a raised garden bed. This is the gardening equivalent of the adage, "eyes bigger than your stomach." While the equation "more room = more plants" is technically true, what this leaves out is the fact that you are still required to tend to those plants. If there is too much space for you to reach over, then you aren't going to be able to get at the plants in the middle of a wide raised bed. This leads to mistreated plants and signs of sickness or infestation going unnoticed until it is too late. So how do we go about making sure that our raised beds aren't too wide?

The best rule of thumb is to make them no wider than four feet across if you have access to each of the sides. If you have a garden bed with a side that you can't get to, because it up against your house for example, then you should knock a foot off that. If you go over this size, you may not have problems getting to the plants in the middle while everything is still just a seedling. But once their foliage really starts to come in and the bed fills out, suddenly is it much harder to get to those tricky-to-reach plants. Keep in mind, this number is an average based on the height and reach of most people. If you are shorter then you should knock half a foot off your width. Taller gardeners can get away with adding a little to the width, but this could be an issue if you need to go away and get someone to watch over your garden.

Height is an easier calculation to make. The average height for a raised bed is between half a foot to three feet tall. However, as we are primarily discussing beds with a bottom, we should stick to at least a foot in height. The taller a bed is, the more soil you have added to it. The roots of your plants are going to spread out in that soil and search for nutrients. A smaller bed in the half a foot range would need to use a mesh bottom in order to prevent critters from accessing your garden from below while also providing the roots access to the natural soil beneath. A small raised bed of this height is going to contradict some of the benefits such as reducing pests or weeds and avoiding contaminated soil. So, what we need is a bed high enough that the roots don't run out of space. That's a foot at the minimum. If you are planting lots in the raised bed, then you may want to go even taller.

So, the secret to a perfectly sized raised garden bed is to keep it at least a foot tall and no more than four feet wide. Beyond that, you are free to do as you want. Just remember that more soil equals more pressure on the frame. Speaking of frames...

10 easy DIY ideas for your raised beds

- Potager Raised Bed Design

A raised bed potager shows the arranged, formal design these beds can bring to a setting. Easy wood frames built from rot-resistant lumber supplies years of rising success. Raised beds give themselves to demanding gardening methods such as inter-planting, succession planting, and square-foot gardening.

- Colorful Raised Bed

When raised beds are created with UV stable poly propylene, they saturate a landscape with beautiful color all year-round. Plastic beds supply long life and don't deteriorate like wood can. Just make sure you select materials that are UV stable to put off quick failure by sun exposure. This design also comes with easy interlocking corners.

- Stone Beds Last Forever

Assembled stones provide a long-lived bed edging that doesn't rot regardless of contact with wet soil. Stones might have a formal arrangement, like the stacked slate raised bed. The stone sucks up the heat and discharges it into the soil inside the raised bed, allowing you to plant sooner in spring and let crops grow longer in fail.

- Informal Stone Raise Bed

A casual stone raised bed design showcases individual boulders loaded and fitted to build a foundation for fruitful gardens. This mounded garden shows a form of raised bed also known as hügelkultur. Plants in hügelkultur raised beds attain mature size faster than in traditional planting bed and required very little watering.

- Metal Gives a Modern Look

Metal raised beds blend craftily into a contemporary style landscape. Any metal is long-lasting and carefree, and this product showcases a steel product known as the Zincalume, which endure a long time. It lasts four times as long as galvanized steel. This exact design supplies the beauty of curved edges that makes the hard look corrugated metal become softer.

- Aim High with Beds

Huge raised beds can cause a small yard look larger by inserting vertical interest. Higher beds take the back pain out of plant maintenance that is going on by getting rid of the stopping necessary to tend in-ground beds. While building taller foundations, try to add simple benches that make use of the raised beds as the backrest.

- Grow up in Raised Beds

Use the frame of raised bed to make a construction platform to host a trellis, and you can fill your garden with climbing flowers or foods such as snow peas. The frame of raised best supplies multiple choices for attaching attached items such as a hanging row cover, frost blanket or mesh fencing to frighten animals.

- Box Your Garden

Extra-large red cedar boxes let you build a custom raised bed garden design. Five boxes of different sizes come as part of a set. Assemble the planter boxes in a design that makes good use of your growing region, sunlight or yard shape. Long-lived cedar is rot-resistant, making it a perfect material for raised bed planters.

- A Bed of Straw

With straw bales, build a raised bed that's fully compostable. Straw beds supply a host of benefits to the landscape. They are not costly, and they also provide a temporary bed solution. After the garden season comes to an end, straw bales can simply be used as winter mulch or transformed into laminating material for building a lasagna garden.

- Trolley Garden Bed

Enjoy pain-free gardening with a raised bed that is tall enough to prevent bending while tending. This high trolley garden provides an abundant 12 square feet of expanding area, as well as the deep adequate pocket to house tall crops such as tomatoes. Place shorter plants like leaf lettuce and radishes through bed edges.

Chapter 3: What and When to Plant in Raised Beds

You can grow virtually any vegetable, flower or fruit in your raised bed garden; provided they are suitable to the climate and water in your region.

Before we discuss what type of plants you should ideally include in the garden, let's first have a look at another important factor - plant spacing.

Plant spacing

Proper spacing of the plants is one key factor that can greatly influence the success of your raised bed garden.

Keep in mind that if planted too close together plants will compete for sunlight and are more susceptible to certain leaf disease. Planted too far apart, and you waste precious planting space, water and soil, as well as allowing sun to reach potential weed seeds between your plants.

The following list should give you an idea the space required between plants in your raised beds.

Again, you can go tighter or wider depending on your goals and available space.

3 Inches between plants

- Beets

- Broccoli

- Carrots

- Onion sets

- Radish

- Spinach

- Corn

(By the way, Onion sets are clusters of small onion starts, easier and more effective than starting from seeds)

7 Inches between plants

- Lettuce (small plants)

- Rutabaga

- Shallots

10 Inches between plants

- Kale

- Chard

- Celery

- Lettuce (larger plants)

20 Inches between plants

- Pepper

- Tomato

- Cauliflower

- Cabbage

- Eggplant

30 Inches between plants

- Watermelon

- Squash

- Large Tomato Plants

- Pumpkin

Choosing the right plants

If you are trying to plant vegetables in your new raised bed garden, it is recommended that you start with transplants rather than growing plants from seeds. This is because transplanting usually results in better yields, especially if you are new to gardening. However, if you are still interested in planting from seeds after one or two successful harvesting, make sure to choose only those variants that are naturally immune from common pests and diseases seen in your locality.

Any raised bed designed to plant vegetables can also be used to plant fruits as well. The overall size of the garden and the size covered by existing plants will determine how many fruit bearing trees the garden can comfortably host. There are more than a handful of fruit bearing trees that you can choose to plant. Some of these trees can enhance the landscape beauty and some can provide shade.

When to plant

Deciding when to plant your garden is as important as your soil composition or what your plant.

The best times to plant for North America vary depending on the severity of the winter and the temperature zone in which you live. Visit the Farmer's Almanac to get an idea of which growing region you fall into. Then click on your region for a detailed list of plants and the dates when they should be planted.

There are two main reasons that timing is so important in planting. The first reason it is so important to time your planting correctly is that most plants, especially when they are young, are easily killed by just one night of frost. In northern regions the last frost can be anywhere from March to July, so it is important to know your region.

Many first-time gardeners are so excited to get started that they put plants in the ground too early. They end up losing all their hard-earned produce in one bad freeze. Be patient, know your climate, and don't let that happen to you.

If you just can't wait, you can build a greenhouse, or watch the weather closely, and cover susceptible plants with sheets at night when frost is anticipated. This can be a lot of work and worry, but it can also extend your growing season if you are ambitious.

The second drawback is that the soil might be too wet for planting. If this is the case, you can dig holes and add dry soil to sow your seeds.

In general, lettuce, peas, carrots, onion sets, spinach and even broccoli are your best bets for early planting.

Tomatoes, peppers, melons and pumpkins should wait for warmer dryer weather.

The bottom line

Raised beds usually deliver maximum efficiency if the plants are spaced at a uniform-distance from one-another rather than being organized in rows. The ideal distance should be such that they just touch and form a canopy upon maturing. The most feasible way to accomplish this is to keep the distance a little more than the suggested spacing in rows, and then using the same distance between rows too. It is usually more productive to plant three rows of vegetables, parallel to the entire bed length rather than sweating over having an equidistant spacing.

Several vegetables such as cucumbers and tomatoes can grow much better in raised beds than they would normally do in a conventional vegetable garden (provided you support them well with a trellis and allow them to grow steadily upward instead of sprawling).

There are certain vegetables such as corn that usually do not display improved growth in raised beds. This is because they need to be anchored better than most other plants we have tackled so far. Larger sprawling vegetables including pumpkins and watermelons are also much better suited for orthodox gardening methods than raised beds. Therefore, it is usually the smaller vegetables such as lettuce and radish (alongside the ones already mentioned) that should be more focused upon while growing a raised bed vegetable garden.

If possible, interplant them according to their respective growing seasons. For example, you can plant lettuce at a suitable time, so it becomes ready to be harvested just before the ideal growing season for tomatoes starts.

What Not to Grow in Raised Beds

Soft fruit bushes such as raspberries, blackberries and so on are not suited to raised beds because of the space they take up. It is far more cost-effective to put them in the ground, unless your soil is not suitable for them, in which case use free standing containers. You can use raised beds for them, but most people will not, preferring to use the space for vegetables.

Autumn fruiting raspberries should always be grown in containers because they propagate by sending out runners. These are incredibly invasive and will get everywhere. I found them growing through the path and invading neighboring plots when I uncovered them on one of my allotments.

Strawberries, though, are well suited to a raised bed but are best grown in a two- or three-layer planter to maximize your use of space. There are plans online for multi-layered planters that you can build, which allow you to grow a lot of strawberries in a small area.

Other permanent plants such as rhubarb are also not suited for raised beds, purely because they are taking up valuable space which could be used for something else. I inherited a bed with rhubarb plants in and the entire bed (as you can see) is taken up by two plants. These are going to be moved at the end of the growing season to be planted directly into the soil. The raised bed will be used for growing annual crops and put into the crop rotation schedule.

Asparagus is another permanent crop that doesn't need to go in a raised bed. However, as they do like to be planted quite deep, you can grow them in a raised bed, planting them at the bottom of it and then building up the ideal soil for them. It is easier in some cases than digging trenches to plant the asparagus crowns in.

This is my asparagus bed, which is about knee height. It is very productive and produces a fantastic grow every year. It was easier to plant the asparagus in this rather than dig a deep hole for it.

Planting Schedule for Outdoors

There is nothing better or more exciting than growing and harvesting your very own vegetables, right from your own backyard, for dinner. However, for vegetables to grow correctly, you will want to be sure to plant them at the correct times. Typically, you will plant vegetables from early spring to late in summer, depending on the hardiness of the plant. When you plant your vegetables in the correct seasons, you ensure that they can survive any inclement weather and produce a yummy crop. Vegetables have four categories: very tender, tender, semi-hardy, and hardy.

Tips for Planting

1) Figure out where you want to plant your vegetable garden early in the spring- you have already done this when you were building your raised bed. You should make sure that your soil is well drained and has full sun. If you haven't already, you should work in some compost to about eight to ten inches.

2) You will plant your hardy vegetables in early spring, as soon as the ground has completely thawed out from winter. These include vegetables such as rhubarb, asparagus, and onions.

3) You will want to plant the semi-hardy vegetables two or three weeks before the last frost in your area. This typically is mid to late spring. These include vegetables such as: carrots, lettuce, and chad.

4) You will want to plant tender vegetables in late spring, after the last freeze in your area. These are vegetables such as corn and beans.

5) You want to plant your tender vegetables two to three weeks after the last frost in your area. This typically happens in mid to late spring, so you can plant in late spring to early summer. These are vegetables such as melons, tomatoes, and peppers.

These are just very general guidelines, of course. The United States is marked off by zones, so figure out what zone you are in and follow your specific planting guidelines.

There are eleven zones in the United States- Zone 1, is the first and coldest. Zone 11 is the last and the warmest. These zones were determined by the lowest recorded temperatures in the area.

So, plants that survive well in Zone 6 do well when the temperature drops to below ten degrees Fahrenheit, but those that do well in Zone 8 will die a good while before it really gets cold. If a zone gets colder than the coldest that a plant can survive in, you should bring these plants indoors if possible.

There are other things such as shade, sun, and wind exposure that have a bearing on the ability of the plant to get through the winter. There are some plants that will be rated across several zones. This means that they can survive winter in the coldest zone, and the warmth of the warmest one.

Unless a plant is grown as an annual- it grows, bears fruit, and dies in one year, then there will be a zone map, or an indication of the appropriate zone will be listed on the seed package or plant tag. Annual vegetables are those tender ones- beans, peppers, and tomatoes.

A couple of extra tips for planting:

Make sure that you plant the small seeds, such as carrots or cabbage about a half an inch deep. This is so that the plant doesn't have as far to go when it begins to sprout.

Make sure to plant your medium sized seeds, such as beets and chard three quarter inch deep and large seeds should be planted deeper- one to one- and one-half inches deep. This is so that when they start to sprout, they don't get pulled out of the ground before they have had a chance to grow.

Chapter 4: How to Choose the Best Soil?

The soil blend that you put in your raised bed is the most crucial ingredient. More gardens fail or collapse due to bad soil than almost anything else.

• Fill the beds with a mixture of topsoil, compost and other organic material, such as manure, to give your plants a nutrient-rich atmosphere (see recipes below). Learn more about soil alteration and soil preparation for planting.

• Note that the soil in the raised bed would dry up more quickly. During the spring and fall, this is perfect, but in the summer, apply grass, mulch, or hay to the top of the soil to help it hold moisture.

• Regular watering with raised beds will be necessary, particularly in the early stages of plant development. Otherwise, elevated beds would require minimal maintenance.

The Garden Planner has a 'Made Garden Bed' option. It also has a unique square foot gardening (SFG) function, which involves dividing the bed into squares to make the organizing of your garden much more straightforward.

Whichever garden you pick, the Garden Planner will show you the number of crops that fit into each area so that you don't overcrowd seed or waste it. There is a companion planting device that lets you plant vegetables that grow at once and avoid plants that hinder each other.

Check our Garden Planner with a free 7-day trial — a ton of time to plan your first garden! If you like the Garden Planner, we hope you can sign up. Otherwise, it is enough time to play around and give it a go.

Plot Out Your Garden

Good soil, good sunlight, and proper drainage are essential criteria for a productive vegetable garden but preparing your garden should not be a last-minute thought. Each garden —

and every gardener — is unique, so make a garden personalized to your space and needs.

Soil Preparation

Every successful gardener will tell you that soil preparation comes first when you aim for a bountiful harvest. Without proper soil, you may as well throw in the towel before you even begin. Initially you should focus all your attention on the condition and quality of soil you are going to use. A good quality soil will ensure that your vegetable plants grow to their full potential and that you will not spend too much valuable time fighting pests and weeds.

Following are a few tips for mixing rich and fertile soil to suit all your planters and garden beds. Your locality may influence the type of soil you will need to a small degree, but these basic principles are applicable everywhere, regardless of where you live.

1.   Topsoil does not Always Contain Organic Matter

Purchased soil often looks quite promising: dark in color, well screened and clean. This might not always be an indication of what it contains. It may well be a good growing medium though without any of the vital organic matter that is essential for growth. Therefore, you should always inquire from the attendant at the garden center what the soil consists of and what its origin is. You should assume that some extra feeding would be necessary to build up this soil to the standards needed for successful gardening.

2.   Revitalize Soil Annually

Usually new gardens will do well during their initial year even though no additional matter was added to amend the soil. The reason for this is that the available nutrients, organic matter and trace minerals have not been tapped yet. However, after one or two seasons of successive gardening, the crops will have used up all the riches in the soil. That is why it is so important that you revitalize your gardening soil regularly.

A wonderful solution is to plant 'green manure' as a cover crop after the first two seasons of growing vegetables. These crops are very easy and simple to grow and have many benefits. As soon as the cover crop has ripened, chop it up and then dig it lightly into your soil. Now your soil has been replenished with fresh organic matter. Consider growing leguminous crops like alfalfa or fenugreek since they will fix the atmospheric nitrogen in such a way that it can be used as nutrients by the plants. This type of green manure has many benefits; their roots will loosen the soil, bringing the deeper nutrients nearer to the surface of your garden beds. While you chop up the manure and work it into the ground as well as the activity of the roots will aerate your soil, thus improving the drainage for future crops.

3.   Soil must be Crumbly, Fluffy and Light

You want to make it as easy as possible for the roots of your plants to be able to work their way through the layers of soil in search of moisture and nutrients. Compacted and dense soil will make this essential task of plant roots very difficult and they will spend so much energy struggling to get to the nutrients that not much will be left for the rest of the plant to grow. You can easily facilitate better root growth by lightening your garden soil. This is turn will lead to better vegetative growth and you will see the positive results when your plants start to flourish.

How do you know if your soil is light enough? A simple test is to push your finger into it. You should have no trouble to poke it in up to the third knuckle of the finger. If you struggle to achieve this then you will have to lighten the soil by adding peat moss and working, it into the top layer. I have already mentioned that peat moss is acidic by nature, so you will most probably have to add lime. Always enquire about the pH level of the soil you purchase. You need to know if lime will be necessary. Acidic soil is commonly found in most areas of our country, so lime is usually needed, although there are regions that have alkaline soil. Many gardeners prefer to use vermiculite for lightening the soil because it does not break down at the same speedy rate as the peat moss.

4.   The Ultimate Amendment for Soil: Compost

Making your own compost is easy and can save you extra expense. Many gardeners have a compost heap in their back gardens. Compost consists of organic material filled with nutrients to turn normal soil into a rich medium for all your plants. Use this valuable resource correctly and wisely and you can be sure of a prolific vegetable garden. Instead of adding compost to the soil right after harvesting, rather postpone it to two or three weeks before you plant your following crop. You want to prevent a sudden downpour from washing away all that wonderful richness in the compost and undo all your hard work.

The general idea amongst many people who consider a compost heap an unsightly, smelly mess is truly a misconception. If you go about it the correct way, your compost heap will be neat and tidy with a wonderful rich and earthy aroma. Veteran gardeners will tell you that active compost heaps should not be smelly. If your plot is too small to allow for a larger compost pile, you can purchase a sealed composter. This device contains smells and is small and tidy in appearance. Because they are sealed, they are immune to dogs, mice, raccoons and such-like critters.

A composter in your garden has an additional benefit; it will take care of all the dead plant matter left after the harvest. After your last tomatoes have been harvested, carefully remove all the 'skeletons' from the plants, break or chop it into smaller pieces and simply throw them into the compost pile. It is a wonderful way to re-use all plant residues in your garden to contribute to the nutrient-rich compost for your future crops. Just inspect the dead plant matter carefully for any diseases before you add it to the composter.

5.   Organic Fertilizers are the Best Choice

Do not be overly enticed by all the many product claims you read on the packaging of chemical fertilizers. They may be true, but the advantages often do not last and are rather short-lived. You will have to reapply them regularly after each planting. In the end, the benefits of these commercial fertilizers may be lessened to some extend because they do not improve the condition of the soil, the most important aspect of successful gardening.

I would therefore suggest that when you find yourself short of compost, to make use of an organic fertilizer. It will also give your little seedlings an instant boost. Canola meal is one of the popular fertilizers. This material is finely ground and lightweight, making it very easy to sprinkle onto your beds. On top of that, it is relatively inexpensive and free of weeds. (Some kinds of manures may include weeds). Make sure to mix the canola meal lightly into the topsoil because mice love it and may attack your beds. For the same reason, take care where you store your bag. It should be well sealed and in any dry spot where mice will not be able to reach.

6.   Rock Phosphate

If you a new gardener, using the plot or raised bed for the first time, you will probably be able to use the basic soil for one or two years. After this, you will have to add some source of phosphorus to it. Your crops will grow steadily and vigorously and mature early because of the addition of this element. You will have larger-sized vegetables and fruit in autumn. Crops, which mature earlier, will better avoid summer drought and be less vulnerable to disease and frost. Rock phosphate also contains several minor elements like zinc, boron, iodine and nickel, all necessary in smaller doses for plants to grow optimally. Furthermore, rock phosphate works long-term, thus releases its elements slowly so that the plant will benefit over a longer period.

Although phosphate is such an essential contributor to plant growth it is often overlooked even by more experienced gardeners. I strongly advise you to buy a bag and sprinkle a handful or two into your beds from time to time. A sack of phosphate will store well and last for years. Make a note to mix some rock phosphate into your raised vegetable beds at least every couple of years.

After reading this, I am sure you understand the importance of paying attention to all the different aspects of your soil; its structure, the organic matter it contains, its drainage and the condition of the bottom or ground soil. If you focus on these elements all your expectations for a lush, high-yielding vegetable garden will be met. Your time will be spent on harvesting rather than on fighting diseases and pests and you will end up a happy, contented gardener.

Chapter 5: Growing Herbs

Details regarding how many seeds to sow, germination period, and times to maturity herbs have been introduced when assessing the top forms for indoor civilization. Finest germination temperatures for many herbs lie in 65°F into 75°F (18--24°C).

Within my adventure, by increasing them at tropical climates and they are going to endure quite high temperatures up to 85--90°F (29.5--32°C) under greenhouse conditions. Don't hesitate to rise most herbaceous plants beneath quite broad temperature ranges, so they'll last.

I strongly recommend planting herbaceous plants in plant towers using perlite, coco, or perlite mix because manufacturing is significantly enhanced through coaching those non-toxic plants at the restricted distance of the house or garden greenhouse.

With diminished to germinate herbs like thyme and rosemary and begin them into Rockwool or even Oasis cubes and transplant rosemary following 6--7 months and rosemary in 8--9 weeks.

Types of herbs

Just about everyone people would want the notion of using freshly juiced herbs in cooking. Though you always have the option to grow these herbaceous plants in dirt, you can benefit from a much healthier herb if grown in raised beds.

In the following pages, you will be able to find out more about creating some blooms Raised Bedally.

Basil

The most effective system to disperse growth is NFT -- move the seedlings into NFT when seedlings are 1 or 2 inches. Seed germination takes 7days; supply a projection of 9 to 12 inches between plants.

You can use vermiculite, soil-less combinations, rock-wool, and coco-peat. Basil thrives and continues to rise at considerable sunshine and requires 1-1 hours. Don't crop ginger on short days as it is vulnerable to ailments. The most typical reasons for the illness are in Aphids and Pythium. USDA hardiness isn't appropriate to Basil.

Chamomile

Chamomile is a yearly herb that's small white blossoms; those blossoms are inserted to tea to provide a different flavor and cause medicinal properties. Chamomile seeds need light to germinate and take 7 to 2 weeks for germination. These herbaceous plants add to a height of 20 to 30 inches and then perform nicely with a diameter of 6 inches between plants. Potential bugs are Aphids and Mealybugs. USDA Hardiness is annual.

Chervil

This herb is owned by the Parsley family and can be chiefly employed as a culinary herb. This herb thrives under cool temperatures (700 to 750 F); avoid exposing it to sunlight. Germination period for Chervil is just about per week transplant the seedlings to NFT once the very first true leaves appear. Spacing between plants must be kept at 1 inch, and then you'll be able to start to harvest at monthly. Chervil is more likely to Aphids, especially during hot days.

Cilantro

Cilantro or Coriander is one of the Parsley family; cilantro tastes like parsley but having a citrus twist. These plants give seeds that can be employed in various color combinations, liquors, and confectioneries. The leaves could be applied as a culinary herb. Cilantro climbs well in the sun; you could use fluorescent lights or HID lighting fixtures. Seed germination normally takes approximately ten weeks as well as the plant could grow as many as two feet tall. Pests that could strike cilantro are Aphids, whitefly, mites, and thrips. USDA Hardiness is Annual.

Dill

Dill, too, is one of the Parsley family and is still an annual / supplement. Dill seeds are traditionally found in pickles along with also the herb itself is traditionally employed as a culinary taste enhancer. All these plants usually reach a height of 24 to 36 inches and must be dispersed 12 to 15 inches apart. It requires approximately ten weeks for your seeds to germinate and the plant grows well in sunlight. Employing HID lights may perform just fine inside. Care must be used never to Over Water Dill plants; USDA hardiness isn't related to Dill. Also, it might be affected by powdery mildew and aphids.

Lavender

A flowering plant which is one of the mint family. Lavender flowers, if dried out a pleasing odor; those blossoms are frequently used in aromatherapy perfumes and oils. Lavender grows to a height of 18 inches; the spacing needs to have been 20 to 24 inches between plants. Seed germination may choose between 10 to 28 days. Lavender needs enough sun; mimic the lighting utilizing HID lights. Lavender might be assaulted by white-fly, spider mites, mealy scales, and bugs. USDA Hardiness is 5a into 9b.

Lemon Balm

This goes back to the mint family and is popularly famous for its soothing properties. It is considered a 'soothing herb'.

Lemon Balm develops well under partial sun and propagates through plants and seeds. Seed germination takes five days and 3 to 30 days to root development. Transplant the seedlings when they are approximately 2 inches tall. Lemon Balm is allergic to White-fly assault, Spider Mite, and Thrip. USDA Hardiness zone is 4a into 9b.

Marjoram

All these are perennial herbaceous plants grown as annuals; you will find two varieties -- sweet and wild. Sweet Marjoram is traditionally employed as a culinary herb. It grows to a height up to 3-6 inches, and the spacing between plants needs to have been 15 to 18 inches. Germination period is 10 to 15 days; those herbaceous plants grow well under the sun. Deficiency of light or bad illumination structures can lead the plant to die to fungal diseases. Marjoram is allergic to many different fungal diseases and white-fly strikes. USDA Hardiness is 6b into 11.

Oregano

A perennial herb also can be particularly referred to as 'bud marjoram.' Oregano Mediterranean herb grows up to 18 inches; the dimension between plants needs to have been 12 to 15 inches. The seed germination period is 8 to 2 weeks and takes approximately four weeks, to begin with, a crop. This herb needs to grow in full sun; usually, do not overcrowd the leaves. It contributes to infections and decay. You have to offer additional light when daylight is briefer compared to 11 hrs. Oregano is allergic to fungal attacks and infections against white-fly, mites, and leaf miners. USDA Hardiness is currently 5a -- 9b.

Parsley.

This is a biennial herb that is grown as an annual. Parsley has many varieties - curled foliage, fern foliage, as well as also rooted. You can grow Parsley entirely exposed to the sun; however, it will grow in partial color too. Utilizing fluorescent bulbs for indoor farming is adequate. All these plants reach a maximum height of 18 inches; distance the plants one foot apart. Seed germination is slow in Parsley – it often takes three weeks to your seedlings to emerge. There aren't a lot of diseases connected with Parsley. Nonetheless, they are sometimes assaulted by Aphids, spider mites, and white fly. USDA Hardiness is currently 5a -- 9b.

Rosemary

Rosemary has many applications; nevertheless, it is used as a culinary herb as well as also in medicine. This herb thrives in well-drained material and necessitates occasional watering. Rosemary has a slow growth rate but can last for years with good winter security. They can grow to a height of 6 feet; seed germination occurs approximately 3 to 30 days. The development rate slows once the daytime drops below 11 hrs. Per day. Rosemary is more prone to fungal diseases like Powdery Mildew and attack from Mites. USDA Hardiness is 7a into 10b.

Sage

Sage is a perennial shrub that's used both for medicinal and culinary purposes. Sage needs enough sun and a minimum of 10.5 hr. Shorter days impact the development of this tree. Seed germination takes approximately weekly, also develops to a height of 3-6 inches. Plant spacing needs to be 2-4 inches apart. Throughout winter, you may use supplemental fluorescent light 14 hours/day to ensure decent growth. Sage is allergic to diseases but may often defeat them; it is more prone to strikes in Mites and White fly. USDA Hardiness is currently 4a -- 11.

Benefits of growing herbs

The advantages of being able to grow and harvest your own herbs are immense. And with a raised bed garden ready to allow you to add these tasty herbs into every recipe all year round, you are well on your way to a culinary trip that you and your family can enjoy.

- Choose roadside growers—meaning herbs that are known for growing in poor, dry soil conditions. This will minimize the upkeep needed to tend to your garden.

- Annual herbs such as dill, basil, calendula and nasturtiums are ones that live from spring through fall. Perennials, on the other hand, are herbs that can survive through winter, such as lavender, rosemary, thyme, oregano, chives and mint. Because raised bed gardens allow you to plant across different seasons, you can continually enjoy and experiment with new flavors.

- Spacing rules for growing herbs require you understanding just how large a full-grown herb can be. Take note that while the herbs are small when they are seedlings, they can grow into leafy plants once they achieve their full size. In general, it would be best to plant the herbs 6 inches apart.

Growing chart

Type of herb	Indoor seed starting or direct sow	When to start indoors (weeks before last expected spring frost)	When to direct sow	Planting depth
Basil	Indoor	6 to 8 weeks		1/4 inch deep
Common Chamomile	Both	6 weeks	After last frost	On soil surface
Chives	Indoor	10 to 12 weeks		1/4 inch deep
Cilantro	Direct sow		1 to 2 weeks before last frost	1/2 inch deep
Dill	Both	6 weeks	After last frost	1/4 inch deep
Lavender	Indoor	10 to 12 weeks		1/8 inch deep
Lemon Balm	Indoor	6 to 8 weeks		1/8 inch deep
Mint	Indoor	10 weeks		1/4 inch deep
Oregano	Indoor	10 to 12 weeks		On soil surface
Parsley	Indoor	10 weeks		1/4 inch deep
Rosemary	Indoor	10 to 12 weeks		
Summer Savory	Both	6 to 8 weeks	After last frost	1/4 inch deep
Thyme	Indoor	14 to 16 weeks		On soil surface

Chapter 6: Growing Plants

Types of plants

Raised beds aren't just for growing delicious and nutritious vegetables. One of the reasons that they are so popular is the simple fact that they can look quite beautiful. With a little bit of time and tender care, a raised bed can be made to look like a natural part of the landscape or even used as a beautiful decoration. It can be filled with flowers of all different colors. This can be used to line pathways or create designs that are beautiful and captivating. It takes a little bit of time and effort, but many flowers can be planted and grown year after year. You can choose to go with long-lasting ones or single season flowers, depending on how much energy you want to invest in the process.

What you plant is going to depend on what colors you want, as well as what season you want it to be the brightest. We'll look at an example of a beautiful and bright display for spring, summer, and fall to see some of the gorgeous flowers that you can use in your raised beds. Keep in mind that this is just an example of one arrangement you could go with but there are even more options for flowers than there are with vegetables.

You will need to consider your local climate when choosing species, but you'll find yourself with shocking amounts of variety.

Starting with spring, we'll grow a mixture of tazetta and jonquil-type daffodils. Tazetta have wide flower petals which peel back to crown the golden center that protrudes outwards. They are a striking flower when they are healthy, and they complement a jonquil-type daffodil quite nicely since these daffodils have white flower petals that sometimes come in yellow with bright yellow centers.

Together, these two can create the main part of a bed. The bed will need to be at least a foot deep in order to support the root system. You can add some hellebores to the bed, which often have a deep purple color. Spread throughout a raised garden bed full of tazettas, these hellebores will really pop out in bold fashion.

Maintaining a spring bed of this fashion isn't very hard. You'll want this to be a partly shaded bed, with the hellebores getting the most shade. Both hellebores and tazetta are perennials and so you can keep these beds alive for several years.

Pay attention to the tazetta and trim away any heads that die or that have faded too much. The hellebores will help to distract from the fading of the tazetta but if you remove the fading ones it will promote new growth and keep the bed bright.

You will want to dig up the tazetta every few years to space them out a little more and reorganize the garden and keep the root system from becoming too tangled up. Keep an eye on watering and add a little bit of fertilizer from time to time and you will have yourself a gorgeous spring arrangement.

For a beautiful summer arrangement, plant a mixture of coreopsis, annual cosmos, and catmint. This will create a really strong contrast in the colors and a more three-dimensional texture due to the height disparity.

Catmint is the easier to pronounce name for nepeta mussinii. It is like its more well-known cousin catnip, aka nepeta cataria.

But catmint produces tall stems which bloom deep purple flowers from soil to tip.

Mixing these in with coreopsis will create the color contrast, since coreopsis are mostly yellow petals around a yellow core. Some types of coreopsis will have dark red, almost black, rings around their center but otherwise they are pure yellow. To bring the arrangement together, some purple or pink annual cosmos are added. These have a shape closer to the coreopsis but a color like the catmint and so when added they create a sense of unity to the arrangement.

Again, this arrangement is made up of perennials which will last you several years if properly tended. To keep them bright and beautiful you will need to use fertilizer on them with a regular schedule.

You will also need to trim back heads which have faded in color. Removing the heads will cause the flowers to bloom again, but this also helps keep the plant healthy and happy in general. It both makes your raised bed garden look better and helps your plant to better distribute its energy.

The annual cosmos will need to be replanted every year, but you can use this as a chance to switch up the colors and try something new. The annual cosmos can also be replaced with another perennial if desired, which will reduce the amount of upkeep required on the raised bed each year.

For fall, we are going to go with similar colors to summer, but our purples will be darker, and our lighter shades will be a little bit more washed out in appearance. Washed out flowers might not sound appealing at first but keep in mind that we are talking about fall, that season where the colors turn deep oranges and reds before fading out. A washed-out flower actually fits with the season perfectly to deepen that natural mood that autumn invokes.

For this washed out look we will use sedum and goldenrod. We set this off against the deep purple shades of asters to create a very rich and moody display.

It should be noted that the sedum is a succulent and this works well for a quick discussion about winter. There aren't many flowers that enjoy the winter weather but there are a few succulents which are planted in fall to grow throughout the winter.
These can keep a raised bed garden looking beautiful throughout the winter, which is especially useful for raised beds that work as pathways or those seeded with annuals.

Some winter succulents that are beautiful include the green and purple royanum, the broad and bold agave, the unique cobweb sempervivum, the rose-like jovibarba, and the adorable orostachys. These are just a few of the succulents that can make your raised bed gardens stand out even in the coldest of weather.

RHUBARB

Rheum rhabarbarum

Rhubarb needs extended temperatures below 40 degrees Fahrenheit. The plants thrive in colder climates and can live up to 15 years. In beds, rhubarb plants should be divided sometime between years 5 and 15, basically when they need to be thinned. Do not eat the leaves—they are toxic. Only eat the stalks.

Family: Polygonaceae

Growing Seasons: spring, late fall in warmer climates

Zones: 3 through 8

Spacing: 3 to 4 feet apart

Seed to Harvest: 365 days to maturity

Indoor Seed Starting: not recommended

Earliest Outdoor Planting: early spring

Watering: 1 inch of water per week

Starting

Location: full sun, part shade

Planting: Plant bare-root plants. Plants require little to no fertilizer.

Growing

Remove flower stalks in the first year.

Harvesting

Leave at least one-third of the plant when harvesting; doing so will strengthen the plant.

Problems

Rhubarb is relatively pest- and disease-free.

SUNFLOWER

Helianthus

Harvest sunflower seeds for your own enjoyment or leave them for your backyard birds and squirrels.

Family: Asteraceae

Growing Seasons: spring, late spring

Zones: 3 through 10

Spacing: 18 to 24 inches

Seed to Harvest: 70 to 90 days

Indoor Seed Starting: directly sow in the garden

Earliest Outdoor Planting: after danger of frost

Watering: soil should be moist, but not wet

Starting

Location: full sun

Seeding: Do not start sunflowers indoors. Plant them directly in the garden.

Planting: Cover seeds with ½ inch of soil. Plant taller varieties north of shorter plants so they don't shade the shorter plants.

Growing

Weeding and watering are the only needed maintenance. Sunflowers do not require fertilizer if grown in good garden soil.

Once the flower is growing, it can handle drought-type conditions.

Harvesting

Sunflowers are ready for harvest once their heads start to droop and their stalks are dry. Cut the heads with 1 foot of stem attached. Hang them in an area with good air circulation until the seeds are dry and ready to eat.

Problems

Some bugs, including beetles, cutworms, and moths, may affect your sunflowers if their growing area is not kept clean and weed-free. If you end up with a problem, apply the human- and pet-safe BT (Bacillus thuringiensis) bacterium as directed on the BT label.

SWEET PEA

L. odoratus

Sweet peas are great for borders and lovely as cut flowers. They are not edible.

Family: Fabaceae

Growing Seasons: early spring to summer; in frost-free areas can be sown in fall

Zones: 3 through 10

Spacing: 3 to 6 inches apart

Seed to Harvest: sweet peas are ornamental flowers that generally bloom within 3 to 4 months after planting

Indoor Seed Starting: not recommended

Earliest Outdoor Planting: early spring

Watering: 1 inch of water per week

Starting

Location: full sun

Planting: Soak seeds in water overnight before sowing. Sweet peas can tolerate a light frost.

Growing

Sweet peas are climbing plants and will need a trellis or some other support. Some dwarf sweet peas do not need the support.

Harvesting

Once the lowest blossom barely opens, cut the stems any time you like. Frequent picking means the plants put their energy into growing more fragrant, beautiful blooms. Regularly deadhead sweet peas to keep them in production.

Problems

Slugs: Remove them by hand.

Powdery mildew: Spray affected areas with a solution of 2 to 3 tablespoons of white vinegar per gallon of water.

Chapter 7: Growing Vegetables in Raised Bed Gardening

Types of vegetables

There are a lot of vegetables you can grow in a raised bed, in fact, you can grow almost anything you want. Here is more information about the many different vegetables and how they will grow in raised beds.

Root Vegetables

Root vegetables such as carrots, beets, parsnips, radishes and so on do well in raised beds. Carrots and parsnips grow deep roots, so you either need an eight to twelve-inch-deep raised bed or you need to have dug down into the soil below to give them the space they need to grow. The deeper root vegetables will not work if you have a shallow bed and either poor soil beneath it or a wire mesh to prevent burrowing pests. Raise your beds up higher (12" is fine) to grow deep rooted veg if the soil below is poor. Because raised beds tend to be free of rocks, you end up with good quality carrots and parsnips with long, well-formed roots. Add horticultural sand to your raised beds to make it drain better, so your carrots grow straighter.

Potatoes, though, aren't particularly suited to raised beds. In smaller beds, they will grow down into the soil beneath and require a lot of digging to get out. In larger beds, you are practically going to have to empty the bed to get all the potatoes out. It is a personal preference, and some people will plant potatoes in raised beds, but I prefer to grow them in bags and then use the spent compost in the beds the following year. The advantage of growing in bags is that you don't find potato plants appearing in your raised beds the following year and nor do you have to do a lot of digging to get them out of the ground.

If you do want to grow potatoes in a raised bed, then you need your soil to be 18–24 inches deep and be able to mound up the earth around the shoots as they grow. They will do well in a raised bed because they need a loose, free draining soil, which is one of the main premises behind raised beds. You will also get a good-sized crop of potatoes, but my personal preference is to avoid it because of the digging involved ... it is far easy just to empty out a bag! Plus, for years afterward you will be finding potatoes growing in the bed which will disturb your other vegetable crops.

Leafy Greens

Most leafy greens such as kale, spinach, cauliflower, lettuce and so on do fantastically in a raised bed. Many of these can be started early in the year, and some, such as kale, pak choi, cauliflower, broccoli, and others can be started soon in the year and overwintered. Because raised beds warm faster than the surrounding soil you can often get a good harvest before summer and they will do very well because they like free draining soil.

Be aware that these will get eaten by pests, particularly slugs, snails, and caterpillars. A tight mesh cage built over the bed will keep the caterpillars off and may prevent larger slugs and snails. You will still need to keep an eye on the plants and act against any slugs that find their way into your raised bed. Young plants are at risk of damage from birds so also need covering. I will often use a plastic poly tunnel for the young plants as they benefit from the extra warmth as well as the protection from birds.

Onions, Leeks, and Garlic

Any member of the onion family does well in a raised bed because they like plenty of organic matter and a free draining soil. They do tend to have a long growing season (grown from seed they can take over 100 days to mature) and raised beds ensure that you can get planting early in the year.

The onion family does not like competition nor do they like drying out. Make sure you keep the weeds down because they will crowd out the onions. In hot weather, water these beds regularly because if they dry out too much, the plants will end up dying and the bulbs will not form properly.

Tomatoes

Tomatoes are greedy feeders and, if you add extra compost to your raised bed, then they will do very well indeed. However, the only issue comes with staking the tomatoes as the stakes are not secure in the loose soil. You can either drive the stakes into the firm soil below your raised bed or fix them to the edges of the bed. I have screwed wooden trellises to the raised bed as support for plants, which worked very well.

Tomatoes ripen with heat rather than just sun, so you may find that you need to fleece your tomato bed to give them some extra warmth, particularly towards the end of the growing season. You can wrap clear plastic over the bed or create a polythene poly tunnel to keep them warm, so they produce a good crop.

Peas and Beans

These will do very well in raised beds though you may have issues with supporting taller crops such as runner beans. Driving supports into the soil beneath your bed or fixing them to the bed itself will help.

Young plants are at risk of damage from birds so will need covering and protecting. With beans you will need to build a frame from bamboo canes, using ten to twelve-foot-high canes for them to climb up. Either lash short canes to these or build a frame of garden twine to help encourage the beans to spread and climb up.

Peas also need supporting, and traditionally pea sticks are used. These are dead branches or specially bought pea sticks. Alternatively, you can build a mesh from garden twine, and the pea plants will use those for support. You can also buy special pea netting which the plants will climb up. Putting a six-foot bamboo cane in each corner plus one in the middle will allow you to build a mesh of twine that will support your peas. Add extra canes as necessary, depending on the size of your raised bed.

Vine Crops

These are not very well suited for raised beds, particularly as squashes are very greedy feeders indeed. The problem with long trailing vines is you run out of space, and they can crowd out neighboring plants. You can build supports for them, and you can grow your cucumbers vertically which will help reduce the space requirements.

Courgettes (zucchini) are available in bush forms which do not take up as much space as the trailing forms and are well suited for raised beds. Other squash plants, such as petty pan squashes, are reasonably compact plants which makes them suitable for a raised bed.

Plants such as pumpkins are generally very rambling and are going to take up vast amounts of space. They will not be contained within a raised bed and will expand outside of their designated area, taking over your vegetable plot.

With the long, trailing vines, you can build a small raised bed to plant them in. This is a variation on the hill method, where the soil is very nutrient rich to give the plant a good start in life.

Because squashes such as pumpkins and butternut squashes grow so big, you should avoid growing them in a raised bed because they are going to grow like crazy and crowd out all your other plants. Although you can grow these large plants vertically, they will still take up a lot of space, and you will have to grow varieties that produce smaller fruits.

Benefits of growing vegetables

Did you realize that raised garden beds are simpler for you? when you use a raised garden bed, it is simpler for your back and knees. You can invest your energy working in your garden and not stress over hurting soon.

- Better for Drainage

Raised vegetable garden beds have better drainage, and this implies plants aren't exposed to a lot of water when it rains. Since one of my errors as a beginner gardener was to over water, I felt this was a superior method to support my plants.

Likewise, since we get those monster rainstorms, we love such a great amount during hot days, I felt that having a better drainage system for my garden was gainful.

- Easier to Build Soil

The reason I didn't begin my garden on the ground was that I felt that it will be too much work. It is much simpler to include soil up than working changes into the ground.

- Simple to Build

Building raised vegetable garden beds are extremely simple. You can make this into a one-day DYI project. Even your children can help to build their garden raised bed!

All you must assemble your raised vegetable garden beds are some accessible devices and material and obviously, an additional pair of hands.

Growing chart

Crop	Number of days for germination	Number of weeks to optimum age for transplanting	Amount of light* required	Number of days from seeding to harvest
Beans	5-8	-	Sun	45-65
Cucumbers	6-8	3-4	Sun	50-70
Eggplant	8-12	6-8	Sun	90-120
Lettuce, leaf	6-8	3-4	Partial Shade	45-60
Onions	6-8	6-8	Partial Shade	80-100
Parsley	10-12	-	Partial Shade	70-90
Pepper	10-14	6-8	Sun	90-120
Radish	4-6	-	Partial Shade	20-60
Squash	5-7	3-4	Sun	50-70
Tomato	7-10	5-6	Sun	90-130

Chapter 8: Watering and Feeding Your Plants

Best practices for hand watering and best irrigation systems

Sometimes, the most tedious part of gardening is the simplest. Take watering, for instance. When maintaining a garden, the most obvious part would of course be watering it. But it would be great if the success of your garden would not be so utterly dependent on this tiresome, mundane but necessary chore.

So, what are your options?

• Take a watering can and find a way to enjoy the mundane task of watering your garden.

• Install an automated, and very likely, expensive irrigation system that can do the job for you.

Surely there is another alternative that will find a happy medium between the tedium of manual watering and the automated and ambitious irrigation set-up of large, professional gardens.

Thankfully, there is. All it takes, as with anything related to gardening, is a little creativity.

What you'll need:

•   Soaker hoses (length depending on what you need for your raised garden)

•   A couple of long nails

How to set it up:

Step 1:

Take the pair of nails and set it up so that it holds up the hose nozzle in place at each edge of the bed.

Step 2:

Allow the hose to slither through the soil and greens, doubling back in loops at each end of the bend until it covers the entire raised garden.

Step 3:

When it is time to water the garden, remove the end cap of the rear exit of the hose and allow water to run through it at low pressure until the soil is moist. Cover the hose in straw mulch to help the plants hold the moisture.

Trickle Irrigation Simplifies and Improves Your Garden

On the off chance that you garden in raised beds, there is no improvement that will spare you time and upgrade results better than trickle water system. The time spent introducing a dribble water system framework will be returned many occasions over in the main season alone, also over the numerous long stretches of utilization you ought to escape a very much arranged framework produced using solid materials. Plants developed utilizing dribble water system develop better since they get increasingly uniform watering. It is simpler to water with ironclad unwavering quality when the errand is diminished to just killing your fixture on and or relegated to a programmed water clock.

There are many dribble water system tubing items available today, however none match the usability, solidness, unwavering quality and fine designing of in-line producer tubing. Our way of thinking: carry out the responsibility well the first run through utilizing top quality materials, and you won't have to do it again at any point in the near future.

In-line producer tubing accompanies pre-introduced producers each 6". You basically roll the tubing off the curl, slice to measure with hard core scissors and introduce it in your beds. The 6" separating between producers gives a nonstop band of water on either side of the tubing. You can plant little seedlings adjoining the producers on either side of the tubing. You can likewise plant seeds.

The standard components of most raised beds are 4' x 8'. While the length of your beds isn't basic when you decide the design of your framework, it is imperative to have the correct number of lines stumbling into the width of your bed. Too hardly any lines and you will have holes in water inclusion. An excessive number of lines and you will squander water, advance weeds and mess the outside of the beds with pointless tubing.

The perfect number of lines in a 4' wide raised bed is three, with one running down the center of the bed and one either side, 16" from the middle line In the event that your beds are 3' wide, two lines 18" separated focused over the center will be carry out the responsibility well.

Cut and Connect

The establishment of your tubing is simple and clear. You essentially cut each line leaving the overall length of each wire around 12" shy of the absolute height of your beds. For instance, if your foundations are 8' long, 7' measures of tubing inset 6" from either end will be enough. Avoid frameworks that require cinches and paste as these are superfluously entangled and not any more successful.

A Manual Control Valve

Use strong feeder line to come up the side of your wooden edges from ground level (see picture at right). If you wish, a shut-off valve can be introduced here so you can kill the water any beds that aren't in dynamic use.

Not with standing interfacing your raised beds, strong feeder line additionally drives back to your spigot. A Y connector on your fixture will permit you to make a changeless association with your raised beds and leaves the opposite side of the Y for a nursery hose. It is enthusiastically suggested that you join a progression of segments to your spigot to channel your water system water and control the weight. We have such a get together, ready-to-use, called Low Volume Control Kit.

How Often and How Long to Run Your System
Low Volume Control Unit

You should run your dribble water system framework day by day for ideal plant development. Vegetable plants develop their best with a consistent stock of water. Protracted interims without water will put weight on your plants. This outcomes in reduced development and lower yields.

To what extent you water every day relies upon a scope of variables: the size and development of your plants, air temperature, wind, cloud inclusion, and the force of the sun. All in all, you need less water from the get-go in the season and more water late in the season when the plants are bigger, come to pass more and are creating organic product.

You'll have to consider these factors alongside the measure of water your tubing administers over a unit of time, i.e., what number of gallons every moment (GPH) per producer. Our raised bed framework uses producers that administer water at the pace of .4 GPH. That is somewhat not exactly ½ gallon every hour. Expecting your plants need about 16 ounces of water for each day right off the bat in the season, utilizing a similar tubing you would run a day by day watering cycle that is 15 minutes in length. Before the finish of the period the watering cycle may be 45 minutes in length toward the beginning of the day, with a shorter, brief cycle toward the finish of long, hot days to recharge water misfortune.

Make a move

It is beneficial to find out about trickle water system, yet even better to venture out introduce your framework. I can guarantee you, the time spent introducing trickle water system in your nursery is time very well spent.

Try not to take on more than you could possibly deal with. On the off chance that you have an enormous nursery, select a segment where dribble water system will give you the greatest value for your money, and afterward start. When you've handled a little task, you'll have the certainty and want to water all pieces of your nursery utilizing trickle water system. The advantages are simply too pragmatic to even think about ignoring.

On the off chance that this sounds like too much effort, go pre-assembled

Watering frameworks are a tremendous assistance for growing an effective home garden and unquestionably rearrange the way toward flooding plants. Add a clock to your framework, and you can turn it on when you leave for work, realizing your nursery won't flood and your plants will be extinguished. In any case, in case you are not the DIY type, don't have the opportunity to focus on building a watering framework, or battle with lopsided watering between plants, you are not up the creek without a paddle.

While not in fact a dribble water system framework, the water stream is flexible from a trickle to a full stream dependent on your plant needs. For those generally intrigued by this area, you'll be glad to realize no instruments are required for the garden grid, you simply press the pre-gathered segments together and place it in your nursery. You'll have a watering framework, as the name infers, in minutes.

Chapter 9: Pest Control for Raised Beds

Types of pests and general directions to prevent most common

Common Pests

The following are common pests and diseases you may run into while gardening, the key to a healthy garden is knowing how to identify and treat common pests and diseases, so take note to ensure you are able to identify these should they (unfortunately) find their way into your garden.

Aphids

Aphids are small white critters that congregate on stems and nodes, they suck the life out of plants. To eliminate Aphids a

strong spray from your garden hose will dislodge them. Ladybugs can also rid Aphids.

Black vine weevils

During late spring and early summer, these weevils are harmless pupae resting in your gardens soil. The adults emerge and eat the foliage of dozens of perennials (and lay eggs for the generation while they are at it). The typical sign is notched leaf edges, particularly lower down on the plant where the insects find more shelter. Starting in early fall, the newly hatched grubs eat roots.

Counterattack in fall by releasing beneficial nematodes (roundworms), available from most garden centers and mail-order sources; apply according to the label's instructions.

Leaf miners

Leaf miners form a brown, tan or clear traceries, tunnels or channels on affected leaves but hardly ever kill the plant. I recommend removing and discarding the affected leaves, the plant will generate new ones.

Root nematodes

Plants affected with root nematodes develop severely distorted growth.

Remove the plants out and discard them before they spread.

Voles

Voles come out of their underground tunnels and chew on perennials, specifically the leaves but also roots, seeds, and bulbs. Voles are slightly larger than mice, with a shorter tail and smaller ears. The best deterrent for Voles is a cat.

Castor oil as a repellent also works quite well.

Integrated Pest Management

Integrated pest management (IPM) is using beneficial insects, backed with organic pesticides (bioagents) to control pests in the greenhouse. It is a natural equilibrium of insects and insects that are beneficial in maintaining the insect population at manageable levels to ensure quite restricted plant harm happens in their existence. It is not to remove the pests altogether because that could exclude the valuable insects from getting adequate meals to keep their presence. Beneficial pests can be predators where they consume their prey (insects), or else they are parasites into the victim by depositing eggs at the victim. As these eggs hatch, they ruin the insects out of the interior, utilizing them because of their food origin.

They are ferocious and competitive insects which cause the passing of numerous insects, but continuously keeping a certain equilibrium in keeping enough quantities of insects to nourish them and their following generations since the cycle reproduces these beneficial insects are unique to certain insects. Biological supply houses, for example, Koppert, back the valuable insects and also market them into farmers.

The providers of beneficial insects additionally provide advice on tracking the improvement of their benefit, along with even the management of their insect population. In many instances, hobby raised bed farmers may use IPM together with assistance from neighborhood shops or the internet at which these benefits can be found.

The secret to achievement would be that the appropriate identification of the insect and obtaining certain insects that are beneficial to control that insect control of these insect population at least a few times per week having sticky cards to draw the pests provide a representative sample of their amounts and whether the inhabitants are growing or staying stable with all the help of their beneficial.

This balancing and monitoring of the two pests and prey is your cornerstone of effective IPM. It is a somewhat more complicated method of controlling insects; however, it is natural with no using pesticides. You might use occasionally organic pesticide (bio agents) sprays to reduce outbreaks in pest populations to help the predators in gaining hands. But these bio agents mustn't be damaging to the beneficial pests Information about the compatibility of their bio agents using all the benefits can be obtained on different sites.

Spraying

When applying pesticides using a sprayer, select the proper equipment to suit precisely the dimensions of your septic system to create the job simpler. In many instances, a backpack sprayer, like the "Solo" sprayer with a potential of 3 liters, is much more than enough for indoor and garden surgeries. It includes a flexible nozzle to distribute the spray out of a flow to a beautiful mist. Mix the pesticide using water-based on this speed instructions precisely according to the tag. Spray throughout the morning until temperatures climb and when at a garden ocean before sunlight becomes extreme, as high temperatures and mild may cause burn the plant leaves.

Overcoming Common Raised Bed Gardening Problems

Raised bed gardens can bring you more benefits than the conventional garden, as far as practicality and logistics are concerned. However, it is inevitable that you will encounter some gardening problems along the way. This part will tackle some of these problems. Along with the main problems are the solutions that you must consider in dealing with these predicaments.

If you decide to build your raised bed gardens higher, this will imply that you must deal with more issues in watering.

One primary factor that causes this problem is gravity. Gravity is responsible for quickly sucking out the water from the entire bed more than you will expect it to. To help you deal with this problem effectively, you must use a sprinkler system or a soaker system. Also, it is important to closely check out the specific water needs of each seed that you have planted in your raised bed garden.

Construction materials may be considered an issue if you are working within a budget.

For this problem, you should strike a balance between cost and durability. Fortunately, there are numerous inexpensive materials that you can use for constructing and maintaining the entire garden. Some of these include pressure treated lumber, cedar planks, railroad ties, rocks, and concrete blocks. It does not really matter what type of materials you will use for the bed. More than the materials, it is the soil quality that matter more importantly.

The seeds that you plant in the raised bed garden may cause problems if you do not pay close attention to air circulation.

Different plants have different space requirements. To help you prevent this problem, you must check out the prescribed distance for each seed variety. It is also important to find out if you still need to space them out as they begin to grow.

You should keep the soil from getting stale by making sure that the soil is rich in nitrogen.

Fish emulsion on the soil surface serves as a good source of nitrogen. You should provide this booster shot on a monthly basis. If you can provide nitrogen weekly, this will be much better for the soil and the plants, especially if you water your plants often.

Each garden may have their own share of advantages and disadvantages over the other setups. Knowing these intricacies, you should readily determine what the possible problems are so you can minimize the harm that may befall your garden if you do not do anything about them.

Chapter 10: Tips & Tricks for Raised Bed Gardening

Now that we have covered most of the important parts, let's consider a few pointers for anyone who wants to be successful at raised-bed gardening. Keep these in mind.

Choose the Right Location

You must choose the right spot. You want to expose your plants to sunlight because sunlight is good for them. It will help them grow and carry out the process of photosynthesis. This also means that you will be able to grow plants a lot faster, regardless of what you intend to grow. Your plants must get at least 6 hours of full sunlight. This will also help get rid of pests, insects, and certain diseases/infections.

Give Your Plants Enough of Water

The danger with raised-bed gardens is that these tend to dry out a lot faster and while full sunlight is great for such plants, this can also affect the compost and fertilizer, which is likely to dry up faster. So, you want to keep watering the plants every 2-3 hours to prevent this from happening. It would be better for your plants if the raised-bed garden was near a source of water. That would also make things easier for you, but if this is not the case, then you must water the plant on your own.

Take Good Care of Your Soil

If you've taken good care of your soil, your plants will turn out to be great. If not, you'll be growing low-quality plants. Some people tend to have soil of great quality, but because they do not take good care of it, they end up ruining everything and their soils get infected. Before they know it, this ends up affecting their plants, crops, and flowers too.

The importance of taking care of your soil cannot be stressed enough. Make use of additives if you must. Plants grown in raised beds tend to have 'limited options' when it comes to nutrients because these are secluded from the surrounding soil. So, they only have access to the nutrients available in the soil that you've planted these in. Stock up on nutrients so that you can add these to the soil whenever you see signs that you need to do so.

Check the Soil for Drainage

If water seeps too fast through it that means your soil won't benefit from rainfall and if the water stands for too long that, too, will be harmful for your soil. Water that stands for too long may infect your plants, especially if it is contaminated water. Another thing you can do is take some soil in your hands and squeeze it so that it forms a ball. If your soil does not form a ball that means that your soil's too sandy. If it breaks into several little pieces (or if it crumbles) that means your soil can be used to grow plants and that it can retain healthy amounts of water. This also means that your soil is perfect for plant growth.

Companion Gardening

Adding plants that complement each other has many benefits, such as helping to protect your plants from pests and insects like mosquitoes, grasshoppers, etc. Growing plants that counteract these conditions will allow you to avoid using dangerous insecticides.

Blood flower is a great herb for those of you who need to get rid of worms. While worms are great for the soil, if you feel that there are way too many worms in your soil, this herb is just what you need to protect your soil. Tansy would help get rid of mosquitoes and grasshoppers too. There are several other herbs you could grow.

Importance of Nitrogen

Nitrogen is so important for plants because it is what plants use when they are photosynthesizing. Always use cash crops to enrich the oxygen content in your soil. You don't want to wait till your plants get yellow and show signs of nitrogen deficiency, because that means it is too late. You want to take good care of your plants and of your soil. Do your plants and yourself a favor by planting cash crops after you have grown vegetables, flowers and plants in the soil. Go for crop rotation if you must.

Avoid Overwatering

In the summertime, go easy on the water. This is when your plants grow. Don't water the soil too much around this time period. You should only do so once or twice a day. Any more than that might prove to be harmful and possibly drown your plants. Something you definitely want to avoid.

Growing Plants Together

You want to protect the soil; if you grow the plants together, they will be able to shelter the soil underneath them. This will protect the soil from evaporation, and this will also help get rid of weeds. You won't need to mulch all over again either.

Subdivide Your Garden

Plan on how you intend on using the soil. You could grow peppers, carrots, and peas on one side while growing onions and cucumbers on the other. You could also choose to grow vegetables on one side and flowers and fruits on the other.

Always Be Prepared

Know that this is what you want or else you are just wasting your time. While raised-bed gardening may seem like an appealing idea; it also involves a lot of work, so you really must want to go for it and be consistent. You'd be wasting a lot of money and time otherwise.

Choose Quality Building Products

Be careful of what you are buying when it comes to purchasing wood for the bed or when it comes to purchasing topsoil for your raised-bed garden. Any material with preservatives could cause more damage than insects, pests and insecticides combined because these preservatives tend to seep into water and can ruin your plants completely.

Chapter 11: Ideal Height for Raised Beds

Consider Drainage

R aised beds have an aesthetic appeal, which speaks to many gardeners, but they also allow for proper drainage of the soil in which your veggies will be grown. In general, most raised beds are eleven inches tall, which is equal to that of two 2 by 6 standard boards. (In fact, the measurements are 1.5 by 5.5 inches).

The reason why this height is most popular is that it provides adequate drainage for most crops. The best results can be achieved if you allow for another twelve inches at least of rich soil underneath your raised bed. That will give your veggie plants up to twenty inches of good soil. Remember that raised beds usually end up not filled to the brim with soil; after every watering the soil will compress somewhat. You will need this extra space to add some mulch.

Two factors contribute to the earlier warming up of the soil in raised beds during the spring: Firstly, the soil is always well above the ground level and the second aspect is the good drainage in these beds.

Gardeners can, therefore, start transplanting much earlier and so lengthen the growing season of their veggies. To shield the young, vulnerable seedlings from a late frost or strong winds, place cold frames over the beds.

Once the seedlings are stronger and better established, these frames can simply be removed and used elsewhere if needed.

Consider Bending Down

Young gardeners who are fit and energetic might not even waste time thinking about this aspect since going on your knees or bending down to attend to your plants is easy and you take it in your stride. People who suffer from backache or strain, or those whose mobility have been impaired will need higher raised beds to help lighten their gardening chores. Beds can be in a range of eight to twenty-four inches high.

You will quickly notice the huge difference between tending these various beds. Taller beds are just so much more comfortable when you must set in transplants, till the soil, weed and harvest. It is not necessary to put extras strain on your back at all.

Cross Supports for Taller Beds

It is commonsense that taller beds will hold more volume, so you must keep this in mind when you construct a raised bed that is taller than twelve inches, (especially if it is longer than five feet).

As mentioned before, after a few watering, the soil will compact slightly, becoming heavier and the pressure may well cause your beds to bulge out on the sides in mid-span. So, for beds of this height you will require cross supports. Place them in the middle of the span, right across the width. This will prevent the two sides from bulging out.

If you purchased your raised beds from a garden center these supports were probably included in the package but if your raised beds are home-made, you will have to make your own, using composite plastic, aluminum or wood.

Soil Depth for Most Vegetables

The Roots Need Adequate Depth

Most nutrients in garden beds are to be found in the top six inches of the soil. The reason is that most vegetable root growth happens in this shallow depth.

The key nutrients like fertilizers and compost are added from the top and then tilled in lightly. Mulches also are applied on the top surfaces of the beds from time to time; they eventually decompose to add extra nutrients to the soil, enriching it.

If moisture and nutrients are available deeper in the soil, tap roots will grow down to reach them. This brings additional trace minerals to the vegetable plants as well. The larger the plant, the deeper the roots will travel.

Deeper roots anchor the plant much firmer into the bed, enabling it to withstand strong winds or heavy rains and saturated soil. Plants with big leaves and shallow root systems like broccoli, cauliflower and Brussels sprouts will need staking to make sure they do not fall over as they develop and reach maturity.

Raised beds which have been set on a gravel surface or a concrete patio will not allow roots to grow any deeper down than the depth of the beds. In this case, make sure you know the depth requirements for the different crops. You can compensate for an impenetrable ground surface by making the beds higher, providing enough root space.

The average raised bed is between eight and twelve inches tall, but experienced gardeners have planted in beds with sides exceeding three feet. While these beds are ideal for crops with deep roots, you must provide good drainage by drilling several holes towards the bottom of your beds, right along the sides.

Chapter 12: Making Your Own Compost

A lot of people try their hand on one old technique which turns garbage to gold, which is known as making compost. However, its making may be mysterious to certain people or just too complex. This belief, however, is not true. If you follow the given directions, you can make compost that is fit for use in your raised bed garden.

The first step is deciding to build piles or even bins in your own yard. You can decide to use drums or even tumbler systems which make compost quick in a space that is small. It also is possible for you to have worms or even larvae incorporated to consume the garbage you place inside and accelerate the composting process.

First, select a spot that is out of direct kind of sunlight and right out of the rain, yet still near raw materials or the garden or the place where this ought to be used.

The second step is gathering materials. You can make use of vegetable scraps, grounds of coffee, tea leaves, fallen leaves, manure, and organic plant materials. However, do not use the manure of humans, cats, dogs, and caged birds. You also must avoid weed seeds, diseased plants, meat, and oil.

You then must shred or even chop materials which are large. In the process of composting, materials of the raw kind to be broken require access to plant surfaces of the moist kind. Chop and even shred things so these do not take long to decompose.

In building your pile, alternate the layer of materials that are brown in color with the green ones. Another option that you have is mixing everything altogether. If necessary, moisten it to make it damp and not too wet. If you happen to make use of piles of the traditional kind, you may decide to have the whole thing left as it is. Nature works quite slowly, breaking down what organic materials are placed in around eight months to a year.

If it happens that you make use of drum, grub, or the worm composters, you will not need to have ingredients layered. All that you need is throwing everything in it. Should you make use of a sphere or a drum system, make sure of rotating or even turning your tumbler so it mixes well. When choosing worms, red wigglers have been known to be the best for processing compost.

Another step, despite being optional, is to have it screened. This allows you to get the larger sticks and even stones right out of the product which is already finished. One sign that your compost is already ready for use is when this is crumbly, rich, and dark. Also, it is ready when you can no longer see the raw materials in it.

The last step is using it in your raised bed garden for planting seeds, added to soil, and for top-dressing the plants that you have. Know that using this material for gardening allows for plants to be healthier and more beautiful.

Chapter 13: Strategies for Planting Seeds in Your Raised Bed Garden

A key to an increase of productivity is the right methods of planting. For a garden to get off to a great start, taking care when planting seeds is important for them to germinate successfully. Highlighted below are the methods that should be used in the planting of seeds in raised bed gardens.

The initial step is checking the resources that are attached to the seeds for any instructions that have to do with planting. Often, this resource is one that has information that have to do with the recommended depth, spacing, along with the required distance right between the rows.

You should always remember the recommended depth for the seed along with its spacing. By planting the seeds in the proper depth, this allows them to truly germinate right under its ideal conditions and will assure the proper development of plant roots. Having these planted in a shallow manner inhibits the support system of the plants, and having the seeds planted in a deep fashion might inhibit its germination or will result in its rotting.

The following step will involve spacing these in rows. This will actually depend on the recommendation that is stated on the seed package. This will allow some room for plants to mature and for the roots to actually grow. Having the vegetables planted closer to the spacing that is recommended usually will result in reduced yields and will risk plant health.

You also need to have the second row of these vegetables planted to the distance for seed spacing. As an example, beans could be planted at around four inches apart.

In raised bed gardens, the rows may be spaced at around four inches rather than the common eighteen until twenty-four inches. Distance between the rows that are being listed is intended for allowing for cultivation right between the rows and just for ease when it comes to harvesting.

Remember this when reading the instructions for planting that you have already accommodated for this space when you designed your boxes. Based on some expert resources, planting some vegetables in a close way in gardens of this sort can help for the conservation of water.

Have the ones which are newly planted watered well for moistening the soil right to the depth that the seeds have. The soil must be kept moist right until the appearance of seedlings. The time of germination will depend on the particular plants.

However, there exist several of them that will just germinate within one or two weeks. Be sure of checking the time of germination that is being stated for you to know the right time when the ones that you happen to have will begin to appear on the gardens that you happen to have.

By using these strategies when planting your seedlings, you can ensure that you get your garden off to the right start. Once your seeds reach the stage of germination, you can thin them out as necessary to provide ample space for growth as they develop into full plants.

A raised bed can be built with any one of several materials, the most popular being timber (treated or untreated). Other materials include, concrete, brick, corrugated sheet metal, sandbags, straw bales or concrete block work. In fact, anything that you must hand that can produce a decent barrier between 4 inched (100mm) and 2-foot (600mm) inches high, can be used to construct a Raised Bed garden.

Raised Bed Dimensions:

As to dimensions, this is really determined by many things including the space you have available, and indeed just exactly what your requirements are. Do you have a large family to feed, or do you intend to sell or barter (bartering is a great way to enjoy a diversity of produce from other gardeners) some of your produce?

With all that considered, a typical raised bed vegetable plot is about 6 foot by 3 foot. This is an ideal size because it allows access from both sides, without you having to step onto the raised bed itself. This enables you to tend to your plants without treading on them in the process – always a good thing! Another popular size is a simple square arrangement around 4-foot (1200mm) square to produce what has become known as a square foot garden. This simple technique can produce an amazing variety of vegetables throughout the growing season As to depth. Overall you should aim for a minimum of 4 inches for a simple herb garden say, and up to 2 foot for root vegetables such as carrots and parsnips.

Bear in mind that the depth of the raised bed does not have to be the height of the sides, to explain a bit further. Say you would like a bed depth of 18 inches (450mm), but you only have timber for 12-inch sides. Simply build your bed in the way described and dig out the interior an extra six inches. This will enable you to fill in the bed with the compost of choice up to the required depth.

It should perhaps be pointed out here though, that this negates the concept of building a raised bed for the advantages to be gained with the height of the bed itself above ground, as will be explained soon in the article.

This system is mainly used where the existing soil is of poor quality and must be replaced/substituted in order to grow the vegetables of your choice.

If you are building multiple raised beds, then they should be placed at least two feet (600mm) apart if possible – more if wheelchair access is required - to allow for easy access between them.

Chapter 14: Building a Timber Raised Bed

The construction of a timber raised bed is fairly simple and straight forward. First of all, level and mark out the area where you would like your raised bed to be. Bear in mind that it should not be under overhanging trees, and in an area where you can have easy access for tending your plants. It should get a minimum of 5-6 hours sunshine per day to produce best results for most vegetables.

For a 6 x 3 x 1.5-foot bed built using traditional decking timber, (I tend to use decking as it is stronger than just plain boards) you will need:

6 lengths decking @ 6' x 6" x 1"

6 lengths decking @ 2'10" x 6" x 1"

10 – 3" x 2" pointed posts @ 30"

Weed control fabric

Galvanized screws or nails

Wire mesh (optional)

Although the following instructions are aimed at an 'anchored' bed, it is also acceptable to simply make the corner posts the same depth as the bed itself and lay the whole frame on the ground – the weight of soil will usually keep it anchored in place.

Begin by marking out with string and pegs, the area of your raised bed, putting down a peg on each corner. This is where you should consider whether or not you are going to dig out any of the existing ground.

Questions to ask yourself are, what depth of compost do I need, versus what height do I want the finished bed to be. If you are growing root vegetables that need depth, but you do not want the finished height to be over 1 foot for instance, then digging out the area to the depth required is your only option. This 'digging out' however may not be necessary if you have good quality topsoil. Simply loosen the existing soil with a garden fork and add your infill mix (more on this soon) to the required level.

Once this decision is made, then we can proceed with building the raised bed. Once you have the pegs in the area that marks out the four corners of your raised bed, you simply take out one peg at a time and replace by hammering down your pointed posts, leaving them a minimum of 18 inches above the ground.

Alternatively, if you make these posts longer then you can use them as handy aids for lifting yourself up when tending your vegetables – just a matter of choice really.

The best way to do this is to put down one post at the end, then temporarily fix the first short end against the post. With this done, then hammer in the second post flush with the end of the 6" x 2" decking plank. Proceed with the two longer sides, then complete the other end. If you just put one screw partially home, then you can easily adjust to suit.

Be sure that you have leveled the timber and that you have left a minimum 12" in height above the first planks, so you are able to complete the job.

I find that it is better to construct with a cordless screwdriver as this does not impact the framework in the same way that hammer, and nails does. Even if you make a slight error it is no trouble to take apart for adjustment.

Once this is done then simply mark out along the inside length two feet from each end, then making sure the construction is straight, hammer in two of the posts to the same height as the others. On the end of the construction, do the same with one post in the center of the framework.

This will give you a strong sturdy construction, which you will need if you do not want the sides of your raised deck to bow under the pressure of the soil.

Point of note:

If you are building with heavier timbers, say 6" x 2" for instance then it may be possible to just put one post in the center of the long side and none on the end. I however tend to lean on the cautious side and would rather aim for stronger option overall. Another tip is to put a cross brace in, if you are concerned about the sides bowing outward.

It is not an exact science, but there are minimum guidelines that must be kept ensuring a construction fit for purpose.

After you have built the sides then just screw down the remaining planking face down along the edge (as in the photograph), to make a comfortable sitting or leaning area for tending to your raised bed.

One thing to consider during this time, is whether or not you are bothered by Gophers or Moles. If you are, then at this point you would place in 1" galvanized wire mesh, covering the bottom of your raised bed. This will be extremely effective in stopping the varmints from destroying your crop and giving you endless grief and heartache!

The weed control fabric should be fixed down the inside of the bed, to keep the wet soil away from the timber. This will help the timber to breathe and make it just that bit longer lasting.

2nd Point of note: Do not use timber that has been treated with creosote, as this may weep through and kill the plants!

If you think you may wish to move them to another location perhaps in the following season, then it is probably best not to hammer the corner posts into the ground and instead make them the actual height of the bed itself.

In other words, your 18-inch-high bed will just need 18-inch-high posts instead of 30 inches or so. These will be fixed in the same way to the corner posts and the infill will hold the whole construction in place – though not as well as the former method!

Here is an example of a larger construction 9 foot in length and 18 inches high. As you can see, this bed is built to sit upon a concrete base. Built with three rows of decking, it has 2 center braces made from 3 x 2 to keep it solid.

Possibly the simplest form of Raised Bed is the 4-foot square model. This can be constructed from decking material by simply adding a short corner post at each corner and fixing it together with decking screws. Everything else is constructed the same way as the larger deck.

Materials needed would be...

2 lengths decking @ 4' x 6" x 1"

2 lengths decking @ 3'10" x 6" x 1"

4 – 2" x 2" pointed posts @ 18"

Weed control fabric

Galvanized screws or nails

Wire mesh (optional)

Again, you have the option to simply use 6-inch posts at the corners if you have no need to 'lock in' to the ground area.

To create a 'Square Foot Garden then simply add a 'grid' as in the picture below using garden canes or even twine to mark out the foot-square areas for planting.

Regarding timber: Some people have concerns over whether or not to use treated or untreated timber to build their raised beds. This is perfectly understandable as more of us become aware of the possibility of contamination regarding chemicals that have been used to treat the timbers.

There are 2 main issues to consider here, and that is the effect that treated timber may have on the plants themselves. And the effect that may be had to the consumer of these same vegetables – if indeed they survive!

Modern timber treatment via tantalization methods according to the soil association is perfectly suitable for gardening structures such as Raised Beds or compost bins – provided the timber has been purchased already treated.

Various blogs will insist that there could be an issue with the chemicals leeching out of the timber, but I have found no evidence for this – although I do agree that it is unwise to use treated timber sawdust in the compost for instance, and that I would not use it on the barbeque where toxins could be released into the atmosphere – and your food!

'Old' methods such as the creosote that would be used on timber railway sleepers however is definitely hazardous to the plants themselves and should be avoided for any planting constructions – unless it is covered or lined with a suitable polythene membrane. In fact, I recommend lining timber Raised Beds anyway as this reduces water leakage and lengthens the life of the timbers.

If the plants foliage comes into contact with creosote then it will wither and die, simple as that.

To sum-up. As far as I can deduct there is no real evidence to show that plants grown in treated timber structures, do in any way absorb the chemicals that have been used to treat the timber.

However – If in doubt simply use untreated timber or line with polythene membrane. Even an untreated timber bed will still give you at least 5-7 years of use before it starts to decay.

Chapter 15: Secrets to Gardening Success

A fair bit of finding your green thumb is trial and error. What works for one gardener may not necessarily prove to be effective for another. However, there is a lot to be said for taking in all the advice and learning what does work for others. That said, here are some of my very own secrets to the gardening success that I enjoy.

Sticking to Favorite Varieties.

There are almost endless options to try in terms of vegetable varieties. It is a great idea to try something new every year. But as you gain your gardening confidence and learn more about how to best use your available space, you may just find that you are sticking to a few favorites. Here are some of my favorite varieties and some must-haves for all vegetable gardens.

Tomatoes. Tomatoes come in all shapes, sizes, colors, and even flavors. For large slicers you simply cannot go wrong with Brandywine. A pink beefsteak, this tomato can reach almost 2lbs per fruit. With bold flavors and an interesting texture, this is a must-have for your garden. It is also found in black, yellow and red varieties, but gardeners tend to agree that the original pink offers the most flavor.

Cherry tomatoes are also popular, and you simply can't go wrong with Sweet 100. Sun Sugar is another tasty variety. Consider also looking for white cherry tomatoes. They taste almost like a dessert fruit when chilled for a few hours. If tomato sauce is on your agenda this year, then you'll have plenty of success with Roma tomatoes.

Peas. Easy to grow and incredibly sweet right out of the pod, peas are a spring must-have. Sugar Pod snap peas are a tasty option that you'll enjoy in stir fries, stews, or just raw right off the vine. Mr. Big is a variety that produces plump peas, and it is a great fun choice for kids to grow. For the best in sweetness, Garden Sweet is a prolific and low-maintenance option.

Beans. Falling under the category of being low maintenance, there are endless options for beans. Some of my favorite pole beans are Kentucky Blue, Monte Gusto (a tasty yellow wax bean), and Purple King. These three should produce well through summer and up to the first frosts. Bush bean favorites are French Stingless, and Italian Rose. With so many options for beans, you should definitely experiment until you find your favorites. Beans are also great for crop rotation as they help to replenish nutrients in the soil for other crops.

Summer squash. Most zucchini and yellow summer squash are prolific and low-maintenance options. But I do like to mix things up a little bit by adding some Green Tiger zucchini, and of course a variety of Patty Pans. The Sunburst Patty Pans offer a rich flavor that you'll quickly find yourself addicted to. Verte et Blanc squash are very similar to Patty Pans, but they are so pretty to grow; and of course, are incredibly tasty.

Winter squash. No garden is complete with growing butternut. Waltham and Butter bush will deliver big. You'll get plenty of squash, with each boasting a rich buttery taste that you will never find in store-bought squash. Buttercup and Lakota winter squash are also tasty, easy options to grow. Any true Hubbard squash will also give you plenty of squash for those pumpkin pies when the holiday season rolls around. A little-known secret is that many pumpkin pies are actually made with Hubbard squash!

Potatoes. Spuds can be enjoyed at any size, so feel free to harvest them at any time. But if you are looking for large potatoes then you simply cannot go wrong with Yukon Gold. The Rio Grande Russet is also a great reliable option. If you are looking for something a little bit different, try growing purple or blue potatoes. The All Blue or Purple Majesty varieties are delicious and hold their color when cooked. Purple mashed potatoes can be a lot of fun for the whole family.

Onions. No winter garden should be without onions. Red Candy is a large and sweet red onion that you'll find easy to grow; for a sweet yellow onion you'll appreciate Walla Walla Sweet. Onions can be one of those subjective flavors, so try a couple of different varieties until you find the ones that best suit your taste buds.

Start with the offerings at your local garden center, and you'll soon find what does and doesn't work for you.

Rain Barrels

Water is certainly easy to gain access to, but one thing I have found to not just be a huge time saver, but also a huge money saver, is to invest in rain barrels. Rain barrels collect and store rainwater that would otherwise be lost as it pours from your roof and other surfaces.

Typically rain barrels are 55-gallon drums, PVC couplings, a vinyl hose, and a screen to keep it free from debris. Relatively easy and budget-friendly to construct, your rain barrels can sit underneath any gutter downspout around your home.

During the summer months your garden is going to need extra water. Watering your vegetables could boost your water bill a fair bit. But during dry periods, having your rain barrel to rely on could make quite a positive difference. Whether you purchase a kit or build one of your own design, you'll find that rain barrels are an incredible addition to your garden.

Raised Bed Materials

There are so many options for building raised beds. I started out with kits using plastic molded frames, and now I've moved on to a design of my own. I've tried out most of the different materials in my pursuit of raised bed perfection. My favorite is pressure treated lumber. It is affordable, durable, and easy to work with. With pressure treated lumber, I can build beds of any size and height to suit my needs exactly. Bricks and cinderblocks also work well.

Garden Twine

To make sure that you always have garden twine on hand when it is needed, simply stick a ball of twine inside of a clay pot. Pull the end of the twine through the drainage hole and set the pot upside down in a convenient location. This way you'll never have to go on the hunt for twine to secure your tomatoes or squash. Those same small clay pots can make great cloches for your tender young plants in the event of an unexpected frost.

Feeding Your Plants

Fertilizers and compost certainly do the job, but there are some little tricks that can give your plants a boost. When you steam or boil vegetables, don't pour the water out. Allow it to cool and then pour it over your garden. You will be impressed at how well your plants respond to this little nutrient boost. Leftover coffee grounds and tea leaves can add a bit of an acid boost for plants that love acidic soil. Rooibos tea is one of the many great tea options you should consider.

Chapter 16: Advantages and Disadvantages of Using Raised Beds

Advantages of Raised Bed Gardening

Accessibility for people who have health challenges such as bad backs because they can't always bend down to the ground, squat or bend over. Growing food in raised beds makes it easily accessible for them to work on their garden thereby erasing the stress and the back pains with other health challenges they may occur during the process.

• The raised bed gardening is known to look more attractive and easier to manage than the traditional garden system. It can be built with simple things like the cedar boxes, which can be placed in yards looking a lot nicer.

• They are not permanent. For example, if you live in an area where you don't want to dig in the ground, or you just can't, for instance if you are renting and the owners don't want you to dig or plant in the ground, then this is a great alternative because you can plant in the boxes and if you move you can just take the boxes apart, throw the dirt away and/or give the plant away and you are good to go.

• The ability to plant over bad soil is another perceived advantage. What I mean by bad is not a contaminated soil, that's another story. By bad soil, I mean if you don't want to take the time to mulch it and create a good soil over some time but you want to plant right away, the raised beds can be placed over the top of the granite and fill it with compost and you will be ready to get started.

Disadvantages of Raised Bed Gardening

•   It is more easily affected by heat and cold in other words, when you are growing in raised beds and you don't have a buffer zone, you don't have an insulation of dirt or soil around it; in the summertime the dirt, soil or compost will dry out a lot quicker thus you'll have to water a lot more. It will also heat up a lot more in the spring, sometimes that can be a benefit but for the most part, it is very hard to control the temperature and the water in a raised bed.

•   Likewise, in the wintertime, raised beds will be affected more by the cold because you can't insulate them unless you've got the giant heating blanket that's 12 feet long that can be wrapped around it.

•   It is harder to put a barrier around it, in other words like a fence or something like that or even if you just want to build up stones and rocks. Some people like to put fences around to keep the deer but they are very persistent, so it is harder to put a border or a fence around it.

• You must replace the material over time no matter what unless of you are using brick or cement blocks. Using this material even creates bigger challenges with lime leach in the summertime when it is 90 degrees outside; those bricks will get seriously hot and that creates another challenge. If you are using wood, you are going to have to replace it over some time.

• Filling the beds with compost is another challenge being faced with raised bed gardening. What compost does over some time is that it settles in, and if you are going to have something permanent in there, for instance, grapes, it is going to just keep settling in and it is going to take the plants down with it as well.

• The challenge of replenishing it after the compost settles in and takes down the plant is another disadvantage as well.

Chapter 17: Types of Growing Beds

How you arrange your garden will hang on upon the analysis you have completed of your site, the particular of climate, topography and dimensions special to it, and what your wish to build from it. However, there are some general principles that most designs will involve, one of which is the sitting of garden beds within Zone 1 of your site.

Your garden beds are where most of your vegetable and herb crops are planted. (Some fruits can be also be Zone 1 crops, although they tend to have specific growing needs, and fruits in Zone 1 tend to be citrus planted in pots rather than beds.) These crops are sited in Zone 1 as they are visited frequently to collect food for the kitchen. Different types of crops benefit from siting in different types of beds, suitable to their preferred growing condition, their structure and the frequency with which you harvest them. Here are some of the more common types of beds that can be adaptable to many kinds of site and may prove useful when making your permaculture design.

• Herb Spiral

The herb spiral has become, arguably, one of the archetypal features of permaculture design. And with good reason. It makes efficient use of space, provides opportunities to create various microclimates and so extending the range of species you can grow in it, it allows for ease of harvesting, and it is an attractive design.

The circular design means that different parts of the spiral get different amounts of sunlight, exposure to wind and vary in temperature. This creates many different niches, which you can also adapt and modify by judicious use of elements such as stones to retain heat, and guild planting to modify soil composition or shade coverage. The top of the spiral tends to be drier that the bottom, as water drains down through the pyramidal structure, while the west side is likely to be the hottest side.

You can grow a large number both edible and therapeutic herb (many have properties of both) on a spiral, including all the cultivars of basils, sages, oregano, thymes, rosemary and tarragons. All herbs need at least some direct sunlight, but plant those that can grow in part shade on the southern side of the spiral. You can easily water your spiral with a single spray head at the top, allowing the water to percolate down through the consecutive beds. Because the beds are fairly shallow, they need to be filled with soil that is rich in organic matter.

• Clipping Beds

Clipping beds are used to plant crops from which you will regularly clip parts, such as leaves and flowers. They are typically placed follow to paths and the inside edges of keyhole beds. They tend to be planted with lower lying species, including chives, dandelions, mustard greens and nasturtiums, that benefit from protection from the wind but access to lots of sunlight.

• Plucking Beds

Typically placed behind the clipping beds, but still within arms-reach for regular harvesting, plucking beds are planted with taller and faster-growing species than their clipping cousins. Suitable plantings include kales, silver beet, broccoli, coriander and zucchini. From these types of plants, you pluck fruit, leaves or seed to eat, and they benefit from frequent harvesting to prevent these edible elements growing too big and so damaging the rootstock.

• Narrow Beds

Species that are most matched to narrow beds involve carrots, peas, radishes, beans, tomatoes and eggplant. They are plants that in the main grow upright and definitely require a lot of direct sunlight in order to flourish and produce good crops. For this reason, narrow beds are generally line up north to south so that they can receive as much sun in both the morning and afternoon as possible. Narrow beds also benefit from the inclusion of some permanent plants, such as asparagus, to help retain the integrity of the soil. Good levels of composing and mulch cover are also recommended for narrow beds.

- **Broad Beds**

Broad beds are set further back from paths than the past beds, and behind the clipping, plucking and narrow beds, as they are generally home to species whose edible parts are harvested only once each growing season, so less frequent access is required. Slower growing species of vegetable make ideal broad bed plantings, and these include pumpkin, cauliflower, sweet corn and cabbages. Other species such as artichokes can be useful as windbreaks and suntraps for companion species within broad beds.

- **Broad Scale Beds**

Broads scale beds are suitable for larger plots as they are used for growing grains. Cultivating grains is a big step towards self-sufficiency as they provide food for people and animals. Corn, wheat, rice, oats and barley are all potential plantings for broad scale beds, depending on the climate conditions of your site. There are different options for crowing your grain. For instance, alley cropping involves growing your grain crop alongside an established tree planting (which offers wind protection) while the Fukuoka grain cropping method which involves planting grains crops alongside rice in winter for harvest in spring.

• Vertical Planting

Types of growing beds. Not all garden beds have to lie horizontally along the ground. There are certain plants that will thrive on a vertical 'bed'. Using trellises, pergolas, fences and the sides of buildings can dramatically increase the size of your available growing space, as well as provide opportunities to modify microclimates (for instance, by locating a pergola opposite a white wall to gain extra heat) and cultivate different types of plant.

There are several species that you can grow vertically, including climbing beans and peas, kiwifruit, cucumbers and grapes.

As with many aspects of permaculture design, instituting garden beds like those outlined above gives plenty of opportunity to increase edge. The herb spiral is a prime example of this, but avoiding straight lines in the design of your other beds, through a keyhole design or similar non-uniform technique, can help maximize your growing area, increase the number of niches, and ultimately expand upon the harvesting potential of your site.

Chapter 18: A Few Reminders for a Successful Application of Raised Bed Gardening Methods

One of the best tips that one should never forget is to make sure that you lay out the beds horizontally so they can face the south of the garden. It will work best if the longest beds are the ones closest to the south.

The reason why this needs to be done is to make sure that all the plants in the garden will receive the proper—and equal amount of lighting. However, by letting the end parts of the beds face the south, you are also limiting your chances of planting more crops, especially when variety is concerned. It will also limit sunlight from reaching small plants at the back. If you can remember, it is said that it is best to plant the tall plants at the back so that the small ones can get sunlight without any blockage.

A balanced diet

Plants need to have a great diet, too! Look for organic fertilizers and make sure that you use certain types of soil amendments that contain the following:

Nitrogen, which is usually found in alfalfa meals, composted manure, and cover crops; Magnesium, which raises PH levels so plants won't dry up, and which can be found in Epsom salts;

Calcium, just like people, plants also need calcium to grow strong. Calcium is usually found in lime or gypsum and provides nutrients most especially for acidic soil;

Potassium, which can be found in greensand or kelp meal;

Phosphorus, which can be found in rock phosphate and bone meal, and;

Sulfur, but only if you are using Alkaline soil and if you need to lower PH levels of extremely acidic plants.

Providing your plants with these nutrients will make you breathe a sigh of relief as it is a sign that nutrient deficiency will be blocked.

Keep those pests away

Pests will do nothing good to your plants and one easy way to keep them away is by making sure that you lay galvanized mesh or hardware cloth across the bottom of the soil once it is on the bed already. Use ½ or ¼" layer of the said mesh cloth, and make sure that it continues up to 3" from where it was first laid on.

However, if you are trying to grow carrots, potatoes, and root crops, you must remember to set the mesh as low as possible or just choose to buy raised garden planters in place of them. These would keep those crops safe.

Mulch between beds

Keep in mind that you should keep a perforated layer of landscape cloth on top of the soil when you are trying to weed out the pathways. Use 2 to 3" of course sawdust or bark mulch to cover this and let it reach up to 1" of the bottom of the bed. After that, you can then staple it to the bed, so you won't have to mulch over and over again. Don't worry about esthetics because mulch will already be able to cover this.

Spread out the soil

By spreading out the soil, you can be sure that every plant you put in there will be able to receive equal amounts of nutrients, water, and sunlight. Of course, you can never be too sure about how equal it is, so you'd just have to add soil amendments, such as lime, compost, or peat and then top it off with topsoil. This way, they can all come together and eventually, you'll notice that they've all been spread out evenly!

Bed Leveling

It may be a bit meticulous to use bed levels, but it will keep those beds safer, which in turn could lengthen their life. This way, you'll be able to use them more in years to come. What you have to do is put a 2 x 4" board on each side of the bed and tap the sides down until you reach the size that you desire.

Root Check

Don't forget to check for roots coming from other plants that may snatch the nutrients that are meant for the plants in your bed. When you see one, pull it out right away. Never ever allow the roots to grow. You can also install a root barrier.

Chapter 19: Chemical Shortcuts

C hemical use in the garden is a balancing act that is often just as likely to kill predators—like this cannibal fly—as pests.

But the reality is that if your crop fails, you'll end up buying replacement food at the grocery store or farmer's market. And every large-scale producer, whether conventional or organic, understands that sometimes you must spray to bring home the harvest. So, without further ado, here are some tips on conventional pesticides that pass the organic test.

Soap and Water

Okay, I really am going to recommend off-the-shelf chemicals shortly. But first, I want to make a plug for water—approved by even beyond-organic gardeners like me.

A few insects—notably aphids and whiteflies—are so tiny that all it takes is one good thunderstorm to wash them so far away from your plants that they have no hope of latching back on. Which means that plants safely protected from storms on your window ledge or in your greenhouse may build up populations of pests that would never make it in the great outdoors.

The solution? A nice hard spray from a garden hose or kitchen faucet can often get rid of an aphid or whitefly infestation before it gets too bad. Just be sure to keep the flow moderate enough so you don't injure the plant. Now that's a type of spray even I will gladly use!

If water isn't enough to do the trick, you might turn to following insecticidal soaps. These relatively innocuous products are like the soaps used in your kitchen but are formulated to be more plant friendly and at the same time more problematic to pests.

What can you kill with soaps? These mild insecticides work by covering up the hole's insects use to breathe and by creeping through the insects' skins to directly harm their cells. As a result, only soft-bodied insects like aphids, lace bugs, mealybugs, mites, psyllids, scale (when young), thrips, and whiteflies are affected. Hard-shelled beetles are immune.

As with any type of chemical, however, soaps come with a few warnings. First, soap will kill soft-bodied beneficial just as easily as they kill similar pest species. And insecticidal soaps don't kill any bugs that show up after the initial treatment, so you'll need to keep reapplying as new insects colonize the soaped-up plant.

The other concern with soaps comes in relation to the plants themselves. Even assuming you carefully steer clear of detergents (which are bad for plant leaves), insecticidal soaps can cause allergic reactions in certain types of plants.

Cucumbers are the only vegetable reputed to be thoroughly anti-soap, but flowers of other types of fruits and vegetables can be harmed by the sudsy spray. Meanwhile, stressed plants of all sorts are likely to react negatively to soap application, as are plants treated during hot, sunny days.

If in doubt, treat a small area and keep an eye out for yellow or brown leaf spotting during the twenty-four following hours before choosing to spray your entire patch.

All of that said, insecticidal soaps are one of the safest organic pesticides on the market.

Just be sure to buy products intended for garden use, apply no more often than once or twice a week, and dilute concentrates with rainwater or other soft water if your tap is full of calcium.

Following those instructions, you are not likely to go too far wrong using soap.

Traps

Flypaper is the classic sticky trap. Here, the glue-coated surface is being used to control fungus gnats in a mushroom fruiting area.

Physical or chemical traps are another type of garden shortcut that are unlikely to cause negative effects in your plot. The theory is simple—pests are attracted to a scent or a color, then they either drown or become stuck to a flypaper-like surface on which they perish. The primary downsides are cost and fiddliness you'll need to refresh traps relatively frequently to maintain their efficacy within the garden. Environmental repercussions, on the other hand, are minimal.

I'll begin with the least useful type of trap—pheromone traps. A pheromone is simply a scent that animals release into the air to communicate with others of their species. In the insect world, pheromones are precursors to sex, attracting males to a female ready to mate.

Sticky traps are in higher demand by the home gardener because they capture both males and females indiscriminately. These simple traps consist of a piece of colored plastic covered by a substance like Tangle foot that makes interested insects stick tight. You can either buy sticky traps ready-made or can purchase a bottle of glue to coat homemade traps of various sorts.

Once again, sticky traps see the most use as monitoring equipment, especially in greenhouses where yellow cards can give managers an idea when pest populations are about to explode. Placement of cards is of prime importance in this scenario—always close to preferred host plants but in various orientations and locations depending on which type of insect is meant to be trapped. For example, fungus gnats are best caught with horizontal sticky cards placed just above the soil surface, while sticky cards close to the crop canopy work better for trips.

But can't you just use sticky cards like flypaper to get rid of all the pests? Red sticky balls (or Red Delicious apples) covered with Tangle foot are often used to great effect by organic orchards intent upon trapping apple maggots while the real apples on the tree are still young. Beyond that example, however, large-scale use of sticky traps for pest eradication runs into several hurdles difficult to overcome.

First comes sheer labor. Sticky traps need to be changed out once or twice a week, which either means purchasing a new premade trap (pricey) or removing and reapplying the Tanglefoot coating from the existing trap. In many cases, sticky traps must be located only a few feet apart for full coverage. And perhaps more daunting from an ecosystem perspective is the tendency of these traps to catch pollinators who mistake the bright colors for a nectar-rich flower. Parasitic wasps are also often found on yellow sticky traps, meaning that your hornworm population may explode even as your winged aphid infestation declines.

Moving on from pheromone and sticky traps, let's consider a DIY trap that's easy to make at home—beer traps for slugs. This old standby consists of taking any shallow dish, filling it partway up with beer, then waiting for the slugs to move in and die. According to a Mother Earth News survey, beer traps are 80 percent effective at trapping slugs . . . but what kind of slug do they catch?

Interestingly, many gardeners report that the fermentation attracts slugs, not the beer itself. So, you can get just as good results by using bread yeast mixed with warm water and sugar to produce a yeasty scent like that found in a can of beer.

This raises a dilemma: if the slugs are being drawn to fermentation, are they really herbivores that graze upon garden leaves? Or are the slugs being drowned instead the beneficial species that help decompose organic matter . . . which is often being worked upon by fungi and thus has a yeasty scent?

Now that I've rained on your parade quite thoroughly, it is time to mention the sole type of trap I would use in my own garden—shingle traps for squash bugs. No, this isn't any type of fancy, purchased product. It is merely a few roofing shingles (or a board) placed at the base of an infested squash plant. Squash bugs like to hide at night under thin objects close to the ground, so they'll congregate beneath the shingles or boards. If you head out to the garden first thing in the morning when the air is cool and the insects are slow, it is easy to lift your trap and push the napping inhabitants into a cup of water. Of course, that brings me back to my favorite type of organic insect control—yes, I am once again telling you to hand-pick.

More Potent Pesticides

Pesticides are most organic gardeners' last resort.

Soaps and traps might not be the solution to your insect explosion, but if you need a shortcut then other organic pesticides are there to help. But there are times when it is better to save your crop with sprays than to give up on a harvest entirely.

There aren't many types of organic pesticides on the home-garden market, so I'm going to give you a quick rundown on each one. The first category is the dormant oils, which are like insecticidal soap. Dormant oils work via suffocation, can damage stressed plants and any type of blossom, must be reapplied frequently, and are going to kill any nearby beneficial just as efficiently as the pests you are targeting with your spray. When applied in winter or early spring to woody plants (like apple trees), though, dormant oils can help protect against aphids, mites, and scales. And they seem to be relatively innocuous to non-insects in the vicinity, which is a major plus.

Although the name is similar, neem oil operates in a different way. Neem oil will smother insects just as dormant oil does upon direct contact, but the inclusion of naturally occurring azedarach has a longer lasting repellent effect upon any insects attempting to suck or chew on the treated plant. Most effective against insects' juvenile stages, neem oil has been shown to target aphids, beetles, caterpillars, lace bugs, leafhoppers, leaf miners, mealybugs, psyllids, trips, and whiteflies for up to two weeks.

The close targeting of neem oil to problematic nibblers is enticing, but there is one distressing feature of the pesticide to be aware of. Neem oil is very toxic to honeybee larvae, so it is best to apply it in late evening or at night after the bees have gone to bed. The goal is for most of the neem to have soaked into the plants by the time pollinators arrive the following morning, protecting honeybees from unintentionally bringing the toxic substance back to their hives.

And now, at last, it is time to address sprays like Bt (used on cabbageworms, tomato hornworms, corn earworms, European corn borers, and squash vine borers), Spinosad (a broad-spectrum insecticide that kills most insects on contact), and pyrethrin's (used on cabbage loppers, cucumber beetles, leafhoppers, stink bugs, and trips) that are very similar to conventional pesticides but are organic certified because they are derived from a natural source. The theory is that chemicals found naturally in the environment are less likely to harm the ecosystem or humans who eventually imbibe small quantities while chowing down on the bug-free crop. True or false?

The jury's still out on that question but is leaning toward "false." A good example is the case of rotenone, an extract from a tropical plant that started being used on organic farms in 1947. Unfortunately, more recent studies discovered that rotenone exposure results in human symptoms like those created by Parkinson's disease, so the product is no longer allowed on shelves in the United States.

The organic pesticides currently on the market are presumed to be safer than rotenone was from a human point of view. However, most are broad-spectrum, affecting any insect they come in contact with. Meanwhile, pyrethrin's are particularly harmful to honeybees. And it is impossible to know which problematic side effects simply haven't been discovered yet.

In the end, when it comes to chemical shortcuts, you'll need to decide for yourself how daring you are willing to be. Anything that kills a bad insect is likely to kill just as many good insects. The question is—are you willing to put up with the associated loss?

Chapter 20: Planting

Before you dive in, be aware of which bearing the sun is originating from—you don't need taller plants to conceal out anything behind them.

I planted once a zinnia at the front of my raised beds without perusing the seed bundle. The blossoms developed to be around three to four feet high! They were clearly not a decent, low mounding assortment.

You need to ensure the warmth cherishing foods grown from the ground that you plant—tomatoes, squash, melons, cucumbers, and so on. — will get in any event six to eight hours of daylight daily (ideally more like eight).

Regardless of whether you are planting seeds or planting seedlings, make certain to peruse the seed parcel or plant tag cautiously, with the goal that you recognize what conditions the plants need to flourish.

When planting root veggies, for instance, you'll need to follow the headings for diminishing once the sprouts begin jabbing through the dirt. While it may appear to be a waste when you are hauling them out, beet grows, for instance, can be spared and prepared in a serving of mixed greens. Carrot seedlings, then again, ought to be covered, as clarified right now diminishing carrots. Diminishing beets, carrots, radishes, turnips, and other root veggies, will energize solid root development and greater vegetables.

For certain plants, like tomatoes, you need to give them enough space with the goal that air can course between the plants. This forestalls illnesses. You likewise need light to arrive at the plants and organic product.

However, you would prefer not to space tomatoes excessively far separated, which can permit weeds to sneak in. Remember these tips for other nightshade veggies, like peppers, eggplants, and tomatillos.

Make certain to set up a customary watering plan with the goal that you remember to hydrate your delicate youthful plants. Cloches or column spread can be used to shield them from a pre-summer ice.

Why planting seriously in raised beds?

Concentrated planting is a procedure that lessens void space in the nursery where weeds can discover a space to develop. Planting seedlings closer together methods the plants themselves go about as a living mulch over the dirt, keeping it cool and diminishing vanishing.

Plants that do well when planted seriously incorporate greens, like arugula, mustard greens, lettuce, and spinach. Our edibles master, Niki Jabbour, plants her veggies in scaled down lines or groups. Also, she just plants a tad bit of each harvest at once to decrease nourishment squander—you needn't bother with 100 heads of lettuce prepared simultaneously!

Progression planting in raised beds

This carries us to progression planting. In case you are pulling out your spring crops, like peas and root veggies, or your garlic reap in the late spring, there is no reason why you cannot add more veggies to that vacant space.

You should give seeds a head starts under your develop lights. When planting, recollect the manure tip: change the dirt to include a few supplements back in and energize a productive reap. Great soil wellbeing is the way into a flourishing nursery.

Include plant bolsters so you have space for additional plants

When planting a raised bed, make certain to give a portion of your plants something to climb—trellises, an old bit of grid, dairy cattle boards, and so on. On the off chance that you've at any point planted a squash seedling in a raised bed, you realize that as it develops, the plant will assume control over half, if not the entire nursery! Including vertical structures will bolster the climbers, like cucumbers, squash, beans, peas, and melons.

Plant a blend of veggies and blossoms in your raised beds.

I like to plant blossoms, like zinnias, nasturtiums, and universe in my raised beds. They pull in pollinators that will thus fertilize my tomato blossoms, squash blooms, and cucumber sprouts (It is success win!). Frequently when I'm in the nursery on a mid-year day, hummingbirds bounce around me, hoping to arrive on my zinnias. Plant a couple of additional blossoms, so you can leave some for the pollinators and cut the rest to assemble summer bunches for containers.

You can likewise use blossoms as common bug control when planting a raised bed. I base a portion of my plantings on the nuisances that have attacked my nursery in past seasons, and others as preventive measures.

Here are a couple of models:

Alyssum pulls in parasitic wasps, which deal with a huge measure of awful bugs, like cabbage worms, cucumber insects, squash vine borers, tomato hornworm, cutworms, vagabond moth caterpillars, and that's only the tip of the iceberg.

Hyssop pulls in the two-spotted smell bug, which devours the hatchlings of the Colorado potato insect—an adversary that likes to unleash destruction on my tomatillos.

Marigolds are planted to repulse nematodes under the dirt. I've likewise perused an ongoing report that says they repulse whitefly from tomato plants.

If it is all the same to you giving up a couple, nasturtiums can be used as a snare crop for aphids.

Conclusion

Starting a raised bed garden is a great way to accommodate that budding little gardener in your family. It is the ideal way for kids to learn about nature; they will see the wonder of a little seedling emerging from the ground, growing tiny leaves and soon develop into a mature plant with fruit. Planting in raised beds will make it convenient for both you and the young ones to reach every plant in the box without ending up with muddy feet or knees full of dirt.

Now that you have all the information needed, it is time to get going. Walk around your available space during the day to find a sunny location. Once you have decided where you want to place your raised bed, you must choose the size and dimensions. The following step is to make a list of everything you will need, from the soil, compost and other materials, to the frames. Once your bed is up and filled up with the soil mixture, it is time to turn your attention to the plants. Select the type of veggies you want to grow according to the guidelines I have provided. If you want to grow plants from seeds, you will have to do some prior planning since it will take time for them to develop into seedlings ready to be planted outside in your box. Otherwise, you can purchase seedlings to plant directly into your raised beds.

Now most of the work is done and the fun part starts. While you wait for your veggies to grow, a little attention is needed; water them regularly and keep your eyes peeled for any pests or weeds. Then wait for the fruit to ripen and start harvesting!

Growing vegetables in raised beds makes gardening a pleasure. With limited time and space, you can grow an abundance of food in a small area. The benefits are numerous; fewer weeds and pests, better drainage, better soil, no compacting of the soil, less pain potential for you, the gardener, to name but a few. Your friends will envy your neat, attractive garden and harvest of healthy, tasty vegetables. If there was ever any need for gardening enthusiasts to exercise creativity and their building know-how in the garden, there is nothing like taking on raised bed gardening as a project to prove it.

From its more obvious advantages such as soil control, easy pest management and overall ease when it comes to maintenance, it is also ideal for anyone with physical disabilities and limitations, as it provides better access for your garden without requiring you to put a strain on your back. In terms of water, it is actually easier to maintain and set up an irrigation system for raised gardens. And if you have pets, you can rest assured that they won't be messing up your garden, as it will be harder for them to get to it.

You've now been equipped with all the necessary knowledge to select the right plants and tools to grow yourself a fantastic raised bed garden that will brighten up your home, as mentioned in the here raised bed gardening has a huge variety of benefits and the feeling of accomplishment felt from growing a successful, vibrant raised bed garden are endless.

Now enjoy your fresh vegetables even during the winter!

Mathematics:
Ideas and Applications

Mathematics: Ideas and Applications

Daniel D. Benice

MONTGOMERY COLLEGE

Academic Press

NEW YORK
SAN FRANCISCO
LONDON
A Subsidiary of Harcourt Brace Jovanovich, Publishers

ACADEMIC PRESS, INC.
111 FIFTH AVENUE, NEW YORK, NEW YORK 10003

UNITED KINGDOM EDITION PUBLISHED BY
ACADEMIC PRESS, INC. (LONDON) LTD.
24/28 OVAL ROAD, LONDON NW1

ISBN: 0-12-088250-7
Library of Congress Catalog Card
Number: 77-91587

PRINTED IN THE UNITED STATES OF AMERICA

In memory of my mother
Rose Laufer Benice

Contents

Preface

Mathematics: Ideas and Applications is designed to provide an exciting semester or two of mathematics for students in liberal arts, general education, and elementary education. The course may be of a general, survey, cultural, or appreciation nature. The book presents fresh and exciting topics, a variety of applications, historical notes where appropriate, and interesting exercises. In search of fresh ideas and applications, I have examined books and journals in many liberal arts disciplines. The result of this effort can be seen here in the application of mathematics to many fields, including: anthropology, archaeology, art, astronomy, biology, business, chemistry, computers and data processing, ecology, economics, electronics, farming, geography, geology, history, linguistics, medicine, mineralogy, music, physics, psychology, sociology, and others. Also presented are applications of mathematics to sports, consumerism, logic, games, tricks, and recreational mathematics.

Students will use arithmetic skills as they study the various applications. Although some of the applications do require a little algebra, manipulation is rarely needed.

There are no strange formulas to memorize, no busy work, and no drill. Instead, students will look at different branches of mathematics from an elementary point of view—complete with an abundance of inspiring applications. The approach is direct, moving quickly to demonstrate the usefulness of the mathematics introduced. Reviewers have used such words as "captivating" and "gemlike" to describe these applications. I expect you too will enjoy them.

Often an entire section is an application. Other times the section develops the mathematical idea and then the exercises present several applications and further development. I cannot overemphasize the importance of the exercises to the content and adaptability of the book. Since many of the exercises are in fact applications, the heading for exercises reads "Applications and Exercises."

For the most part, sections can be omitted freely, and the eight chapters can be taught in almost any order. Flexibility in topic selection and in handling of each topic chosen are built in. Although specific guidelines and outlines are presented in the *Instructor's Manual*, a note seems in order here. Chapter 1 is intended to be a stimulus and starting point for the further investigation that is presented in Chapters 2 through 7. Chapter 8 on computers can be covered at any point and then used throughout the remainder of the course. My personal preference is that Chapter 8 be used last because of its summary nature. The *Instructor's Manual* includes teaching suggestions, references to outside sources, additional exercises, and the answers to those exercises which are not answered in the text.

The book is intended to convey the importance of mathematics as well as its beauty. I expect that in the end students will have enjoyed a mathematics course, gained an appreciation for mathematics, and raised their level of understanding and ability.

I am pleased to acknowledge the assistance provided by the editorial and production staffs at Academic Press. I would also like to credit the following people who reviewed the manuscript for Academic Press and made many helpful suggestions: Bernard Eisenberg (Kingsborough Community College), Redford Fowler Yett (University of Southern Alabama), Eugene Gover (Northeastern University), James T. Hardin (formerly of Philadelphia Community College), Kenneth Retzer (Illinois State University), Donald Short (San Diego State University), and James Snow (Lane Community College).

DANIEL D. BENICE

Mathematics:
Ideas and Applications

Patterns

"A mathematician, like a painter or poet, is a maker of patterns." These words from G. H. Hardy's *A Mathematician's Apology* may not seem consistent with the way you see mathematics. Perhaps you think of mathematics as mostly calculations and manipulations. If you do, then there is a pleasant surprise for you as you read this book. This chapter and much of the rest of the book are designed to show you the beauty and fascination of patterns in many areas of mathematics. With this chapter we hope to whet your appetite. Each of the chapters that follows presents a different branch of mathematics from both an intuitive and a practical point of view. In several instances you will see that what begins as "fun and games" often leads to important applications.

FIBONACCI SEQUENCES AND OTHER PATTERNS

Patterns are often present in *sequences* of numbers. Such sequences arise in a variety of settings, as you will soon see. Before we look at the first application, however, a bit of orientation is in order. Here are three sequences and a brief explanation or description of each.

1, 2, 3, 4, 5, . . .	The counting numbers, or natural numbers
2, 4, 6, 8, 10, . . .	Positive even numbers
1, 4, 9, 16, 25, . . .	Squares of natural numbers

The three dots after the numbers of each sequence indicate that the pattern continues indefinitely. Each number of a sequence is called a *term* of the sequence.

The following puzzle yields an interesting sequence.

How many pairs of rabbits can be produced from a single pair of rabbits in a year, if each pair produces a new pair every month, deaths do not occur, and only rabbits that are at least one month old reproduce?

At the beginning there is 1 pair of rabbits. After one month there is still 1 pair of rabbits, but now they are able to produce a pair of rabbits. So, after two months there are 2 pairs of rabbits. One of these pairs is capable of producing and one pair is not yet able to do so. After three months there are 3 pairs of rabbits. Two of the 3 pairs are capable of producing, so at four months there are 5 pairs of rabbits. The first two terms of the sequence being generated are 1, after which each term is the sum of the two preceding terms of the sequence.

$$1, 1, 2, 3, 5, 8, 13, 21, 34, \ldots$$

Leonardo Fibonacci
(1180–1250)

This sequence was originally presented, along with the rabbit problem, by Leonardo of Pisa in 1202 when he introduced algebra into Italy. He was also known as Leonardo Fibonacci (Leonardo, son of Bonacci) and is considered the greatest mathematician of the thirteenth century. The sequence 1, 1, 2, 3, 5, 8, 13, 21, 34, etc. is called the *Fibonacci sequence.*

It is not difficult to see why the Fibonacci sequence contains terms that are the sum of the two preceding terms. Note, for example, that when there are 21 pairs of rabbits, 13 of the pairs have been around for a month and are therefore capable of producing more rabbits. This means that those 13 pairs will produce 13 pairs. Combine these 13 pairs of offspring with the present 21 pairs of rabbits to get the next total of 34 pairs of rabbits.

Numbers from Fibonacci's sequence occur in a variety of places in nature. A sunflower blossom has spirals that go in opposite directions. The number of spirals going in one direction and the number that go in the opposite direction are nearly always two consecutive numbers from the Fibonacci sequence.

A similar relationship also exists for pineapples, evergreen cones, daisies, and some other plants. The number of petals of some flowers are numbers from the Fibonacci sequence: lily (3 petals), buttercup (5), delphinium (8), marigold (13), aster (21), daisy (34, 55, or 89).

Those of you with backgrounds in electronics may be interested to know that the numbers of the Fibonacci sequence can be generated by a specially designed electrical circuit. If all of the elements indicated by ⋛ in the circuit below are 1-ohm resistors, and the current in the last branch is 1 ampere, then the voltages across the resistors are (from right to left) the Fibonacci numbers 1, 1, 2, 3, 5, 8, 13, 21, 34, 55, ...

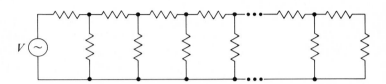

The sequence 1, 1, 2, 3, 5, 8, 13, . . . is often considered to be *the* Fibonacci sequence because it is the original Fibonacci sequence. But any sequence in which each term after the second is the sum of the two preceding terms can be considered a Fibonacci sequence. In this sense, the following are two more examples of Fibonacci sequences.

$$4, 7, 11, 18, 29, 47, \ldots$$
$$5, 1, 6, 7, 13, 20, 33, \ldots$$

It does not matter what the first two terms of the sequence are. As long as each of the other terms is the sum of the two terms preceding it, the sequence is called a Fibonacci sequence.

French mathematician Edouard Anatole Lucas (1842–1891) introduced the sequence 2, 1, 3, 4, 7, 11, 18, . . . and derived some relationships among the numbers of other individual Fibonacci sequences. Consequently, Fibonacci sequences other than the original Fibonacci sequence are sometimes called Lucas sequences. Astronomers have noticed that eclipses of the sun and moon show certain patterns of repetition every 6, 41, 47, 88, 135, 223, and 358 years. Notice that these numbers form a Lucas sequence.

Here's a magic trick that uses a Fibonacci sequence. You (the

Little Pinkie; 5 petals

Cosmos: 8 petals

Tithonia: 13 petals

magician) can quickly determine the sum of any ten consecutive Fibonacci numbers that anyone writes down in sequence. How? The sum is always 11 times the seventh number in the sequence. For the numbers 3, 5, 8, 13, 21, 34, 55, 89, 144, 233, the sum is equal to 11 times 55, $11 \cdot 55$, which is 605. (You might want to check this by adding all the numbers.) All you need is a quick way of multiplying 11 times any number n. Here are two ways. One way: $11 \cdot n$ is the same as $10 \cdot n + 1 \cdot n$ or $10 \cdot n + n$. For example, $11 \cdot 12 = 10 \cdot 12 + 12 = 120 + 12 = 132$. Another way: To multiply 11 times any number, write the number and write the same number below it but shifted one place to the left, and add. Thus, $11 \cdot 12$ is

$$\begin{array}{r} 12 \\ 12 \\ \hline 132 \end{array}$$

which is a shortcut for

$$\begin{array}{r} 12 \\ 11 \\ \hline 12 \\ 12 \\ \hline 132 \end{array}$$

Make up a few Fibonacci sequences and verify that this trick works. In Application 4 we'll see *why* it works.

APPLICATIONS AND EXERCISES

1. Solve Fibonacci's problem: How many pairs of rabbits can be produced in a year?

2. Fill in the blanks in the following Fibonacci (or Lucas) sequences.
   (a) 2, 6, 8, _14_ , _22_ , _36_ , _58_ , _94_.
   (b) 2, 3, 5, _8_ , _13_ , _21_ , _34_ , _55_ , _89_
   (c) _12_ , _19_ , _31_ , _50_ , _81_ , 131, 212
   (d) _3_ , _10_ , _13_ , _23_ , 36, _59_ , 95
   (e) 35, _____, 58, _____, _____, _____

3. If a_n is any term (the nth term) of a sequence, then a_{n+1} is the term after it and a_{n-1} is the term before it.

$$\ldots, a_{n-1}, a_n, a_{n+1}, \ldots$$

Use a_{n-1}, a_n, and a_{n+1} to express the relationship among the terms of a Fibonacci sequence.

4. Now let's find out *why* the magic trick presented in this section does indeed work. Let the first of the ten terms of a Fibonacci sequence be called x, and let the second term be y. Then the third term is $x + y$, the sum of the first two terms.

(a) Show that the fourth term is then $x + 2y$.
(b) Show that the fifth term is $2x + 3y$.
(c) Find the sixth through tenth terms. As a check, note that the tenth term is $21x + 34y$.
(d) Add all ten terms. You should get $55x + 88y$ as the total.

Now look at the seventh term, which is $5x + 8y$. What is the relationship between the seventh term, $5x + 8y$, and the sum, $55x + 88y$? The sum is 11 times $5x + 8y$. In other words, the sum is 11 times the seventh term of the sequence.

5. One of the first sequences we looked at in this section was a sequence consisting of the squares of numbers. Do you know why 3^2, or $3 \cdot 3$, is called 3 *squared?* Examine the illustration below and write a brief explanation.

6. The cost of sending a letter changed from 3¢ in 1957 to 13¢ in 1976. The sequence of costs: 3¢, 4¢, 5¢, 6¢, 8¢, 10¢, 13¢.

(a) Show that the increase from 4¢ to 5¢ represents a 25% increase in cost.
(b) Which cost change represents the smallest percentage increase?
(c) Which cost change represents the largest percentage increase?

Pascal's Triangle   The array of numbers shown below is not a sequence, but it is a pattern with applications in the study of probability (see page 340). It is called *Pascal's triangle*, after the French mathematician Blaise Pascal, who introduced it to the Western world in 1665. The triangle had appeared more than 200 years earlier, however, in publications by the Chinese mathematicians Yan Yui and Chu shih-chieh.

7. (a)   The triangle shown contains only five rows. There is a sixth row, a seventh row, and so on. The numbers in each row are determined by the numbers in the row above it. Study the triangle to determine the pattern used to obtain a row from the row that precedes it. (*Hint:* An arithmetic operation is used.)
    (b)   Obtain row six.
    (c)   Obtain row seven.
    (d)   There are other kinds of patterns apparent in Pascal's triangle. If the 1 at the top of the triangle is ignored, then the triangle becomes

$$
\begin{array}{ccccccc}
 & & 1 & & 1 & & \\
 & 1 & & 2 & & 1 & \\
1 & & 3 & & 3 & & 1 \\
\end{array}
$$
$$
\begin{array}{ccccccccc}
1 & & 4 & & 6 & & 4 & & 1 \\
\end{array}
$$

Now the second number in each row is always the row number. Other patterns are less obvious and involve the adding and subtracting of elements. Find and describe several other patterns. You'll find this easier to do if the next two rows (obtained in parts (b) and (c)) are included in the triangle.

Data Processing Card   Patterns extend to many areas of application, as you will see throughout this chapter. Some of these applications concern computers. Data processing cards are coded according to a pattern. A typical card is shown next. It has twelve horizontal rows in which punches (perforations) can be made in order to record information. At the bottom of the card there is a row of 9's. Just above it is a row of 8's, and so on. Near the top of the card is a row of 0's. The row above the zeros, although unlabeled, is a row of 11's; the row above that is an unlabeled row of 12's. Machines record any letter of the alphabet in a vertical column by making two different punches in that column. The letter A is represented by a 12 punch and a 1 punch, abbreviated 12-1. The letter L is 11-3; Y is 0-8.

8. (a) Examine the card. Then describe the pattern for representing the letters A through I.
   (b) Describe the pattern for representing the letters J through R.
   (c) Describe the pattern for representing the letters S through Z.
   (d) Explain why "junior," which is abbreviated "JR," is the key to remembering the entire card code for letters.

SEQUENCES AND ASTRONOMY

Observing a pattern led German mathematician J. D. Titius to realize a rule for the successive distances of planets from the sun. He published the rule in 1766. Several years later, German astronomer Johann Elbert Bode called attention to Titius' rule, which has since been named *Bode's law*. First have a look at the following table. Then we'll examine the rule.

Planet	Bode's distance	Actual distance[a]
Mercury	4	3.9
Venus	7	7.2
Earth	10	10.0
Mars	16	15.2
—	28	—
Jupiter	52	52.0
Saturn	100	95.3

[a]See Application 5 for the units of measure.

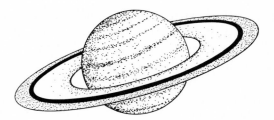

Bode's law, the rule that yields the distances in the table, is based on the sequence 0, 3, 6, 12, 24, 48, 96, ... If the number 4 is added to each of the terms of this sequence, the results are Bode's distances 4, 7, 10, 16, 28, 52, 100. This sequence is Bode's law for the relative distances of planets from the sun. Perhaps you have noticed that 28 is missing in the table and you may know that there are other planets beyond Saturn, yet they are not given in the table. At the time Bode's law was first presented, only the entries shown in the table were known. What has happened since then is presented in the exercises and applications that follow.

APPLICATIONS AND EXERCISES

1. The planet Uranus was discovered by William Herschel in 1781 at a distance of 192. How does this compare with Bode's distance for the next planet beyond Saturn?

2. After the discovery of Uranus and its agreement with Bode's law, astronomers were disturbed that there was no planet to correspond to the Bode distance 28. Then, in 1801, the first (and largest) of the asteroids was discovered at an actual distance of 27.6. Large numbers of such minor planets travel around the sun in a path that is basically between Mars and Jupiter.

Using Bode's law as a starting point, astronomers discovered Neptune in 1846 at a distance of 301. How does this compare with Bode's distance?

3. Pluto was discovered in 1930 at a distance of 396. How does this distance fit Bode's law?

4. Bode's law is the result of observing a pattern in a sequence of numbers. In the end, unfortunately, the law fails for the distant planets. Does this make you feel that the law should be deleted from the history of astronomy? Explain.

5. The actual distances of planets given in the table are measured in tenths of astronomical units (AU). For common usage, Earth is considered to be 1 AU from the sun, that is, one tenth of the value shown in the table is the actual distance of the planet from the sun.
   (a) Convert all of the other actual distances in the table to astronomical units.
   (b) Since the earth is 93 million miles from the sun, 1 AU equals _____ miles.
   (c) How many miles is Jupiter from the sun?

6. If Mercury is ignored and Venus is considered the first planet, then the Bode distance (call it B) can be computed from the planet's position p (for Venus $p = 0$, for Earth $p = 1$, etc.) by the formula $B = 3 \cdot 2^p + 4$. Verify this formula for Venus, Mars, the asteroids, and Saturn. (Note that $2^0 = 1$.)

7. Study the illustration that follows. What relation does it suggest between the number of moons a planet has and its

distance from the asteroid belt? The numbers indicate how many moons each planet has.

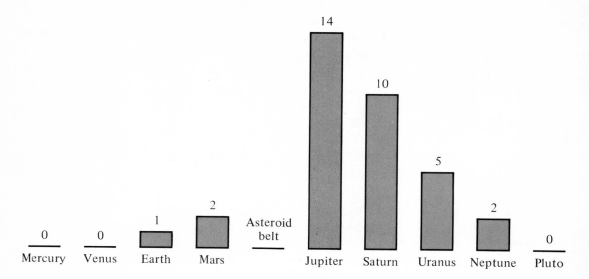

ARITHMETIC AND GEOMETRIC SEQUENCES

Sequences in which successive terms differ by a constant are called *arithmetic sequences*. The sequence 1, 3, 5, 7, . . . is arithmetic because each term is 2 more than the term before it. The sequence 9, 12, 15, 18, . . . is also arithmetic. Can you determine the next term after 18? You should have noted that each term is 3 more than the term to its left. So the term after 18 should be 3 more than 18, that is, 21. The sequence 35, 29, 23, 17, . . . is arithmetic because each term is 6 less than the term before it.

Sequences in which each term is a constant times the term before it are called *geometric sequences*. The sequence 1, 2, 4, 8, . . . is geometric because each term is 2 times the term before it. The sequence 3, 12, 48, 192, . . . is also geometric. Can you determine the next term after 192? You'll probably need pencil and paper. You should have noticed that each term is 4 times the term to its left. So the term after 192 is 4 times 192, that is, 768.

A variety of applications of arithmetic and geometric sequences is presented in the exercises that follow. One interesting observation was made in 1798 by English economist Thomas R. Malthus. He pointed out that populations (such as man) produce far more offspring than are needed to replace themselves; thus, such populations grow geometrically. On the other hand, food for the population grows only arithmetically. The implication for the future is obvious. To fully appreciate the problem, you might like to compare the following two sequences. Both begin with the same term. The first sequence is arithmetic, with a difference of 2 between terms. The second is a geometric sequence in which each term is 2 times the term before it.

Arithmetic: 1, 3, 5, 7, 9, 11, 13, 15, 17, 19, 21, . . .

Geometric: 1, 2, 4, 8, 16, 32, 64, 128, 256, 512, 1024, . . .

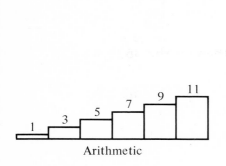
Arithmetic

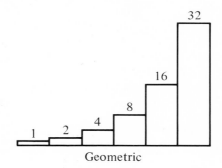
Geometric

APPLICATIONS AND EXERCISES

1. Suppose you are paid every Friday and your first check this month is on the fifth.
    (a)   What are the dates of the other pay days this month?
    (b)   What kind of sequence do the dates form?

2. For each of the following sequences, determine the next term and indicate whether or not it is an arithmetic sequence.
    (a)   2, 4, 6, 8, . . .   (b)   2, 4, 8, 16, . . .
    (c)   5, 8, 11, 14, . . .   (d)   0, 10, 20, 30, . . .
    (e)   1, 3, 6, 10, 15, . . . (f)   20, 18, 16, 14, . . .

3. For each of the following sequences, determine the next term and indicate whether or not it is a geometric sequence.

(a) 1, 3, 9, 27, . . .   (b) 10, 20, 40, 80, . . .
(c) 5, 10, 15, 20, . . .   (d) 1, 10, 100, 1000, . . .
(e) 100, 200, 300, 400, . . .   (f) 48, 24, 12, 6, . . .

4. Here is an example of a *chain letter* that is based on geometric sequences. You receive a letter with a list of six names. You are asked to mail a dollar to the person at the top of the list, cross that name off the list, and add your name to the bottom. Then you mail copies of the letter to six friends. Each friend is supposed to mail a dollar to the person at the top of the list, then delete that name and add his name to the bottom. Finally, each of the six friends sends out six letters as directed. If the chain remains unbroken, this will continue for a while and will have quite a large payoff for you when your name gets to the top of the list. In practice you won't have the opportunity to get rich by means of chain letters, because such chain letters are against the law.

(a) If the chain is unbroken, your name will be on the 6 letters you send first, then on the 36 letters sent by your six friends (each of the six friends sends six letters, for a total of 36 letters they send), and so on. What kind of sequence do the numbers 6, 36, . . . form?

(b) What is the third number in the sequence?

(c) How much money will you receive if the chain is unbroken?

5. Here is another form of chain letter. This one is of the "pyramid" variety. You send a letter to a friend requesting him to send you a dollar and to forward your letter to a friend who will send both of you a dollar and continue the chain. (As before, such chain letters are against the law.)

(a) The first person must pay out $1, the second person $2, and so on. What kind of sequence do the payments form?

(b) Explain why the word "pyramid" is used to describe this chain.

(c) Why is the chain likely to be broken soon?

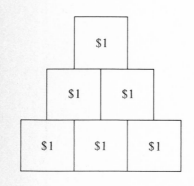

6. Consider a game in which you bet a certain amount of money. If you win, you win an amount equal to your bet. If you lose, then you lose the amount of your bet. Some gamblers believe that in such games it is good betting strategy to double your bet each time you lose. In this way, each time you win you get back more than the total of the previous losses. Assume a gambler bets $1 and loses, then bets $2 and loses, then $4 and loses, and so on.

   (a)   If he loses five times in a row, beginning with $1, how much has he lost altogether?

   (b)   If he then wins the sixth time (after losing the first five), how much does he win the sixth time, and how much is he ahead after all six bets?

   (c)   Comment on the advantages and disadvantages of this approach to gambling.

   (d)   What kind of sequence do a loser's bets form?

7. A piece of paper is 1/256 of an inch thick. Suppose you begin by folding it in half. Then you fold the result in half. Continue this process until you have made 12 folds.

   (a)   What kind of sequence do the consecutive thicknesses obtained form?

   (b)   How thick is the paper after 12 folds?

   (c)   Could you continue the process in the classroom for four more folds? Explain your answer.

8. This problem doesn't really have much to do with sequences, but it is interesting and related to the thickness feature of the previous exercise. The Federal Government spends billions on this and billions on that. Just how much is a billion dollars ($1,000,000,000) physically? A dollar is about 4/1000 of an inch thick. If a billion dollar bills are piled one on top of the other, approximately how high is the billion-dollar pile? (Note: 12 inches = 1 foot, 5280 feet = 1 mile.)

The remaining applications are from a variety of unrelated fields, yet they all have a common link—mathematical sequences.

9. The *Richter scale* is used by seismologists to measure the relative magnitudes of earthquakes. A quake of magnitude 4 has ten times the intensity of a quake of magnitude 3. Similarly, a quake of magnitude 5 has ten times the intensity of a quake of magnitude 4 on the Richter scale.

(a) What kind of sequence do the magnitude numbers 3, 4, 5, . . . form?

(b) What kind of sequence do the intensities form?

(c) How many times as intense is an earthquake of magnitude 6 than an earthquake of magnitude 3?

10. A piano has eight keys named C. Beginning from the left, each successive C note has twice the frequency of the one before it.

(a) How many times greater is the frequency of the last C note than that of the first C note?

(b) What kind of sequence do the frequencies of the C notes form?

11. The sounds of two different instruments playing the same note can be distinguished because of the difference in *tone color*. Our ears identify the basic note, called the *fundamental frequency*, and several additional frequencies, called *overtones*. Each instrument has its own pattern of strengths and weaknesses among its overtones, and this pattern accounts for its distinctive tone color. If an instrument is playing a fundamental of 1500 cycles per second, its overtones (multiples of the fundamental) are

3000, 4500, 6000, 7500, . . .   cycles per second

(a) What is the next overtone in the sequence?

(b) What kind of sequence is this?

(c) Many people cannot hear frequencies above 10,000 cycles per second. How many overtones of a 1200 cycles-per-second fundamental would such people hear?

12. Read the nursery rhyme and answer its question.

> As I was going to Saint Ives,
> I met a man with seven wives.
> Every wife had seven sacks.
> Every sack had seven cats.
> Every cat had seven kits.
> Kits, cats, sacks, and wives,
> How many were going to Saint Ives?

13. If you have seen the answer to the previous problem, you

may feel that you've been tricked. Okay, have it your way. Assuming that everything mentioned in the rhyme was indeed going to Saint Ives, how many things were going there?

14. Election years for presidents of the United States form an interesting sequence. The sequence from 1960 onward appears as

$$1960, 1964, 1968, 1972, 1976, 1980, \ldots$$

(a) What kind of sequence is this?
(b) Is 2000 an election year?
(c) Was 1950 an election year?
(d) Was 1850 an election year?

Photos by I. J. Neubart

15. A star of magnitude 0 is approximately $2\frac{1}{2}$ times as bright as a first-magnitude star. Similarly, a first-magnitude star is approximately $2\frac{1}{2}$ times as bright as a second-magnitude star, and so on.

(a) How many times as bright is a star of magnitude 0 than a star of magnitude 2?
(b) How many times as bright is a star of magnitude 0 than a star of magnitude 3?
(c) Actually, 2.512 is a better approximation to the brightness factor than is $2\frac{1}{2}$ (2.5). The magnitude scheme is set up so that when the brightness factor is raised to the fifth power the result is 100. Verify that $(2.512)^5$, or $2.512 \times 2.512 \times 2.512 \times 2.512 \times 2.512$, is considerably closer to 100 than is $(2.5)^5$. Use a calculator if you have one.

16. A doubling cube is used in *backgammon* to double the stakes of the game. It is shaped like a die (singular of dice),

and the numbers on it form a geometric sequence beginning 2, 4. What are the other four numbers on the cube?

BACKGAMMON

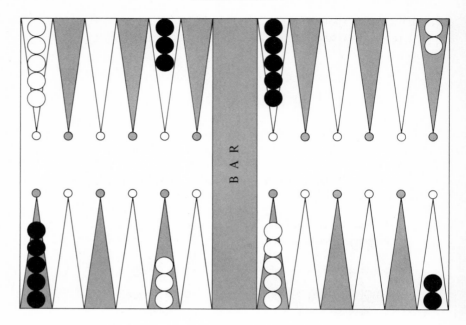

Compound Interest   If you invest $3000 at 5% annual interest, then at the end of one year you will have $3000 + .05($3000). This expression can be written as 1($3000) + .05($3000), or as (1 + .05)$3000. It simplifies to (1.05)$3000. In other words, if you invest money at 5% annual interest, you will have 1.05 times as much at the end of a year. So if you invest all of this money accumulated during the year (that is, principal plus interest) for a second year, you will have (1.05)(1.05)$3000 or $(1.05)^2$$3000 at the end of the second year. Such reinvestment of interest this way is called *compounding* of interest. Here is the sequence of amounts you have at the beginning, after one year, after two years, after three years, and so on.

$$\$3000, (1.05)\$3000, (1.05)^2\$3000, (1.05)^3\$3000, \ldots$$

17.   (a)   What is the next term in the sequence?
     (b)   What kind of sequence is this?

(c) The expression $(1.05)^2\$3000$ represents the return after two years on $3000 invested at 5% compounded annually. Write the expression that represents the return after three years on $5000 invested at 6% compounded annually.

(d) Write the expression that represents the return after n years on $8000 invested at 5% compounded annually.

---

18. In a computer environment, the following units of measure are used for time: second, millisecond, microsecond, nanosecond, picosecond. For example, the prefix "milli-" means one thousandth, so a millisecond is a thousandth of a second.

milli	$\dfrac{1}{1000}$	thousandth
micro	$\dfrac{1}{1,000,000}$	millionth
nano	$\dfrac{1}{1,000,000,000}$	billionth
pico	$\dfrac{1}{1,000,000,000,000}$	trillionth

(a) A microsecond is a _____ of a second. A nanosecond is a _____ of a second. A picosecond is a _____ of a second.

(b) In the order in which they are introduced in part (a), each term is ____ times the term following it.

(c) What kind of sequence is formed by the terms second, millisecond, microsecond, nanosecond, and picosecond?

(d) If the sequence is extended, the next two terms are *femtosecond* and *attosecond*. Write each as a fraction.

(e) How many times longer is a millisecond than a picosecond?

METRIC SYSTEM

The last application involved the units of time used in a computer environment. The prefixes used, such as milli and micro, are also applied to basic units in the *metric system*. The United States is now in the process of converting from the English system to the metric system.

In the English system, length is measured in inches (in.), feet (ft), yards, and miles. In the metric system the basic unit is the *meter* (m) and all lengths are measured in terms of meters. In the English system, capacities are measured in ounces, quarts, and gallons. In metric it's *liters* (l). In the English system, weights are measured in ounces, pounds, and tons. In metric it's *grams* (g).*

A meter is a little longer than a yard. Specifically, a yard is 36 inches and a meter is about 39.37 inches.

A liter is slightly more than a quart. Specifically, a liter is 1.06 quarts. (And a quart is about .95 liters.)

A gram is much smaller than an ounce. Specifically, an ounce is equal to about 28.35 grams.

*Physicists make the distinction that pounds are a measure of force, whereas grams are a measure of mass.

The most common prefixes used in the metric system are given next.

kilo	1000	thousand
centi	$\frac{1}{100}$	hundredth
milli	$\frac{1}{1000}$	thousandth
micro	$\frac{1}{1,000,000}$	millionth

Here are some examples of the use of these prefixes. A kilogram (kg) is 1000 grams (or about 2.20 pounds). On the other hand, a milligram (mg) is only one thousandth of a gram. A microgram (mcg) is but a millionth of a gram. Pharmacists work with small weights like these; you may notice the abbreviations mg and mcg on some drug labels. A centimeter is one hundredth of a meter.

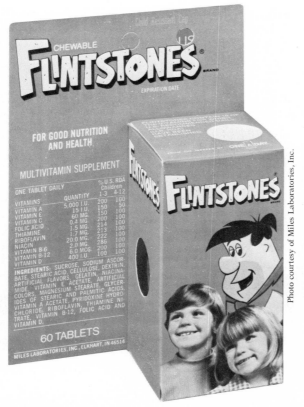

Photo courtesy of Miles Laboratories, Inc.

1. (a) A *millimeter* (mm) is a _____ of a meter. A dime is just slightly more than a millimeter in thickness.

   (b) A centimeter (cm) is a _____ of a meter. An aspirin tablet is about a centimeter in diameter.

   (c) How many millimeters are there in a centimeter?

2. The scale below can be used to measure lengths up to 80 millimeters, or 8 centimeters.

   (a) How many millimeters is the diameter of a dime? Measure one to find out.

   (b) How many millimeters wide is a dollar bill?

   (c) Approximately how many millimeters wide is a regular (small) size first class postage stamp?

   (d) Although they are not now widely issued or used, your parents may remember the *merchant tokens* issued by drugstores, cigar stores, pool halls, bars, cafes, grocery stores, and other local merchants. Each token had a specific value and served as an incentive for customers to return. Now, many people collect such tokens as a hobby, and they measure the width of their tokens in millimeters for descriptive purposes. Determine the width of each token illustrated here.

Photos by I. J. Neubart

3. (a) A *milliliter* (ml) is a _____ of a liter.

(b) A liter is ____ milliliters.

(c) The volume of 1 teaspoon is equal to 5 milliliters. So ____ teaspoons make a liter.

4. (a) A pound is 16 ounces. How many grams is this?

(b) How many milligrams are there in a gram?

(c) How many micrograms are there in a gram?

(d) How many grams are there in a kilogram?

(e) How many milligrams are there in a kilogram?

5. There are other prefixes used in the metric system.

hecto	100	hundred
deka	10	ten
deci	$\frac{1}{10}$	tenth

What kind of sequence do the following measures form: millimeter, centimeter, decimeter, meter, dekameter, hectometer, kilometer? Explain.

6. Conversions from one unit of measure to another can be made by multiplying fractions. Below, conversions are made between feet and inches in order to demonstrate the procedure. To change 5 feet to inches:

$$\frac{5 \text{ ft}}{1} \cdot \frac{12 \text{ in.}}{1 \text{ ft}} = \frac{5 \text{ ft}}{1} \cdot \frac{12 \text{ in.}}{1 \text{ ft}} = 60 \text{ in.}$$

To change 78 inches to feet:

$$\frac{78 \text{ in.}}{1} \cdot \frac{1 \text{ ft}}{12 \text{ in.}} = \frac{78 \text{ in.}}{1} \cdot \frac{1 \text{ ft}}{12 \text{ in.}} = \frac{78}{12} \text{ ft} = 6\tfrac{1}{2} \text{ ft}$$

(a) Since 1 foot equals 12 inches, what is the value of the fractions 1 ft/12 in. and 12 in./1 ft? That is why such a fraction can be used in the procedure just shown. Multiplication by such a fraction changes only the units, not the size of the quantity.

(b) A liter is about 1.06 quarts. Use the fraction

$$\frac{1.06 \text{ quarts}}{1 \text{ liter}}$$

to convert 4 liters to quarts.

(c) Use the fraction

$$\frac{1 \text{ liter}}{1.06 \text{ quarts}}$$

to convert 9 quarts to liters.

(d) A pound is equal to 454 grams. Use fractions to convert 3 pounds to grams and 950 grams to pounds.

(e) A kilogram is about 2.20 pounds. Convert 6 kilograms to pounds and convert 8 pounds to kilograms.

(f) A meter is equal to about 39.37 inches. Use fractions to convert 200 inches to meters.

(g) Convert 8 inches to meters.

(h) A meter is equal to 39.37 inches. A kilometer (km) is 1000 meters. How many inches are in a kilometer?

(i) Use your answer to part (h) to determine how many feet there are in a kilometer.

(j) There are about 2.54 centimeters in an inch. Convert

15 centimeters to inches and convert 15 inches to centimeters.

BINARY NUMBERS

Patterns play a significant role in the internal representation of data in computers and in computer operation. However, the machines do not use our familiar numbers 0 through 9. Before we look at the *binary numbers* used by computers, let us look more closely at the patterns present in our system of decimal numbers.

The numbers that have been used so far in this book are called *decimal* numbers or *base ten* numbers. Such numbers are composed of digits chosen from the following: 0, 1, 2, 3, 4, 5, 6, 7, 8, 9. The contribution of any digit to the total value of a number depends not only on what the digit is but also on where it is placed in the number. For example, in 2873 the 7 contributes 70, but in 2783 the 7 contributes 700. The number 4956 can be written as

$$4956 = 4000 + 900 + 50 + 6$$

Photo courtesy of IBM

or as

$$4956 = 4 \times 1000 + 9 \times 100 + 5 \times 10 + 6 \times 1$$

or in a chart as

1000	100	10	1
4	9	5	6

Notice that the column values are 1, 10, 100, and 1000. If the chart is continued one more place to the left, in order to include one more digit, what would be that next column's value? Perhaps you notice the pattern—each column value is ten times that of the column to its right. That is why such numbers are called *base ten* numbers. Applying this concept, we multiply ten times 1000 to determine the next column, which is 10,000. Let's put an 8 in the new column.

10,000	1000	100	10	1
8	4	9	5	6

The new number is 84,956, from

$$8 \times 10,000 + 4 \times 1000 + 9 \times 100 + 5 \times 10 + 6 \times 1$$
$$= \quad 80,000 + 4000 + 900 + 50 + 6$$
$$= \quad 84,956$$

Although people can record numbers by writing various combinations of the digits 0 through 9, computers are more restricted. A computer can only record data internally by using combinations of "on" and "off" settings of switches, magnetic memories, and the like.

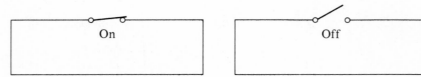

On   Off

The on and off settings are the computer's internal representation of the two digits 0 and 1. These two digits are used to form the *binary* or *base two* numbers. The column values of the binary chart are shown next. Notice that for base two numbers, each column value is twice the value of the column to its right.

. . .	16	8	4	2	1

Here is a typical binary number: 10110. Notice that it consists only of zeros and ones. We'll write 10110 as $(10110)_2$ so we won't forget that it's a binary number. After all, it could be misinterpreted as the decimal number "ten thousand one hundred ten." Now let's see what $(10110)_2$ is equal to in terms of base ten, our familiar base.

16	8	4	2	1
1	0	1	1	0

$$(10110)_2 = 1 \times 16 + 0 \times 8 + 1 \times 4 + 1 \times 2 + 0 \times 1$$
$$= 16 + 0 + 4 + 2 + 0$$
$$= (22)_{10}$$

So we find that $(10110)_2 = (22)_{10}$; the binary number 10110 is the same as the decimal number 22. You might want to study carefully the process by which we changed the binary number to a decimal number, since we will use it several times in the next few pages.

The reverse process, that of converting a decimal number to binary, can be done by fitting the decimal number to a binary chart. As an example, let's change $(53)_{10}$ to binary. In making up the binary chart, we need go only as far as the 32's column, since the next column heading is 64, and 64 is larger than the number (53) that is being converted.

64	32	16	8	4	2	1

Place a 1 in the 32's column to indicate that one 32 is contained in 53. Removing the 32 leaves a remainder of 21 to be placed in the other columns.

32	16	8	4	2	1
1					

$53 - 32 = 21$ left

There is a 16 contained in the 21 that remains. So place a 1 in the 16's column. The amount remaining is then 5.

32	16	8	4	2	1
1	1				

$21 - 16 = 5$ left

There is no 8 in the 5 that remains, so place a 0 in the 8's column.

32	16	8	4	2	1
1	1	0			

5 left

There is a 4 in the 5 that remains. So place a 1 in the 4's column. The amount remaining is then 1.

32	16	8	4	2	1
1	1	0	1		

$5 - 4 = 1$ left

The 1 that remains is clearly no 2's and one 1.

32	16	8	4	2	1
1	1	0	1	0	1

This means that $(53)_{10} = (110101)_2$.

1. The number 1000 can be written as 10^3 (which means $10 \cdot 10 \cdot 10$). In this form, 10 is called the *base* and 3 is the exponent, or power.

    (a)   What is the value of 2^3?

    (b)   Explain why decimal numbers are also called *base ten* numbers.

    (c)   Explain why binary numbers are also called *base two* numbers.

2.   (a)   What kind of sequence do the column headings 1, 10, 100, 1000, . . . form?

    (b)   What kind of sequence do the column headings 1, 2, 4, 8, 16, . . . form?

3. As you move to the left in a base ten chart, each column is ten times the column before it. On the other hand, as you move to the right, each column is one tenth of the column before it.

    (a)   Based on this analysis, fill in the three missing column headings in the following chart.

10,000	1000	100	10	1			

    (b)   What name is given to the small round dot that should be placed between the 1's column and the column to the right of it?

    (c)   Fill in the three missing column headings in the following binary chart.

16	8	4	2	1			

4. Change each number from binary to decimal.

    (a)   1101   (b)   1001

    (c)   10101   (d)   11011

    (e)   11111   (f)   100011

    (g)   1000000   (h)   1100000001

5. Change each number from decimal to binary.

    (a)   12   (b)   23
    (c)   35   (d)   60
    (e)   73   (f)   95
    (g)   100   (h)   127

6. Complete this table.

Decimal	Binary
0	
1	
2	
3	
4	
5	
6	
7	
8	

7. If you have done Exercise 6 correctly, your results should be 0, 1, 10, 11, 100, 101, 110, 111, 1000. Study this sequence to find a pattern, then convert the decimal numbers 9 through 19 to binary by extending the pattern.

8. Convert each of the following binary numbers to decimal. Then examine the binary pattern and the decimal values. Explain the apparent relationship. The binary numbers: 101, 1010, 10100, 101000.

RELATIONSHIPS

When two things interact, there is a relationship between them. Relationships often involve change. If we can spot a pattern in the changes, then we may be able to draw conclusions and make useful predictions.

An endless number of relationships exist in nature and in human affairs, as well as in mathematics. In this section we will look at a few of these relationships, including some important ones between numbers.

The size a distant object appears to a viewer depends on the distance from which the viewer is observing. If the viewer's distance from the object is doubled, the height of the object will seem to be reduced to half its original height. If the distance from the object is tripled, its height will be only a third. On the other hand, if the viewer's distance from the object is reduced to half the original distance, the object will appear to be twice as high. If we let h represent the apparent height of an object and d the relative distance of the viewer from the object, then the following table summarizes the relationship between h and d just explained. Can you determine an equation for h in terms of d?

d	3	2	1	$\frac{1}{2}$
h	$\frac{1}{3}$	$\frac{1}{2}$	1	2

In the table, h is always the reciprocal of d. This means that the equation is $h = 1/d$.

The next table shows a relationship between numbers x and y. Can you state the relationship in words? Can you express it as a formula?

x	1	2	3	5	9
y	2	4	6	10	18

There are two straightforward ways of stating this relationship. One way: y is twice x. Another way: x is half of y. In formula form, the expression becomes $y = 2x$ and $x = \frac{1}{2}y$, respectively. (Note that $\frac{1}{2}y$ can also be written as $y/2$.) The equation $y = 2x$ provides y as a function of x; that is, if you supply an x, you'll get a y dependent on the x supplied. Use 4 for x and you get 8 for y. Use 20 for x and you get 40 for y. The equation $x = \frac{1}{2}y$ provides x as a function of y; that is, if you supply a y value, you'll get a corresponding x dependent on the y supplied. Use 12 for y and you'll get 6 for x.

Now let's see several areas of application.

1. Amoebas reproduce by dividing in half. Thus, one amoeba becomes two amoebas. If both of these amoebas divide, then there will be four amoebas. In theory this process can continue indefinitely, assuming a suitable environment.

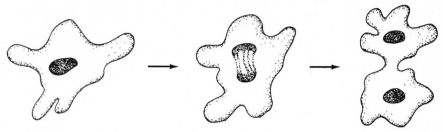

   (a) Complete the table, noting that at time zero ($t = 0$ at the beginning) the number of amoebas is just one. Time is measured in days.

Time (t)	0	1	2	3	4	5
Number (n)	1	2				

   (b) Write a formula for n in terms of t. You might find this easier to do if you ignore the first pair, in which $n = 1$ when $t = 0$. If your formula is correct for $t = 1$, 2, 3, 4, and 5, it will also be correct for $t = 0$. You can check it after you obtain the formula.
   (c) What kind of sequence do the values of n form?
   (d) Some amoebas are only 5 microns in diameter. A micron is a thousandth of a millimeter. If you could line up amoebas one right next to the other, how many would it take to equal 1 millimeter of amoebas?

2. The speed of some chemical reactions (that is, the rate at which the end product is formed) is approximately doubled when the temperature is increased by 10°C.

   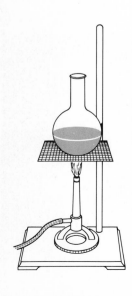

   (a) Complete the table.

Temperature (t)	100	110	120	140
Speed (s)	1			

(b)   What is the value of t when s is 8?

(c)   What is the value of s when t is 170?

3.   It has been observed that the number of chirps a cricket makes per minute depends on the temperature. The warmer it is, the more chirps a cricket makes in a given period of time. Furthermore, a cricket does not chirp at 40°F or below. Here are some recorded observations of chirps per minute and corresponding Fahrenheit temperatures.

Number of chirps (n)	0	4	8	12	40	60
Temperature (t)	40	41	42	43	50	55

(a)   Study the table above for a pattern. Then complete the following table, assuming that the pattern can be extended (which it can).

Number of chirps (n)	16	80	88		
Temperature (t)				75	85

(b)   Determine the temperature when a cricket chirps 94 times in 1 minute.

(c)   Determine the number of times per minute a cricket will chirp when it is 81°F.

(d)   A cricket has just chirped 10 times in a 15-second interval. What is the approximate temperature?

4.   According to some historians, the famous Italian scientist Galileo performed several experiments from atop the leaning tower of Pisa. He determined that if you drop an object, the distance it travels depends only on time (and not on the weight of the object). The table that follows gives the distance traveled (d) in feet as a function of time (t) in *quarter seconds*.

Galileo Galilei
(1564–1642)

t	0	1	2	3	4
d	0	1	4	9	16

(a) How far will an object fall in 5 quarter seconds?

(b) Express distance (d) in feet as a function of time (t) in quarter seconds by means of an equation or formula.

(c) Express time in quarter seconds as a function of distance in feet.

(d) How far will an object fall in 2 *seconds?* In 3 seconds? In 4 seconds?

(e) Express the distance (d) in feet as a function of time (t) *in seconds.*

5. If an object is thrown downward with a beginning speed of 50 feet per second (rather than dropped), then the distance (d) it travels in t seconds is $d = 16t^2 + 50t$.

(a) How far does the object travel in 2 seconds? (Note: $16t^2$ means 16 times the square of t.) How does this compare with the distance traveled by the object of Application 4, which was merely dropped rather than thrown downward?

(b) How far has the object traveled the instant it is thrown? (Ask yourself what the value of t must be the instant the object is thrown.)

(c) A ball is thrown down from the top of a building. If it strikes the ground exactly 3 seconds after it is thrown, how high is the building?

6. Galileo made discoveries that led to the invention of the pendulum clock. One such discovery is the relationship between the time of one full swing of a pendulum and the length of the pendulum. Here is his set of data.

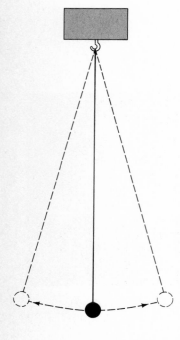

Time of swing (t)	1	2	3	4
Length of pendulum (l)	1	4	9	16

(a) If t is 5, what is l?

(b) Write a formula expressing l in terms of t.

(c) If l is 36, what must t be?

(d) Express t in terms of l.

7. Stereo enthusiasts are often concerned with *watts* and *decibels*. The following table shows a comparison between these two different units of power that an amplifier can deliver to speakers.

Watts	.1	1	10	100
Decibels	−10	0	10	20

(a) How many watts correspond to 30 decibels?

(b) How many decibels correspond to .01 watt?

8. The distance that a golf ball will carry (or travel in the air before bouncing) depends on the speed with which it leaves the club. Assuming there is no wind and that the ball is well hit, the number of yards the ball will carry is given by the relationship

$$\text{Carry} = 1.5 \cdot \text{Velocity} - 103$$

The velocity is in feet per second.

(a) If the ball leaves the club at 176 feet per second (120 miles per hour), how many yards will it carry?

(b) Suppose the ball is not well hit—that the velocity is only 70 feet per second (about 48 miles per hour). What is the carry? Can you see that this formula is questionable for poorly hit drives?

Florida Department of Commerce

(c) Verify that 176 feet per second is equivalent to 120 miles per hour by carrying out the following conversion.

$$176 \frac{\text{ft}}{\text{sec}} = 176 \frac{\text{ft}}{\text{sec}} \cdot \frac{60 \text{ sec}}{1 \text{ min}} \cdot \frac{60 \text{ min}}{1 \text{ hr}} \cdot \frac{1 \text{ mile}}{5280 \text{ ft}}$$

(d) Change 30 miles per hour to feet per second.

9. A sequence such as 2, 4, 6, 8, . . . can be studied in a table in order to obtain a formula stating the relationship between each member of the sequence and its position in the sequence. Consider the following table, which represents the sequence 2, 4, 6, 8, ...

Position (n)	1	2	3	4	. . .
Member (a_n)	2	4	6	8	. . .

From the table it becomes clear that each member of the sequence is twice its position number. This observation can be stated symbolically using the following notation. Let a_1 represent the first member of the sequence, a_2 the second member, and so on. For this sequence, then, $a_1 = 2$, $a_2 = 4$, $a_3 = 6$, $a_4 = 8$, and so on. In general, $a_n = 2n$; that is, a_n is twice n for this sequence.

(a) Find a_5 and a_6 of the sequence above.

Determine a formula for a_n for each of the following sequences. You might find making a table helpful.

(b) 3, 6, 9, 12, . . .
(c) 1, 4, 9, 16, . . .
(d) 7, 7, 7, 7, . . .
(e) 1/1, 1/2, 1/3, 1/4, . . .
(f) 1/3, 2/3, 1, 4/3, . . .
(g) 2, 3, 4, 5, . . .
(h) 2, 4, 8, 16, . . .

In Application 1 (page 30) it was noted that if you begin with one amoeba, the number (n) of amoebas present after t days is given by $n = 2^t$. The growth of the amoeba population, as indicated by the formula, is an example of *exponential growth* of a population.

10. (a) Bacteria are capable of extremely rapid growth. Under ideal conditions cells can divide every 20 minutes. This means that the bacteria population can double every 20 minutes. If we begin with just one bacterium, how many will there be an hour later?

    (b) It has been stated that $n = 2^t$ specifies an exponential growth. Which number is the exponent? Which number is the base?

_____

Radiocarbon dating is used in archaeology to determine the age of findings. The technique was devised in 1948 by Dr. Willard Libby of the University of Chicago, and is based on the fact that all living animals contain the same amount of carbon-14 per unit of weight. They acquire it from the atmosphere through respiration. Once the animal dies, however, it no longer obtains carbon-14. Furthermore, the amount of carbon-14 it contained at the time of death decays (that is, changes into a different form of carbon). It takes 5730 years for the amount of carbon-14 to drop to half of its original level.

11. (a) Complete the following table. Assume the original amount of carbon-14 is 64 grams.

Time in years	0	5730	11,460	
Grams of carbon-14	64			8

    (b) Complete the following table.

Time in years	0	5730	11,460		
Percent of carbon-14 remaining	100			$12\frac{1}{2}$	$6\frac{1}{4}$

    (c) Why do you think this application is considered "decay" rather than "growth?"

Logarithms

In this application, you will have the chance to see another form in which exponential relationships can be written. Let's explore these "logarithmic" relationships.

12. (a) The first column of the table indicates that $4^2 = 16$. The second column says that $2^3 = 8$. Complete the table.

Base	4	2	5	9	4	3	6	10	2	3	10
Exponent	2	3	2	2	3						
Result	16	8			9	36	100	16	27	10,000

(b) The exponential relationship $4^2 = 16$ can be written in a form that displays the exponent by itself. This alternative form of $4^2 = 16$ is

$$\log_4 16 = 2$$

The word "log" is an abbreviation for the word "logarithm." *A logarithm is an exponent.* Above, we have $\log_4 16 = 2$, which is read as "the *logarithm* of 16 to the base 4 *is 2*." In more familiar words, the *exponent* to which 4 must be raised to produce 16 *is 2*. If the exponential relationship $2^3 = 8$ is written as a logarithmic relationship, it is $\log_2 8 = 3$. Rewrite each of the following exponential relationships as logarithmic relationships.

(i) $2^5 = 32$ (ii) $7^2 = 49$
(iii) $5^3 = 125$ (iv) $10^4 = 10,000$

(c) Rewrite each logarithmic relationship as an exponential relationship.

(i) $\log_4 64 = 3$ (ii) $\log_2 1024 = 10$
(iii) $\log_5 625 = 4$ (iv) $\log_{10} 1,000,000 = 6$

Logarithms were invented in 1614 by John Napier, a Scottish baron. Traditionally, logarithms have been used to simplify calculations. However, the recent widespread use of computers and the availability of hand calculators have reduced the need for logarithms for calculations. On the other hand,

John Napier (1550–1617)

logarithms are used extensively in calculus (See Application 12, page 315), statistics, and many other applications. In many fields, relationships among variables are easier to express when logarithms of the numbers involved are used. Here are a few examples of such relationships.

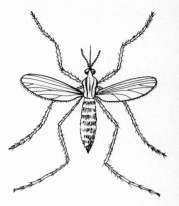

In ecology, a study of the development of certain mosquito larvae yielded the following formula for duration of development with respect to the temperature of the environment: $\log_{10} D = a - b \log_{10} T$. In this formula, D is the duration of a given stage of development and T is the temperature. The numbers represented by a and b are constants, where a is the number of day-degrees (a product of days times degrees) required for completion of a developmental stage and b is the minimum temperature at which development can proceed.

A relationship between the age of a leaf and the temperature range over which photosynthesis occurs is given by the formula $\log_{10} T = m + n \log_{10} A$. Here A is the age of the leaf in days and T is the temperature range over which photosynthesis occurs. The numbers m and n are constants whose values depend on location. For example, the constants for northern California are different from those of Maine or Florida. The formula $\log_{10} P = a - b \log_{10} A$ gives a relationship between the rate (P) at which photosynthesis occurs and the age (A) of the leaf.

The two applications above involve *common logarithms*, that is, logarithms that use 10 as the base. The next example involves *natural logarithms*, that is, logarithms using as a base the number e, which is approximately equal to 2.718.

A study of 100 cuttings was taken in order to determine a relationship between the diameter of a leaf (in centimeters) and the dry weight of the leaf (in grams). The relationship between the two was found to be of the form $\log_e Y = a + b \log_e x$, where x is the diameter of the leaf and Y is the dry weight of the leaf.

Some further appreciation for the number e can be gained from Application 11 on page 302. A calculus definition of the natural logarithm is given in Application 12 on page 315. Often, the following abbreviated notations are used with logarithms.

$$\log x \quad \text{to mean} \quad \log_{10} x$$
$$\ln x \quad \text{to mean} \quad \log_e x$$

2	7	6
9	5	1
4	3	8

MAGIC SQUARES

Next in our study of patterns we'll have a look at a completely different type of pattern—one that is displayed as a square array of numbers. The square array of numbers here is called a square of third order, because each side of the square is composed of three numbers. If you examine its rows, columns, and diagonals, you may discover the special property this square possesses. Are you able to discover the special property of this square? If not, think "addition" and try again. You should have discovered that the three numbers in each row (2–7–6, 9–5–1, 4–3–8), in each column (2–9–4, 7–5–3, 6–1–8), and in each of the two diagonals (2–5–8, 4–5–6) add up to the same total. That sum is 15, and it is called the *magic sum* of this *magic square*. Most squares containing arrangements of the numbers 1, 2, 3, 4, 5, 6, 7, 8, and 9 do not possess this property. Furthermore, algebra can be used to prove that the center number of a third-order magic square must be 5.

The magic square above is credited to the Chinese emperor Yu the Great, who lived more than 4000 years ago. The Hindus investigated magic squares more than 2000 years ago. In medieval days, magic squares were used as good luck charms to protect against evils. The fourth-order magic square shown next appears in the print *Melancholia* by the sixteenth-century artist Albrecht Dürer.

16	3	2	13
5	10	11	8
9	6	7	12
4	15	14	1

Detail from *Melancholia*
by Albrecht Dürer

What is the magic sum for this square? Verify your answer by showing that all four rows, all four columns, and both diagonals yield that number. You might also want to verify that the corners (16, 4, 13, 1), the four center numbers (10, 11, 7, 6), and each of the two-by-two corner squares (16, 3, 10, 5), (2, 13, 8, 11), (9, 6, 15, 4), (7, 12, 1, 14) also yield the magic sum.

More recently, magic squares and other related squares have proved useful in the design of statistical experiments.

APPLICATIONS AND EXERCISES

Photo by I. J. Neubart

1. The formula for the magic sum s of any magic square of order n (that is, n numbers by n numbers) is $s = \frac{1}{2}n(n^2 + 1)$.

   (a) Verify the formula for the magic square of order three.
   (b) Verify the formula for the magic square of order four.
   (c) According to the formula, what must be the magic sum of the magic square of order five?

2. Use the method of trial and error to find another magic square of order four. Keep in mind that all the natural numbers from 1 through 16 must be used and only once each. Also, you know what the magic sum must be.

3. The magic square of order three contains all the natural numbers from 1 through 9. The magic square of order four contains all the natural numbers from 1 through 16.

   (a) The magic square of order five contains the natural numbers from 1 through ____ .
   (b) The magic square of order n contains the natural numbers from 1 through ____ .

4. In your own words, explain what is meant by a magic square of order n.

5. Suppose 1 is added to each number in a magic square of order n. Does the resulting square possess any magic? If so, what is the magic sum?

6. Illustrated next are *magic triangles* of order four and order five. In the magic triangle of order four, the sum of the four numbers composing each side (called the *magic sum*) is 20. The magic sum of the magic triangle of order five is

32. A magic triangle of order four uses the natural numbers from 1 through 9. A magic triangle of order five uses 1 through 12.

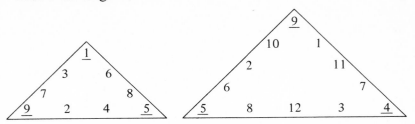

The underlined numbers in each triangle are called the *vertices* of the magic triangle.

(a) Construct a magic triangle of order four with vertices 4, 5, and 6 and having magic sum 20.

(b) Construct a magic triangle of order four with vertices 2, 3, and 7 and having magic sum 19.

(c) Construct a magic triangle of order five that does not have vertices 4, 5, and 9.

7. A *Latin square of order three* contains three rows and three columns and uses three different symbols (1, 2, and 3), and each row and column contains all three symbols. Here is such a Latin square.

$$3 \quad 2 \quad 1$$

$$1 \quad 3 \quad 2$$

$$2 \quad 1 \quad 3$$

(a) Note that one of the diagonals contains all 3's. See if you can create a Latin square in which all three numbers on a diagonal are 2's. Next, try to create a Latin square in which all three numbers on a diagonal are 1's.

(b) If the first and second *columns* of the original square above are interchanged, is the result a Latin square? What do you notice about one of the diagonals? If instead the second and third *rows* are interchanged, is the result a Latin square? What do you notice about one of the diagonals?

(c) Construct a Latin square of order four consisting of the letters A, B, C, and D. Your experience with patterns in parts (a) and (b) should make the problem easier to solve.

(d) Construct a Latin square of order five consisting of the Roman numerals I, II, III, IV, and V.

8. The excavators of Pompei found this "magic square" scratched upon one of the pillars of the stadium. In what way is this square magical?

R	O	T	A	S
O	P	E	R	A
T	E	N	E	T
A	R	E	P	O
S	A	T	O	R

9. The famous Swiss mathematician Leonhard Euler (1707–1783) invented the unusual square of order eight that is shown here.

1	48	31	50	33	16	63	18
30	51	46	3	62	19	14	35
47	2	49	32	15	34	17	64
52	29	4	45	20	61	36	13
5	44	25	56	9	40	21	60
28	53	8	41	24	57	12	37
43	6	55	26	39	10	59	22
54	27	42	7	58	23	38	11

(a) What is the sum of any row or any column?
(b) What is the sum of the first four or last four numbers in any row or column?
(c) In *chess*, the move of a knight looks like the letter L—two squares horizontally and then one square vertically *or* two squares vertically and then one square horizontally. So the knight (horse) shown in the next illustration can reach any one of the lettered squares from its present position. Now imagine there is a knight on the square numbered 1 in Euler's square. Do you see that in one move it can be in the square numbered 2? Also, from the square numbered

2 it can move next into the square numbered 3. Continue this so-called "knight's tour" by moving the knight so that it hits numbered squares in the sequence 1, 2, 3, 4, 5, ... Can you cover the entire board in this manner?

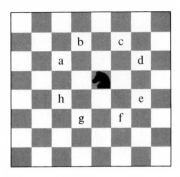

10. Benjamin Franklin created an interesting square.
    (a) What is the sum of any row?
    (b) What is the sum of the first four or last four numbers in any row?
    (c) What is the sum of the four corners?

52	61	4	13	20	29	36	45
14	3	62	51	46	35	30	19
53	60	5	12	21	28	37	44
11	6	59	54	43	38	27	22
55	58	7	10	23	26	39	42
9	8	57	56	41	40	25	24
50	63	2	15	18	31	34	47
16	1	64	49	48	33	32	17

11. An *antimagic square* or *heterosquare* of order three contains the natural numbers from 1 through 9 such that all

rows, columns, and diagonals have different sums. Construct an antimagic square of order three by beginning with 1 in the center and spiraling out from there, using consecutively the numbers 2 through 9.

THE 15 PUZZLE

In 1878, Sam Loyd invented the 15 Puzzle. You might note that it bears some resemblance to a fourth-order magic square. The puzzle consists of a square frame enclosing 15 small movable square blocks numbered from 1 through 15. Because there is room for 16 blocks, there is also an open square space the size of one block. The position shown here is called the *normal position*.

1	2	3	4
5	6	7	8
9	10	11	12
13	14	15	

Since the blocks cannot be lifted out of the frame, it is the open space that permits the 15 blocks to be moved about into different locations. The number of different positions possible is more than 20 trillion (20,000,000,000,000). An explanation of how this number was determined is given in the study of permutations in Chapter 7.

The 15 Puzzle was extremely popular in Europe for years and is still readily available in stores throughout the United States. Tournaments were held and large cash prizes were offered to anyone who could obtain a particular arrangement beginning from the normal order shown in the illustration. Naturally, this competition had wide appeal, since the game seemed simple enough. However, no one ever won the prizes, because the required solutions were impossible.

The proof that certain positions are impossible was published in 1879 by two American mathematicians. As it happens, half of the 20 trillion arrangements are possible and half are impossible to reach from the normal position shown. Although the proof itself is complicated, the resulting test is relatively easy to apply. If the total number of inversions is even, then the position is indeed obtainable from the normal position. If the total number of inversions is odd, then the position cannot be obtained from the normal position. *What is an inversion?* Beginning at the top left position and going across, if a number precedes a number smaller than itself, that is an *inversion*. Consider the position shown next.

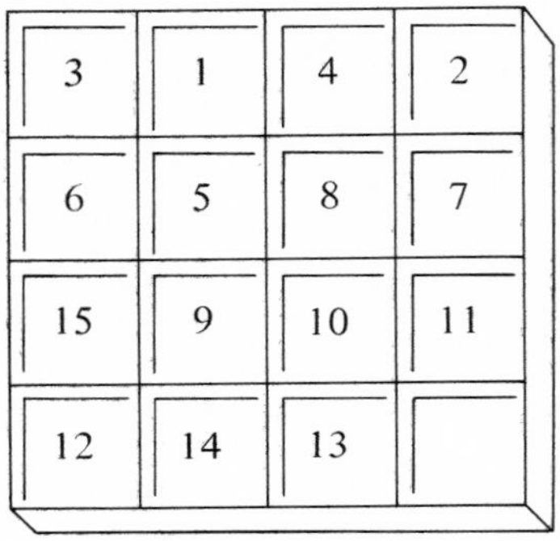

3	1	4	2
6	5	8	7
15	9	10	11
12	14	13	

Here 3 precedes 1 and 2. So that's two inversions. Also, 4 precedes 2. That's another inversion, a total of three so far. Then 6 precedes 5, and 8 precedes 7. That's two more inversions, a total of five inversions thus far. Then 15 precedes 9, 10, 11, 12, 14, and 13. That's six more inversions, or 11 inversions so far. Finally, 14 precedes 13. So the total number of inversions in this position is 12, which is even, so the position can indeed be obtained beginning from the normal position.

1. Count the number of inversions for each position shown here and then decide whether the position is possible or impossible to obtain from the normal position.

1	3	5	7
2	4	6	8
9	11	13	15
10	12	14	

(a)

1	5	9	13
2	6	10	14
3	7	11	15
4	8	12	

(b)

1	2	3	4
12	13	14	15
5	6	7	8
11	10	9	

(c)

1	3	5	7
9	11	13	15
2	4	6	8
10	12	14	

(d)

12	2	1	15
7	9	10	4
11	5	6	8
	14	13	3

(e)

15	14	13	12
11	10	9	8
7	6	5	4
3	2	1	

(f)

2. If possible, obtain a 15 Puzzle. Then try to move the squares into the positions shown in Exercise 1, assuming they are possible. Reset the puzzle to normal position before beginning each time.

3. Did you notice that the position in Exercise 1, part (e), is a magic square "of sorts." Explain how it resembles a magic square, yet why it is not a magic square.

MORE MAGIC

Earlier, we saw some "magic" based on Fibonacci sequences. In this section we'll examine some magic tricks that are based on arithmetic and elementary algebra. In each case only the natural numbers (that is, $1, 2, 3, 4, 5, \ldots$) will be used. Here's the first trick.

Write down the year of your birth, but omit the "19" part (for example, 1958 becomes 58). Add to it the year of some important event in your life. Now add your age to this total. Finally, add the number of years since that important event took place. *The result will be twice the current year!* Let's see why this works.

---

year of birth:	x	(Here x is 58, if the year is 1958.)
year of event:	$x + n$	(n years after x)
your age:	$C - x$	(C is the current year, so age is $C - x$.)
years since event:	$C - x - n$	
sum:	$2C$	(All the rest adds up to zero.)

Don't try this trick more than once in the same group of people. Why not?

Here's another trick. Think of a natural number. Add 15 to it. Double the result. Add the original number. Divide by 3. Subtract the original number. *The result is 10.* To see what's happening, let x be the number you select.

Think of a number.	x
Add 15 to it.	$x + 15$
Double the result.	$2x + 30$
Add the original number.	$3x + 30$
Divide by 3.	$x + 10$
Subtract the original number.	10

Whatever number is used for x, the result will always be 10, so don't try this trick more than once in the same group of people. Perhaps you can see that many variations of this trick are possible.

For the third trick, think of a natural number. Multiply it by 5. Now add 7 to the product. Multiply this result by 4, and then add 1. Finally, multiply the total by 5. *I can determine the number you began with by removing the last two digits and then subtracting 1 from the number that is left.* Why? Let's call your number x. By following the specified steps, you create the expression

$$[(5 \cdot x + 7)4 + 1]5$$

which reduces to $(20x + 28 + 1)5$, then to $(20x + 29)5$, and finally to $100x + 145$. Whatever natural number x is used, the last two digits of $100x$ are zeros. (Let $x = 17$, for example. Then $100x = 1700$.) So when you remove the last two digits, the 45 disappears, leaving $100x + 100$, which can be written as $100(x + 1)$. But removing two digits also changes the place value, and in effect divides the number by 100. So the result is $x + 1$. (Using $x = 17$ and $100x = 1700$ again, $100x + 145 = 1700 + 145 = 1845$. Removing 45 gives 18, which is one more than x.)

Now, the final trick: Select any two numbers from the following list. Add them. Then remove any digit from that sum. Finally, add the remaining digits. Tell me the total and I'll tell you what digit you removed.

5211	4302	2466
9423	3330	9531

Here is an explanation of how the trick works. Each number in the list is a multiple of 9. A multiple of 9 is 9 or 18 or 27 or 36, and so on. This means that the sum of the digits of any number in the list is also a multiple of 9 (see Chapter 3). Furthermore, the sum of the digits of the sum of any two numbers from the list is also a multiple of 9. So if you give me the sum of all the digits but one, I merely compute which number is needed to bring the total to 9 or 18 or 27, and so forth. Suppose, for example, you select 5211 and 9423. The sum of those numbers is 14,634. Before adding the digits of 14,634, remove one digit, say 3. The sum of the remaining digits is 15, which you report to me. I note that 3 must be added to your 15 to get 18, the next multiple of 9. So I report that you removed a 3 from the sum.

APPLICATIONS AND EXERCISES

1. Make up some variations of the second trick and try them on your friends.

2. The third trick is based on the fact that

$$[(5 \cdot x + 7)4 + 1]5$$

is equal to $100x + 145$, or $100x + 100 + 45$. Consider the following algebraic expressions, all of which are variations of the one above. Determine which expressions can be used for the same trick because only the last two digits change when the value of x changes.

(a) $[(5x + 8)4 + 1]5$
(b) $[(5x + 7)4 + 6]5$
(c) $[(5x + 7)5 + 1]5$
(d) $[(4x + 7)5 + 2]5$
(e) $[(2x + 3)5 + 1]10$

3. For each expression in Exercise 2 that can indeed be used for the third trick, explain each step in words as if you were showing someone the trick. Begin "Think of a number. Multiply it by. . . ."

4. Which lists of numbers can be used for the fourth trick, the one involving multiples of 9?

(a)	(b)	(c)	(d)
7416	1944	9063	1053
8802	2853	2196	2223
9045	3780	7201	5400
5103	4815	4554	7542
6030	4914	5823	4446

5. Think of a number (call it x). Add 2 to it. Triple the result. Add 4. Subtract twice the original number. The result is ____ more than the original number. In other words, if you want to try this trick on a friend, and he tells you that the result is 38, you know that the original number was ____.

REGULAR POLYGONS

So far we have considered only patterns of numbers, yet patterns are not restricted to numbers. There are many important patterns in geometry, some of which we will examine now, as we conclude the chapter with a look at regular polygons. A *regular polygon* is a geometric figure whose sides are equal and whose angles are equal. The Greeks studied polygons more than 2000 years ago, and most of the names of polygons reflect this. (More is said on this in Chapter 5, *Introduction to Topology*.) Illustrated next are the five most common regular polygons.

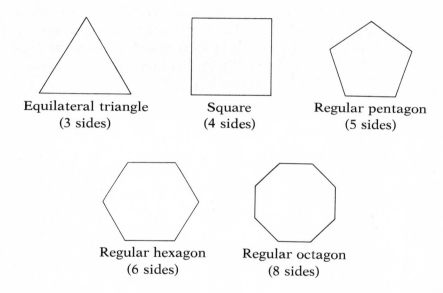

Equilateral triangle
(3 sides)

Square
(4 sides)

Regular pentagon
(5 sides)

Regular hexagon
(6 sides)

Regular octagon
(8 sides)

Bees design their honeycombs with cells having the shape of regular hexagons. Although equilateral triangles or squares might seem more obvious and simpler, by using hexagons bees need less wax to enclose an equal amount of space. Hexagons are also a better shape for the roundish larvae, which are reared in the small chambers. Furthermore, the hexagonal design is stronger than comparable designs employing triangles or squares. Curiously, IBM's modern computer mass storage system (shown next) uses honeycomb storage compartments.

Honeycomb computer storage

In organic chemistry, regular polygons are used to illustrate formulas for compounds, as shown in the following illustrations.

Codeine

Adenine, a DNA component

In automobiles equipped with ignition points, the points open and close according to the movement of a cam. For an eight-cylinder engine, the cam is a regular octagon. For a six-cylinder engine, the cam is a regular hexagon. In each case, the points make contact when the rubbing block fits flatly against a side of the polygon. This is shown in the next illustration.

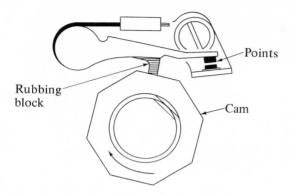

One of the IgM antibodies found in human blood (they protect the body against disease) is five sided or ten sided, depending on your perspective. Examine this IgM antibody.

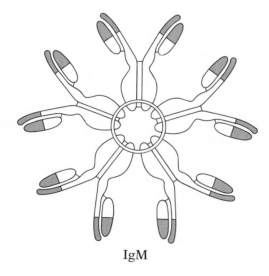

IgM

The light-sensitive nerve cells in the retina of the human eye are of two types, rods and cones. The ends of the cones (the receptors that give us color vision) form a mosaic of hexagons. The average width of each cell is only .003 millimeter.

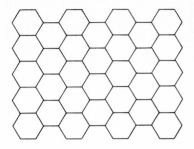

Color theory has been studied with the aid of various color circles. Albert Munsell's color circle is based on five colors and thus contains an inscribed pentagon.

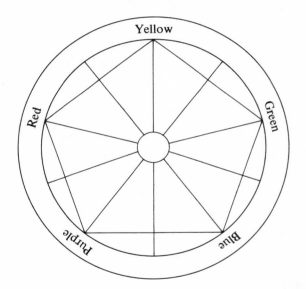

Johann Wolfgang von Goethe's color circle contains a six-pointed star.

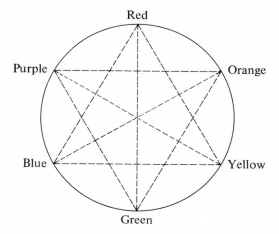

Natural ice crystal forms are based on hexagons. Here are a few forms.

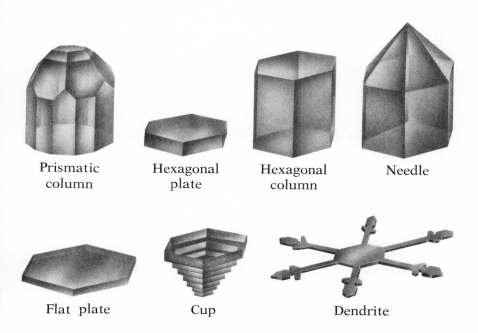

Prismatic column   Hexagonal plate   Hexagonal column   Needle

Flat plate   Cup   Dendrite

Some diatoms (algae) have the shape of regular polygons.

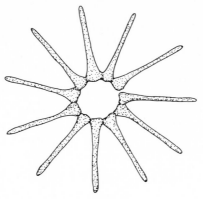

Diatom

Some minerals crystalize into forms having faces (flat surfaces) that are regular polygons. For example, pyrite (fool's gold) crystals have faces that are regular pentagons. In three dimensions the entire crystal is a regular dodecahedron, a 12-sided solid all of whose faces are identical regular pentagons. On the other hand, real gold crystals are regular octahedrons, eight-faced solids all of whose faces are identical regular triangles. Tiny sea animals called radiolaria have a skeletal structure that approximates various regular polyhedra. Some small viruses, such as herpes virus, tipula iridescent virus, adenovirus, and polyoma virus, are regular icosahedrons. An icosahedron is a 20-sided solid all of whose faces are identical equilateral triangles. In Chapter 5, polyhedra will be illustrated and examined.

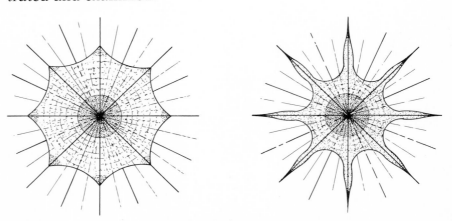

Radiolaria

1. Examine the illustrations given for the triangle, square, pentagon, hexagon, and octagon. As the number of sides of a regular polygon increases, the polygon begins to look more and more like a _____. If this is not obvious, try making a rough drawing of a 16-sided regular polygon.

2. Which regular polygon is used for stop signs?

3. The Defense Department has a huge office building in Washington, D.C. called the _____ because of its shape.

4. What kind of precipitation is composed of regular hexagons?

5. A regular pentagon has five diagonals. If all five are drawn, the figure formed is called a *pentagram*. It has the same general shape as a particular "fish." Draw the diagonals and have a look.

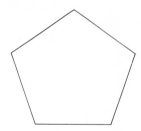

6. Extend all five sides of the regular pentagon below. (Extend each until it meets another extended side.) What is formed?

7. Extend all six sides of the regular hexagon below. (Extend each until it meets another extended side.) What is formed?

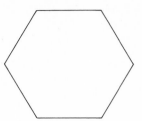

8. What happens when you extend all four sides of a square? Compare this result with the results of Exercises 6 and 7. Can you explain why this one is different?

9. In addition to the polygons mentioned in this section, there are others whose names are used occasionally. They include heptagon, nonagon, decagon, and dodecagon. Look up these words in a dictionary in order to determine how many sides each has. The British 50-pence coin is a heptagon. Malta's 50-cent piece is a decagon. The Australian 50-cent piece is a dodecagon.

10. The numbers 1 through 12 can be placed in the circles of the star shown here in order to create a magic six-pointed star. If the magic sum of each line of the star is 26, create the magic star. (It is interesting to note that it is impossible to create a magic five-pointed star. The proof that such a star cannot be made involves mathematics beyond the scope of this book.)

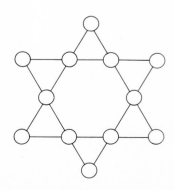

11. The most common shape for floor tiles is the square. What other regular polygons could be used for tiles?

12. On page 49 it is stated that a regular hexagon uses less material to enclose the same area as an equilateral triangle or a square. Illustrated next is a regular hexagon, a square, and an equilateral triangle. All have approximately the same area. Which polygon has the smallest perimeter; that is, which would require the least material, such as very thin wire or wax, to make? You may want to use a string or a ruler to measure all three polygons for comparison.

Hex   The game of hex is played on a board composed of rows and columns of hexagons. The board can have three rows and three columns, four rows and four columns, or more. Here are two sample hex boards.

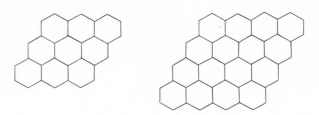

The two players (call them A and B) take turns writing their letters in the hexagons. The first player writes an A in any hexagon. Then the second player writes a B in a different hexagon. The process continues. The first player wins if he joins the top of the hex board to the bottom of the board with a chain of A's in adjacent hexagons. The next figure shows one way that A can win a game.

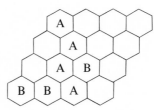

The second player wins if he joins the left edge of the hex board to the right edge of the board with a chain of B's in adjacent hexagons. The next figure shows one way that B can win.

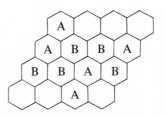

13. Here are some hex boards. Enjoy a few games of hex. Incidentally, a game of hex can never end in a draw; one player must win.

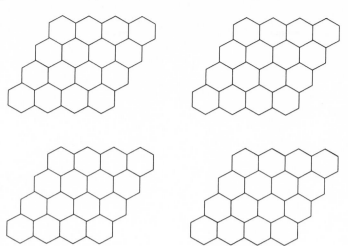

A Taste of Logic

Bode's law is a rule that gives the relative distances of planets from the sun (see page 8). The rule was suggested by observing an apparent pattern and concluding that the pattern could be extended. Reasoning in which people make observations, notice patterns, and then draw general conclusions is called *inductive reasoning*. Inductive reasoning is used frequently in science, often to draw conclusions based on experimental data. You, too, use inductive reasoning in many everyday applications. You have seen the sun rise in the east and set in the west so many days, you expect the same thing to happen tomorrow as well. If you subscribe to a daily newspaper, then you have been conditioned inductively to expect a newspaper every day. By inductive reasoning, you expect certain flowers to bloom in the spring.

Although many important conclusions are drawn by inductive reasoning, such reasoning does not *guarantee* that the conclusion is true. In the case of Bode's law, for example, the law happens to fail for the distant planets. Many conclusions obtained by inductive reasoning are true, but inductive reasoning itself does not *guarantee* they are true.

There is, however, another kind of reasoning that *is* used to prove that a conclusion follows from certain assumptions. It is called *deductive reasoning*. Deductive reasoning is used to prove that the conclusion is true whenever the assumptions are true. In deductive reasoning, statements that are accepted as true are used in a step-by-step logical process to draw a conclusion. As a simple mathematical example, we'll use deductive reasoning to solve the equation $\frac{1}{2}x - 15 = 6$. In this instance we are more concerned with the logic than with the algebra.

The conclusion will be a statement concerning the value of x. We begin by using an application of the statement "If the same number is added to each of two equal numbers, the two resulting sums are equal to each other." Specifically, we'll add 15 to $\frac{1}{2}x - 15$ and to 6. The result is $\frac{1}{2}x = 21$. This can be simplified further by using an application of the statement "If each of two equal numbers is multiplied by the same number, the two resulting products are equal." Specifically, we'll multiply both $\frac{1}{2}x$ and 21 by the number 2. Thus, $\frac{1}{2}x = 21$ becomes $2(\frac{1}{2}x) = 2(21)$, or $x = 42$. The conclusion that x is 42 is the type of conclusion we want when solving an equation. We have shown by deductive reasoning that *if $\frac{1}{2}x - 15 = 6$, then $x = 42$*. The assumption is that $\frac{1}{2}x - 15 = 6$. The conclusion is that x is 42. This means, of course, that if 42 is substituted for x in the original equation $\frac{1}{2}x - 15 = 6$, the two sides of the equation will indeed be equal.

The deductive reasoning applied to solving the equation $\frac{1}{2}x - 15 = 6$ included the use of two *axioms*. An axiom is a statement that is assumed to be true; often it is a property that is obvious. We used the axiom "If a number is added to each of two equal numbers, the two resulting sums are equal to each other" and the axiom "If each of two equal numbers is multiplied by the same number, the two resulting products are equal."

In English, the word axiomatic is used to mean obvious or self-evident. For example, it is axiomatic that students who study do better on exams than those who do not study.

When deductive reasoning yields a conclusion that is considered important enough to be used frequently, the assumptions together with the conclusion are usually called a *theorem*. The theorem may be used directly to solve problems, or it may be used with other true statements in order to derive other theorems by deductive reasoning. Here are some examples of theorems we will encounter in later chapters.

THEOREM (from Chapter 3) *An integer is divisible by 3 if the sum of its digits is divisible by 3.*

THEOREM (from Chapter 4) *In all right triangles, $a^2 + b^2 = c^2$, where c is the length of the hypotenuse and a and b are the lengths of the other two sides.*

THEOREM (from Chapter 5) *In any polyhedron, V + F = E + 2, where V is the number of vertices, F is the number of faces, and E is the number of edges.*

Some words used in the statements of axioms and theorems are undefined because they are understood, whereas other words must be precisely defined. Before deductive reasoning can be used, we must know exactly what all the words of our axioms and theorems mean. Thus, there must be some precise *definitions*. In the theorems just stated, the terms divisible, hypotenuse, polyhedron, and others must be clearly defined. We will look at the careful use of axioms and definitions to prove and develop theorems in Chapter 3.

Now we can make a comparison. Although inductive reasoning is often used to *discover* mathematical facts and theorems, it is deductive reasoning that is used to *prove* those facts and theorems.

As a different example of deductive reasoning, consider the following statements:

> All dogs are mammals.
> All mammals are warm-blooded animals.

If you accept these two statements as true, then you must also accept the obvious conclusion:

> All dogs are warm-blooded animals.

This conclusion follows from the two statements by deductive reasoning. In this chapter, you will learn how to determine whether a conclusion does indeed follow logically from given statements. Many examples are not nearly as obvious as the one just given, so a formal procedure for evaluating reasoning is often useful—especially when you want to test the validity or logical soundness of an argument offered by a lawyer, a politician, a writer, or an advertiser. You cannot rely on how the person impresses you or on what you would like the validity of the person's argument to be.

1. Use inductive reasoning to solve each problem.

   (a) Determine the tenth member of the sequence 5, 8, 11, 14, ...

   (b) It has been raining for nine days straight. What will tomorrow's weather be?

   (c) Determine the first member of the sequence ____, ____, ____, 5/9, 6/10, 7/11, ...

   (d) Franz Schubert wrote nine symphonies, one of which is called the *Unfinished* because the last two movements were never completed. Which of the nine symphonies would you expect to be the *Unfinished?*

   (e) From the top of a high bridge you drop four objects into the water below. The first is a penny. The second is a 15-pound rock. The third is a marble. The fourth is an old math book. On your way to the police station, you have a chance to study the data on how long it took each object to reach the water. In each case it took approximately 5 seconds. What is your conclusion?

2. Solve each problem. The reasoning that you will use, whether you realize it or not, is deductive reasoning.

   (a) Solve for x: $5x + 2 = 32$.

   (b) Rockefeller is richer than Kennedy. Kennedy is richer than Heinz. Who is richer, Heinz or Rockefeller?

   (c) A teacher gives her class a test. To discourage cheating, she uses two different tests. The first row gets test A, the second row test B, the third row test A, the fourth row test B, and the fifth row test A. Afterward she notices that Mark has test B, but all his answers are the correct answers for test A. What deduction might the teacher make?

   (d) The drive from your home to your condominium in Florida is 1350 miles. The car you plan to drive there has a 24-gallon tank and gets 17 miles per gallon. What is the minimum number of gasoline stops you will need to make, assuming that you start out with a full tank of gas?

(e) In a presidential election the candidate receiving the most votes in a given state gets all of the electoral votes of that state. The candidate receiving the most electoral votes wins the election. What is the minimum number of states a candidate can win to guarantee that he or she is elected? Here is a list of states and their electoral votes.

Alabama	9	Alaska	3
Arizona	6	Arkansas	6
California	45	Colorado	7
Connecticut	8	Delaware	3
D.C.	3	Florida	17
Georgia	12	Hawaii	4
Idaho	4	Illinois	26
Indiana	13	Iowa	8
Kansas	7	Kentucky	9
Louisiana	10	Maine	4
Maryland	10	Massachusetts	14
Michigan	21	Minnesota	10
Mississippi	7	Missouri	12
Montana	4	Nebraska	5
Nevada	3	New Hampshire	4
New Jersey	17	New Mexico	4
New York	41	North Carolina	13
North Dakota	3	Ohio	25
Oklahoma	8	Oregon	6
Pennsylvania	27	Rhode Island	4
South Carolina	8	South Dakota	4
Tennessee	10	Texas	26
Utah	4	Vermont	3
Virginia	12	Washington	9
West Virginia	6	Wisconsin	11
Wyoming	3		

(f) Using the method of election suggested in part (e), is it possible for the most popular candidate to lose the election? In other words, can a candidate receive more of the people's votes but lose because he received fewer electoral votes?

(g) Can a candidate win a presidential election with less than half of the electoral votes cast for him?

(h) Why do some states get more electoral votes than others? Study the list.

3. Label each example of reasoning as either inductive or deductive.

   (a) John reasons that if doughnuts are $2.40 a dozen, then one doughnut costs 20¢.
   (b) A child examines several insects and concludes that all insects have six legs.
   (c) It has snowed in January in each of the last five years, so it will snow again this January.
   (d) The perimeter of a square is 12 meters, so each side is 3 meters.
   (e) Sandy has disliked every math course she ever took, so she will dislike this one too.
   (f) The product of two numbers is negative. One number is known to be positive. So the other is negative.
   (g) Bill notices the writing 14/75 on a lithograph. He is told this means that 75 prints were made from the original stone before it was destroyed, and that this is the fourteenth of those 75 prints. Bill concludes that if he buys the lithograph, it is unlikely that any of his friends will also have one like it.
   (h) Experience has shown that the movies are more crowded on Saturday night than on Tuesday night.
   (i) If you divide 3 into a number and the remainder is 0, and you divide 4 into the same number and the remainder is also 0, then you should get 0 as a remainder if you divide 12 into that same number.
   (j) Richard stretches a rubber band to lengths of 3 inches, 4 inches, 5 inches, and 6 inches. He concludes that he can stretch the rubber band to any length.

4. What opinion does this anthropologist's graph convey?

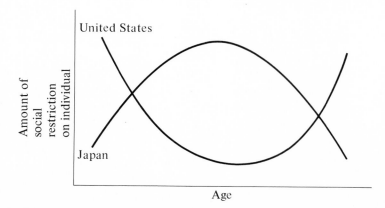

5. The Turkish language has eight different vowel sounds. Each is made with the tongue in a different position and formation. The tongue is positioned either high (H) or low (L) in either the front (F) or back (B) of the mouth. Furthermore, the tongue can be positioned either rounded (R) or unrounded (U). The following three-dimensional system illustrates the eight sounds possible using different combinations of H or L, F or B, and R or U.

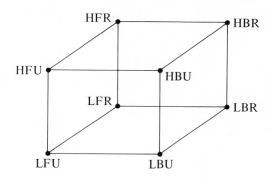

Specify the region of the cube associated with all vowel sounds in which the tongue is

(a) high   (b) low   (c) front
(d) back   (e) rounded   (f) unrounded

6. Kpelle children of Liberia play a game in which 16 stones are lined up in two rows of eight each, like this:

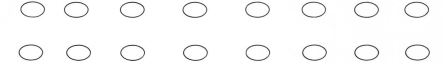

One child is sent away while the others choose, but do not remove, a stone. The child then returns and attempts to determine the selected stone. He or she may ask four times in which row the stone is located. After each reply the child may rearrange the stones between the two rows. He or she must identify the chosen stone after the fourth reply. Explain in steps how this can be done correctly every time. *Hint:* Make each guess eliminate half of the stones about which there is any doubt; that is, eliminate eight stones the first time, then four, and so on.

7. Use some form of deductive reasoning (such as trial and error or algebra) to determine what numbers must go in each circle, if the number in each square is the sum of the numbers in the two circles connected to it.

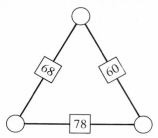

8. When a chord is drawn connecting two points on a circle, the region inside the circle is divided into two subregions. If there are three points, then there will be four subregions. For four points there are eight subregions.

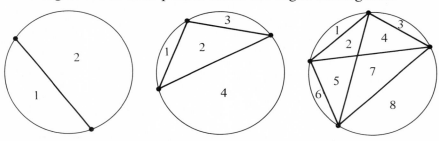

   (a) Draw a circle and show that for five points there are 16 subregions.

   (b) What number should replace the question mark in the following table?

Number of points	2	3	4	5	6
Number of subregions	2	4	8	16	?

   (c) Check your answer to part (b) with the answer at the back of the book. Does inductive reasoning always yield true conclusions? Explain.

9. In some computers, a character of information is represented by eight bits. A *bit* is a *binary digit*. In one popular system, for example, the letter **A** is represented by the binary digit pattern 11000001. A scheme called *parity* is used in order to permit a computer to check errors it can cause when moving information around within the

system. A ninth bit, called a parity bit, is attached to the character. Here are 12 examples. The underlined bit is the parity bit.

<u>1</u>11000011   <u>0</u>11000001   <u>0</u>11000100   <u>1</u>11000101

<u>0</u>11110001   <u>0</u>11110100   <u>0</u>11111000   <u>0</u>11110111

<u>1</u>11111001   <u>1</u>11110110   <u>1</u>11110101   <u>1</u>11110011

Study the examples above. Count the number of 1 bits (excluding the underlined parity bit) in each example. See if you can determine under what condition the parity bit is made a 1 and under what condition it is made a 0.

10. (a) Study the table and use inductive reasoning to determine by what number a fraction must be multiplied in order to change it to a percent.

Fraction	Percent
1/2	50
1/4	25
1	100
1/10	10
9/10	90

(b) Use the result of part (a) to change each of these fractions to a percent.

(i) $\dfrac{7}{10}$ (ii) $\dfrac{3}{5}$ (iii) $\dfrac{1}{20}$

11. Study the two statements in each of the following pairs of sentences. Then determine what conclusion might be drawn in each case. Do not concern yourself with whether or not the conclusion suggested is logically sound. We'll examine that problem in the next section.

(a) All cats are mammals.
All mammals are warm-blooded animals.

(b) All books have pages.
All magazines have pages.

(c) All teachers are poor.
All poor people are on welfare.

SOME SYLLOGISMS

In the preceding section, you saw the statements

> All dogs are mammals.
> All mammals are warm-blooded animals.

and the conclusion

> All dogs are warm-blooded animals.

The three statements constitute what is called a logical argument. An *argument* is an assertion that some statements (called *premises*) lead to another statement (called a *conclusion*). The argument above might be written in the form

> All dogs are mammals.
> All mammals are warm-blooded animals.
> _____
> Therefore, all dogs are warm-blooded animals.

This argument is an example of a syllogism. More specifically, arguments in which there are two premises followed by one conclusion are called *syllogisms*. (This means, of course, that not all arguments are syllogisms. An argument might have three premises, for example.) In this section we'll look at some syllogisms and use diagrams to help determine whether or not a given syllogism is valid. To say that an argument is *valid* means that the conclusion is true whenever all the premises are true. In other words, an argument is *valid* if the conclusion follows from the premises. The foregoing argument is valid because if you assume that the premises ("All dogs are mammals" and "All mammals are warm-blooded animals") are true, then the conclusion ("All dogs are warm-blooded animals") is also true.

The special diagrams we will use to test the validity of logical arguments were invented and used by the eighteenth-century mathematician Leonhard Euler. They are often called *Euler circles*. (In the nineteenth century, John Venn used a variation of these diagrams, so they have also come to be known as *Venn diagrams*.) The statement "All dogs are mammals" can be diagramed as one region (representing all dogs) within another region (representing all mammals). In this way you can see that all dogs are mammals.

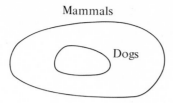

Should you conclude from this diagram that all mammals are dogs? No, all mammals are represented by the larger region. *Some* mammals (see M in the next diagram) are dogs.

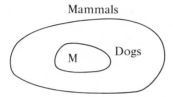

Some (see M in the following diagram) are not dogs.

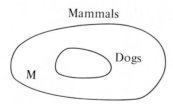

See if you can draw a logic diagram for the statement "All mammals are warm-blooded animals." Check your diagram with the one shown here.

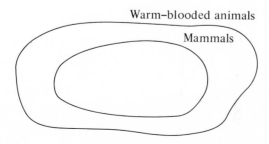

If we put together the two diagrams

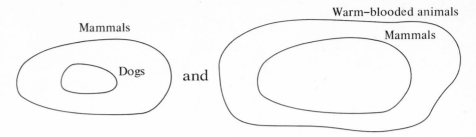

and

we get the diagram

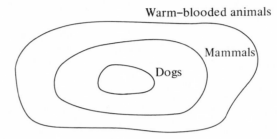

All dogs are mammals.
All mammals are warm-blooded animals.
_____
All dogs are warm-blooded animals.

It follows from the diagram that "All dogs are warm-blooded animals," since the "dogs" region is completely within the "warm-blooded animals" region. So according to this last diagram, the argument in question is valid—that is, the conclusion is true whenever the premises are true.

Next, let's consider the following argument.

All cats are mammals.
All dogs are mammals.
_____
Therefore, all cats are dogs.

Your knowledge of cats and dogs leads you to believe that this argument is not valid. But just why isn't it a valid argument? The premises are obviously true—all cats are indeed mammals _and_ all dogs are indeed mammals—yet the conclusion is obviously false. Recall that for an argument to be valid, the conclusion must be true whenever all the premises are true.

Any argument that is not valid is called a *fallacy*. The argument above is an example of a fallacy.

Now let's diagram the argument in order to see how the drawings will point out the fallacy. After all, we spotted the fallacy because we know something about cats and dogs. Sometimes you will not be so well informed, yet you will have to decide if an argument is valid or is a fallacy. First we diagram the premises "All cats are mammals" and "All dogs are mammals":

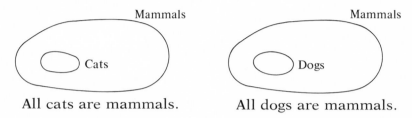

All cats are mammals.   All dogs are mammals.

How should these two illustrations be combined in order to consider a conclusion? Because you know cats and dogs are different, you would naturally draw

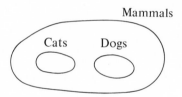

But how would you draw this situation if you were not familiar with dogs and cats? The following are three possibilities.

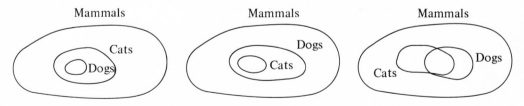

Since there is no statement given that says "All dogs are cats," you have no right to use the first drawing. Similarly, you cannot use the second drawing, since there is no statement of the form "All cats are dogs." On the other hand, the third drawing is accurate, *assuming* that you know nothing about the relationship between cats and dogs. In this way, a cat (C in the drawings shown next) may or may not be a dog.

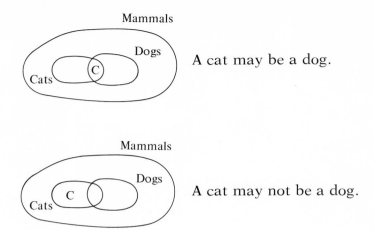

A cat may be a dog.

A cat may not be a dog.

The second diagram shows that you cannot draw the conclusion "All cats are dogs." It does not follow from "All cats are mammals" and "All dogs are mammals" that "All cats are dogs," and this diagram shows this without any additional assumptions or knowledge about cats and dogs.

The preceding argument is a fallacy because the premises are true, yet the conclusion is false. *Be careful that you do not confuse the validity of an argument with the truth of its conclusion.* (Recall that an argument is valid if the conclusion follows from the premises.) A valid argument may have a false conclusion, or a fallacy may have a conclusion that is true. This point is examined in Exercise 4.

From the discussion of the last example, you can probably see immediately that the statement "No cats are dogs" is diagramed as

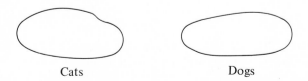

How about "Some people are liars?" Draw it the way you think it should be. Then compare yours with the following illustration.

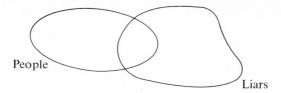

The statement "Some people are liars" should be drawn using overlap. In this way, we can see that some people (P in the drawings that follow) are liars

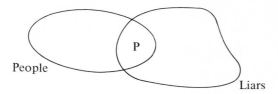

and that some people (P) are not liars, as shown next.

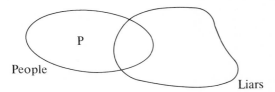

Both possibilities are reasonable. In logic, "some" means at least one.

But what about the suggestion of this diagram that there are liars (see X in the next drawing) who are not people?

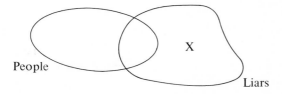

On the one hand, this observation points out a possible weakness of this diagram approach to studying logic. On the other hand, there may be monkeys or Martians who lie. There are definitely newspapers and magazines that stretch the truth or print things that they must later retract. At the very least, we cannot be certain that all liars are people, so the diagram seems to be correct as it stands.

1. Use diagrams to test each argument for validity. Do not prejudge them.

    (a) All Ukrainians are Russians.
    All Russians are Europeans.

    Therefore, all Ukrainians are Europeans.

    (b) All senators earn more than $40,000 per year.
    All doctors earn more than $40,000 per year.

    Therefore, all senators are doctors.

    (c) All right triangles contain a right angle.
    All rectangles contain a right angle.

    Therefore, all right triangles are rectangles.

    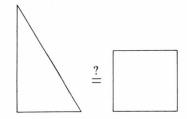

    (d) All silkscreens are serigraphs.
    All serigraphs are stencils.

    All silkscreens are stencils.

    (e) All glubs are zogs.
    All zogs are mips.

    All glubs are mips.

    (f) All trees are green.
    All plants are green.

    All plants are trees.

2. Did you notice in Exercise 1 that there are really only two different patterns, or *forms*, presented.

All A are B		All A are B
All B are C	and	All C are B
All A are C		All A are C

Use diagrams to show that arguments of the first form are always valid and those of the second form are always fallacies. Now you should be able to recognize some arguments as valid or not simply by the form!

3. Statements of the form "If . . . , then . . ." can be translated into statements of the form "All . . ." for use with diagrams. For instance, the statement "If he is a politician, then he is insincere" can be considered as "All politicians are insincere." In general, "If A, then B" translates into "All A are B." Now translate each of the following statements into an "All . . ." form.

(a) If he is a lawyer, then he is wealthy.
(b) If it is a bird, then it has feathers.
(c) If it is a lithograph, then it is an original print.
(d) If she is liberal, then she is a Democrat.
(e) If she is a Republican, then she is conservative.
(f) If it is a green plant, then it produces chlorophyll.
(g) If it is a symphony, then it is not an overture.

4. (a) The following argument has a conclusion that is true, yet the argument is a fallacy. Use a diagram to show that it is indeed a fallacy.

> All trees are green.
> All plants are green.
> _____
> All trees are plants.

If you have done Exercises 1 and 2, then from the latter you might recognize this as the form of a fallacy. From Exercise 1 you might note that this argument is of the same type as (b), (c), and (f), all of which are fallacies.

(b) For a valid argument (for example, the first form in Exercise 2) to have a conclusion that is false, one of the premises must be false. The following argument has a conclusion that is false, yet it is a valid argument. Use a diagram to show that it is indeed a valid argument.

> All apples are bananas.   (Or "If apples are bananas.")
> All bananas are yellow.
> _____
> All apples are yellow.

5. Use diagrams to test the validity of each argument.

   (a)   If it is a zebra, then it has stripes.
         All referees have stripes.
         _____

         All referees are zebras.

   (b)   If it is a fossil, then it is old.
         If it is a prehistoric bone, then it is old.
         _____

         All fossils are prehistoric bones.

6. Use diagrams to test each argument for validity. Do not prejudge them, test them.

   (a)   All dinosaurs are prehistoric.
         Some rocks are prehistoric.
         _____

         Some dinosaurs are rocks.

   (b)   All x's are y's.
         No y's are z's.
         _____

         Some x's are not z's.

LOGIC CIRCUITS

You have just seen how diagrams can be used to test the validity of logical arguments. A completely different approach was offered over a hundred years ago by George Boole, an English mathematician. In 1854, Boole published a book that

Courtesy of the Library of Congress

George Boole (1815–1864)

explained how logical statements could be transformed into mathematical symbols. He also explained how to calculate the truth or falsity of related statements by using rules designed for just that purpose. The mathematics that Boole developed is known as *Boolean algebra*.

Boolean algebra created little interest until a practical application was found in the 1930s. Then, Claude Shannon showed how Boolean algebra could be applied to the design and simplification of complex circuits involved in electronic computers. Still later, Boolean algebra even found its way into many grade school and high school mathematics programs in the form of set theory, a part of the so-called new math.

In this section we'll take a brief look at this "switching logic," as it is sometimes called. Our interest will be in the logic of the circuit, not in the electronics. Here is the notation we will use:

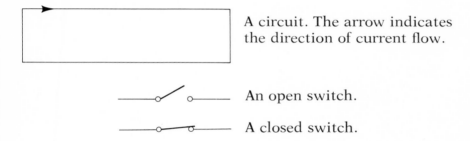

A circuit. The arrow indicates the direction of current flow.

An open switch.

A closed switch.

In the next circuit, the switch is open. No current will flow through it.

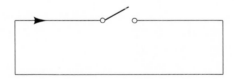

In the following circuit, the switch is closed. Current will flow through it.

Let's look at the next circuit. Can you see what must be the status (open or closed) of the switches A and B for current to flow through the circuit?

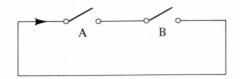

Both switches must be closed for current to flow. This means that A *and* B must be closed. If either switch is open, then there is a break in the circuit and current will not flow. We will denote

A and B

by

$$A \cdot B$$

Examine the circuit below and see if you can write in symbols the condition under which current flows.

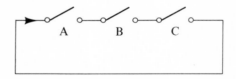

Did you observe that current will flow only when A and B and C are all closed? This condition, A *and* B *and* C, is written symbolically as $A \cdot B \cdot C$.

    The two circuits above, $A \cdot B$ and $A \cdot B \cdot C$, are examples of *series* circuits. All switches must be closed for current to flow through a series circuit.

    Next, look at the following circuit. See if you can determine under what condition current will flow through it.

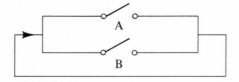

You probably realize that current will flow through the circuit if either A *or* B (or both) is closed. If A is closed, current flows through the top branch. If B is closed, current flows through the bottom branch. If both switches are closed, then current flows through both branches. We will denote

$$A \quad or \quad B$$

by

$$A + B$$

Examine the following circuit and see if you can write in symbols the condition under which current flows.

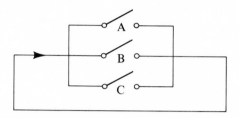

Current will flow if A or B or C is closed. The condition A *or* B *or* C is written symbolically as A + B + C. (By A or B or C is meant that any one or more of these switches must be closed for current to flow.)

The two circuits just discussed, A + B and A + B + C, are examples of *parallel* circuits. Current will flow through a parallel circuit if any (one or more) of the switches is closed.

Circuits may consist of combinations of series and parallel. An example is the circuit shown next.

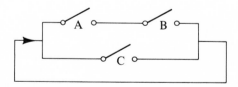

Current will flow through the top branch if A and B are closed or through the bottom branch if C is closed. So the label that describes the condition for current flow is

$$(A \text{ and } B) \text{ or } (C)$$

or, in symbols,

$$(A \cdot B) + (C)$$

Here's another example. In this circuit

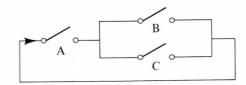

current will flow if A and B are closed or if A and C are closed. Based on this analysis, the label for current flow is

$$(A \text{ and } B) \text{ or } (A \text{ and } C)$$

or

$$(A \cdot B) + (A \cdot C)$$

Let's consider another approach to labeling this circuit. Can you see that A must be closed or there is no chance for current to flow through the circuit? Also, either B or C must be closed. So the label can be

$$A \text{ and } (B \text{ or } C)$$

which is written symbolically as

$$A \cdot (B + C)$$

Since both $(A \cdot B) + (A \cdot C)$ and $A \cdot (B + C)$ are labels for the same circuit, a logical deduction is that

$$A \cdot (B + C) = (A \cdot B) + (A \cdot C)$$

This equality is called a *distributive property*.

Suppose we reverse the process, and draw the circuit that corresponds to a given symbolic label. To draw the circuit $(A + B) \cdot (C + D)$, consider that $A + B$ is

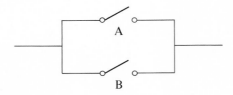

and that C + D is

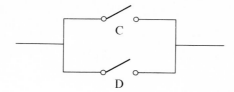

We want

$$(A + B) \quad \text{and} \quad (C + D)$$

that is,

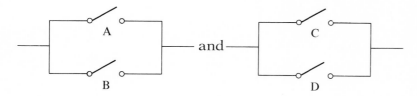

The "and" specifies series, so the result is

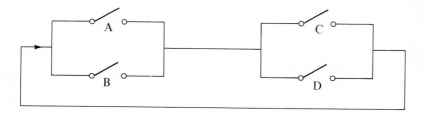

1. Label each circuit to indicate under what conditions current will flow.

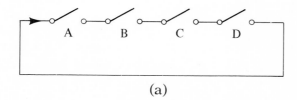

(a)

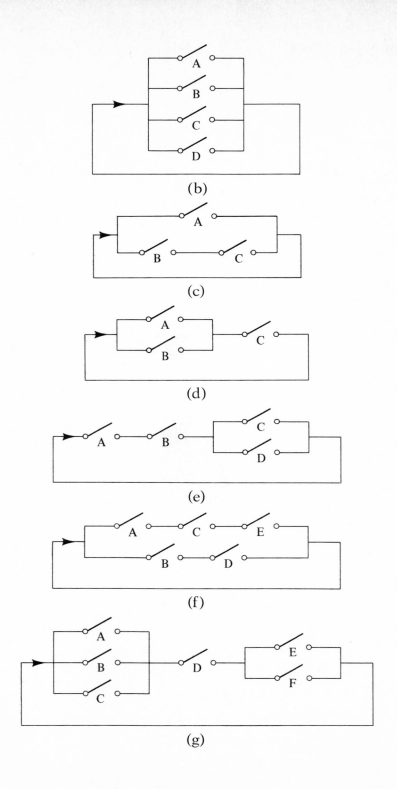

(b)

(c)

(d)

(e)

(f)

(g)

2. Draw the circuit indicated by each label.

    (a)   (A) + (B · C)   (b)   (A) · (B + C)

    (c)   (A + B) · (C) · (D)   (d)   (A · B · C) + (D)

    (e)   (A · B · C) + (D · E)   (f)   (A · B) + (C · D) + (E · F)

    (g)   (A) · (B + C) · (D)

SETS

Most of you have undoubtedly learned about sets from previous mathematics courses, so we will not cover the topic in depth. Instead, we'll present some basic notation and definitions and show some of the relationships between sets and logic.

Sets were introduced about a hundred years ago by the German mathematician Georg Cantor. The original theory has been expanded over the years and now serves as a basic tool in many areas of advanced mathematics.

Georg Cantor (1845–1918)

To begin, a *set* is a collection of things. In mathematics, the things are usually numbers. The set consisting of the numbers 1, 3, 4, and 9 is written {1, 3, 4, 9}. The braces indicate that it is a set. The things in the set, called *members* or *elements*, are separated by commas. The order in which the elements are written does not matter, in the sense that {4, 9, 1, 3} is the same set as {1, 3, 4, 9}.

Set operations are different from ordinary arithmetic operations. The operation of *intersection*, denoted by ∩, is explained next by means of examples. Study them and see if you can explain in general what results from the intersection of two sets.

$$\{1, 2, 3, 4\} \cap \{2, 3, 4, 5\} = \{2, 3, 4\}$$
$$\{5, 6, 7, 9\} \cap \{5, 9\} = \{5, 9\}$$
$$\{1, 2, 3\} \cap \{4, 5, 6\} = \{\ \}, \qquad \text{a set with no elements}$$

In general, the intersection of two sets is a set containing all elements that are common to both sets. Thus, {3, 7, 10} ∩ {1, 9, 10} = {10}, since 10 is the only element common to both sets. By the way, the set { } is called the *empty set* or *null set*. Sometimes it is denoted by ∅, a symbol derived from a Scandinavian letter.

Venn diagrams, used in the section on syllogisms, are also used to illustrate relationships between sets. If two sets, *A* and *B*, have some elements in common, then circles representing the sets can be drawn like this.

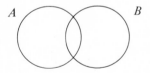

The intersection, then, is represented by the portion these sets have in common. This area is shaded in the next drawing.

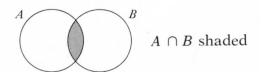

$A \cap B$ shaded

The operation of *union,* denoted by ∪, is explained next by means of examples. Study them and see if you can explain in general what results from the union of two sets.

$$\{1, 2, 3\} \cup \{4, 5, 6\} = \{1, 2, 3, 4, 5, 6\}$$
$$\{1, 2, 3, 4\} \cup \{3, 4, 5\} = \{1, 2, 3, 4, 5\}$$
$$\{5, 6, 7, 9\} \cup \{5, 9\} = \{5, 6, 7, 9\}$$

In general, the union of two sets is a set containing all elements that are in one set or in the other set or in both sets. Thus, $\{4, 5, 7, 9\} \cup \{4, 6, 9, 10\} = \{4, 5, 6, 7, 9, 10\}$.

If two sets A and B have some elements in common, then the circles representing the sets can be drawn as

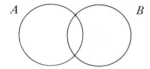

The union is represented by the portions shaded in the next diagram.

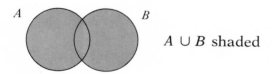

$A \cup B$ shaded

Sometimes it is desirable to discuss what is *not* in a set. In such instances we must know what is to be considered, so a *universe* $\mathcal{U}$ is chosen for each setting. For example, let $\mathcal{U} = \{1, 2, 3, 4, 5, 6, 7, 8, 9, 10\}$ and let $A = \{1, 2, 3\}$ be a set of elements chosen from the universe. Then the set of elements that are not in A is $\{4, 5, 6, 7, 8, 9, 10\}$. This set is denoted by A' and is called the *complement* of A. As another example, let $\mathcal{U} = \{5, 6, 7, 8, 9, 10, 11, 12\}$, $A = \{6, 8, 10, 12\}$, $B = \{8, 9, 10\}$. Can you determine A' and B'? You should have reasoned that since A' is the complement of A, it is the set of all elements of the universe that are not in A. Thus, $A' = \{5, 7, 9, 11\}$. Similarly, $B' = \{5, 6, 7, 11, 12\}$.

1. Although the order in which the elements of a set are written "does not matter," perhaps you can see that some orders may be superior to others. Comment on this.

2. Determine the result of each operation.
   (a) $\{1, 2, 3, 4, 5\} \cap \{1, 3, 5\}$
   (b) $\{1, 3, 5, 7, 9\} \cap \{5, 7, 9, 11, 13\}$
   (c) $\{1, 3, 5, 7\} \cap \{2, 4, 6, 8\}$
   (d) $\{5, 8, 13, 19\} \cap \{1, 3, 9, 13\}$
   (e) $\{1, 2\} \cup \{3, 4\}$
   (f) $\{1, 3, 5, 7, 9\} \cup \{2, 4, 6, 8, 10\}$
   (g) $\{9, 12, 16, 23\} \cup \{4, 9, 23, 35, 67\}$
   (h) $\{1, 2, 3\} \cup \{1, 2, 3\}$

3. Shade the intersection.

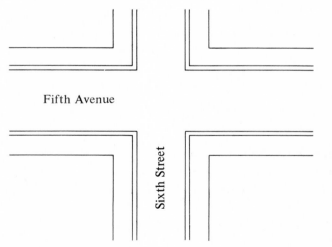

Fifth Avenue

Sixth Street

4. (a) Shade $A \cap B$ in each case.

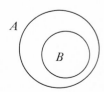

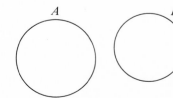

(b) Shade $A \cup B$ in each case.

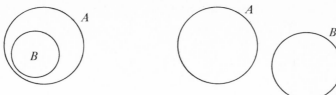

5. (a) Current will flow through the circuit below if A is closed *and* B is closed. Similarly, an element is in the intersection of sets A and B if it is in set A *and* in set B. This suggests a similarity between _____ of sets and _____ circuits.

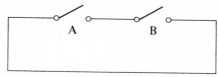

(b) Current will flow through the circuit below if A is closed *or* B is closed or both are closed. Similarly, an element is in the union of sets A and B if it is in set A *or* in set B or in both sets. This suggests a similarity between _____ of sets and _____ circuits.

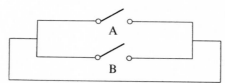

6. (a) The intersection of three sets is a set consisting of all elements common to all three sets. Shade $A \cap B \cap C$ in the following drawing.

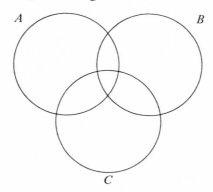

(b) The union of three sets is a set consisting of all elements that are in at least one of the sets. Shade $A \cup B \cup C$ in the following drawing.

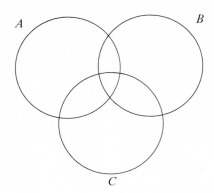

7. (a) Let $\mathscr{U} = \{1, 2, 3, 4, 5, 6, 7\}, A = \{1, 4, 7\}, B = \{5, 6, 7\}$. Determine A' and B'.
   (b) Let $\mathscr{U} = \{2, 3, 5, 7, 8, 12\}, E = \{2, 3\}, F = \{3, 7, 12\}, G = \{2, 3, 5, 7, 8, 12\}$. Determine E', F', and G'.

ARCHAEOLOGICAL DECIPHERMENT

This concluding section describes an application of deductive reasoning in the field of archaeology. Archaeologists attempting to read inscriptions written in an ancient language face serious obstacles because no living person uses or knows the language, and often only a small amount of the written language is available. Sometimes a bilingual text is found that has the same message in two languages (one of which may be known). Deciphering is then easier. On the other hand, archaeologists rarely discover bilingual texts. The Rosetta Stone is an exception. Found by Napoleon's army in 1799 near Rosetta, Egypt, the Rosetta Stone contains forms of Ancient Egyptian along with a Greek translation. This rare find provided the key to the deciphering of Egyptian hieroglyphics in 1822.

Early in this century excavators discovered another ancient language in Greece and in Crete. Unfortunately, there was no bilingual text available to aid the decipherers of Linear B, as this language came to be known. The decipherers decided to collect words that began the same but ended differently, or else

The Rosetta Stone

Archaeological Decipherment   91

began differently but ended the same way. Since the syllables in Linear B were simple—one vowel (V) or one consonant plus one vowel (CV)—the pattern could be written and analyzed logically in a table such as the one shown here. The table is called a *syllabic grid*. In it, C_1 represents one consonant, C_2 another, C_3 still another, and so on. Similarly, V_1 represents one vowel, V_2 another, V_3 still another, and so on. The expression C_1V_2, for example, represents the syllable formed by combining the first consonant with the second vowel.

	V_1	V_2	V_3	$\cdots$
C_1	C_1V_1	C_1V_2	C_1V_3	
C_2	C_2V_1	C_2V_2	C_2V_3	
C_3	C_3V_1	C_3V_2	C_3V_3	
C_4	C_4V_1	C_4V_2	C_4V_3	

If the syllable C_4V_1 is shown (or guessed) to represent, say, *n i*, then C_4 is *n* and V_1 is *i*. If it is also discovered that C_2V_3 is *t e*, then C_2 is *t* and V_3 is *e*. Based on this information, what must be the value of C_2V_1? The value of C_2V_1 can be readily determined. Since C_2 is *t* and V_1 is *i*, it follows that the value of C_2V_1 is *ti*. This deductive process is called *triangularization*. A brief look at the following table will convince you that the process is appropriately named.

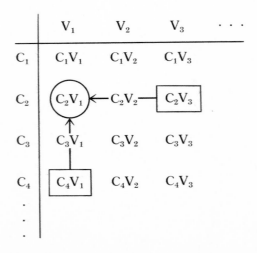

Another entry in the table is also readily determinable by this triangularization procedure. Which entry is it, and what is its value? You should have determined that the entry is C_4V_3, and its value is *ne*, since C_4 is *n* and V_3 is *e*. Observe the triangularization in the next table.

	V_1	V_2	V_3	$\cdots$
C_1	C_1V_1	C_1V_2	C_1V_3	
C_2	C_2V_1	C_2V_2	$\boxed{C_2V_3}$	
C_3	C_3V_1	C_3V_2	C_3V_3	
C_4	$\boxed{C_4V_1}$ —	$C_4V_2 \rightarrow$	$\bigcirc\; C_4V_3$	

Shown next is an actual syllabic grid used by archaeologist Michael Ventris to decipher Linear B.

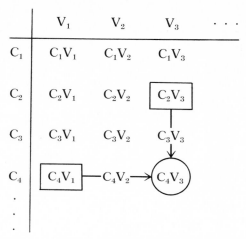

LINEAR B SYLLABIC GRID

THIRD STATE : REVIEW OF PYLOS EVIDENCE

FIGURE II
WORK NOTE 17
20 FEB 1952

Prepared by Michael Ventris; copy supplied by Emmett L. Bennett, Jr.

1. Consider the following table.

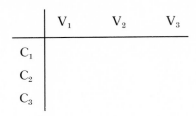

	V_1	V_2	V_3
C_1			
C_2			
C_3			

(a) If C_1V_3 is *du*, then $C_1 = $ _____ and $V_3 = $ _____.
(b) If C_3V_1 is *ra*, then $C_3 = $ _____ and $V_1 = $ _____.
(c) What is the value of C_3V_3, based on the results of parts (a) and (b)?
(d) If C_2V_2 is *ke*, then $C_2 = $ _____ and $V_2 = $ _____.
(e) Based on the preceding results, what are the values of C_3V_2, C_2V_3, and C_1V_2?
(f) What must be the values of C_2V_1 and C_1V_1?

2. Assume that $C_1V_1 = to$, $C_2V_4 = na$, $C_3V_3 = bi$, and $C_4V_2 = re$. Use triangularization to determine the values of the 12 missing entries.

	V_1	V_2	V_3	V_4
C_1	*to*			
C_2				*na*
C_3			*bi*	
C_4		*re*		

3. In the four-by-four table of Exercise 2, four entries were given. This enabled you to determine all the other entries. Is it always true that knowing any four entries is sufficient to enable you to determine the other twelve entries by triangularization? Make tables and triangularize until you can make a deduction.

4. (a) Here is the Chinese version of Pascal's triangle, published a few hundred years before Pascal was born. Compare the symbols within the circles of the Chinese triangle with the numbers of Pascal's triangle (page 6, Application 7) and determine the numerical value of each Chinese symbol.

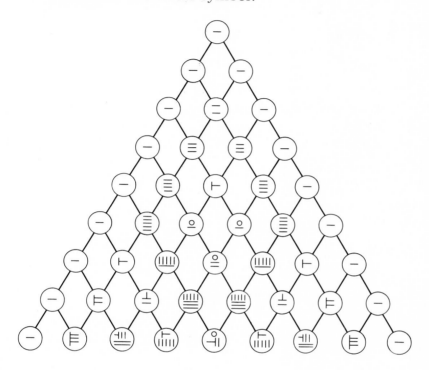

(b) Study the results of part (a) and look for a pattern. Then write the Chinese symbol you believe corresponds to each of the following numbers: 12, 20, 26, 30, 33, 50, 57, 60.

Number Theory

3

Number theory is the branch of mathematics that includes the study of the integers. In other words, in number theory we study the properties and interrelationships of the numbers 0, 1, $-1, 2, -2, 3, -3, 4, -4, \ldots$. Such studies have intrigued people for thousands of years. The ancient Chinese and Babylonians were active in this area more than 4000 years ago.

Magic squares, presented in Chapter 1, are one of the topics explored in number theory. In this chapter, we shall study prime numbers, divisibility, and modular arithmetic, and look at some applications in these areas of number theory. We will begin by introducing some basic definitions, which will be further developed in the next two sections.

DIVISORS AND PRIME NUMBERS

The words "divisor" and "factor" are synonyms used frequently in number theory. See if you can determine what these words mean by studying the following statement. The numbers 1, 2, 3, 4, 6, and 12 are the divisors (or factors) of 12. Here is the explanation. The numbers 1, 2, 3, 4, 6, and 12 are divisors (or factors) of 12 because when 12 is divided by any one of them, the remainder is zero. In general, integer a is a *divisor* of integer b if there is an integer c such that $ac = b$. In the example, 4 is a divisor of 12 because there is an integer 3 such that $4 \cdot 3 = 12$. This also means that 3 is a divisor of 12. Why? You should now be able to explain why 2 is a divisor of 12 and why 12 is a divisor of 12. If a is a divisor of b, we also say that b is *divisible* by a. (This means that b is divisible by a, if there is an integer c such that $b = ac$.) Since 4 is a divisor of 12, we say that 12 is divisible by 4. Here are some questions to consider before going on to the next paragraph.

1. What are the divisors of 18?

2. Is 20 divisible by 5? Why?

3. Is 21 divisible by 5? Why?

The divisors of 18 are 1, 2, 3, 6, 9, and 18. Yes, 20 is divisible by 5, because 5 is a divisor of 20; that is, there is an integer 4 such that $5 \cdot 4 = 20$. No, 21 is not divisible by 5, because there is no integer c such that $5 \cdot c = 21$.

A *prime number* is an integer that is greater than 1 and has no positive divisors (or factors) other than 1 and itself. The numbers 2, 3, 5, 7, and 11 are examples of prime numbers. On the other hand, 4 is not prime because it is divisible by 2. The number 6 is not a prime because it is divisible by 2 and by 3. The numbers 4 and 6 are examples of *composite numbers*, integers greater than 1 that are not prime numbers.

One method for finding primes was first suggested by the Greek mathematician Eratosthenes about 230 B.C. It is called the *Sieve of Eratosthenes*. Here is how the sieve method is used to find all the primes less than 50. First write the integers from 1 to 50.

1	2	3	4	5	6	7	8	9	10
11	12	13	14	15	16	17	18	19	20
21	22	23	24	25	26	27	28	29	30
31	32	33	34	35	36	37	38	39	40
41	42	43	44	45	46	47	48	49	50

Now proceed through the list, crossing out numbers that are not primes and circling those that are primes. Begin this procedure by crossing out 1, which is not a prime. Next, circle 2, the first prime number, and cross out 4, 6, 8, 10, and the other multiples of 2. Next, circle 3 and cross out 6, 9, 12, 15, and other multiples of 3. (We will see in the next section why this works.) Of course, some multiples of 3 are also multiples of 2, so they have already been crossed out. Next, circle 5 and cross out 10, 15, 20, 25, and so on. Continue the process until all numbers have been either circled or crossed out. All prime numbers less than 50 are circled in the following sieve.

1̸ ② ③ 4̸ ⑤ 6̸ ⑦ 8̸ 9̸ 1̸0̸
⑪ 1̸2̸ ⑬ 1̸4̸ 1̸5̸ 1̸6̸ ⑰ 1̸8̸ ⑲ 2̸0̸
2̸1̸ 2̸2̸ ㉓ 2̸4̸ 2̸5̸ 2̸6̸ 2̸7̸ 2̸8̸ ㉙ 3̸0̸
㉛ 3̸2̸ 3̸3̸ 3̸4̸ 3̸5̸ 3̸6̸ ㊲ 3̸8̸ 3̸9̸ 4̸0̸
㊶ 4̸2̸ ㊸ 4̸4̸ 4̸5̸ 4̸6̸ ㊼ 4̸8̸ 4̸9̸ 5̸0̸

This brief section was intended to acquaint you with prime numbers and some basic terminology. These concepts will be extended and amplified in the sections that follow. Then, applications will be presented.

APPLICATIONS AND EXERCISES

1. For each of the following numbers, list all of its divisors.
   - (a) 10
   - (b) 14
   - (c) 16
   - (d) 28
   - (e) 50
   - (f) 100
   - (g) 48
   - (h) 64
   - (i) 81

2. (a) List all the factors of 120.
   (b) List all the factors of 150.

3. Use the Sieve of Eratosthenes to find all prime numbers less than 100.

4. Use the sieve prepared for Exercise 3 to determine the first 20 composite numbers.

5. Is every odd number a prime number?

6. Is every even number a composite number?

7. A theorem states: *The sum of any two prime numbers greater than two is always even.* Verify this theorem for five different pairs of prime numbers.

8. Mathematician Christian Goldbach (1690–1764) claimed that every even integer greater than two can be expressed as the sum of two prime numbers. The conjecture has not yet been proved. For each of the following numbers, verify

Goldbach's conjecture by finding two primes whose sum is that total. The Sieve of Eratosthenes might be helpful here.

(a) 12   (b) 32   (c) 60   (d) 84

9. Prime numbers such as 11 and 13 that differ by two are called *twin primes*. Mathematicians believe there are an infinite number of such pairs. List six other pairs of twin primes.

10. Many formulas have been devised to generate some prime numbers. The expression $4n - 1$ produces many primes for positive integer values of n. It also produces some numbers that are not primes. Compute the value of $4n - 1$ for $n = 1, 2, 3, 4, 5, 6,$ and 7. Specify which results are prime numbers and which are not.

11. The expression $2^p - 1$ produces some primes for positive integer values of p. Use $p = 1, 2, 3, 4, 5, 6,$ and 7. Specify which results are prime numbers and which are not.

12. The expression $n^2 - n + 41$ generates prime numbers when any integer between 1 and 40 is used as the value of n. Verify this for $n = 1, 2, 3, 4, 5, 6, 7,$ and 8. Can you see why this formula fails when n is 41? Explain.

13. Define or explain in terms of divisibility what is meant by an *even number*.

14. The early Greeks called some natural numbers "perfect." A natural number is *perfect* if the sum of all its divisors (excluding the number itself) is equal to the number. For example, the divisors of 6 are (excluding 6 itself) 1, 2, and 3. The sum $1 + 2 + 3$ is 6, the number in question. So 6 is a perfect number. Test the numbers 9, 16, 20, and 28 to see if any of them are perfect numbers.

15. The Greeks considered the number 12 to be *abundant*, because the sum of its divisors (excluding 12) is greater than itself. The divisors are 1, 2, 3, 4, and 6. Their sum is 16, which is greater than 12. Similarly, the number 14 is considered to be *deficient*, because the sum of its divisors, 1, 2, and 7, is less than 14. Test the numbers 4, 15, 18, 24, and 100 to determine which ones are abundant and which are deficient.

16. Every positive integer can be expressed as the sum of four or fewer squares of integers.

   (a)   Verify that 5 can be expressed as $1^2 + 2^2$; 30 can be expressed as $1^2 + 2^2 + 3^2 + 4^2$; and $35 = 1^2 + 3^2 + 5^2$.

   (b)   Express 53 as the sum of two squares.

   (c)   Express 91 as the sum of three squares.

   (d)   Express 96 as the sum of three squares.

   (e)   Express 142 as the sum of four different squares.

LEAST COMMON MULTIPLE

In this section we will look at some more useful concepts that involve prime numbers. Every composite number can be expressed as a product of prime numbers. We shall use some examples to illustrate this *prime factorization* concept. The number 10 can be written as $2 \cdot 5$, and both 2 and 5 are prime numbers. Thus,

$$10 = 2 \cdot 5 \qquad \text{(prime factorization)}$$

The number 24 can be written as $2 \cdot 12$. But 12 is not prime. However, 12 can be factored further as $2 \cdot 6$, and 6 can be written as $2 \cdot 3$. Thus, $24 = 2 \cdot 2 \cdot 2 \cdot 3$. When a factor appears more than once, exponents are used to simplify the factorization. Since $2 \cdot 2 \cdot 2 = 2^3$, we have

$$24 = 2^3 \cdot 3 \qquad \text{(prime factorization)}$$

See if you can obtain the prime factorization for 18. Then check with the answer that follows. You should have found that the desired factorization is $2 \cdot 3^2$. Perhaps you did this as $18 = 2 \cdot 9 = 2 \cdot 3 \cdot 3 = 2 \cdot 3^2$.

To factor a number, try dividing the number by the primes 2, 3, 5, 7, 11, . . . (in that order) until you find a divisor. Consider, for example, finding the divisors of 455. First, 2 is not a divisor. Next, 3 is not a divisor. Next, 5 is a divisor, since $455 \div 5 = 91$, or $455 = 5 \cdot 91$. Now search for a divisor of 91. The smallest prime number that is a divisor of 91 is 7; $91 = 7 \cdot 13$. Thus, $455 = 5 \cdot 7 \cdot 13$.

Next, we'll apply our knowledge of prime factorization in

order to find what is called the *least common multiple* of two or more numbers. You probably recall that in order to add two or more fractions, you must find a common denominator for the fractions. The smallest common denominator is the same as the least common multiple or *LCM* of the denominators. It is the smallest denominator divisible by all of the other denominators. For example, the LCM of 8 and 6 is 24, since 24 is the smallest number divisible by both 8 and 6. If you were adding fractions having denominators of 6 and 8, you would select 24 as the smallest common denominator. The LCM of two or more numbers can be found by trial and error or by using prime factorization. Let's see how to find the LCM of 6 and 8, written LCM(6, 8), by using prime factorization. Here is the factorization:

$$6 = 2 \cdot 3$$
$$8 = 2^3$$

For the LCM we select all the different prime factors displayed (namely, 2 and 3) and we retain the highest power of each prime that is raised to a power in any of the prime factorizations. Thus,

$$LCM(6, 8) = 2^3 \cdot 3 = 24$$

Check your understanding of this process by finding LCM(50, 45). The work is shown next. $50 = 2 \cdot 5^2$ and $45 = 3^2 \cdot 5$. Thus, LCM(50, 45) $= 2 \cdot 3^2 \cdot 5^2 = 450$.

In the next section you will have a chance to apply the concept of least common multiple to the balancing of chemical equations.

APPLICATIONS AND EXERCISES

1. Determine the prime factorization of each number.

    (a) 30   (b) 70   (c) 63   (d) 72
    (e) 150   (f) 180   (g) 490   (h) 441
    (i) 325   (j) 891

2. Find the least common multiple (LCM) of each pair of numbers.

   (a) 12, 15   (b) 25, 30
   (c) 48, 42   (d) 40, 100
   (e) 72, 54   (f) 120, 35
   (g) 70, 49   (h) 320 150

3. Find the LCM of each triplet of numbers. Part (b) is *worked out* in the answer section.

   (a) 2, 3, 4   (b) 10, 15, 20
   (c) 18, 24, 32   (d) 24, 40, 42
   (e) 45, 50, 60   (f) 80, 32, 28

4. Determine the common denominator that should be used to add each group of fractions. But do not actually add the fractions; that will be done in Application 5.

   (a) $\dfrac{17}{26} + \dfrac{12}{39}$ (b) $\dfrac{7}{36} + \dfrac{5}{27}$

   (c) $\dfrac{1}{2} + \dfrac{3}{8} + \dfrac{7}{20}$ (d) $\dfrac{8}{55} + \dfrac{12}{65} + \dfrac{19}{143}$

   (e) $\dfrac{25}{144} + \dfrac{9}{60} + \dfrac{13}{84}$

5. Add the fractions in each part of Application 4.

6. The German mathematician Leibniz (1646–1716), a co-inventor of calculus, discovered an interesting triangle while working on summation of infinite series of numbers.

$$\frac{1}{1}$$
$$\frac{1}{2} \quad \frac{1}{2}$$
$$\frac{1}{3} \quad \frac{1}{6} \quad \frac{1}{3}$$
$$\frac{1}{4} \quad \frac{1}{12} \quad \frac{1}{12} \quad \frac{1}{4}$$

Every number within the triangle is equal to the sum of the two numbers below it.

   (a) Verify that $\frac{1}{4} + \frac{1}{12} = \frac{1}{3}$ and $\frac{1}{12} + \frac{1}{12} = \frac{1}{6}$.
   (b) Note the pattern of the numbers running down the sides of the triangle. Assuming the pattern holds, which it does, what is the first number and the last number of the next row of the triangle?
   (c) Generate the entire fifth row of the triangle.

7. When examining a number n in order to determine its prime factorization, there is no need to test any number larger than $\sqrt{n}$. In seeking the prime factors of 144, test for divisibility only as far as 12. Larger numbers need not be tested. Similarly, in seeking the prime factors of 211, test only numbers smaller than $\sqrt{211}$. Now $\sqrt{211}$ is between 14 and 15, since $\sqrt{196}$ is 14 and $\sqrt{225}$ is 15. So test for divisibility only as far as 14. In other words, the only possible prime factors of 144 are 2, 3, 5, 7, and 11. The only possible prime factors of 211 are 2, 3, 5, 7, 11, and 13. Examine the prime factorization of the numbers 26, 100, and 169. Then explain why the method suggested here is indeed sufficient.

CHEMISTRY AND LCM

We will now look at an application of the least common multiple (LCM): the balancing of chemical equations.

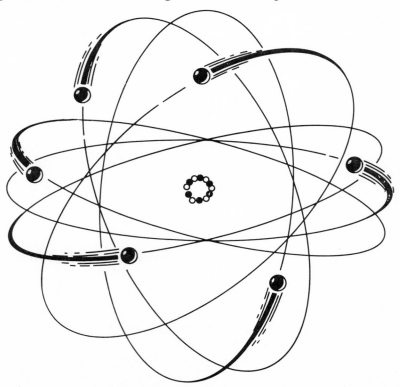

Chemistry is concerned with matter and the changes it undergoes. Our environment includes matter undergoing change, and the change can be expressed by chemical equations. These equations show the manner in which atoms and molecules combine or decompose to produce other atoms and molecules. Consider the rusting of iron, which is the combining of iron with oxygen from the air to produce iron oxide (commonly called rust). The equation for this chemical reaction is

$$4Fe + 3O_2 \longrightarrow 2Fe_2O_3$$

The arrow means "yields." The equation says that iron (its symbol is Fe) plus oxygen (O) yields rust (Fe_2O_3). You will soon find out why the formula for rust is Fe_2O_3 rather than, say, FeO or FeO_2 or something else. You will also learn why 4Fe appears rather than just Fe; and you will see that the process of balancing equations of this type closely resembles the addition of fractions. In each case, a least common multiple (LCM) or common denominator must be found.

Before you can balance equations, though, you need to know how atoms combine to form molecules. Mathematically, the combining ability of an atom is expressed by its *valence*. Here is a table of a few common elements and their valences.

Element	Symbol	Valence
Hydrogen	H	+1
Chlorine	Cl	−1
Sodium	Na	+1
Oxygen	O	−2
Calcium	Ca	+2

When you examine formulas for chemical compounds, you will see that the total valence of all atoms or molecules composing each compound will add up to zero. Notice how this condition, which is a physical necessity, can be expressed very simply mathematically. For example, sodium chloride (table salt) has the formula NaCl, where the valence of Na is +1 and Cl is −1; the total valence is zero.

Often, subscripts appear after one or more of the elements in a compound. For example, water is H_2O rather than HO, because the valence of H is +1 and the valence of O is −2. Physically, two H atoms are needed to balance each O atom. This is made clear mathematically by writing H_2O rather than HO. Here is a table of other compounds. Read it over to be sure you agree with the valence comments.

Common name	Chemical name	Formula	Comments on valence
Sand	Silicon dioxide	SiO_2	Si is $+4$, O is -2
Lime	Calcium oxide	CaO	Ca is $+2$, O is -2
Laughing gas	Nitrous oxide	N_2O	N is $+1$, O is -2
Chalk	Calcium carbonate	$CaCO_3$	Ca is $+2$, C is $+4$, O is -2
Washing soda	Sodium carbonate	Na_2CO_3	Na is $+1$, C is $+4$, O is -2
Carbon monoxide	Carbon monoxide	CO	C is $+2$, O is -2

Perhaps you noticed that carbon (C) has a valence of $+4$ in $CaCO_3$ and $+2$ in CO. For some elements, the valence of the atom depends on the compound.

Now let's begin balancing equations. Iron, as we said, rusts by combining with oxygen to form iron oxide (Fe_2O_3). Since oxygen exists naturally as O_2 rather than as O, we can start by writing the equation as

$$Fe + O_2 \longrightarrow Fe_2O_3$$

But this is not yet a balanced equation. To see this, look first at the O_2 on the left and the O_3 on the right. For the equation to be balanced, there must be an equal number of oxygen atoms on each side. Right now there are two on the left and three on the right. Noting that LCM(2, 3) = 6, multiply O_2 by 3 and Fe_2O_3 by 2, so that in both cases the quantity of oxygen will be changed to 6. The result is an equal number of oxygen atoms on each side.

$$Fe + 3O_2 \longrightarrow 2Fe_2O_3$$

Although the quantity of oxygen is now balanced, the iron is not. On the right there are four iron atoms specified (from $2Fe_2$), yet there is only one iron atom on the left. Since LCM(1, 4) = 4, just put a 4 in front of the iron on the left. This last step does nothing to disturb the balance of the oxygen, so the equation is now balanced.

$$4Fe + 3O_2 \longrightarrow 2Fe_2O_3$$

The balanced equation shows the same number of atoms of each element before and after the reaction. Before, there are four iron atoms and six oxygen atoms. After, there are also four iron atoms and six oxygen atoms.

Suppose instead that you began to balance the equation

$$Fe + O_2 \longrightarrow Fe_2O_3$$

by balancing the iron first. There is one iron on the left and two on the right. Since $LCM(1, 2) = 2$, just multiply the Fe on the left by 2.

$$2Fe + O_2 \longrightarrow Fe_2O_3$$

Balancing the oxygen is done as before. Since $LCM(2, 3) = 6$, multiply the O_2 by 3 and the Fe_2O_3 by 2. The result is

$$2Fe + 3O_2 \longrightarrow 2Fe_2O_3$$

But note that on the right the Fe_2 has also been multiplied by 2. So now there are four iron on the right (yet only two on the left, still). This means that we'll have to multiply the Fe on the left by still another 2, making it four altogether. The final result is the same as we obtained the first time we balanced this equation.

$$4Fe + 3O_2 \longrightarrow 2Fe_2O_3$$

As another example, let's balance the equation involving the reaction of aluminum (Al) with hydrochloric acid (HCl) to produce aluminum chloride ($AlCl_3$) and hydrogen gas (H_2). The unbalanced equation is

$$Al + HCl \longrightarrow AlCl_3 + H_2$$

There are three chlorine on the right, but only one on the left. Since $LCM(3, 1) = 3$, multiply the HCl on the left by 3 to create three chlorine on the left.

$$Al + 3HCl \longrightarrow AlCl_3 + H_2$$

Now there are three hydrogen on the left, but only two on the right. Since LCM(3, 2) = 6, multiply the 3HCl by 2 to make it 6HCl (for six hydrogen) and multiply the H_2 by 3 (for six hydrogen).

$$Al + 6HCl \longrightarrow AlCl_3 + 3H_2$$

Unfortunately, this changes the balance of chlorine. On the left there are now six chlorine, but on the right there are still three. Since LCM(6, 3) = 6, multiply the $AlCl_3$ by 2 to obtain six chlorine.

$$Al + 6HCl \longrightarrow 2AlCl_3 + 3H_2$$

Now the aluminum is not balanced: there is only one on the left whereas there are two on the right. Since LCM(1, 2) = 2, multiply the Al on the left by 2. At last, the equation is balanced.

$$2Al + 6HCl \longrightarrow 2AlCl_3 + 3H_2$$

APPLICATIONS AND EXERCISES

1. Assume that you know only the valences of hydrogen (+ 1), oxygen (− 2), calcium (+ 2), and chlorine (− 1). Then for each of the following compounds, determine the valence of the element specified.
   (a) Potassium (K) in potassium oxide, K_2O
   (b) Magnesium (Mg) in magnesium chloride, $MgCl_2$
   (c) Sulfur (S) in hydrogen sulfide, H_2S
   (d) Carbon (C) in calcium carbide, CaC_2
   (e) Aluminum (Al) in aluminum oxide, Al_2O_3
   (f) Nitrogen (N) in nitrogen pentoxide, N_2O_5
   (g) Carbon (C) in carbonic acid, H_2CO_3
   (h) Sulfur (S) in sulfuric acid, H_2SO_4

2. Balance each equation.
   (a) Oxygen (O_2) becomes ozone (O_3) as a result of static electricity discharge, such as sparks from an electric motor or lightning.

$$O_2 \longrightarrow O_3$$

(b) Sodium (Na) and chlorine gas (Cl_2) can be combined to form table salt (NaCl).

$$Na + Cl_2 \longrightarrow NaCl$$

(c) Silver (Ag) is not affected by oxygen (O_2) at room temperature, but ozone (O_3) does attack silver and combine with it, producing tarnish.

$$Ag + O_3 \longrightarrow Ag_2O$$

(d) When copper ore (Cu_2S) is heated in air, it produces copper (Cu). It also produces the pollutant sulfur dioxide (SO_2). Before the SO_2 was reclaimed in the exhaust stacks, it polluted the air and killed nearby vegetation.

$$Cu_2S + O_2 \xrightarrow{\text{heat}} Cu + SO_2$$

(e) Magnesium inside a flashcube burns in oxygen to produce a bright flash of light.

$$Mg + O_2 \longrightarrow MgO$$

(f) Aluminum and oxygen combine to form aluminum oxide.

$$Al + O_2 \longrightarrow Al_2O_3$$

(g) Phosphorous (P) and oxygen combine rapidly under combustion.

$$P + O_2 \longrightarrow P_2O_5$$

(h) Two pollutants produced by the gasoline automobile engine are carbon monoxide (CO) and nitric oxide (NO). When an appropriate catalyst is used, they can be combined chemically to produce carbon dioxide (CO_2) and nitrogen gas (N_2), neither of which is a pollutant.

$$CO + NO \xrightarrow{\text{catalyst}} CO_2 + N_2$$

Be careful; oxygen appears twice on the left.

Catalytic converter

(i) Lime (Ca) is used at some water treatment plants to remove phosphates (PO_4).

$$Ca + PO_4 \longrightarrow Ca_3(PO_4)_2$$

(j) Baking soda ($NaHCO_3$) is used in baking bread because when it is heated it releases carbon dioxide (CO_2), which causes the bread to rise.

$$NaHCO_3 \longrightarrow Na_2CO_3 + H_2O + CO_2$$

Be careful; oxygen appears three times on the right.

3. The use of sulfur-containing fuels may lead to unpleasant environmental effects due to the acidity of the rain produced in the polluted air. The sulfur trioxide haze (SO_3) mixes with water in the air to produce sulfuric acid (H_2SO_4).

$$SO_3 + H_2O \longrightarrow H_2SO_4$$

Later, this rain may cause structural deterioration of marble and limestone structures ($CaCO_3$).

$$CaCO_3 + H_2SO_4 \longrightarrow H_2O + CO_2 + CaSO_4$$

The sulfuric acid in the rain can also eat away metal (iron is Fe).

$$Fe + H_2SO_4 \longrightarrow FeSO_4 + H_2$$

What do you notice about "balancing" in these three equations?

4. In algebra, when you multiply one side of an equation by a number, you must multiply the other side by the same number. Furthermore, in multiplying one side of an equation by a number, you must multiply all terms on that side by the number. Explain how balancing of chemical equations differs from this.

DIVISIBILITY TESTS

We have seen how divisibility is applied to factoring and determining the LCM. Some applications were given and others will be presented later. What we can use now are some short-cut methods for determining whether one number is divisible by another number. These methods are called *divisibility tests*. One such test will show us quickly that the number 74,625 is divisible by 3. Without the test we would actually have to divide 74,625 by 3 to see if the remainder is zero. Another divisibility test will tell us quickly that 714 is not divisible by 4, but that 1324 is. Divisibility tests are also useful in reducing fractions, as we shall see in Application 18.

Our study of divisibility tests begins with the statement and discussion of two simple theorems. To prove these theorems requires deductive reasoning using axioms and definitions. We illustrate the nature of these proofs by using concrete examples. The two theorems are then used to prove Theorems 3 and 4, and the process continues. Eventually, we will accumulate a useful list of divisibility tests.

THEOREM 1 *If an integer is divisible by n, then any multiple of that integer is also divisible by n.*

EXAMPLE

Since 12 is divisible by 4, $5 \cdot 12$, or 60, is also divisible by 4.

WHY IT WORKS

The number 12 is divisible by 4. So it can be written as 4 times some integer. Specifically, $12 = 4 \cdot 3$. We can see that any multiple of 12 is also divisible by 4 by considering a number such as 60, which is a multiple of 12. Specifically, $60 = 5 \cdot 12$. We want to show that 60 is divisible by 4 because 12 is divisible by 4. Since $60 = 5 \cdot 12$, and $12 = 4 \cdot 3$, it follows that $60 = 5 \cdot 4 \cdot 3$. This leads to $60 = 4 \cdot (5 \cdot 3)$, or $60 = 4 \cdot 15$. Since 60 can be written as 4 times some integer, this means that 60 is divisible by 4.

A complete proof of this theorem would sound much like the preceding discussion, but would be more abstract. We would consider x being divisible by n rather than 12 being divisible by 4.

THEOREM 2 *If two integers x and y are each divisible by n, then their sum is also divisible by n.*

EXAMPLE

Since 12 is divisible by 4 and 100 is divisible by 4, their sum, 112, is divisible by 4.

WHY IT WORKS

Here is an example that follows the outline of a complete proof of this theorem. The number 12 is divisible by 4, since

$12 = 4 \cdot 3$. Similarly, 100 is divisible by 4, since $100 = 4 \cdot 25$. So $12 = 4 \cdot 3$ and $100 = 4 \cdot 25$. Adding yields $112 = 4 \cdot 3 + 4 \cdot 25$. This can be factored, as $112 = 4 \cdot (3 + 25)$, or $112 = 4 \cdot 28$. This shows that 112 is divisible by 4, since 112 is now written as 4 times some integer.

THEOREM 3 *An integer is divisible by 2 if its last (rightmost) digit is divisible by 2.*

EXAMPLE

Numbers such as 74, 58, 20, 5632, and 116 are divisible by 2, since the last digit of each (4, 8, 0, 2, and 6, respectively) is divisible by 2.

WHY IT WORKS

A two-digit number such as 76 can be written as $7 \cdot 10 + 6$. The three-digit number 538 can be written as $53 \cdot 10 + 8$. Integers having more than three digits can be written similarly. Now let's examine 538 in the form $53 \cdot 10 + 8$. Since 10 is divisible by 2 (that is, $10 = 2 \cdot 5$), we know that $53 \cdot 10$ is divisible by 2. This follows from Theorem 1. Applying Theorem 2 we see that the sum of $53 \cdot 10$ and 8 is divisible by 2 because $53 \cdot 10$ is divisible by 2 and 8 is divisible by 2. Furthermore, all integers can be written as $a \cdot 10 + b$ for some integers a and b, where b is the last digit of the number. Observe.

$$7539 = 753 \cdot 10 + 9 \qquad (a = 753, b = 9)$$
$$62 = 6 \cdot 10 + 2 \qquad (a = 6, b = 2)$$
$$7 = \quad 0 \cdot 10 + 7 \qquad (a = 0, b = 7)$$

So whether or not a number is divisible by 2 depends entirely on the last digit. If the last digit is 0, 2, 4, 6, or 8, then it is divisible by 2 and thus the entire number is divisible by 2.

As an application of Theorem 3, which of the numbers 176, 93, 5961, 1032, 4447, and 3514 are divisible by 2? You should have determined that 176, 1032, and 3514 are divisible by 2 because their last digits are 6, 2, and 4, respectively. The other numbers are not divisible by 2. Now let's look at a more subtle theorem involving division by 3.

THEOREM 4 *An integer is divisible by 3 if the sum of its digits is divisible by 3.*

EXAMPLE

According to the theorem, 852 is divisible by 3, since the sum of its digits (8 + 5 + 2) is 15, and 15 is divisible by 3. On the other hand, 413 is not divisible by 3, since the sum of its digits (4 + 1 + 3) is 8, and 8 is not divisible by 3.

WHY IT WORKS

We shall prove the theorem for three-digit numbers only. The extension to larger numbers should be apparent. Consider a three-digit number n. Call the digits x, y, and z. The number can be written as $n = 100x + 10y + z$. (For example, $856 = 100 \cdot 8 + 10 \cdot 5 + 6$.) Clearly, $100x = 99x + x$, $10y = 9y + y$, and $z = z$. In other words,

$$n = 100x + 10y + z$$
$$= 99x + x + 9y + y + z$$
$$= 99x + 9y + x + y + z$$

Note that 99 is divisible by 3 and 9 is divisible by 3. Thus, $99x + 9y$ is also divisible by 3. Now if $x + y + z$ is divisible by 3, then the number $n = 99x + 9y + x + y + z$ is divisible by 3, since it is then the sum of numbers divisible by 3.

Can you determine which of the numbers 75, 523, 102, 99, 313, 704, 991, and 765 are divisible by 3? You should have determined that only 75, 102, 99, and 765 are divisible by 3.

Perhaps you noticed that $99x + 9y$ is divisible by 9 as well as by 3. That observation yields the next theorem.

THEOREM 5 *An integer is divisible by 9 if the sum of its digits is divisible by 9.*

Test each of the following numbers for divisibility by 9: 75, 523, 102, 99, 313, 704, 991, 765. You should have determined that only 99 and 765 are divisible by 9.

THEOREM 6 *An integer is divisible by 4 if the number formed by the last two digits is divisible by 4.*

EXAMPLE

According to the theorem, 7316 is divisible by 4 because the number 16 (formed by the last two digits) is divisible by 4. Similarly, 8528 is divisible by 4, but 4414 is not divisible by 4.

WHY IT WORKS

The proof of this theorem is similar to that of Theorem 3 concerning divisibility by 2. Consider a four-digit number such as 7316. It can be written as $73 \cdot 100 + 16$. The number 100 is divisible by 4, so $73 \cdot 100$ is divisible by 4. Then the entire number $73 \cdot 100 + 16$ is divisible by 4 because 16 is divisible by 4.

THEOREM 7   *An integer is divisible by 8 if the number formed by the last three digits is divisible by 8.*

EXAMPLE

According to the theorem, the numbers 79,200 and 15,344 are divisible by 8 because 200 and 344 are divisible by 8.

THEOREM 8   *An integer is divisible by 5 if its last digit is 5 or 0.*

EXAMPLE

The numbers 195, 600, 9435, and 12,000 are divisible by 5 because each has either 0 or 5 as its last digit.

Up to this point, we have examined tests for divisibility by 2, 3, 4, 5, 8, and 9. Tests are also known for 7, 11, and 13, but they are too complicated and take too much time to apply to be worthwhile for most problems. To check such divisibility, just divide the number in question by 7, 11, or 13 to see if 7, 11, or 13 is a divisor. But how about divisibility by 6, 10, 12, and other numbers? The following theorem, stated without proof, suggests tests for such divisibility.

THEOREM 9   *If a number is divisible by a and by b, and a and b have no factors in common, then the number is divisible by the product $a \cdot b$.*

EXAMPLE

The number 2538 is divisible by 2 and by 3. (Check this.) The numbers 2 and 3 have no factors in common, so the number 2538 is divisible by 6. The number 156 is divisible by 3 and by 4, and 3 and 4 have no factors in common, so 156 is divisible by 12. The number 1340 is divisible by 2 and divisible by 4. *But* 2 and 4 have a factor (2) in common. So we cannot conclude that 1340 is or is not divisible by 8 based on this test alone.

1. Test each number for divisibility by 2, 3, 4, 5, 8, and 9.
   (a) 124   (b) 342   (c) 360
   (d) 285   (e) 672   (f) 1414
   (g) 7136   (h) 1550   (i) 5280
   (j) 1776   (k) 9990   (l) 11,111

2. Use Theorem 9 in order to determine whether the following numbers are divisible by 6, 10, 12, and 15.
   (a) 522   (b) 650   (c) 264
   (d) 255   (e) 238   (f) 420

3. Explain how you would test a number for divisibility by 30. Apply your method to test 660, 540, 645, and 610.

4. What is probably the quickest way to determine if a number is divisible by 14? Apply your method to test 4237, 6496, 7770, and 8514.

5. If a number is divisible by 8, must it also be divisible by 2? By 4? Explain.

6. If a number is divisible by 3, must it also be divisible by 9? Explain.

7. If a number is divisible by 9, must it also be divisible by 3? Explain.

8. No discussion is provided for Theorem 7, although the discussion would be similar to that of Theorems 3 and 6. Give an explanation of why Theorem 7 works. Use the number 15,344 in your discussion.

9. Examine Theorems 3, 6, and 7, and see if you can determine a test for divisibility by 16.

10. Prove Theorem 8 for any three-digit number having digits a, b, and c; that is, prove the theorem for positive integers of the form $100a + 10b + c$.

11. Determine a one-step test for divisibility by 10, and explain why it works.

12. The Internal Revenue Service (IRS) suggests that a common error on tax returns is the interchanging of two

adjacent digits; for example, 7583 might be incorrectly written as 7853 or as 7538. This type of error is a relatively easy one for a computer to find, because the difference between the correct number and the incorrect number is divisible by 9. In other words.

$$\text{correct} - \text{incorrect} = 9 \cdot (\text{some integer})$$

Form 1040

US Department of the Treasury—Internal Revenue Service
Individual Income Tax Return

Consider a two-digit number whose digits are m and n.

(a)   If the correct form of the number is $10m + n$, represent the incorrect form in which the digits m and n are interchanged.

(b)   Now compute the value of "correct minus incorrect" by using the correct form $10m + n$ and the incorrect form determined in part (a).

(c)   If you have not already done so, simplify the expression obtained in part (b) and factor it.

(d)   If m and n are both integers, then so is $m - n$ an integer. Keeping this in mind, examine the result of part (c) and explain why the difference between the correct number and incorrect number is divisible by 9.

13.   In a formal proof of Theorem 2 it might be stated that *if y is divisible by n, then $y = nq$ for some integer q.* What is the reason for this being true? That is, what right do we have to claim that if y is divisible by n, then $y = nq$ for some integer q?

14.   Write in your own words the standard algebra axiom that is used to proceed from $x = np$ and $y = nq$ to $x + y = np + nq$ by adding the two equations. The axiom is needed in order to prove Theorem 2.

15.   In a formal proof of Theorem 2 it would be assumed that if p is an integer and q is an integer, then the sum $p + q$ is also an integer. Does this seem like a reasonable axiom? Give some examples and comments.

16. The discussion of Theorem 3 suggests that all positive integers can be written as $a \cdot 10 + b$ for some integers a and b, where b is the last digit of the number. Write each of these positive integers in the form $a \cdot 10 + b$.

(a) 24   (b) 159
(c) 7836   (d) 9

17. Let $p = q \cdot r$, where p, q, and r are all integers, none of which equals 1 or -1.

(a) Must p be divisible by q? Why or why not?
(b) Must p be divisible by r? Why or why not?
(c) Must q be divisible by p? Why or why not?
(d) Must qr be divisible by p? Why or why not?

Your knowledge of divisibility should enable you to reduce fractions more efficiently than before. As an example, consider the fraction

Reducing Fractions

$$\frac{84}{132}$$

Both 84 and 132 are divisible by 4, since 84 is divisible by 4 and 32 is divisible by 4. Also, both numbers are divisible by 3, since $8 + 4 = 12$ (which is divisible by 3) and $1 + 3 + 2 = 6$ (which is divisible by 3). Because both numbers are divisible by 4 and by 3, they are each divisible by $4 \cdot 3$ or 12. Applying this divisibility yields

$$\frac{84}{132} = \frac{12 \cdot 7}{12 \cdot 11} = \frac{7}{11}$$

The fraction is reduced.

18. Reduce each fraction completely by first testing numerator and denominator for divisibility.

(a) 78/90   (b) 60/105   (c) 108/117
(d) 60/220   (e) 63/98   (f) 180/252
(g) 210/330   (h) 135/360   (i) 60/462
(j) 315/390   (k) 272/304   (l) 1080/1260

19. Here is a test for *divisibility by 11*. The proof itself is considered in Exercise 20. Beginning at the left end of the number, combine the digits by alternating subtraction and addition. If the result is zero or a multiple of 11, then the number is divisible by 11. For example, consider 9372. The digits 9, 3, 7, and 2 are combined as $9 - 3 + 7 - 2$, which is 11. Since this result is a multiple of 11, the number 9372 is divisible by 11. Test each of the following numbers for divisibility by 11.

(a) 7183   (b) 9812   (c) 583
(d) 1890   (e) 10857   (f) 36938
(g) 12096   (h) 9999   (i) 99999

20. To prove the divisibility by 11 test for a four-digit number, let the digits be *a*, *b*, *c*, *d* from left to right. Assume $a - b + c - d$ is divisible by 11 and show, by following steps (a)–(d), that the original number must be divisible by 11.

(a) Explain why the original number is $1000a + 100b + 10c + d$.

(b) Add $a - b + c - d$, which is divisible by 11, to the original number $1000a + 100b + 10c + d$. What is the sum?

(c) Is 11 divisible by 11? Is 99 divisible by 11? Is 1001 divisible by 11? Why then must the number $1001a + 99b + 11c$ be divisible by 11?

(d) Consider this general assertion: If $x + y$ is divisible by w and y is divisible by w, then x must be divisible by w. Apply this assertion to explain why the original number $1000a + 100b + 10c + d$ is divisible by 11.

MODULAR ARITHMETIC

It is natural to think of the quotient as more "important" than the remainder. In the last section, we were concerned with divisibility tests—where there is no remainder (that is, a remainder of zero). But sometimes the remainder is more important than the quotient, as you will find out in this section.

To begin, try to imagine a setting in which the following statement is true: $8 + 7 = 3$. Suppose it is now 8 o'clock and you plan to study for 7 hours. What time will it be when you have finished studying? It will be 3 o'clock, of course. In this setting, 8 + 7 = 3. Here 8 + 7 ≠ 15 because the only numbers on the clock are 1, 2, 3, 4, 5, 6, 7, 8, 9, 10, 11, and 12. After 12, we begin again at 1.

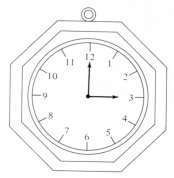

Here are a few clock arithmetic exercises for you. In each case, determine the number that will fill in the blank based on a 12-hour clock.

$$9 + 7 = \underline{\hspace{2em}}$$
$$3 + 15 = \underline{\hspace{2em}}$$
$$2 + 9 = \underline{\hspace{2em}}$$
$$12 + 15 = \underline{\hspace{2em}}$$

Now that you have finished, compare your results with the answers: 4, 6, 11, 3. In each instance, the answer is the *remainder* when the sum is divided by 12. Observe.

$9 + 7 = 16$ and $16 \div 12 = 1$ with *remainder 4*

$3 + 15 = 18$ and $18 \div 12 = 1$ with *remainder 6*

$2 + 9 = 11$ and $11 \div 12 = 0$ with *remainder 11*

$12 + 15 = 27$ and $27 \div 12 = 2$ with *remainder 3*

Let's pursue this a little further. If 12 is added to 3, the result is 15. If another 12 is added, the result is 27. If still another 12 is added, the result is 39; and so on. All of these numbers (15, 27, 39, . . .) are equal to 3 in the sense that when they are divided by 12, their remainders are 3. Another way of looking at the relationship of 15, 27, and 39 to 3 is to note that when the difference between any of them and 3 is divided by 12, the remainder is zero.

$$15 - 3 = 12 \quad \text{and} \quad 12 \div 12 = 1 \quad \text{with remainder zero}$$
$$27 - 3 = 24 \quad \text{and} \quad 24 \div 12 = 2 \quad \text{with remainder zero}$$
$$39 - 3 = 36 \quad \text{and} \quad 36 \div 12 = 3 \quad \text{with remainder zero}$$

These examples suggest the notions of congruence and modular arithmetic, originally introduced by the great German mathematician Carl Friedrich Gauss. We say that two numbers are *congruent modulo n* if the difference between them is divisible by n. For example, 27 is congruent to 3 modulo 12, since the difference between 27 and 3 is 24, and 24 is divisible by 12. Recall that "divisible by" implies with a remainder of zero. Write this as $27 \equiv 3 \pmod{12}$, where the $\equiv$ means "is congruent to." In symbols, $a \equiv b \pmod{n}$ if $a - b$ is divisible by n. Similarly, 15 and 39 are also congruent to 3 modulo 12.

Courtesy of Columbia University Library

Carl Friedrich Gauss (1777–1855)

$$15 \equiv 3 \pmod{12}$$
$$39 \equiv 3 \pmod{12}$$

Also,

$$39 \equiv 15 \pmod{12}$$

since $39 - 15 = 24$, and 24 is divisible by 12.

Notice that 12 and 0 are congruent modulo 12

$$12 \equiv 0 \ (\text{mod } 12)$$

since $12 - 0$ is divisible by 12. The clock system that led us to modular arithmetic is based on the numbers 1 through 12, and any other integers can be reduced to one of these 12. In mathematics, zero is usually used instead of 12 when discussing mod 12. In other words, the basic numbers to which all others reduce mod 12 are 0, 1, 2, 3, 4, 5, 6, 7, 8, 9, 10, and 11. Here are some examples.

$14 \equiv \ \ 2 \ (\text{mod } 12)$, since $14 - 2 = 12$ is divisible by 12.

$29 \equiv \ \ 5 \ (\text{mod } 12)$, since $29 - 5 = 24$ is divisible by 12.

$59 \equiv 11 \ (\text{mod } 12)$, since $59 - 11 = 48$ is divisible by 12.

$36 \equiv \ \ 0 \ (\text{mod } 12)$, since $36 - 0 = 36$ is divisible by 12.

To what number is 64 congruent modulo 12? Divide 64 by 12 and look at the remainder.

$$64/12 = 5 \quad \text{with remainder } 4$$

Thus, 64 is congruent to 4 modulo 12.

$$64 \equiv 4 \ (\text{mod } 12)$$

As a check, note that $64 - 4 = 60$ is divisible by 12.

APPLICATIONS AND EXERCISES

1. Which statements are true and which are false?
   (a) $16 \equiv 4 \ (\text{mod } 12)$. (b) $12 \equiv 0 \ (\text{mod } 12)$.
   (c) $23 \equiv 8 \ (\text{mod } 12)$. (d) $31 \equiv 7 \ (\text{mod } 12)$.
   (e) $72 \equiv 0 \ (\text{mod } 12)$. (f) $29 \equiv 4 \ (\text{mod } 12)$.

2. Find the number (0, 1, 2, 3, 4, 5, 6, 7, 8, 9, 10, or 11) to which the given number is congruent modulo 12.
   (a) 19   (b) 37   (c) 47
   (d) 52   (e) 108 (f) 230

3. (a) Use the definition of congruence modulo n to explain what it means to say that two numbers are congruent modulo 7.
   (b) True or false? $31 \equiv 5 \pmod 7$. Explain.
   (c) True or false? $51 \equiv 2 \pmod 7$. Explain.
   (d) $69 \equiv ? \pmod 7$. Select for your answer either 0, 1, 2, 3, 4, 5, or 6. Explain your choice.

4. Find a number that satisfies $x \equiv 2 \pmod 5$. Can you find another? How many numbers do satisfy $x \equiv 2 \pmod 5$?

5. Consider negative integers mod 5. To which number (0, 1, 2, 3, or 4) is -3 congruent modulo 5? The number is x such that $-3 - x$ (the difference between the two numbers) is divisible by 5. So x is 2, since $-3 - 2 = -5$, and -5 is divisible by 5. Thus, $-3 \equiv 2 \pmod 5$. Find a value for x for each of the following congruences.

   (a) $-9 \equiv x \pmod 5$.   (b) $-9 \equiv x \pmod 7$.
   (c) $-3 \equiv x \pmod 9$.   (d) $-23 \equiv x \pmod 9$.
   (e) $-19 \equiv x \pmod 3$.   (f) $-1 \equiv x \pmod{13}$.

6. Complete the following addition table using modulo 4. Entries should be either 0, 1, 2, or 3 only. Two entries are already filled in, and here is the reasoning. First, $0 + 2 = 2$, and 2 is congruent to 2 modulo 4. Second, $3 + 1 = 4$, and 4 is congruent to 0 modulo 4.

+	0	1	2	3
0			2	
1				
2				
3		0		

7. Suppose $a \equiv c \pmod n$ and $b \equiv c \pmod n$.
   (a) Is $a \equiv b$?
   (b) Is $b \equiv a$?
   (c) Is $a = b$? Explain.

8. Determine positive values for x that make each congruence true.
   (a) $x + 25 \equiv 3 \pmod 7$.   (b) $x + 25 \equiv 3 \pmod 5$.

9. Congruence modulo 5 partitions the positive integers into five *equivalence classes.* The numbers in one class are all congruent to 0 modulo 5; the numbers in another class are all congruent to 1 modulo 5, and so on. Each number is in precisely one and only one class.

Class I: 0, 5, 10, 15, 20, 25, 30, . . .
Class II: 1, 6, 11, 16, 21, 26, 31, . . .
Class III: 2, 7, 12, 17, 22, 27, 32, . . .
Class IV: 3, 8, 13, 18, 23, 28, 33, . . .
Class V: 4, 9, 14, 19, 24, 29, 34, . . .

(a)   How many equivalence classes are there for congruence of positive integers modulo 7?

(b)   List the equivalence classes for congruence of positive integers modulo 7.

10. To the Chinese, 1977 was the year of the snake. In fact, the Chinese have a 12-year cycle in which each year is named after an animal. They believe that people born in a particular year possess the characteristics of the animal associated with that year. Consider the twentieth century and write 1900 as 0, 1901 as 1, 1974 as 74, and so on. The 12 equivalence classes are as follows.

Rat:	0, 12, 24, . . .	Horse:	6, 18, 30, . . .
Ox:	1, 13, 25, . . .	Sheep:	7, 19, 31, . . .
Tiger:	2, 14, 26, . . .	Monkey:	8, 20, 32, . . .
Rabbit:	3, 15, 27, . . .	Rooster:	9, 21, 33, . . .
Dragon:	4, 16, 28, . . .	Dog:	10, 22, 34, . . .
Snake:	5, 17, 29, . . .	Boar:	11, 23, 35, . . .

(a)   What animal is associated with the year in which you were born? When will the year of that animal occur next?

(b)   Two years are in the same equivalence class if their difference is divisible by ____, that is, if their difference is a multiple of ____.

(c)   Are the years 1993 and 1962 associated with the same animal? Explain.

(d)   Are the years 1999 and 1951 associated with the same animal? Explain.

11. The nomadic Mbuti (Pygmies) of the Congo used modular arithmetic to outwit visitors who stopped at their camps. When the visitors demanded food, the Mbuti challenged them to a game of "panda." In panda, a specified number of beans are thrown on the ground, and one of the visitors scoops up a handful. The Mbuti must estimate at a glance how many are needed to make up a multiple of four. The Mbuti requests that many (0, 1, 2, or 3) beans, and if the new total is indeed a multiple of four, the Mbuti wins, and the visitors leave with nothing. Otherwise, the visitors get the food they want.

    (a) The Mbuti approach this problem by using numbers modulo ____ .

    (b) Explain how they might determine the number of beans to be added to make up a multiple of four.

    (c) If the Mbuti were just guessing, would they have been more likely to win or lose? Explain.

12. Fill in the following blanks with integers between 0 and 8 inclusive.

    (a) $15 \equiv$ ____ (mod 9).   (b) $18 \equiv$ ____ (mod 9).
    (c) $26 \equiv$ ____ (mod 9).   (d) $20 \equiv$ ____ (mod 9).
    (e) $29 \equiv$ ____ (mod 9).   (f) $43 \equiv$ ____ (mod 9).

There are several approaches you might have taken. Perhaps you used trial and error. Or perhaps you determined what number must be subtracted in order to create a multiple of 9. Still another approach is to subtract 9's from the original number until it is reduced to a number between 0 and 8 inclusive.

————

Casting Out Nines   The preceding exercise was intended to prepare you to examine a process, called *casting out nines,* that can be used as a partial check of arithmetic operations. Among the theorems of congruence that are applied in the process is: *Any integer is congruent to the sum of its digits modulo nine.* According to this theorem, $357 \equiv 3 + 5 + 7 \equiv 15 \equiv 6 \pmod 9$. Note, when 357 is divided by 9, the remainder is 6, so indeed $357 \equiv 6 \pmod 9$.

    This example shows how casting out nines can be used to check addition. Here first is the original addition:

$$937$$
$$524$$
$$\underline{143}$$
$$1604$$

Next, here is the check by casting out nines. See if you can follow the work.

$$937 \longrightarrow 9 + 3 + 7 = 19 \equiv 1 \ (\text{mod } 9)$$
$$524 \longrightarrow 5 + 2 + 4 = 11 \equiv 2 \ (\text{mod } 9)$$
$$\underline{143} \longrightarrow 1 + 4 + 3 = \ \ 8 \equiv 8 \ (\text{mod } 9)$$
$$1604   11 \equiv 2(\text{mod } 9) \ \nearrow$$
$$ \searrow \ 1 + 6 + 0 + 4 = 11 \equiv 2(\text{mod } 9) \ \nearrow$$

In both cases the sum is congruent to the same number, 2. This completes the partial check. Had the two results yielded different numbers, it would have suggested an error either in the original addition or in the check.

13. Perform each addition and check the result by casting out nines.

(a) $\ \ 538$ (b) $\ \ 893$ (c) $\ \ 175$ (d) $\ \ 351$
$ 217$ $ 476$ $ 298$ $ 499$
$ \underline{492}$ $ \underline{855}$ $ 663$ $ 753$
$ \underline{247}$ $ \underline{628}$

14. Here is the application of casting out nines to checking *multiplication*. Study the example. Then perform each multiplication and check it by casting out nines.

$$284 \longrightarrow 2 + 8 + 4 = 14 \equiv \ \ 5 \ (\text{mod } 9)$$
$$\underline{679} \longrightarrow 6 + 7 + 9 = 22 \equiv \ \ \underline{4 \ (\text{mod } 9)}$$
$$2556 20 \equiv 2 \ (\text{mod } 9) \ \nearrow$$
$$1988$$
$$\underline{1704}$$
$$192836 \longrightarrow 1 + 9 + 2 + 8 + 3 + 6 = 29 \equiv 2 \ (\text{mod } 9) \ \nearrow$$

(a) $\ \ 93$ (b) $\ \ 513$ (c) $\ \ 694$ (d) $\ \ 8162$
$ \underline{87}$ $ \underline{78}$ $ \underline{785}$ $ \underline{3497}$

15. A theorem of number theory states that if $a \equiv b \ (\text{mod } n)$ and $c \equiv d \ (\text{mod } n)$, then $(a + c) \equiv (b + d) \ (\text{mod } n)$. Let $n = 10$ and verify this theorem for several different choices of a, b, c, and d. Just be sure you choose a, b, c, and d such that $a \equiv b \ (\text{mod } 10)$ and $c \equiv d \ (\text{mod } 10)$.

WHAT DAY OF THE WEEK . . . ?

Have you ever wondered on what day of the week you were born? As years pass, birthdays and anniversaries occur on different days of the week. Whatever day of the week your birthday falls on this year, it will not be on the same day of the week next year. Let's see how modular arithmetic can help us find a way to determine the day of the week of past and future dates.

A particular date does not fall on the same day of the week each year, because the number of days in a year (365 or 366) is not divisible by 7, the number of days in a week. When 365 is divided by 7, the remainder is 1. Thus, the number of days in ordinary years is congruent to 1 modulo 7, or $365 \equiv 1 \pmod 7$. Similarly, when 366 is divided by 7, the remainder is 2. So the number of days in leap years is congruent to 2 modulo 7, or $366 \equiv 2 \pmod 7$. This means that with respect to days of the week, a 365-day change is a 1-day change. This in turn means that for an ordinary year the weekday of a specific date will increase by one in the next year. For example, if October 16 is on a Tuesday one year, it will be on a Wednesday the year after that. Applying this in reverse, if October 16 is a Tuesday one year, it occurred on a Monday the year before.

Unfortunately, the day of the week changes by *two* for each leap year. So you have to make allowances for leap years. They can be recognized readily because they are divisible by 4.* Do you recall the test for divisibility by 4? A number is divisible by 4 if the number formed by the last two digits is divisible by 4. Thus, 1960, 1972, 1976, and 1980 are some leap years. On the other hand, 1951, 1978, and 1994 are not leap years.

In order to determine days of the week, it is also necessary to have a calendar to use as a reference with which to begin. Any year will do. Without a calendar, a complicated formula is needed. A 1977 calendar is presented here for reference.

As an example, note that October 16 occurred on Sunday in 1977. On what day of the week will it occur in 1985? From 1977 to 1985 is eight years, of which two (1980 and 1984) are leap years. So the day of the week moves ahead a total of ten days (six years at one day each plus two years at two days each). This means that October 16, 1985, is a Wednesday.

* The exception is any year ending in 00 that is not divisible by 400. Thus, 2000 will be a leap year, but 1700, 1800, and 1900 were not leap years.

1977

JANUARY

S	M	T	W	T	F	S
						1
2	3	4	5	6	7	8
9	10	11	12	13	14	15
16	17	18	19	20	21	22
23/30	24/31	25	26	27	28	29

FEBRUARY

S	M	T	W	T	F	S
		1	2	3	4	5
6	7	8	9	10	11	12
13	14	15	16	17	18	19
20	21	22	23	24	25	26
27	28					

MARCH

S	M	T	W	T	F	S
		1	2	3	4	5
6	7	8	9	10	11	12
13	14	15	16	17	18	19
20	21	22	23	24	25	26
27	28	29	30	31		

APRIL

S	M	T	W	T	F	S
					1	2
3	4	5	6	7	8	9
10	11	12	13	14	15	16
17	18	19	20	21	22	23
24	25	26	27	28	29	30

MAY

S	M	T	W	T	F	S
1	2	3	4	5	6	7
8	9	10	11	12	13	14
15	16	17	18	19	20	21
22	23	24	25	26	27	28
29	30	31				

JUNE

S	M	T	W	T	F	S
			1	2	3	4
5	6	7	8	9	10	11
12	13	14	15	16	17	18
19	20	21	22	23	24	25
26	27	28	29	30		

JULY

S	M	T	W	T	F	S
					1	2
3	4	5	6	7	8	9
10	11	12	13	14	15	16
17	18	19	20	21	22	23
24/31	25	26	27	28	29	30

AUGUST

S	M	T	W	T	F	S
	1	2	3	4	5	6
7	8	9	10	11	12	13
14	15	16	17	18	19	20
21	22	23	24	25	26	27
28	29	30	31			

SEPTEMBER

S	M	T	W	T	F	S
				1	2	3
4	5	6	7	8	9	10
11	12	13	14	15	16	17
18	19	20	21	22	23	24
25	26	27	28	29	30	

OCTOBER

S	M	T	W	T	F	S
						1
2	3	4	5	6	7	8
9	10	11	12	13	14	15
16	17	18	19	20	21	22
23/30	24/31	25	26	27	28	29

NOVEMBER

S	M	T	W	T	F	S
		1	2	3	4	5
6	7	8	9	10	11	12
13	14	15	16	17	18	19
20	21	22	23	24	25	26
27	28	29	30			

DECEMBER

S	M	T	W	T	F	S
				1	2	3
4	5	6	7	8	9	10
11	12	13	14	15	16	17
18	19	20	21	22	23	24
25	26	27	28	29	30	31

APPLICATIONS AND EXERCISES

1. On what day of the week will October 16, 1990, occur?

2. Determine on which day of the week your birthday will occur in 1987.

3. (a) On what day will Christmas (December 25) fall in 1980?

   (b) In what years from now until 1999 will Christmas fall on a Sunday?

4. February 5, 1977, and June 11, 1977, are both Saturdays, yet February 5, 1984, is a Sunday whereas June 11, 1984, is a Monday. Explain the apparent discrepancy.

5. On what day of the week did Halloween (October 31) occur in 1965?

6. When was the last year that Valentine's Day (February 14) came on a Sunday?

7. Determine on which day of the week you were born.

CRYPTOGRAPHY AND CRYPTANALYSIS

In this section you'll see how modular arithmetic can be applied to *cryptography*. Cryptography is the art of secret writing, that is, of writing coded messages. The process of converting a message into secret language is called *enciphering*. *Cryptanalysis* is the solution and reading of such cryptic messages. Obtaining the original message from the secret form is called *deciphering*. Both cryptography and cryptanalysis are pursued by experts for intelligence agencies such as the CIA (Central Intelligence Agency) of the United States. Cryptographic methods are also used in modern computer security systems in order to prevent unauthorized personnel from obtaining confidential data from computer files. Two elementary cryptanalysis techniques are presented in this book. A technique based on the frequency distribution of the letters of the alphabet is explained in Chapter 7. The other technique involves the use of modular arithmetic, and it is explained next.

Julius Caesar (100–44 B.C.) used a system, now called the Caesar cipher, in which each letter of the original message was replaced by the letter three places beyond it in the normal alphabet.

Table I

Normal alphabet:	A B C D E F G H I J K L M N O P Q R S T U V W X Y Z
Caesar cipher:	D E F G H I J K L M N O P Q R S T U V W X Y Z A B C

To encipher the message "ET TU BRUTE THEN FALL CAESAR," begin by writing the original message.

ET TU BRUTE THEN FALL CAESAR

Next, locate each letter of the message in the normal alphabet and copy the corresponding Caesar cipher. Here is the result:

Original message:	ET	TU	BRUTE	THEN	FALL	CAESAR
Enciphered message:	HW	WX	EUXWH	WKHQ	IDOO	FDHVDU

To decipher a message known to be coded in Caesar cipher, reverse the process. In other words, replace each letter in the coded message by the corresponding letter of the normal alphabet. For example, the enciphered message

EHZDUH WKH LGHV RI PDUFK

is translated as

BEWARE THE IDES OF MARCH

If numbers are used to represent letters in the normal sequence, then enciphering and deciphering can both be accomplished without actually writing the cipher alphabet. To encipher we'll use

Table II

A	B	C	D	E	F	G	H	I	J	K	L	M	N	O	P	Q	R	S	T	U	V	W	X	Y	Z
1	2	3	4	5	6	7	8	9	10	11	12	13	14	15	16	17	18	19	20	21	22	23	24	25	26

and the following process: First, replace each letter of the original message by the corresponding number in Table II. Next, add 3 to each of the numbers obtained. Finally, locate each new number in Table II and copy the letter written above it. Thus,

	E	T	T	U	B	R	U	T	E	
becomes in steps										
	5	20	20	21	2	18	21	20	5	(replacing letters by numbers)
	8	23	23	24	5	21	24	23	8	(adding 3)
	H	W	W	X	E	U	X	W	H	(replacing numbers by letters)

To decipher, reverse the process. First replace each letter of the enciphered message by the corresponding number in Table II. Then, subtract 3 from each number obtained. Finally, locate each new number in Table II and copy the letter written above it. Thus,

H W   W X   E U X W H

becomes in steps

8 23   23 24   5 21 24 23 8   (replacing letters by numbers)
5 20   20 21   2 18 21 20 5   (subtracting 3)
E T   T U   B R U T E   (replacing numbers by letters)

The role of modular arithmetic begins to become apparent when we try to encipher X, Y, or Z by the numerical process.

    X   Y   Z
    24   25   26   (replacing letters by numbers)
    27   28   29   (adding 3)
    ?   ?   ?   (replacing numbers by letters)

The numbers 27, 28, and 29 are not in Table II, so it seems that we cannot complete the process. Yet we know (from looking at Table I) that X, Y, and Z correspond to A, B, and C, respectively. But Table II shows that 1 (not 27) is A, 2 (not 28) is B, and 3 (not 29) is C. So in this setting we want 27 to be equivalent to 1, 28 equivalent to 2, and 29 equivalent to 3; and they are, if we use congruence modulo 26!

$$27 \equiv 1 \pmod{26}, \text{ since } 27 - 1 \text{ is divisible by 26.}$$

$$28 \equiv 2 \pmod{26}, \text{ since } 28 - 2 \text{ is divisible by 26.}$$

$$29 \equiv 3 \pmod{26}, \text{ since } 29 - 3 \text{ is divisible by 26.}$$

To convert any number larger than 26 to a number between 1 and 26, divide it by 26 and use the remainder. There is one exception, however. If the remainder is 0, use 26 rather than 0. This is reasonable, since there is no 0th letter and since $26 \equiv 0 \pmod{26}$.

$27 \div 26 = 1$, and the *remainder is 1*. Thus, $27 \equiv 1 \pmod{26}$.
$28 \div 26 = 1$, and the *remainder is 2*. Thus, $28 \equiv 2 \pmod{26}$.
$29 \div 26 = 1$, and the *remainder is 3*. Thus, $29 \equiv 3 \pmod{26}$.

There is a related problem to which modular arithmetic can also be applied. If the *coded* message contains A, B, or C, then deciphering by the numerical process yields

A	B	C	
1	2	3	(replacing letters by numbers)
−2	−1	0	(subtracting 3)
?	?	?	(replacing letters by numbers)

From Table I we see that enciphered A, B, and C correspond to normal X, Y, and Z. But Table II shows that 24 (not −2) is X, 25 (not −1) is Y, and 26 (not 0) is Z. So the desired congruences modulo 26 are

$$-2 \equiv 24 \pmod{26}, \text{ since } -2 - 24 = -26 \text{ is divisible by 26.}$$
$$-1 \equiv 25 \pmod{26}, \text{ since } -1 - 25 = -26 \text{ is divisible by 26.}$$
$$0 \equiv 26 \pmod{26}, \text{ since } \quad 0 - 26 = -26 \text{ is divisible by 26.}$$

For a code of this type, any number smaller than 1 can be converted to a number between 1 and 26 by adding 26 to it.

$$-2 \longrightarrow -2 + 26 = 24$$
$$-1 \longrightarrow -1 + 26 = 25$$
$$0 \longrightarrow \quad 0 + 26 = 26$$

APPLICATIONS AND EXERCISES

1. Use Table I (the Caesar cipher) to encipher each message.
   (a) HELP
   (b) GOOD MORNING
   (c) I CAME I SAW I CONQUERED
   (d) CALL THE POLICE
   (e) WHAT TIME IS IT

2. Use Table I (the Caesar cipher) to decipher each message.
   (a) KDLO FDHVDU
   (b) LW LV VQRZLQJ
   (c) L KDYH D KHDGDFKH
   (d) GR BRX HQMRB PDWKHPDWLFV

3. Use the table below to encipher each message.

A	B	C	D	E	F	G	H	I	J	K	L	M	N	O	P	Q	R	S	T	U	V	W	X	Y	Z
K	L	M	N	O	P	Q	R	S	T	U	V	W	X	Y	Z	A	B	C	D	E	F	G	H	I	J

(a)   I AM CONFUSED
(b)   WHEN IS THE CLASS OVER
(c)   THIS IS THE THIRD EXERCISE

4. Use the table in Exercise 3 to decipher each message.

(a)   XEWLOB DROYBI
(b)   YXO WYBO NKI
(c)   PSH DRSC MKB

5. Use Table II and the Caesar cipher to encipher each message.

(a)   IN CHAPTER
(b)   TWO WE
(c)   STUDIED LOGIC

6. Use Table II and the Caesar cipher to decipher each message.

(a)   WKH SURRI
(b)   NQRZ QRW L
(c)   KRZ WR GR

7. Use Table II and the Caesar cipher to encipher each message.

(a)   YES I SAW AN OX AT THE ZOO
(b)   RELAX AND BE LAZY TODAY

8. Use Table II and the Caesar cipher to decipher each message.

(a)   LQWURGXFWLRQ WR PDWKHPDWLFV
(b)   UHDG FODVVLFV

9. When numbers larger than 26 were produced when enciphering with the Caesar cipher, they were reduced by dividing by 26 and using the remainder. Recall that the Caesar cipher shifts the alphabet 3 places.

(a)   Will this same approach (division by 26) work if the cipher is changed so that the alphabet is shifted 7 places instead of 3?

Normal:	A	B	C	D	E	F	G	H	I	J	K	L	M	N	O	P	Q	R	S	T	U	V	W	X	Y	Z
Cipher:	H	I	J	K	L	M	N	O	P	Q	R	S	T	U	V	W	X	Y	Z	A	B	C	D	E	F	G

    (b)   If your answer to part (a) was yes, what numbers larger than 26 can be produced and what do they reduce to? If your answer was no, suggest a different approach.

    (c)   What negative numbers can be produced when deciphering with this new code, and to which letters of the normal alphabet do they correspond?

10. (a) Use the cipher suggested in Exercise 9, part (a), to encipher this message:

FIVE IS A NATURAL NUMBER

    (b)   Use the same cipher to decipher the following message.

AOPYAF PZ JVUNYBLUA AV ADV TVKBSV ZLCLU

11. Use the cipher suggested by the table in Exercise 3, but use the *numerical* process to encipher each of these messages.

    (a)   WITH MALICE TOWARD NONE
    (b)   SPEAK FOR YOURSELF JOHN
    (c)   TO BE GREAT IS TO BE MISUNDERSTOOD

12. Use the cipher suggested by the table in Exercise 3, but use the *numerical* process to decipher each of these messages.

    (a)   ZRICSMSKX ROKV DRICOVP
    (b)   QBOKD WOX KBO XYD KVGKIC GSCO
    (c)   NKBUXOCC GRSMR WKI LO POVD

13. At the beginning of this section, it is stated that Julius Caesar lived from 100–44 B.C. Should it really be stated as 44–100 B.C., or is it correct as originally presented? Explain.

Excursions into Geometry

4

In this chapter, you will have an opportunity to explore some aspects of geometry that are quite different from those you may have worked with in earlier courses. There are many applications of geometry to the world we live in. This section includes some applications to art, architecture, and drama. Later sections offer other applications, some theory, some relationships between geometry and algebra, and some novel views of a familiar number and a familiar theorem.

Geometry has influenced art and architecture for thousands of years. The pyramids, built over 4000 years ago, reflect a basic knowledge of geometry. The *golden section*, or *golden ratio*, was used in ancient Greece by architects in designing the dimensions of their buildings and columns. The golden ratio is the ratio of the length to the width of a specially constructed rectangle called a *golden rectangle*. To construct such a rectangle, you must first construct a square and locate the midpoint (*m*) of the base. Then you draw an arc of the circle (as done in the drawing) whose center is at *m*. Now if you extend the base, it will meet the arc at a point (*p*). This defines the length of the rectangle. The completed golden rectangle is shown here.

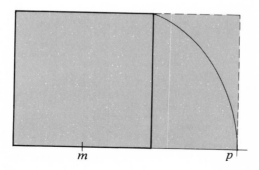

Leonardo da Vinci suggested proportions for an ideal human figure in terms of the golden ratio. Even paintings by such modern artists as Mondrian and Dali demonstrate the use and appearance of the golden ratio.

Renaissance artists turned to mathematics in order to reproduce nature more accurately. They introduced the visual effect of depth in an attempt to convey the same visual impression in their painting as that of the actual scene. This they accomplished by using *perspective* in their work. These artists introduced new concepts in geometry, which in turn led to the more formal development of *projective geometry*. Concepts of projective geometry were also applied by mapmakers to project the sphere that represents the world onto the flat surface of a piece of paper.

The parallel walls of a room or the parallel sides of a road were not drawn or painted parallel by the Renaissance artists. Instead, to create an illusion of depth they were drawn or painted so that they would meet if they were extended. Notice how perspective is used to create depth in this fifteenth century painting of *The Annunciation* (first picture at the right). Specifically, the walls are farthest apart in the foreground, and they appear to get closer and closer together as they recede into the background. In this setting, parallel lines appear to meet if extended far enough. This is a distinguishing feature of projective geometry; in the more traditional Euclidean geometry, parallel lines never meet.

Dutch artist Maurits Escher is famous for his use of perspective to create extraordinary illusions. The second picture at the right, called *Waterfall*, is an example.

Symmetry has been used in art since long before the Renaissance. Here are two examples that are intended to explain the concept of symmetry with respect to a line. The letter A (shown next) is symmetric with respect to the vertical dashed line drawn through its tip.

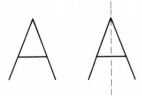

This means that the image on the left side of the dotted line is the same as the image on the right side. If a mirror is placed on

The Annunciation
by Master of the Barberini Panels

Waterfall
by M. C. Escher

the dotted line and viewed from the left, the right side of the letter will appear in it. If the mirror is viewed from the right, the left side of the letter will appear in it. As another example, the letter E shown here is symmetric with respect to the horizontal line drawn.

The concept of symmetry is applied to the theater, where there is concern with the visual balance of one side of the stage with the other. A "symmetrically balanced" stage includes mirrorlike duplication of objects and designs on either side of the center line. The result of such balance is to convey a formal, dignified, or static feeling. Accordingly, such balance is usually reserved for plays that reflect an artificial, formal, or imper-

Excursions into Geometry   137

Symmetric balance

Asymmetric balance

sonal tone. On the other hand, "asymmetric balance" (also called "occult balance") conveys a feeling of movement and excitement by balancing large or heavy-appearing objects on one side of the stage with smaller objects on the other side of the stage. The larger objects may sometimes only appear larger or more significant because of their color, shape, texture, or attractiveness.

APPLICATIONS AND EXERCISES

1. Use perspective in each drawing.

   (a) Draw railroad tracks to create an illusion of depth; that is, make them appear to get farther and farther away from the viewer as he follows them "into" the background of the drawing.

   (b) Draw a cube. Your drawing should give depth to the cube, making it appear as close to three dimensional as possible.

2. For each letter drawn, draw a line that could serve as a mirror, reflecting what is on one side onto the other side of the line, to point out the symmetry of the letter.

   (a)

   (b)

(c)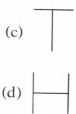

(d)

3. Complete each illustration, assuming it is supposed to be *symmetric* with respect to the dashed line. (In other words, assume the dashed line serves as a mirror.)

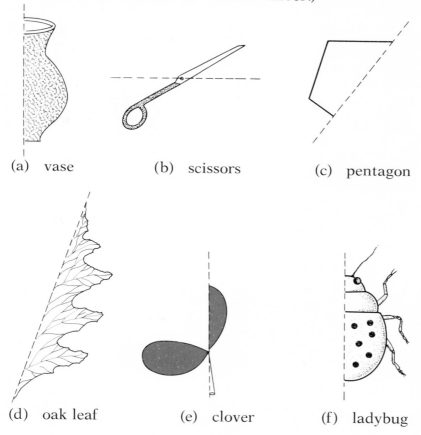

(a) vase

(b) scissors

(c) pentagon

(d) oak leaf

(e) clover

(f) ladybug

4. Each tooth is assigned a number representing approximately the contribution it makes to the chewing process. These numbers appear in the following illustration. The sum of the contributions of all teeth present is called the *coefficient of mastication.*

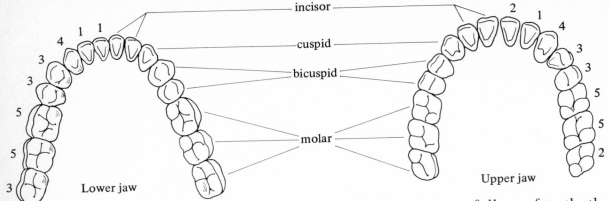

Upper jaw

Lower jaw

(a) Using symmetry and assuming a full set of teeth, the coefficient of mastication for such a perfect set of teeth is ____ .

(b) If two molars are missing (and the other 30 teeth are present), the coefficient of mastication can be no less than ____ and no more than ____ .

(c) If two cuspids are missing, and all other teeth are present, then the coefficient of mastication is ____ . Expressed as a percentage of the coefficient for a perfect set of teeth, this is ____%.

5. In Euclidean geometry, parallel lines never meet. In projective geometry, parallel lines do meet. Is one kind of geometry right and the other wrong? Explain, perhaps with the aid of a few justifying applications.

6. Consider a line segment consisting of two parts, one of length a and one of length b. The total length of the segment is $a + b$. The *golden ratio* is the number b/a that satisfies the proportion

$$\frac{b}{a} = \frac{a + b}{b}$$

The desired solution of this equation turns out to be

$$\frac{b}{a} = \frac{1 + \sqrt{5}}{2}$$

(a) The square root of 5 is approximately 2.2. What then is the approximate value of the golden ratio?

(b) If $a = 1$, what should be the approximate value of b so that b/a is the golden ratio? Use the answer to part (a) to help you solve this problem.

(c)   Draw a line segment of length 1 inch. Draw another segment of length b, so that b/a is approximately the golden ratio.

(d)   If $b = 8$, what should be the value of a so that b/a is approximately the golden ratio?

(e)   If $a + b = 52$, what should be the values of a and b so that b/a is approximately the golden ratio?

A relationship between the golden ratio and the Fibonacci sequence will be explored when limits are presented (see page 302).

GEOMETRIC CONSTRUCTIONS

Geometric constructions have been known and applied for thousands of years. The design of Egyptian pyramids and that of Greek temples are two such ancient applications. In his organization of geometry, Euclid included theorems on geometric constructions that can be made with a compass and

Courtesy of Columbia University Library

Euclid (330–275 B.C.)

straightedge. The compass is used to draw arcs of circles and the straightedge is used to draw straight line segments. Unlike a ruler, a straightedge cannot be used to measure; it can be used only to draw straight line segments. This section presents geometric constructions, many of which are still used by draftsmen, architects, surveyors, and archaeologists.

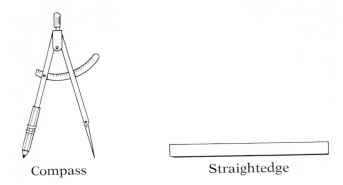

Compass   Straightedge

The first construction to be presented is *bisecting a line segment*, that is, dividing a line segment into two equal parts. Suppose you are given points *A* and *B* and the connecting line segment *AB*, which you want to bisect.

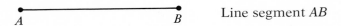

Line segment *AB*

To begin, place the point of your compass on *A*, open the compass until it reaches more than halfway to *B*, and draw a large arc.

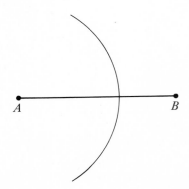

Without changing the compass setting, place its point on B and draw another large arc that intersects the original arc twice (once above and once below segment AB).

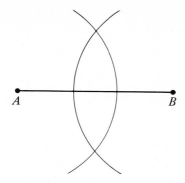

Finally, draw a line through the two points of intersection of the arcs.

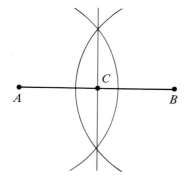

The point C where the line crosses segment AB is the midpoint of segment AB. So line segment AB has been bisected. Since this line that bisects segment AB happens also to be perpendicular to segment AB, it is called the *perpendicular bisector* of line segment AB.

It is believed that Egyptian architects used basic geometric constructions in order to position pyramids to face precisely north, south, east, and west. They may have drawn the perpendicular bisector of the line segment joining the sun's rising and setting positions at equinoxes. (Equinoxes are the two days a year on which day and night are of equal length.) This is illustrated next.

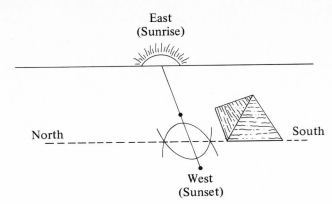

The next construction is that of a *line passing through a given point and perpendicular to a given line.* This would be useful if you were going to run an irrigation ditch from a canal to a field several hundred meters away. You would want the shortest path for the ditch, to minimize the cost of constructing it; and the shortest distance is the perpendicular from the field to the canal. We begin the construction with given point P and given line l.

$P_{\bullet}$

$\overline{\hspace{3cm}}\ l$

Put the point of the compass at P and open the compass far enough so that you can draw an arc that will cross line l in two points (say A and B). Draw the arc.

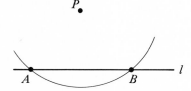

Now you can proceed as in the first construction. Draw arcs from A and B large enough so that they intersect each other twice (at C and at D).

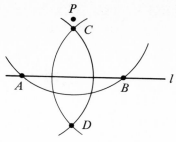

Finally, draw a line through C and D. This then is the perpendicular bisector of line l. It passes through P and is perpendicular to line l.

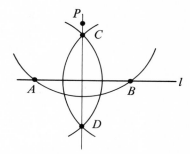

Next, let's *bisect a given angle,* that is, divide it into two equal angles. Call the vertex of the angle V.

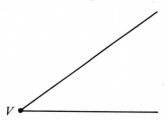

Begin by placing the point of the compass on the vertex of the angle and drawing an arc that intersects the sides of the angle at two points. Call the points A and B.

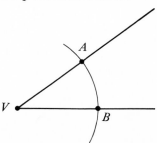

Now from both *A* and *B* draw arcs of equal length as shown next. They will meet at a point *P* midway between the sides of the angle.

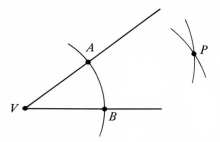

So draw a line through *P* and vertex *V* in order to bisect the angle.

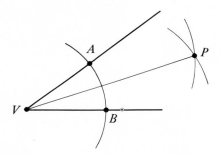

An *angle can be copied* onto a given line. Below, the angle with vertex *V* will be copied onto line *l*.

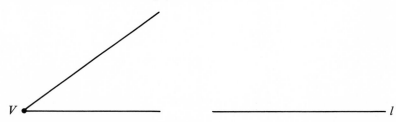

Mark a point *A* anywhere on line *l*.

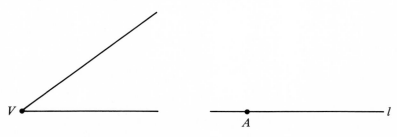

Place the compass at vertex V of the original angle and draw an arc that crosses both sides of the angle at points we'll call B and C. Without changing the compass setting, draw a similar arc with the point of the compass on A. The arc will cross line l at a point. Call the point D.

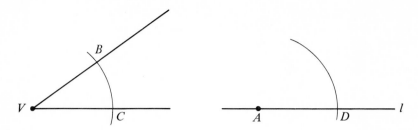

Now use the compass to measure the distance from B to C. This can be done by placing the point on C and opening the compass until the pencil is on B. Then, use the same compass setting to draw an arc with the point of the compass on D. This creates a point E at the intersection of the two arcs.

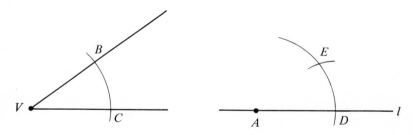

Finally, draw a line from A through E. The resulting angle is the same measure as the original angle.

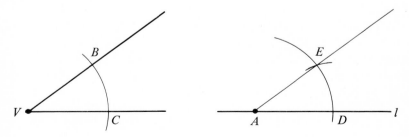

This last construction is used next as a part of the following more complicated construction. Through a given point P, a *line can be constructed* that is *parallel to a given line l.*

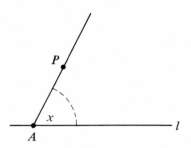

Start by choosing any point A on line l and drawing a new line from A through P.

Now copy the angle (called x) at P on the new line. The steps:

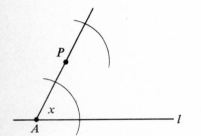 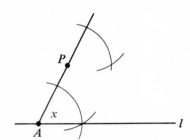 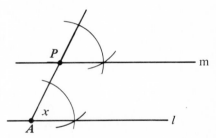

The line m passes through point P and is parallel to line l. If you are not convinced that line m is indeed parallel to line l, or if you do not follow the reasoning, you may prefer the approach suggested in Exercise 6. Either way, this construction will be needed for the cardiology application of the next section. It is also used in the following construction.

A *line segment can be divided into as many equal parts as desired.* Dividing line segment AB, shown next, into three equal parts will demonstrate the general technique.

Draw a line l through A at any angle.

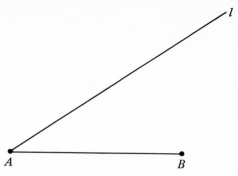

Select a point somewhere on l, preferably one that is near A. Call the point C.

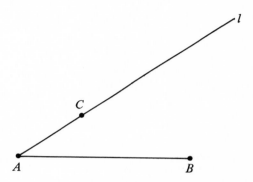

With a compass, measure the distance from A to C. Then, beginning at C, mark off this distance twice along line l, thus creating points D and E. This means, of course, that $AC = CD = DE$.

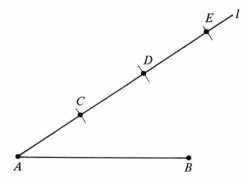

Connect the points B and E to create segment BE.

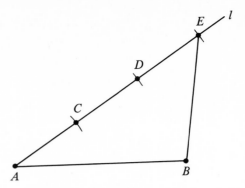

Through point *D* construct a line parallel to segment *BE*.
Through point *C* construct a line parallel to segment *BE*.

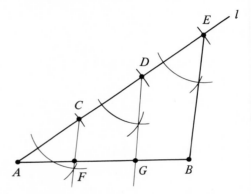

Segments *AF*, *FG*, and *GB* are equal in length. In other words, segment *AB* has been divided into three equal parts.

An architect might use this last construction to lay out elements of a repetitive nature, for example, stairs. Mapmakers could use this method to subdivide a map scale. For example, an inch may represent 20 miles on the map, and the inch may be subdivided into five equal parts.

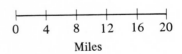

Miles

APPLICATIONS AND EXERCISES

1. In bisecting a line segment *AB*, it was suggested that the compass be opened until it reached more than halfway from A to B. Why? What would happen if it were opened to only about a third of the length of the segment? Try it.

2. Draw a line segment 3 inches long. Then use a compass and straightedge to bisect it. Afterward, measure the two parts of the segment with a ruler. Are they equal?

3. On line l construct a line segment the same length as AB. Label it CD. Do you need both compass and straightedge to do this?

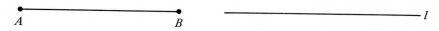

4. Construct a line m perpendicular to line l and passing through point T.

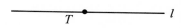

5. Using the compass and straightedge only, construct a right angle (that is, a 90° angle). Begin with a line l and point A on that line. Note that a right angle is formed by the intersection of two perpendicular lines.

6. Construct a line parallel to line l and passing through point T by constructing two perpendicular lines, both of which pass through T.

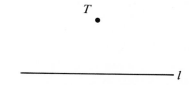

7. Draw a line. Then construct a 45° angle with respect to that line. *Hint:* What is the relationship between the desired angle and a right angle?

8. Divide the following line segment into four equal parts.

9. Divide the next line segment into five equal parts.

10. Divide a line segment into three equal parts. Then copy the original segment and divide it into eight equal parts. Use your results to determine which is larger: 2/3 or 5/8. Then use arithmetic to check your conclusion.

11. Draw a circle. Without changing the compass setting, select any point on the circle (call it *A*) and mark off a point *B* by using the compass as it was set when the circle was drawn. Continue along the circle by marking off points *C*, *D*, *E*, and *F*. Draw line segments *AB*, *BC*, *CD*, *DE*, *EF*, and *FA*. Describe the resulting geometric figure.

12. Construct a regular 12-sided polygon (called a dodecagon). The process resembles that of Application 11, up to a point, but is a little more complex.

13. An interesting design can be made by following the procedure of Application 11 until points *A*, *B*, *C*, *D*, *E*, *F* are marked off. Then, without changing the compass setting, put the compass point on *A* and draw an arc from *B* to *F*. Then put the compass point on *B* and draw an arc from *C* to *A*. Continue in this manner all the way along the circle.

14. Use a variation of the technique of Application 11 to draw an equilateral triangle, that is, a regular three-sided polygon.

15. There is a much simpler way to construct an equilateral triangle than by the method of Application 14. How? *Hint:* Begin with a line segment.

16. Draw a circle and one of its diameters. Next, construct the perpendicular bisector of this diameter. Now, what regular polygon can easily be made? Construct the polygon.

17. Use a variation of Application 16 to construct a regular octagon (eight-sided polygon).

18. Construct a triangle having a right angle (90°) and a 45° angle.

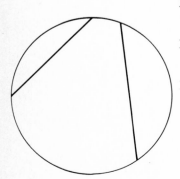

19. A *chord* of a circle is any line segment whose endpoints are on the circle. The perpendicular bisector of any chord of a circle passes through the center of the circle. Use this information and any needed constructions to locate the center of the circle at the left. Two chords are given, and it will be necessary to use them both.

20. Construct a circle through the three points shown here. *Hint:* See Application 19.

21. Can you find two points on the line below that are equidistant from the point *P*? There is an infinite number of pairs of such points.

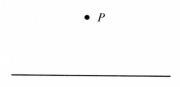

22. Can you find a point equidistant from the two given points? There is an infinite number of such points.

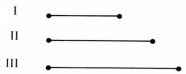

23. Construct a triangle using the three sides given here.

I

II

III

24. Construct a triangle using the two sides and angle given here. The angle is to be included between the two given sides.

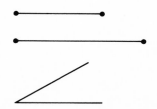

25. Use the two angles and the side given here to construct a triangle. The side is to be included between the two given angles.

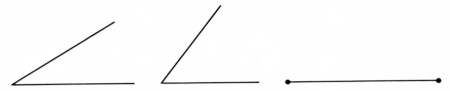

26. Construct a *golden rectangle*. Begin with a line segment, which will become one side of the square you must construct during the procedure. You might want to reread the explanation of the golden rectangle on page 135.

27. The German mathematician Carl Friedrich Gauss (1777–1855) discovered that it is possible to construct regular polygons with only straightedge and compass, provided the number of sides of the polygon is $(2^m) \cdot (2^n + 1)$, where m and n are whole numbers and $2^n + 1$ is a prime number.

    (a)   Let $m = 1$ and $n = 1$ and consider the formula above. What number does $2^n + 1$ become if n is 1? Is it prime? How many sides will this polygon have?

    (b)   Let $m = 2$ and $n = 3$. Can the polygon be constructed according to Gauss's assertion? Explain.

EINTHOVEN'S TRIANGLE

There are applications of geometric constructions that are quite different from those involved in positioning pyramids and making geometric designs. One such application deals with cardiology and is presented next.

An electrocardiogram (EKG) is used to measure the electrical activity of the heart in relation to three points. The points (or leads) usually used are (I) the right shoulder, (II) the left shoulder, and (III) the navel. The figure formed by connecting those three points is an equilateral triangle. The triangle is called *Einthoven's triangle*, for Willem Einthoven, a famous German cardiologist and inventor of the modern EKG.

Einthoven's triangle is used to determine the orientation of the heart; that is, to find the angle at which the heart is tilted.

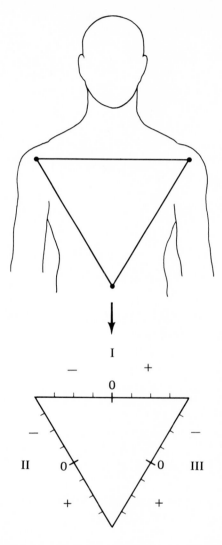

Data provided by the EKG can be plotted on the triangle. The information obtained at each lead consists of upward (+) and downward (−) deflections. For example, lead I may show an upward deflection of 3 and a downward deflection of 1. Those deflections are denoted + 3 and − 1, respectively. On the electrocardiograph, this would appear as follows:

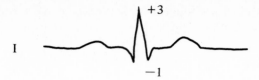

The sum of these deflections is the net deflection, +2.

Suppose leads II and III show the deflections illustrated next. What then is the net deflection in each case? See if you can figure it out.

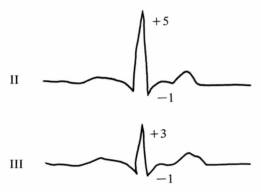

The net deflection at lead II is +4. The net deflection at lead III is +2. So for this example we have

lead I: +2
lead II: +4
lead III: +2

Here is how these net deflections can be plotted on Einthoven's triangle. The midpoint of each side of the triangle is labeled zero.

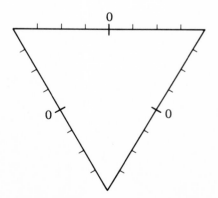

Next, positive values can be plotted on one side of zero and negative values on the other side.

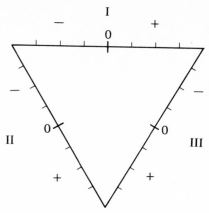

Thus, the specific case of $+2$ at lead I, $+4$ at lead II, and $+2$ at lead III is represented as follows:

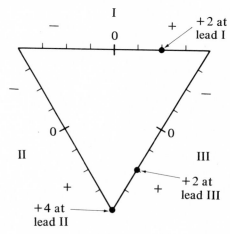

Through each of the three points on the triangle, perpendicular lines are constructed. All three perpendiculars meet in a single point, which we will call P.

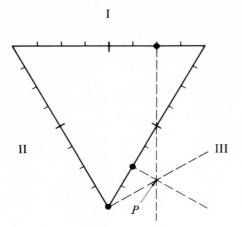

The other point we shall use is the point of intersection of the perpendicular lines drawn from the "zero" of each side of the triangle. We will call that point of intersection B.

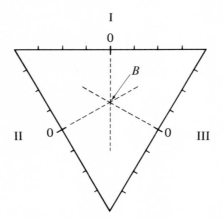

Combining the preceding two triangles (the one that shows point *P* and the one that shows point *B*), we obtain

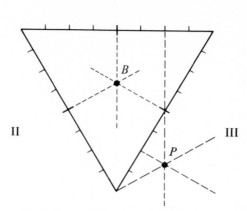

A line can be passed through points *P* and *B*. That line is called the *electrical axis* of the heart. It shows the angle at which the heart is oriented.

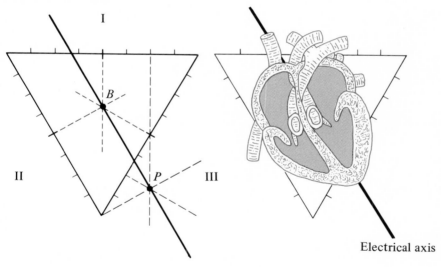

Electrical axis

The actual angle of the heart can be measured as the angle between the electrical axis and the base line. The *base line* is the line through B and parallel to side I of the triangle.

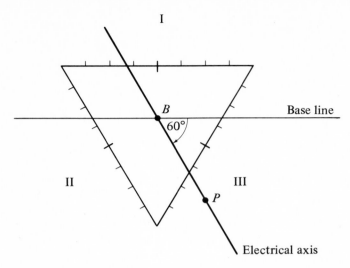

In this example the angle of the heart is 60°. The average for adults is 58°.

APPLICATIONS AND EXERCISES

1. Determine the net deflection of each wave.

(a)

(b)

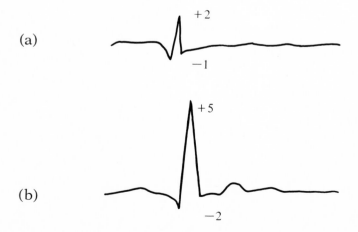

(c)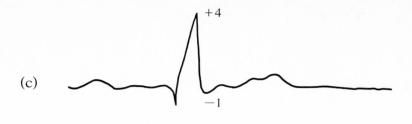

(d)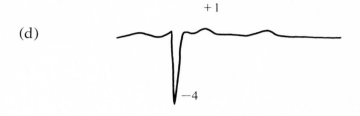

2. Use compass and straightedge to construct the base line of the Einthoven triangle shown here. Begin by constructing a line perpendicular to each side of the triangle and passing through the zero of that side. (This type of construction was done in Exercise 4, page 151.) Note that all three perpendicular lines intersect at a point. Next, construct a line through that point of intersection and parallel to side I. (This is the same type of construction you did in Exercise 6, page 151.) This line is, of course, the base line.

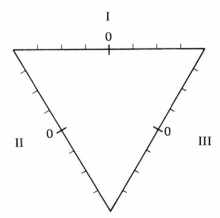

3. For each set of net deflections given, use an Einthoven triangle to determine and construct the electrical axis of the heart.

(a) I: +1
    II: +2
    III: +1

(b) I: +2
    II: +3
    III: +1

(c) I: +1
    II: +3
    III: +2

(d) I: +3
    II: +4
    III: +1

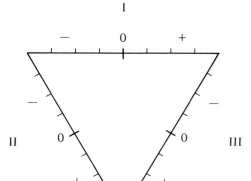

4. The electrocardiogram readings at I, II, and III are such that all three perpendicular lines meet at one point *P*. If you pick arbitrary points on the triangle sides I, II, and III, the perpendicular lines will seldom meet at a point. Verify this by checking the values suggested in (a)–(d).

(a) I: +2
    II: +3
    III: +2

(b) I: +3
    II: +1
    III: +1

(c) I: +1
    II: +4
    III: +2

(d) I: +3
    II: +1
    III: +2

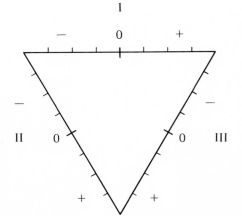

5. In Exercise 4, you saw four cases of false readings. In each instance the perpendiculars failed to meet at one point. Listed next are four readings for which the perpendiculars will meet at one point. (You may wish to verify this.) Study the following data in search of a pattern. There is a relationship among the readings at I, II, and III. Once you see it, write down the relationship. Then verify that this relationship exists for the data of the original text example and for the data in Exercise 3 as well. Finally, show that all of the data in Exercise 4 fails to satisfy the relationship.

    (a) I: +4   II: +5   III: +1

    (b) I: +1   II: +4   III: +3

    (c) I: +2   II: +5   III: +3

    (d) I: +3   II: +5   III: +2

6. Einthoven's triangle is equilateral; that is, all sides are of equal length. Use compass and straightedge to construct an equilateral triangle. Begin by drawing a line segment that will become one of the sides of the triangle.

MINERALOGY GRAPHS

The presentation of Einthoven's triangle demonstrated the application of geometric constructions to medicine. The application of equilateral triangles was also included there. In this section, you will see still another use of equilateral triangles.

Mineralogy is the study of minerals, the naturally occurring elements and compounds making up the solid parts of the earth. Among other things, mineralogists study the composition of rocks. If a mineral consists of *two* compounds, it can be represented in a so-called *binary* system. The graph for such a system consists of a labeled horizontal line segment. If the mineral is composed of two compounds called A and B, then the graph is labeled as the one shown here.

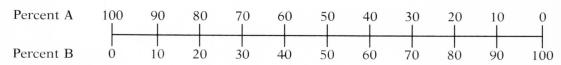

Three minerals, each composed of compounds called A and B, are graphed next. Mineral X is 90% compound A and 10% compound B. Mineral Y is 100% compound B. Mineral Z is 45% A and 55% B.

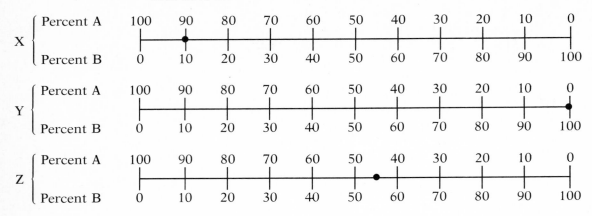

Minerals consisting of *three* compounds can be represented in a so-called *ternary* system. The graph for the system is a large equilateral triangle like the one shown next for minerals consisting of three compounds, A, B, and C. Such graphs are also called *triangle graphs*.

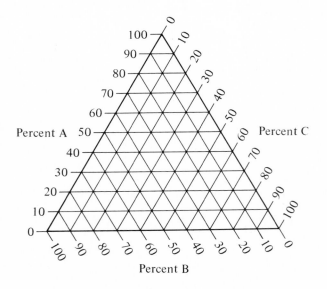

Consider the mineral *t* represented on the next graph.

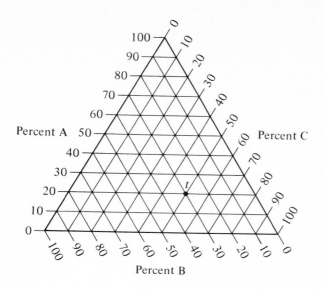

Can you see that it is at the intersection of the lines representing 20% A, 30% B, and 50% C? If you cannot see this, try to follow the lines in from 20 under percent A, 30 under percent B, and 50 under percent C. Those three lines meet at t.

To check your understanding of the graph, determine the percentage of compounds A, B, and C that make up the mineral labeled r in the following graph.

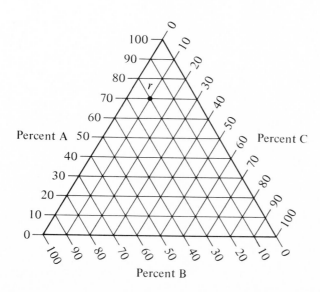

The mineral called *r* in this graph is 70% A, 20% B, and 10% C.

Mineralogists make frequent use of ternary systems and binary graphs. However, they often extend the graphs to include such things as time and temperature and their effect on mineral formation. These extended graphs are considerably more complicated because they are three dimensional, and they will not be presented.

Triangle graphs are used in disciplines other than mineralogy. A few such other applications are given with the exercises that follow.

APPLICATIONS AND EXERCISES

1. Determine the percentages of A, B, and C that make up each mineral (*w*, *x*, *y*, and *z*) graphed here.

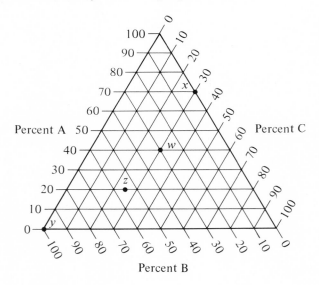

2. Graph each mineral based on its composition.

   (a)   50% A, 10% B, 40% C   (b)   75% A, 15% B, 10% C
   (c)   25% A, 0% B, 75% C   (d)   15% A, 70% B, 15% C

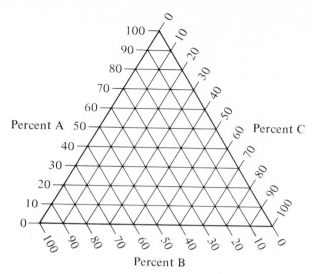

3. Consider the soil in your garden to be a mineral composed of compounds. On the graph on the following page, represent the soil described in parts (a) and (b).

   (a)   Soil called loam is desirable for most gardens. Loam consists of clay, sand, and humus. Represent a loamy soil consisting of 25% clay, 35% sand, and the rest humus. Label the percentage scale of each of the three compounds (previously labeled A, B, and C) as clay, sand, and humus.

   (b)   Beets require a light sandy soil so they can push their roots (the beet) and grow properly. Represent a soil that is 1/10 clay, 1/2 sand, and the rest humus on the following graph. Be sure to label each percentage scale.

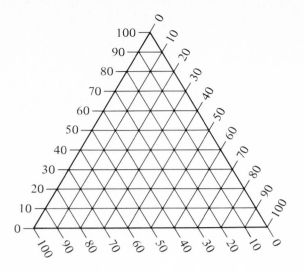

4. Cholesterol-type gallstones form when the relative amounts of cholesterol, lecithin, and bile salts are altered from the normal amounts. The darkened region in the next graph represents the conditions conducive to formation of cholesterol crystals. According to the graph, which of the following conditions could lead to cholesterol-type gallstone formation?

(a)   65% lecithin, 5% cholesterol, 30% bile salt
(b)   70% bile salt, 8% cholesterol, 22% lecithin
(c)   10% cholesterol, 90% bile salt
(d)   40% bile salt, 5% cholesterol, 55% lecithin
(e)   2% cholesterol, 90% bile salt, 8% lecithin

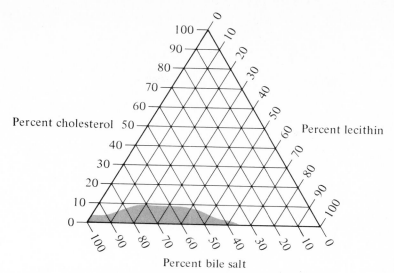

Percent cholesterol

Percent lecithin

Percent bile salt

5. Ecologists have studied the ways that birds seek out insects. They found that birds either fly after airborne insects or they walk through or hover near foliage to catch insects sitting on leaf surfaces. Read the following graph and determine what percentage of each insect-seeking activity is engaged in by these birds: (a) vireo; (b) gnatcatcher; (c) warbler.

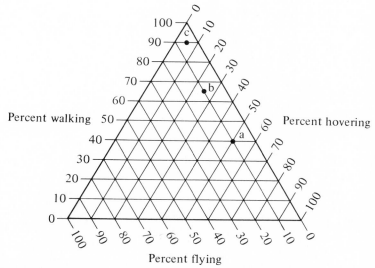

Percent walking

Percent hovering

Percent flying

6. Which kind of reasoning—inductive or deductive—might lead you to conclude that insect-eating birds spend little time trying to catch insects by flying after them?

Epilogue   It is interesting to note that physicist James Clerk Maxwell introduced a triangle graph in order to express the composition of colors in terms of the three primary colors, red, green, and blue.

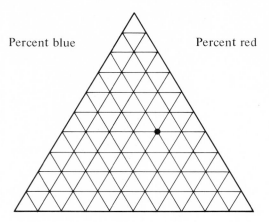

Percent blue   Percent red

Percent green

The importance of Maxwell's graph is that if two colors are measured the same way and are found to have the same percentages of primary colors, then it can be stated with certainty that the two sources (colored lights in the case of Maxwell's experiments) will match exactly if they are placed next to each other; and this statement can be made without having seen the two lights next to one another.

PYTHAGOREAN THEOREM

Next, we move from equilateral triangles to right triangles, with still another application of geometric constructions to come later in the section.

The *Pythagorean theorem* is perhaps the most famous theorem in mathematics. It is believed to have been proved first in the sixth century B.C. by the Greek philosopher Pythagoras, although there is evidence that the Babylonians knew of it more than a thousand years before him. Pythagoras led a group of mathematically inclined philosophers called Pythagoreans. The purpose of the Pythagorean school was to study the unchangeable elements in nature and society—geometry, arithmetic (number theory), astronomy, and music.

Pythagoras (580–500 B.C.)

The Pythagorean theorem states: *In all right triangles,* $c^2 = a^2 + b^2$, *if the length of the hypotenuse is called c and the lengths of the other two sides are called a and b.* The *hypotenuse* of a right triangle is the side opposite the right angle. (It also happens to be the longest side.) Here is a right triangle. Note that c is the hypotenuse. The other sides are labeled a and b. It does not matter which side is called a and which is called b, as long as the hypotenuse is called c in order to fit the formula of the theorem.

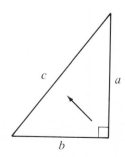

Consider the right triangle below. The hypotenuse is not given, but it is known that the other two sides are 3 and 4 units long.

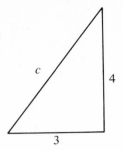

The Pythagorean theorem tells us that $c^2 = a^2 + b^2$, from which

$$c^2 = 3^2 + 4^2$$
$$= 9 + 16$$
$$= 25$$

or

$$c = 5$$

The hypotenuse is 5. The three numbers $3-4-5$ are called a Pythagorean triple or Pythagorean numbers, because they satisfy the Pythagorean theorem. Such triples were known before the time of Pythagoras, however. Verify that $6-8-10$ is also a Pythagorean triple.

Here is a proof of the Pythagorean theorem. The next illustration includes an arrangement of four identical right triangles. We'll show that $a^2 + b^2 = c^2$ for the right triangle.

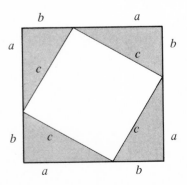

The entire figure is a square with sides $a + b$. This means that the entire area is $(a + b)^2$, since the area of any square is a side squared. The total area can also be considered as the sum of the areas of the four triangles and the square with side c. The area of a triangle is half of its base times its height. So the area of one triangle is $\frac{1}{2}ab$. The area of all four triangles, then, is $4 \cdot \frac{1}{2}ab = 2ab$. The area of the square with side c is c^2. This approach to the calculation tells us that the area of the entire figure is $2ab + c^2$. Earlier, we came up with $(a + b)^2$ as the area. So, since the areas are the same,

$$(a + b)^2 = 2ab + c^2$$

Do you remember that $(a + b)^2$ is the same as $a^2 + 2ab + b^2$? (There is a geometric proof of this basic algebra result suggested in Exercise 7.) If we substitute $a^2 + 2ab + b^2$ for $(a + b)^2$ in the equation above, the result is

$$a^2 + 2ab + b^2 = 2ab + c^2$$

or, after adding $-2ab$ to each side,

$$a^2 + b^2 = c^2$$

This is the desired result. We have proved the Pythagorean theorem!

The Pythagorean theorem, combined with some basic constructions, can be used to construct a line segment that is exactly $\sqrt{2}$ units in length. Begin with a line segment and mark on it a point, say A.

With the compass point on A, draw an arc that crosses the segment at a point, and call the point B.

Let's agree that the segment *AB* is 1 unit in length, for reference. Next, construct a line perpendicular to the original segment and passing through point *A*.

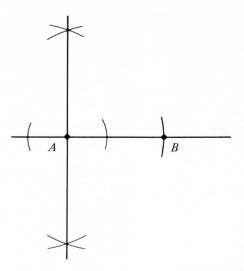

Measure with your compass the distance from *A* to *B* and mark off this distance on the new line—from *A* to a new point *C*.

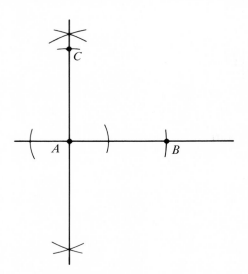

Draw the line segment *BC*.

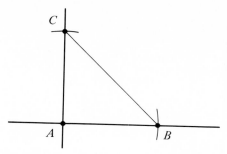

If *AB* is 1 unit, and *AC* is 1 unit, and triangle *ABC* is a right triangle, how long is *BC*? Use the Pythagorean theorem to determine it.

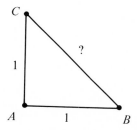

You should have determined that *BC* is $\sqrt{2}$ units long. Using $a^2 + b^2 = c^2$, you get $1^2 + 1^2 = c^2$, $1 + 1 = c^2$, $2 = c^2$, and finally $c = \sqrt{2}$. So the hypotenuse of this triangle is the desired length, $\sqrt{2}$ units. If you would like to see directly how $\sqrt{2}$ units compares with 1 unit, open the compass and measure *BC*. Then mark off this distance along the original line, beginning at *A*.

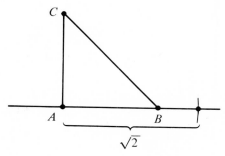

1. Use $a^2 + b^2 = c^2$ to determine which of the following are Pythagorean triples.

   (a) 9–12–15 (b) 4–5–6
   (c) 5–12–13 (d) 1–2–4
   (e) 7–9–11   (f) 5–10–15
   (g) 10–24–26 (h) 7–24–25
   (i) 10–12–16 (j) 3–7–11

2. You can create your own Pythagorean triples. Choose any two different natural numbers. Call the larger one m and the smaller one n. Pythagorean triple a–b–c can be computed from

$$a = m^2 - n^2$$
$$b = 2mn$$
$$c = m^2 + n^2$$

   (a) The smallest Pythagorean numbers result from using 2 for m and 1 for n. What are a, b, and c in this case?
   (b) Let $m = 3$ and $n = 2$. Find a, b, and c.
   (c) Use some m and n values of your own choosing to create Pythagorean triples. Then verify for each triple a–b–c you create that $a^2 + b^2 = c^2$.

3. A surveyor may be measuring the distance between two points (A and B in the following sketch), and there may be a pond or other obstacle in the path.

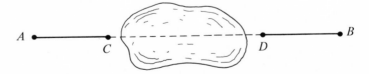

The distance between C and D can be determined indirectly by going around the pond from C to E and then from E to D in such a way that CE is perpendicular to ED. See the drawing on the next page.

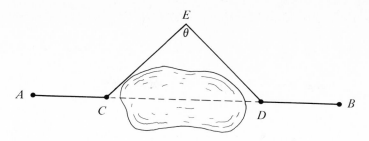

(a) Since *CE* is perpendicular to *ED*, the angle theta (θ) created is a _____ angle, so the triangle is a _____ triangle.

(b) If *CE* is 300 meters and *ED* is 400 meters, then *CD* is _____ meters.

4. A baseball diamond is a square, each side of which is 90 feet. Approximately how far must a catcher (C) throw the ball in order to reach second base (2)? See the arrow in the diagram.

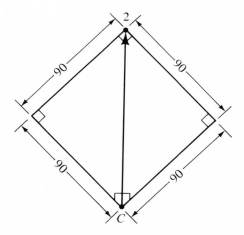

5. State the Pythagorean theorem for a right triangle in which the hypotenuse is called *a* and the other sides are *b* and *c*.

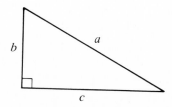

6. (a) Use trial and error to find two integers a and b such that $a^2 + b^2 = 5$.

   (b) Knowing the answer to part (a), and having read the last example of the section, construct a line that is exactly $\sqrt{5}$ units in length.

   (c) If a right triangle has a hypotenuse of $\sqrt{3}$ units, and one side is 1 unit, how long is the other side?

   (d) Use the result of part (c) to construct a line segment that is exactly $\sqrt{3}$ units in length.

7. Use the following figure to prove geometrically that $(a + b)^2 = a^2 + 2ab + b^2$. Use appropriate areas.

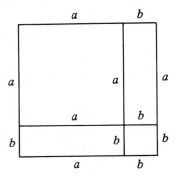

8. Here are the illustrations for a different proof of the Pythagorean theorem. Study them and answer the questions that follow.

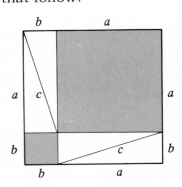 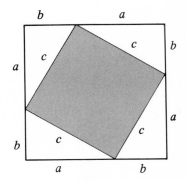

   (a) Look at the diagram on the left. What is the area of the small shaded square? What is the area of the larger shaded square in that same drawing?

   (b) What is the area of the shaded square in the drawing on the right side?

(c)   What is the area of the entire left figure? What is the area of the entire right figure?

(d)   What is the combined area of all four triangles in the left figure? What is the combined area of all four triangles in the right figure?

(e)   Examine all of the information you have obtained about the two figures from parts (a)–(d). Explain why $a^2 + b^2 = c^2$.

PI

It was known thousands of years ago that there is a relationship between the circumference of a circle and its diameter; that the fraction

$$\frac{\text{circumference}}{\text{diameter}}$$

is constant and approximately equal to three. The ancient Greeks named this ratio π (pi), and that name is still used today. The Old Testament describes a basin in Solomon's temple (about 1000 B.C.) as 10 cubits from brim to brim and 30 cubits in circumference, thus suggesting the value of three for pi. The Egyptians (about 1650 B.C.) used 3.16 for π.

In the third century B.C., Archimedes used polygons to obtain

Archimedes (287–212 B.C.)

an excellent approximation for π. He determined that π was between 3.1409 and 3.1429 by using regular polygons of 96 sides. Using four-sided polygons, we'll demonstrate his technique. Begin with a circle whose diameter is equal to one. In this way

$$\frac{\text{circumference}}{\text{diameter}} = \pi$$

becomes

$$\text{circumference} = \pi$$

Draw two squares, one inside (that is, inscribed) and one outside (or circumscribed).

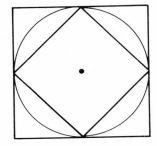

Let C be the circumference of the circle, P be the perimeter of the large square, and p be the perimeter of the smaller square. The value of C is smaller than P but larger than p. So if we get values for P and p, we'll have *bounds* for C; that is, C will be between (or bounded by) p and P. First, let's find P in this setting. Since the diameter of the circle is 1, each side of the square is also 1 unit. So the perimeter P is 4.

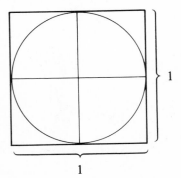

To find p we'll use the Pythagorean theorem. In the next figure, the radius of the circle is $\frac{1}{2}$, since the diameter is 1. The other two sides of the triangle created by drawing the perpendicular line are equal. We'll call each of them x.

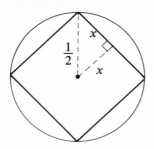

So from the Pythagorean theorem, $a^2 + b^2 = c^2$ becomes

$$x^2 + x^2 = (\tfrac{1}{2})^2$$

This simplifies to

$$2x^2 = \tfrac{1}{4}$$

or

$$x^2 = \tfrac{1}{8}$$

This means

$$x = \sqrt{\tfrac{1}{8}}$$

One side of the square has length $2x$, so the perimeter of the square is $4 \cdot 2x = 8x$. So $p = 8x = 8\sqrt{1/8} \doteq 2.828$. The symbol $\doteq$ means "approximately equal to." The approximation was obtained by using a calculator. We now conclude that the circumference (in this case pi) is between 2.828 and 4.

Although this approximation of pi is not very good, the technique used can yield good results. If the same method is used with regular polygons of eight sides, pi is determined to be between 3.06147 and 3.31371, a considerable improvement. We will not go through the calculation here, but notice how much closer both polygons are to the circle itself in the following drawing.

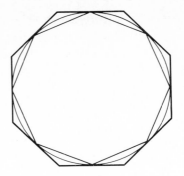

Here is a table of approximations obtained by using other regular polygons.

Number of sides	p	P
4	2.82842	4.00000
8	3.06147	3.31371
32	3.13655	3.15172
64	3.14033	3.14412
512	3.14157	3.14163

The value of π correct to five decimal places is 3.14159.

APPLICATIONS AND EXERCISES

1. (a) State the well-known formula for circumference that can be seen directly from the relationship

$$\frac{\text{circumference}}{\text{diameter}} = \pi$$

Use the letters C for circumference, d for diameter, and π.

(b) The radius of a circle is always half the diameter. Restate the formula you determined in part (a) by using the radius rather than the diameter.

2. Archimedes also derived a formula for the area of the region inside a circle. One way this can be written is $A = \pi d^2/4$.

   (a) What is the area of the region inside a circle whose diameter is 2? (*Note:* Leave the π in your answer; do not approximate it.)

   (b) Using 3.14 as an approximation for π, what is the answer to part (a)?

   (c) Repeat parts (a) and (b) for a circle with diameter 4.

   (d) Use the formula $A = \pi d^2/4$ to find the area when the *radius* is 3.

   (e) Use the formula $A = \pi r^2$ to find the area when the radius is 3. Was this easier than part (d)?

   (f) Show or explain how the formula $A = \pi r^2$ is derived from the formula $A = \pi d^2/4$.

3. Approximation of the number called π can be computed by using terms of this infinite series.

$$\pi = \frac{4}{1} - \frac{4}{3} + \frac{4}{5} - \frac{4}{7} + \cdots$$

The series is usually credited to Gottfried Wilhelm Leibniz, seventeenth-century mathematician and co-founder of the calculus. (Isaac Newton is the other independent co-founder.)

   (a) Write down the next three terms of the series.

   (b) Find an approximation to π (in decimal form) by using the first seven terms. This approximation will not be satisfactory. Many more terms are needed to obtain a value near 3.14.

4. Presented as steps (a)–(f) is a procedure you can follow to obtain the formula for the area of a circle ($A = \pi r^2$, r = radius, A = area). The method is called *rearrangement*, for reasons that will become apparent as you follow the steps. Begin with the fact that the distance around a circle (that is, its circumference) is $2\pi r$. This is shown in the next illustration. The shaded region within the circle is the area

we seek, and we will slice it up and manipulate it to see that $A = \pi r^2$.

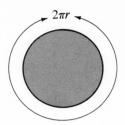

Now go through steps (a)–(f) and explain exactly what is happening in each of them. In the end, you will see that $A = \pi r^2$.

Courtesy of the Golden Press, Box 1342, Boulder, Colorado 80306

(a)

(b)

(c)

(d)

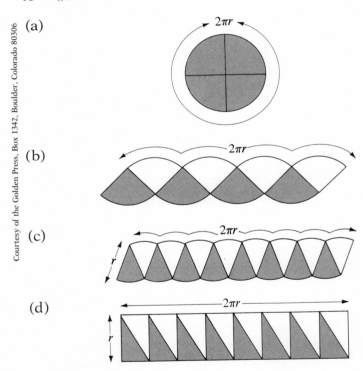

(e) Recall that the area of a rectangle is length × width. Here, the area is $2\pi r^2$. The slices of the original circle constitute only *half* of the rectangle. So, $2\pi r^2$ is twice A.

(f) $A = \pi r^2.$

5. The following circle has a diameter of 2. From the point X, move along the arc of the circle a distance t. In doing this, an angle θ (theta) is created.

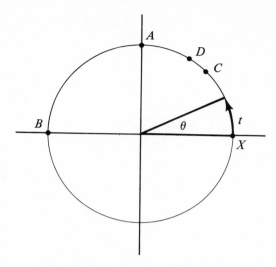

(a) What is the radius of the circle? Can you see why this particular circle is called a *unit circle?*

(b) What is the distance all the way around this circle? Use $C = 2\pi r$ or $C = \pi d$. Leave π in your answer; do not approximate it.

(c) What is the distance from X to A along the arc of the circle? How many degrees are in the angle θ created by moving this distance?

(d) What is the distance from X to B along the arc of the circle? How many degrees are in the angle θ created by moving this distance?

(e) The point C is halfway between X and A. Determine the angle θ (in degrees) and arc length t corresponding to C.

(f) The point D is two thirds of the way from X to A. Determine the angle θ (in degrees) and arc length t corresponding to D.

ANALYTIC GEOMETRY

Analytic geometry was developed by the French mathematician René Descartes to provide a natural union of algebra and geometry. His work, published in 1637, helped lead to the development of calculus less than 50 years later.

Courtesy of the Library of Congress

René Descartes (1596–1650)

In his *Cartesian coordinate* scheme, or *rectangular coordinate system*, any point in a plane (flat surface) can be located by means of two numbers called coordinates. At the beginning, a reference point is chosen at the intersection of two perpendicular axes. This point is called the *origin*. Then for every point in the plane, the first coordinate specifies a position right (+) or left (−) of the origin. The second coordinate specifies a position above (+) or below (−) the origin. The next illustration shows two points plotted in the Cartesian coordinate plane.

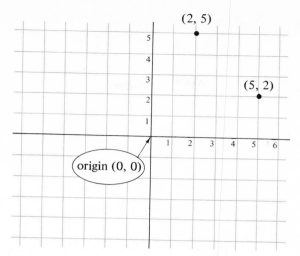

The point (2, 5) is 2 units to the right and 5 units above the origin. Thus, from the origin it is over 2 to the right and up 5. On the other hand, the point (5, 2) is over 5 to the right and up 2. Often, the horizontal axis is labeled x and the vertical axis y. So points are of the form (x, y). A few points are plotted in the next diagram. Check all of them to be sure you agree that their position is consistent with their coordinates.

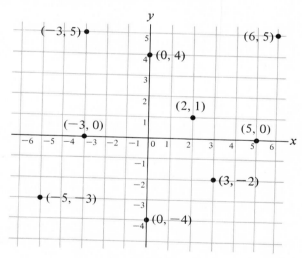

If an algebraic equation such as $y = 2x + 1$ is used to obtain points, and those points are plotted in the plane, then a smooth curve can usually be passed through the points. In the case of $y = 2x + 1$, the smooth curve is a straight line. One way to obtain points is to select values for x and compute the corresponding values of y.

x	$y = 2x + 1$	(x, y)
0	$y = 2(0) + 1 = 1$	$(0, 1)$
1	$y = 2(1) + 1 = 3$	$(1, 3)$
2	$y = 2(2) + 1 = 5$	$(2, 5)$
3	$y = 2(3) + 1 = 7$	$(3, 7)$

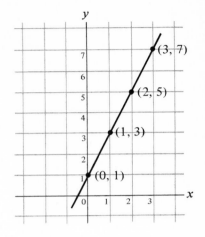

Straight lines and other curves provide a visual interpretation of the relationship between two quantities. Here the two quantities are x and y. Some of the relationships presented in Chapter 1 appear as straight lines when graphed. The graph of the relationship between the temperature and the number of chirps a cricket makes per minute is a straight line. So is the graph of the relationship between the distance a golf ball will carry and the speed at which it leaves the club. Some of the other relationships from Chapter 1 yield different kinds of curves when graphed.

The remainder of this section will be devoted to the study of curved lines. Specifically, you will be introduced to the four curves known as *conic sections*, or "conics" for short. They are called conics because their shapes result when a plane is passed through a cone. The angle of the intersecting plane determines which of the four curves results. Conics were originally studied by the early Greeks, and named by Apollonius about 225 B.C.

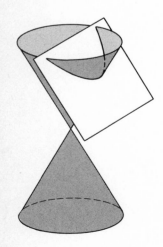

If the intersecting plane cuts the cone as shown at the left, the resulting conic is a *parabola*. In Chapter 1 there are several relationships whose graphs are parabolas, including relationships between distance and time. The graph of the relationship between the rate of photosynthesis of some green plants and the temperature of the air is very nearly a parabola. Such findings are very useful to ecologists.

The next graph shows the path of a car driven off a cliff at a speed of 100 feet per second (approximately 68 miles per hour). Its path is half of a parabola.

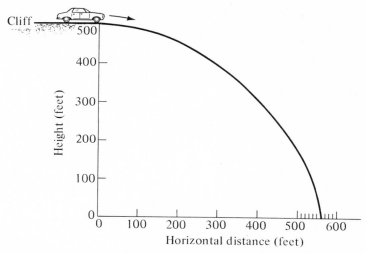

Can you determine from the graph how high the cliff is and approximately how far the car travels in the horizontal direction? You should have determined that the cliff is 500 feet high and the car travels about 560 feet in the horizontal direction.

The center of gravity of a leaping porpoise describes a parabola. Parabolas are used frequently in studies of the paths of freely falling objects.

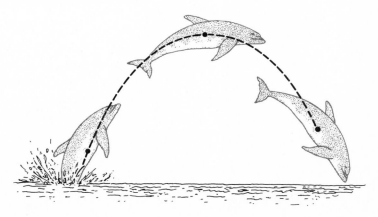

The graph of $y = x^2$ is a parabola. Below, the values 0, 1, −1, 2, −2, 3, and −3 are used for x to obtain corresponding values for y. A smooth curve is then passed through the plotted points.

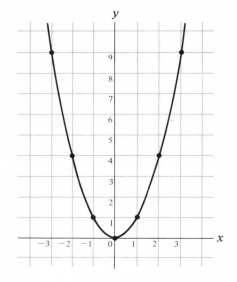

x	$y = x^2$	(x, y)
0	$y = 0$	$(0, 0)$
1	$y = 1$	$(1,1)$
−1	$y = 1$	$(−1, 1)$
2	$y = 4$	$(2, 4)$
−2	$y = 4$	$(−2, 4)$
3	$y = 9$	$(3, 9)$
−3	$y = 9$	$(−3, 9)$

There are many uses for parabola-shaped objects: automobile headlights, searchlights, and flashlights have parabolic mirrors. The light source (for example, the bulb of the flashlight) is placed at a point called the *focus* of the parabola. Then all light rays leaving the light source and striking the parabolic mirror will be reflected as parallel rays, that is, as a powerful concentrated beam in one direction.

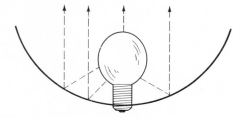

Reflecting telescopes use parabolic mirrors to concentrate (at the focus) the amount of light received from faint objects in the heavens. Radio, TV, and radar waves can be beamed efficiently with minimal loss in peripheral directions when they come from the focus of a parabolic transmitter. Similarly, parabolic radio and TV antennas and radio telescopes help produce a strong signal at the receiving focus.

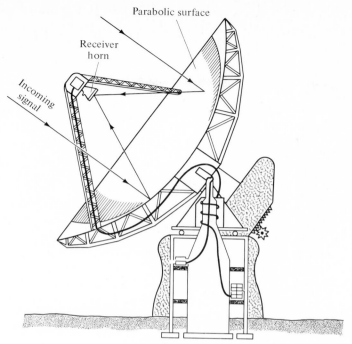

Radio telescope

The French have built a huge oven that uses an eight-story parabolic mirror. The sun's rays are reflected and concentrated to a point at the focus of the parabola, and that is where the oven is placed. Temperatures of more than 6000 degrees Fahrenheit have been achieved. The oven looks like this:

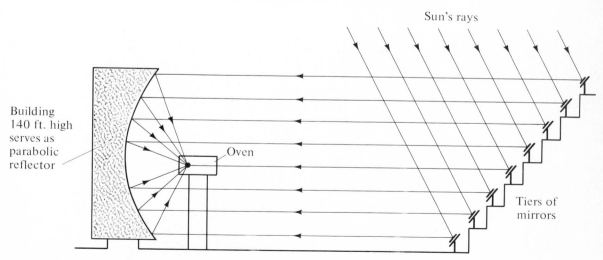

The second conic we shall consider is a *circle*. It is produced by a plane that cuts the cone as shown here.

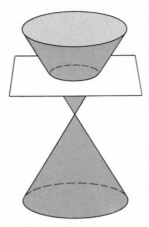

An important characteristic of circles that leads to many applications is that all points on a circle are the same distance from the center. A roll of tape is made circular so that the tape can be taken off smoothly and evenly. Imagine how strangely your car would ride if the tires were not round! How common are drinking glasses or soup cans that do not have circular rims? How would you like to use a telephone dial that was not circular?

The following photo is an eight-hour exposure of the region surrounding the north celestial pole. It shows how the stars move to create concentric circles, that is, concentric circular paths, with respect to the pole.

Lick Observatory Photograph

Center-pivot irrigation, shown in the next photo, is an automatic irrigation system that is based on the properties of a circle. Water is pumped through a pipe that runs from the center of the field out to the edge of the circle. (In other words, the pipe is a radius.) Along this radius pipe there are dozens of sprinkler outlets through which water can be released and applied to the land. The long radial pipe is mounted on wheels and driven by electric power. The pipe sweeps around the entire field in much the same way that a clock hand sweeps around the face of the clock. The photo below shows the use of center-pivot irrigation in western Nebraska.

U.S. Department of Agriculture, Soil Conservation Service

Now that we have seen some applications of the properties of circles, we will see how a circle is graphed. The graph of $x^2 + y^2 = 25$ is a circle. In the following table, the values of $0, 3, -3, 4, -4, 5,$ and -5 are used for x to obtain corresponding values for y.

x	$x^2 + y^2 = 25$	$y^2 =$	$y =$	(x, y)
0	$0 + y^2 = 25$	$y^2 = 25$	$y = 5, -5$	$(0, 5), (0, -5)$
3	$9 + y^2 = 25$	$y^2 = 16$	$y = 4, -4$	$(3, 4), (3, -4)$
-3	$9 + y^2 = 25$	$y^2 = 16$	$y = 4, -4$	$(-3, 4), (-3, -4)$
4	$16 + y^2 = 25$	$y^2 = 9$	$y = 3, -3$	$(4, 3), (4, -3)$
-4	$16 + y^2 = 25$	$y^2 = 9$	$y = 3, -3$	$(-4, 3), (-4, -3)$
5	$25 + y^2 = 25$	$y^2 = 0$	$y = 0$	$(5, 0)$
-5	$25 + y^2 = 25$	$y^2 = 0$	$y = 0$	$(-5, 0)$

These numbers were carefully chosen to avoid square roots of numbers that are not perfect squares. For example, if $x = 2$, then $y = +\sqrt{21}$ or $y = -\sqrt{21}$, and such square roots are more difficult to plot. Once the points are obtained, they are plotted and a smooth curve is passed through them. The graph looks like this:

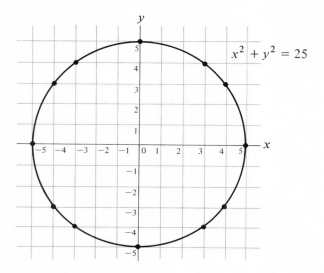

$$x^2 + y^2 = 25$$

If the plane cuts the cone as shown here, the resulting conic is an *ellipse*.

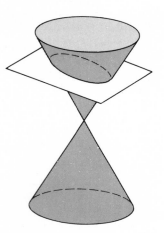

The graph of $4x^2 + 9y^2 = 36$ is an ellipse. In the next table, the values 0, 3, and -3 are used for x to obtain corresponding values for y. These numbers were carefully chosen to avoid square roots of numbers that are not perfect squares. If such square roots do arise, they can always be approximated, but it is better to avoid them unless you have a calculator or table of square roots.

x	$4x^2 + 9y^2 = 36$	$y^2 =$	$y =$	(x, y)
0	$0 + 9y^2 = 36$	4	$2, -2$	$(0, 2), (0, -2)$
3	$36 + 9y^2 = 36$	0	0	$(3, 0)$
-3	$36 + 9y^2 = 36$	0	0	$(-3, 0)$

The graph of this ellipse is

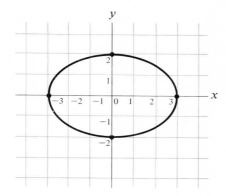

The paths of planets and some comets are ellipses. The large ellipse in the next illustration represents the path of Halley's comet with respect to the sun (black dot). Also shown is the smaller elliptical path of the earth. Man-made satellites orbit

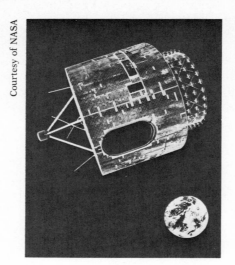

Courtesy of NASA

the earth in paths that are ellipses. Artists and architects know that when a circle is inclined with respect to the plane of the illustration, it will appear as an ellipse. Consequently, ellipses often must be drawn to represent circles.

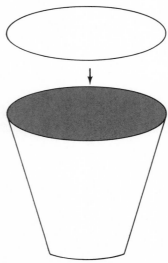

Ellipse representing circle

If the plane cuts the cone as shown next, the resulting conic is a *hyperbola*.

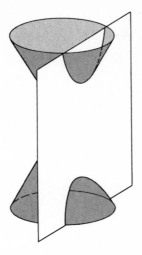

The graph of $y = 1/x$ is a hyperbola. In the following table, the values 1, 2, 3, 4, $\frac{1}{2}$, $\frac{1}{3}$, and $\frac{1}{4}$ are used for x to obtain corresponding values for y.

x	$y = 1/x$	(x, y)
1	1	$(1, 1)$
2	$\frac{1}{2}$	$(2, \frac{1}{2})$
3	$\frac{1}{3}$	$(3, \frac{1}{3})$
4	$\frac{1}{4}$	$(4, \frac{1}{4})$
$\frac{1}{2}$	2	$(\frac{1}{2}, 2)$
$\frac{1}{3}$	3	$(\frac{1}{3}, 3)$
$\frac{1}{4}$	4	$(\frac{1}{4}, 4)$

The solid curve graphed on the following page passes through the points listed in the table. If the negative numbers $-1, -2, -3, -4, -\frac{1}{2}, -\frac{1}{3}$, and $-\frac{1}{4}$ are used for x, then the corresponding y values are $-1, -\frac{1}{2}, -\frac{1}{3}, -\frac{1}{4}, -2, -3$, and -4, respectively. The curve through those points with negative coordinates is shown dashed on the following graph. This graph suggests that there are two separate curves that constitute a hyperbola. The illustration of the plane cutting a cone also suggests this. In fact, it is true in all graphs of hyperbolas, but in practice it often

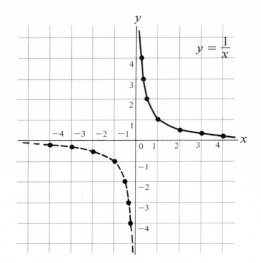

happens that only half the hyperbola is needed or used, yet it is still called a hyperbola.

The shock wave associated with the sonic boom created by jet aircraft flying faster than the speed of sound has the shape of a cone. So if the plane flies parallel to the ground, the shape of the shock wave on the ground is a hyperbola. Some comets have paths that are the shape of a hyperbola. The graph of the relationship between the size an object appears to a viewer and the distance from which the viewer is observing is a hyperbola. The relationship itself was discussed in Chapter 1 (see page 29). The shadow created on the wall by the lampshade of a table lamp approximates a hyperbola.

The arch of the upper jaw of humans has several forms, each form being named for a conic section that it resembles. The forms are (1) hyperbolic, in which the ends of the jaw diverge; (2) parabolic, parallel ends; and (3) elliptic, ends approaching one another.

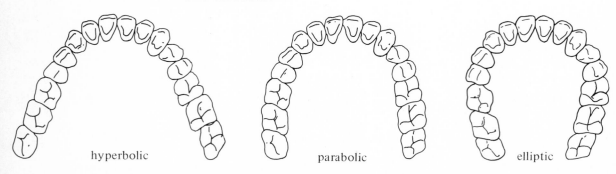

hyperbolic   parabolic   elliptic

1. For each line described in parts (a)–(c), obtain four points and graph it.

   (a) If you earn $3 per hour, then your income (call it y) depends on the number of hours (call them x) that you work. Specifically, $y = 3x$ dollars.

   (b) If a bicyclist travels at 8 miles per hour, then $y = 8x$ gives the distance y in miles that he travels in x hours.

   (c) In Chapter 1 we saw the relationship between the Fahrenheit temperature and the number of cricket chirps per minute. If the temperature is called y and the number of chirps x, then $y = \frac{1}{4}x + 40$. Let $x = 0$, 4, 8, and 12 in order to obtain four points to graph the line.

2. When a frog leaps, its path through the air is a parabola. Suppose a particular frog's path is $y = (2x) - (\frac{1}{4}x^2)$, where y is the frog's height in flight and x the horizontal distance from where it began to leap. All measurements are in feet. Note that $\frac{1}{4}x^2$ means $\frac{1}{4}$ times x^2.

   (a) The frog begins at $(0, 0)$. Explain why.

   (b) Let $x = 1, 2, 3, 4, 5, 6, 7,$ and 8. Determine corresponding y values.

   (c) Plot the points obtained in parts (a) and (b). Pass a parabola through them.

   (d) How far (horizontally) does the frog leap?

   (e) How high does the frog leap?

3. Consider the circle $x^2 + y^2 = 9$. Let $x = 0$ and find the two corresponding y values. Let $y = 0$ and find the two corresponding x values. Plot the four points. Knowing that $x^2 + y^2 = 9$ is indeed a circle, complete the sketch of the graph without obtaining any additional points.

4. Consider the ellipse $x^2 + 4y^2 = 4$. Let $x = 0$ and find the two corresponding y values. Let $y = 0$ and find the two corresponding x values. Plot the four points and pass an ellipse through them.

5. Consider the hyperbola $y = 2/x$. Let $x = 1, 2, 3, 4, 5, 6, 8,$ $20, \frac{1}{2}, \frac{1}{4},$ and $\frac{1}{8}$. Determine corresponding y values. Use the

11 points obtained to sketch the half of the hyperbola suggested by the points.

Recalling the discussion of *symmetry* in the first section of this chapter, look through the present section on analytic geometry and study the graphs of $y = x^2$, $x^2 + y^2 = 25$, $4x^2 + 9y^2 = 36$, and $y = 1/x$.

6. (a) Which graphs are symmetric with respect to the y axis?
   (b) Which graphs are symmetric with respect to the x axis?
   (c) Which graphs are symmetric with respect to both the x and y axes?
   (d) Which graphs are not symmetric with respect to either the x or y axes?

7. Let's study the points of $y = x^2$ to see algebraically why its graph is symmetric with respect to the y axis.
   (a) What point is the mirror image of (3, 9), and what point is the mirror image of (2, 4)?
   (b) What point would be the mirror image of (9, 81) with respect to the y axis?
   (c) Explain the relationship between the coordinates of a point of this graph and of its mirror image with respect to the y axis.

8. Let's consider symmetry with respect to the x axis. Examine the points of the graph of $x^2 + y^2 = 25$.
   (a) What point is the mirror image of (3, 4) with respect to the x axis, and what point is the mirror image of (4, 3)?
   (b) What point would be the mirror image of (-4, 3) with respect to the x axis?
   (c) Explain the relationship between the coordinates of a point of this graph and its mirror image with respect to the x axis.

9. Complete each graph by assuming the type of symmetry suggested.

(a)   Symmetric with respect to the *y* axis only.

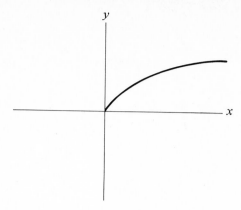

(b)   Symmetric with respect to the *x* axis only.

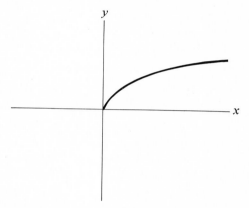

(c)   Symmetric with respect to both the *x* axis and the *y* axis.

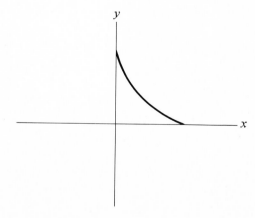

10. The most obvious thing to create by using a compass is a circle. Explain how a compass can be used to make a circle and why it works.

11. You can draw an excellent ellipse by using a piece of string, two tacks and a pencil. Tack down the ends of the string keeping it loose. Then place a pencil against the string, making the string taut. Finally, move the pencil while keeping the string taut.

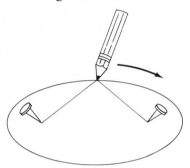

Obtain the materials and draw an ellipse this way.

The points at which the tacks are placed are called the *foci* (plural of *focus*) of the resulting ellipse. The inside of the Mormon Tabernacle in Salt Lake City is approximately elliptical. The reading desk is near one of the foci. Listeners at the far end of this large building and near the other focus can hear the sound made by dropping a pin on the reading desk. The two curved end surfaces act as elliptical sound mirrors.

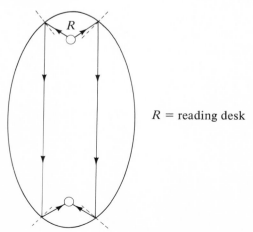

R = reading desk

12. Explain how pencil and string can be used to draw a circle. *Hint:* Refer to Exercises 10 and 11.

13. Suppose the wood piece illustrated next is lying on a large table top. A nail is driven into hole 1, and a pencil is placed in hole 2 and used to rotate the piece of wood about 1. What does the pencil draw?

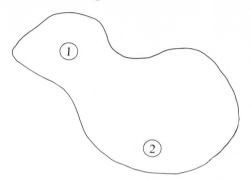

14. The collection of all points that are the same distance from a fixed point is called a _____. The fixed point is called its _____. The distance is called its _____.

15. Obtain a flashlight containing fresh batteries. Turn it on and look at it for a second or two only. Then shine it against a wall. Observe the powerful beam of light. Then take the flashlight apart, remove the parabolic reflecting mirror, and put it back together again without the mirror. How does the brightness and the beam of the bulb alone compare with the original brightness and beam?

16. Anthropologists have several different classifications of human skull shapes. Match up the classifications *ellipsoid, pentagonoid,* and *spheroid* with the following illustrations. Each drawing is a top view. Use a dictionary if necessary, but first examine each word carefully and think.

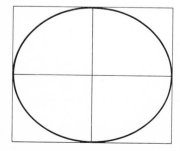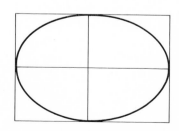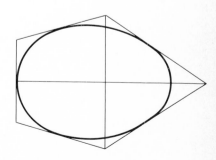

17. In center-pivot irrigation (see page 193), the amount of water that is released through each sprinkler along the radial pipe can be controlled. Where along the radial pipe would you release the most water, and where would you release the least water? Explain why.

18. The distance between two points can be determined using the Pythagorean theorem. Consider the points A (2, 1) and B (6, 4).

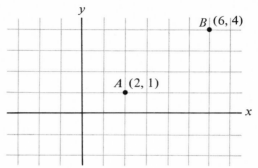

The point C (in the next diagram) is the third vertex of a right triangle that can be formed.

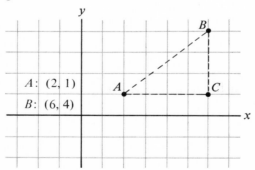

(a) What are the coordinates of C?

(b) What is the distance (number of units) from A of C? Note that A and C have the same y coordinate.

(c) How far is it from B to C? Note that B and C have the same x coordinate.

(d) From parts (b) and (c) you know the lengths of two sides of a right triangle. Apply the Pythagorean theorem to find the length of the hypotenuse. The hypotenuse is, of course, the distance between A and B.

(e) Use steps (a)–(d) to find the distance between (4, 3) and (9, 15).

HONEYBEES AGAIN

Honeybees use a coordinate system quite different from the traditional rectangular coordinate system described in the preceding section. They use *polar coordinates*. Points are located a distance *r* and an angle θ (theta) from the origin, rather than a distance right/left and up/down from the origin. Polar coordinates were described by Isaac Newton about 1671.

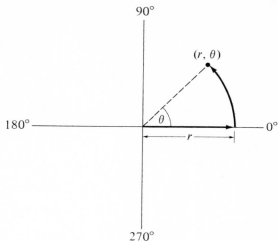

Bees use polar coordinates to tell other bees at the hive where desirable food is located. The returning bee brings a small quantity of food in order to make the smell known to the others. Then it dances in semicircles on the hive. The number of semicircles per minute specifies the food's distance *r* from the hive. During the dance, the bee duplicates the angular direction of the food with respect to the sun. Thus, the bee uses

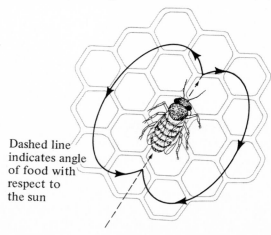

Dashed line indicates angle of food with respect to the sun

polar coordinates to locate food for other bees. It specifies a distance r and an angle θ.

The next illustration shows the orientation of the honeybee in each of three cases. First (a), the nectar is in the same direction as the sun's rays. In the second instance (b), the nectar is at an angle of 65° with respect to the sun's rays. In the last case (c), the nectar is at an angle of 120° with respect to the sun's rays. Polar coordinates are a natural method for the bee, since it need only orient itself to the sun at the same angle at which it originally was oriented when flying to or from the food.

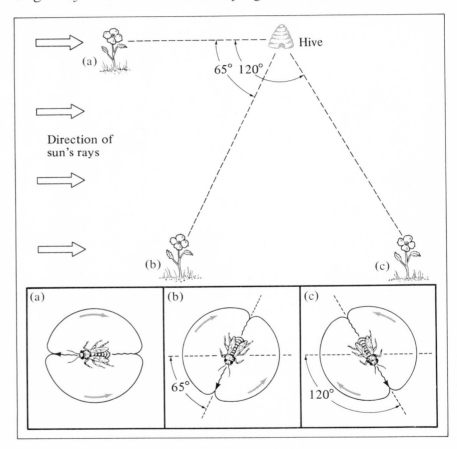

You may be wondering how anyone became aware of the way in which bees directed one another to food. One technique used to study honeybees was to attach small magnets to bees and use coils and recording equipment to measure their activity. Another technique involved dummy bees, rigged to dance well enough to get others to go off in the prescribed direction.

1. Each point is given in polar coordinate form (r, θ). Plot each one. Then look at the plotted point and determine to what rectangular coordinate point (x, y) it is equal.

   (a) $(2, 90°)$ (b) $(3, 180°)$ (c) $(5, 0°)$ (d) $(0, 30°)$
   (e) $(0, 90°)$ (f) $(4, 270°)$ (g) $(1, 360°)$ (h) $(6, 450°)$

2. Although it is the Earth that makes one complete revolution on its axis every 24 hours, to an observer on Earth it appears that the sun revolves about the Earth.

   (a) The "sun moves" through a full revolution of 360° in 24 hours. Through what angle does the sun move in one hour?

   The *sundial* clock works on the principle suggested in part (a). You tell the time of day by the angle the sun's rays make with respect to a post placed perpendicular to the ground. In the accompanying drawing, it is assumed that the sun is overhead at noon, so that the sun's shadow will be at the arrow when it is noon.

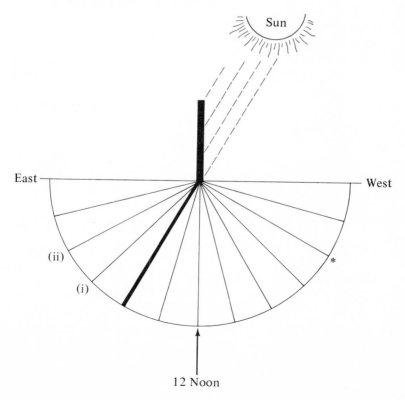

Honeybees Again   **207**

(b) Each of the sections in the drawing contains an angle of 15°. How long does it take the sun's shadow to move through one of these sections, for example, to move from (i) to (ii)?

(c) The sun moves from east to west. What time is it when the shadow is at the asterisk?

3. What would happen if a honeybee waited for an hour after returning to its hive and then gave the other bees directions to the food source?

4. Why do think it is that bees use polar coordinates rather than rectangular coordinates?

TRIGONOMETRY OF RIGHT TRIANGLES

You have already had a brief look at right triangles and the Pythagorean theorem. Now you'll have a chance to learn about the development and application of right triangle trigonometry. Such mathematics was developed to provide an indirect means of measuring distances that could not be measured directly, for example, the distance from the Earth to the moon.

Hipparchus (about 140 B.C.) and Ptolemy (about 150 A.D.) are considered to be the founders of trigonometry. They devised techniques to catalog the positions of stars relative to the earth. Much of the early interest in trigonometry was due to its natural application to astronomy, cartography (mapmaking), and navigation. Before we can consider an application, some definitions are needed.

In a right triangle, the side opposite the right angle is called the *hypotenuse*. The side opposite a specified nonright angle (call the angle θ) is called the *opposite side*. The remaining side next to angle θ is called the *adjacent side*. Which side is opposite and which side is adjacent depends on which angle you choose to refer to. This is demonstrated by the next two illustrations.

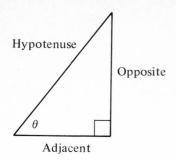 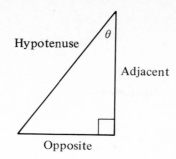

Three trigonometric functions are defined by ratios involving the lengths of the hypotenuse, opposite, and adjacent sides.

$$\text{sine of } \theta = \sin \theta = \frac{\text{opposite}}{\text{hypotenuse}}$$

$$\text{cosine of } \theta = \cos \theta = \frac{\text{adjacent}}{\text{hypotenuse}}$$

$$\text{tangent of } \theta = \tan \theta = \frac{\text{opposite}}{\text{adjacent}}$$

As an example, $\sin \theta$, $\cos \theta$, and $\tan \theta$ are computed for the following triangle. Check each of these yourself.

$$\sin \theta = \frac{\text{opposite}}{\text{hypotenuse}} = \frac{4}{5} \text{ or } .8000$$

$$\cos \theta = \frac{\text{adjacent}}{\text{hypotenuse}} = \frac{3}{5} \text{ or } .6000$$

$$\tan \theta = \frac{\text{opposite}}{\text{adjacent}} = \frac{4}{3} \text{ or approximately } 1.3333$$

Approximate values for the sine, cosine, and tangent of an angle can be looked up in Table I (page 213). To be sure you can read the table, look up sin 24°, cos 81°, and tan 53°. Then check your results with those given here. The ≐ means "approximately equal to."

$$\sin 24° ≐ .4067$$

$$\cos 81° ≐ .1564$$

$$\tan 53° ≐ 1.3270$$

The same table can be used to determine the angle when either the sine, cosine, or tangent is known. Just reverse the table-look-up process used earlier. If sin θ is .9744, how many degrees are in angle θ? If cos θ = .5878, what is the value of θ? If tan θ = .2867, what is θ? When you have finished using Table I to determine these values of θ, check your answers with the results given here.

$$\text{If } \sin θ = .9744, \text{ then } θ ≐ 77°.$$

$$\text{If } \cos θ = .5878, \text{ then } θ ≐ 54°.$$

$$\text{If } \tan θ = .2867, \text{ then } θ ≐ 16°.$$

Now let's see how trigonometry was used to determine the approximate distance from the Earth to the moon. At an appropriate time of the month and night, two points called P and Q on the Earth's equator are selected for observing the moon.

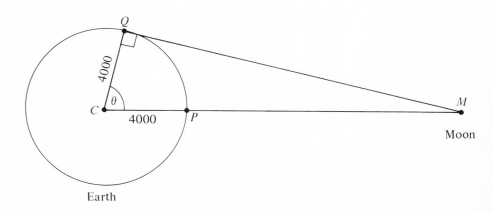

Point P is chosen with the moon overhead, so that the moon (M) can be considered a point on the line from the center of the Earth (C) through P (see the drawing). Point Q is chosen so that the moon is just visible from it. In other words, the moon is clearly visible from points closer to P, but not from points farther away from P than Q is. Selecting Q in this manner makes the line through MQ tangent to the Earth at the equator, and a theorem of geometry tells us that radius CQ is perpendicular to the tangent, thus forming a right angle. We also know that the radius of the Earth is approximately 4000 miles and angle θ is determined to be 89.067°. We seek the distance between P and M, the distance from the Earth to the moon. We will use trigonometry to determine CM. Then we'll subtract 4000 (the length of CP) from it to get the length of PM. Here is the triangle by itself.

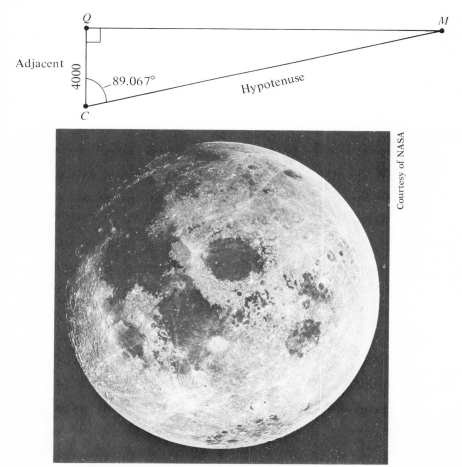

The known side (4000 miles) is the adjacent side with respect to angle θ, which is 89.067°. The unknown side CM is the hypotenuse. The trigonometric function involving the adjacent side and the hypotenuse is cosine. From

$$\cos \theta = \frac{\text{adjacent}}{\text{hypotenuse}}$$

we obtain the approximation

$$\cos 89.067° \doteq \frac{4000}{CM}$$

From tables available elsewhere, $\cos 89.067°$ is found to be approximately .0163. Thus,

$$.0163 \doteq \frac{4000}{CM}$$

or

$$.0163(CM) \doteq 4000$$

or

$$CM \doteq \frac{4000}{.0163} \doteq 245,400$$

So CM is approximately 245,400 miles. To determine the value of PM (the distance from Earth to the moon), simply subtract 4000 miles (the radius of the Earth) from the 245,400 miles. So the approximate distance from the Earth to the moon is 241,400 miles.

APPLICATIONS AND EXERCISES

1. Use Table I to look up sin 20° and cos 70°. What do you notice? Look up sin 35° and cos 55°. Look up sin 80° and cos 10°. State a general conclusion, in words. Now let θ

Table I Values of Trigonometric Functions

Angle	Sin	Cos	Tan	Angle	Sin	Cos	Tan
0°	.0000	1.0000	.0000				
1°	.0175	.9998	.0175	46°	.7193	.6947	1.0355
2°	.0349	.9994	.0349	47°	.7314	.6820	1.0724
3°	.0523	.9986	.0524	48°	.7431	.6691	1.1106
4°	.0698	.9976	.0699	49°	.7547	.6561	1.1504
5°	.0872	.9962	.0875	50°	.7660	.6428	1.1918
6°	.1045	.9945	.1051	51°	.7771	.6293	1.2349
7°	.1219	.9925	.1228	52°	.7880	.6157	1.2799
8°	.1392	.9903	.1405	53°	.7986	.6018	1.3270
9°	.1564	.9877	.1584	54°	.8090	.5878	1.3764
10°	.1736	.9848	.1763	55°	.8192	.5736	1.4281
11°	.1908	.9816	.1944	56°	.8290	.5592	1.4826
12°	.2079	.9781	.2126	57°	.8387	.5446	1.5399
13°	.2250	.9744	.2309	58°	.8480	.5299	1.6003
14°	.2419	.9703	.2493	59°	.8572	.5150	1.6643
15°	.2588	.9659	.2679	60°	.8660	.5000	1.7321
16°	.2756	.9613	.2867	61°	.8746	.4848	1.8040
17°	.2924	.9563	.3057	62°	.8829	.4695	1.8807
18°	.3090	.9511	.3249	63°	.8910	.4540	1.9626
19°	.3256	.9455	.3443	64°	.8988	.4384	2.0503
20°	.3420	.9397	.3640	65°	.9063	.4226	2.1445
21°	.3584	.9336	.3839	66°	.9135	.4067	2.2460
22°	.3746	.9272	.4040	67°	.9205	.3907	2.3559
23°	.3907	.9205	.4245	68°	.9272	.3746	2.4751
24°	.4067	.9135	.4452	69°	.9336	.3584	2.6051
25°	.4226	.9063	.4663	70°	.9397	.3420	2.7475
26°	.4384	.8988	.4877	71°	.9455	.3256	2.9042
27°	.4540	.8910	.5095	72°	.9511	.3090	3.0777
28°	.4695	.8829	.5317	73°	.9563	.2924	3.2709
29°	.4848	.8746	.5543	74°	.9613	.2756	3.4874
30°	.5000	.8660	.5774	75°	.9659	.2588	3.7321
31°	.5150	.8572	.6009	76°	.9703	.2419	4.0108
32°	.5299	.8480	.6249	77°	.9744	.2250	4.3315
33°	.5446	.8387	.6494	78°	.9781	.2079	4.7046
34°	.5592	.8290	.6745	79°	.9816	.1908	5.1446
35°	.5736	.8192	.7002	80°	.9848	.1736	5.6713
36°	.5878	.8090	.7265	81°	.9877	.1564	6.3138
37°	.6018	.7986	.7536	82°	.9903	.1392	7.1154
38°	.6157	.7880	.7813	83°	.9925	.1219	8.1443
39°	.6293	.7771	.8098	84°	.9945	.1045	9.5144
40°	.6428	.7660	.8391	85°	.9962	.0872	11.4301
41°	.6561	.7547	.8693	86°	.9976	.0698	14.3007
42°	.6691	.7431	.9004	87°	.9986	.0523	19.0811
43°	.6820	.7314	.9325	88°	.9994	.0349	28.6363
44°	.6947	.7193	.9657	89°	.9998	.0175	57.2900
45°	.7071	.7071	1.0000	90°	1.0000	.0000	

represent one of the angles of a pair such as 20° and 70°, or 35° and 55°, or 80° and 10°. State the relationship between sine and cosine of such pairs by using symbols rather than words.

2. Don't look in the table. What is the value of sin 0°? *Hint: The definition of sine might help. Explain your answer.*

3. Table I offers four-place values of the sine, cosine, and tangent of various angles. You could generate your own such table. Use a protractor to draw a right triangle having a specific angle, say 30°. Make one side of the triangle at least 3 inches long. Label the 30° angle. Also label the sides with respect to the 30° angle as hypotenuse, adjacent, and opposite. Next, use a ruler to measure the lengths of the sides. If fractions arise in the measurements, change them to decimals. (Keep one place after the decimal point for these measurements.) To find cos 30°, divide the length of the adjacent side by the length of the hypotenuse, thus using the definition of cosine. How does your result compare with the entry in Table I? How would you redraw the triangle in order to improve your approximation? Try it. Compute sin 30° and tan 30° from the measurements of your drawing. Finally, repeat the entire process for angles of 45° and 70°.

4. (a) The sum of the three angles of any triangle is 180°. All right triangles have a 90° angle. This means that in any right triangle, the sum of the two nonright angles is ____.

   (b) If one of the nonright angles of a right triangle is 40°, how large is the other nonright angle?

   (c) Suppose you plan to make a table of sine, cosine, and tangent values for angles in whole degrees from 1° through 89°. What is the least number of right triangles you must draw, assuming you are using the method of Exercise 3 to make the table?

5. The next drawing shows how to compute the approximate radius of the moon. The angle of .25° is known. Also known, as a result of the earlier example, is the length of

EM—the distance from Earth to moon is 241,400 miles. Determine which trigonometric function (sine, cosine, or tangent) is needed, set up the equation, and use whichever value (sin .25° ≐ .0044, cos .25° ≐ .9999, tan .25° = .0044) is needed in order to find the approximate length of the radius of the moon.

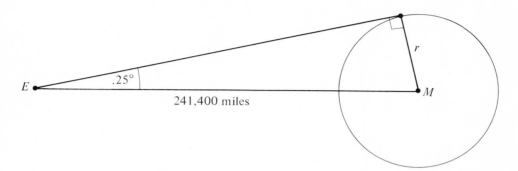

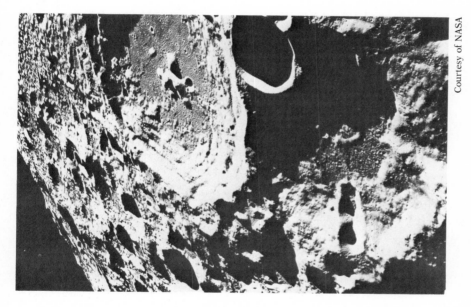

6. The next drawing suggests a way to determine the distance from the planet Venus to the sun. (Some error is introduced by assuming Venus has a circular orbit around the sun.) Determine the length of segment *VS*, the approximate distance from Venus to the sun.

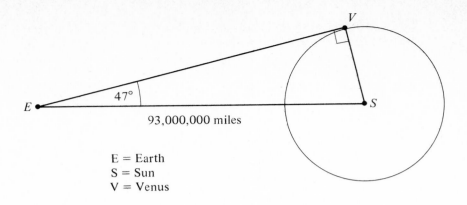

E = Earth
S = Sun
V = Venus

7. Attempting to block field goals is a common defensive tactic in football.

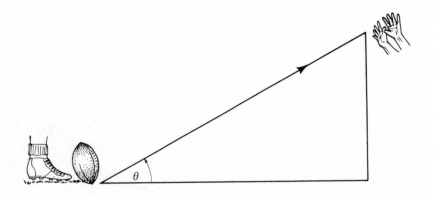

(a) To the nearest foot, how high must the defensive player get his hand to block the ball if it is kicked at an angle of $\theta = 30°$ and the defensive player is $17\frac{1}{2}$ feet from where the ball is originally kicked? The $17\frac{1}{2}$-foot distance between the defensive player and the ball is measured along the ground.

(b) To the nearest foot, how high must the defensive player get his hand to block the ball, if it is kicked at an angle of 35° and the defensive player is $17\frac{1}{2}$ feet from where the ball is originally kicked?

(c) A good defensive player can get his hand up to a height of 11 feet. If the ball is kicked at an angle of

40°, how close must the player be to the ball in order to block the kick?

8. In forestry, right triangle trigonometry is sometimes used to determine the height of a tree. The observer measures his distance (d) from the tree and the angle of inclination (θ) of his line of sight to the top of the tree.

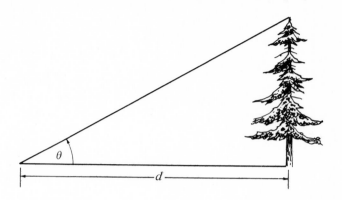

(a) Which trigonometric relationship (sine, cosine, or tangent) should be used to determine the height of the tree?

(b) To the nearest foot, what is the height of the tree if the distance of the observer from the tree is 65 feet and the angle of inclination is 53°?

More advanced trigonometry is used to measure indirectly the upper stem diameters of standing trees.

9. Airports use ceilometers to measure the height of a cloud cover in order to determine whether to allow planes to land and take off. A *ceilometer* (see next page) consists of a light beam projector, a detector, and a recorder. The projector directs an intense beam of light vertically up into the clouds. The detector (a photocell) is located on the ground a fixed distance from the projector. Where the light from the projector hits the cloud base, a spot is created. The detector senses the light spot. The angle between the ground and the light spot is then given by the recorder. Finally, the use of right triangle trigonometry gives the height.

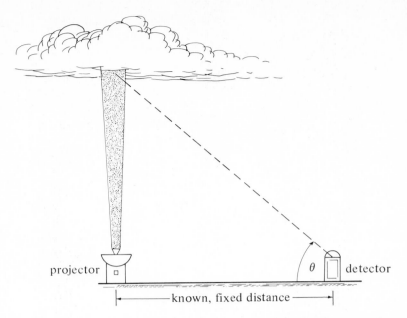

If the known fixed distance along the ground is 200 feet and the angle θ given by the recorder is 42°, how high is the cloud cover?

10. The distance across a river can be determined indirectly by the use of right triangle trigonometry.

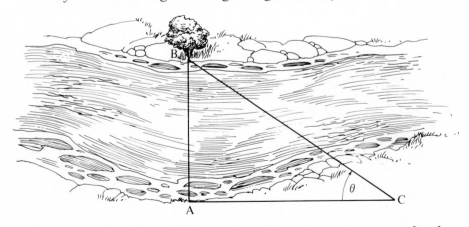

Walk along the shore until you are opposite a tree, bush, large rock, or other reference point on the other shore. Call the point you are standing at A and call the reference on the other shore B. Then walk along the shore until you are perhaps 100 or 200 feet from A. Call this new point C. Now approximate the angle θ between AC and the reference point on the opposite shore. Knowing *AC* (the distance from *A* to *C*) and angle θ, you should be able to approximate the length of *AB*, the distance across the river. Assume that *AC* is 200 feet and that angle θ is 65°. Determine the distance across the river.

11. The string of a kite is attached to the ground. The angle formed between the string and the ground is 58°. If the length of the string is 1000 feet (that is, you have let out 1000 feet of string), how high is the kite?

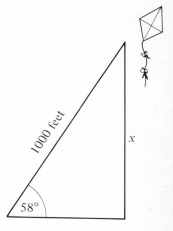

12. An archaeologist may need to determine the horizontal distance between two points (*A* and *B* in the illustration here) at opposite ends of a small valley. This distance is indicated by the dashed line.

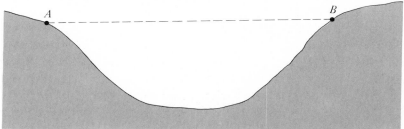

He can determine the distance indirectly by using right triangle trigonometry. He walks through the valley and measures the distances along the surface of the ground. These distances are the lengths of *AC, CD, DE, EF,* and *FB* in the next illustration. With the aid of an instrument called an *Abney level*, he measures the angles (called θ in the illustration) of the ground with respect to the horizontal.

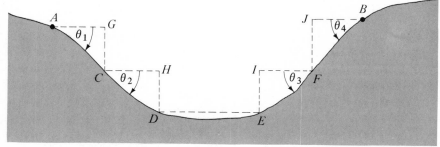

This is enough information to compute the length of the horizontals labeled *AG, CH, DE, IF,* and *JB*. The sum of these five distances is the same as the distance from *A* to *B*.

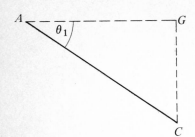

(a) Consider the first right triangle created. If AC is measured to be 75 meters and angle θ_1 is 35°, what is the length of AG to the nearest meter?

(b) Suppose $\theta_2 = 28°$, $\theta_3 = 30°$, $\theta_4 = 36°$, $CD = 100$ meters, $EF = 80$ meters, and $FB = 90$ meters. To the nearest meter, what are the lengths of CH, IF, and JB?

(c) If DE is 150 meters, what is the approximate horizontal distance from A to B?

13. (a) Compute the value of

$$(\sin \theta)^2 + (\cos \theta)^2$$

for each of these right triangles. Simplify the result as much as possible.

 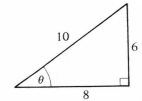 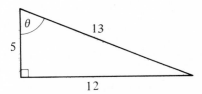

(b) Based on the results of your calculations in part (a), what should go in the blank to complete the following statement?

$$(\sin \theta)^2 + (\cos \theta)^2 = \underline{}$$

(c) Is your conclusion in part (b) based on inductive or deductive reasoning? Explain.

14. There are three other trigonometric functions in addition to sine, cosine, and tangent. They are listed and defined next.

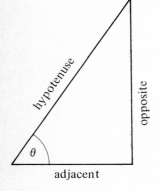

$$\text{cotangent of } \theta = \cot \theta = \frac{\text{adj}}{\text{opp}}$$

$$\text{cosecant of } \theta = \csc \theta = \frac{\text{hyp}}{\text{opp}}$$

$$\text{secant of } \theta = \sec \theta = \frac{\text{hyp}}{\text{adj}}$$

(a) What is the relationship between cotangent and tangent?

(b) What is the relationship between secant and cosine?

(c) If $\csc \theta = 3$, then $\sin \theta = $ _____ .

15. The force (F) that propels a skier parallel to the slope he is descending is computed by multiplying the weight of the skier (W) by the sine of the angle of the slope. In symbols, $F = W \cdot \sin \theta$.

(a) Verify that the entries in the second row of the chart are correct to the nearest pound, assuming the skier weighs 160 pounds. Angles are measured in degrees. Force is measured in pounds.

Angle	0	5	10
Force	0	14	28

State of Colorado, Division of Commerce and Development

(b) Complete the following table, which is an extension of the one in part (a).

Angle	0	5	10	15	20	25	30	35	40	45
Force	0	14	28							

PREDATOR–PREY INTERACTION

The interdependence of animal species sometimes produces fluctuations in animal populations in a given territory. In one instance, Charles Darwin used such interdependence to explain why there are more bumblebees near towns than there are in the country. He noted that near towns there are more cats. This in turn means fewer field mice, and since mice are the chief ravagers of bees' nests, bees are safer near towns.

Sometimes the interdependence of two animal species will result in a fluctuation in both species. Consider, for example, a territory inhabited by lynxes (the predators) and rabbits (their prey), the rabbits being the main food of the lynxes. The following graph illustrates the interdependence of the two species.

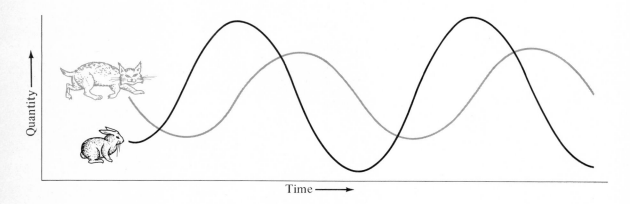

Naturalists have observed an apparently similar relationship between two different species of buttercups observed along a series of ridges and furrows. Unlike the interrelationship of lynx and rabbit, here the growth or decline of one species has nothing directly to do with the growth rate of the other. Instead, it is the topography. One species prefers the furrows, which are often soggy with excess moisture. The other species prefers the ridgetops, which usually are freely drained. The next graph shows the results of these preferences.

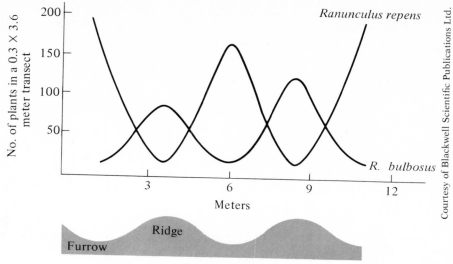

Courtesy of Blackwell Scientific Publications Ltd.

Michael Faraday discovered the principle of the electric generator in 1831. He found that an electric current can be generated by rotating a coil of wire in a magnetic field. The voltage produced alternates between positive and negative, as shown in the next diagram.

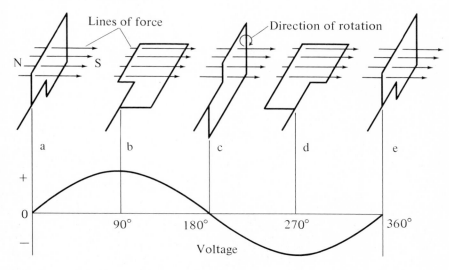

It is interesting to note that this graph resembles the predator–prey graph. Many other examples of this type of relationship exist. In mathematics, they can be written as $y = \sin \theta$ or $y = \sin t$, and so on. The graphs are examples of so-called *sine waves*. Yes, this is the same "sine" that was presented in the trigonometry section. An explanation of why it is the same sine is beyond the scope of this book, but such explanations are readily available in textbooks on trigonometry.

Tides have the same cyclical nature. The following illustration shows the height of water in a harbor at different times of the day.

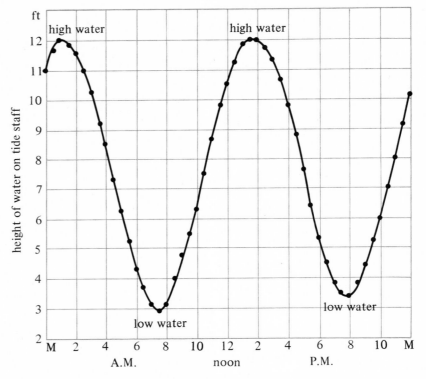

The bean plant orients its leaves so that they are perpendicular to the sun's rays during the day; at night, it folds them. The leaves or flowers of many other plants behave similarly. If the movements of the leaves are recorded, the graph generated (shown on the next page) is an example of a sine wave.

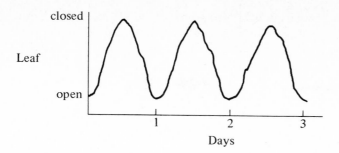

1. Several sections of the following predator–prey graph are numbered. Match the numbers of the sections of the graph with the descriptions below. Read all four descriptions carefully before trying to match any of them.

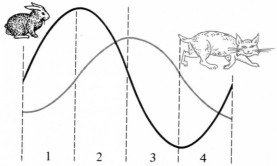

_____ The lynx population has increased to the extent that the rabbit population is actually decreasing.

_____ The lynx population has decreased to the point that the rabbit population is now increasing.

_____ The rabbit population has become abundant, so the lynx population is increasing.

_____ The rabbit population has decreased to the extent that the lynx population is actually decreasing.

2. The cycle of interdependence of lynx and rabbit populations can be illustrated in a different way, as shown here.

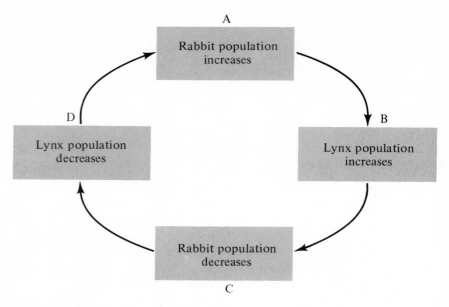

Describe in words one entire cycle:

(a) Beginning with box A.
(b) Beginning with box B.
(c) Beginning with box C.
(d) Beginning with box D.

3. Ecologists refer to the relationship of the lynx and the rabbit as a predator–prey interaction. Examine the following graph to determine which (A or B) is the predator and which is the prey. Explain your answer.

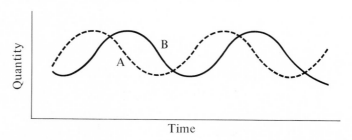

4. Which of the following relationships are likely to have graphs that resemble sine waves?

(a) The relationship between temperature and time of day.

(b) The relationship between the amount of moon visible (assuming no clouds) and the day of the month.

(c) The relationship between a person's age and income.

(d) The relationship between the value of an automobile and its age.

Introduction to Topology

5

From geometry we turn next to topology, a branch of mathematics that resembles geometry because in it geometric figures are often used and studied. Applications of topology can be found in such diverse fields as biology, sociology, and electronics. Logical solution of certain puzzles and games involves basic topological concepts. Topology is concerned with the properties that figures continue to possess even after they have been distorted by stretching, shrinking, twisting, or bending. Unlike geometry, topology is not concerned with measurement, length, shape, angles, or volume. Because of this, topology is sometimes referred to as "rubber sheet geometry" or the "mathematics of distortion." As an example, consider the following figures. They are all *topologically equivalent* (or *homeomorphic*), because any of them can be obtained from any other by twisting, bending, stretching, or shrinking.

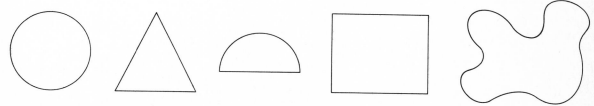

Note, for example, how the circle can be transformed into a triangle:

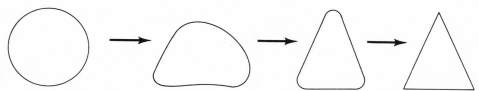

Distortions that make the figure cross itself or touch itself are not permitted. No two of the following figures are topologically equivalent.

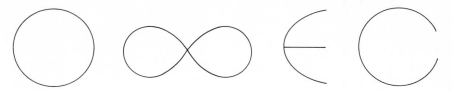

A doughnut with a hole in it is topologically equivalent to a coffee cup with a handle on it. In a series of stretchings, the hole of the doughnut becomes the handle of the cup.

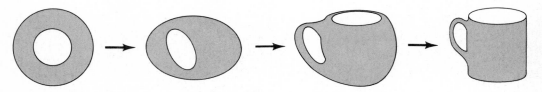

Although several mathematicians before him had solved problems and introduced concepts of a topological nature, the French mathematician Henri Poincaré is credited with

Henri Poincaré (1854–1912)

founding and organizing the branch of mathematics that is now called topology. Beginning in 1895, Poincaré published a series of essays on topology. His interest was in the branch of topology called *combinatorial topology*, and this is the kind of topology we will look at in this chapter.

Another branch of topology, called *point-set topology*, more closely resembles the field of mathematics designated as analysis. Point-set topology was founded by Felix Hausdorff (1868–1942) after Georg Cantor completed developing the theory of sets in 1895.

APPLICATIONS AND EXERCISES

1. Consider these three figures:

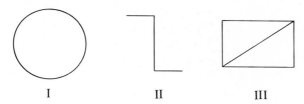

I   II   III

Now examine figures (a)–(i) and determine to which figure (I, II, or III) each is topologically equivalent.

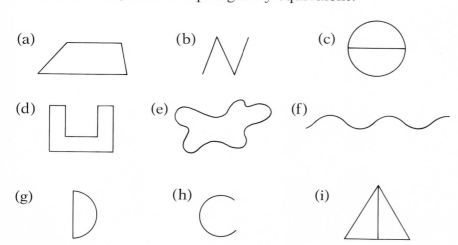

(a)   (b)   (c)

(d)   (e)   (f)

(g)   (h)   (i)

2. Consider these three items:

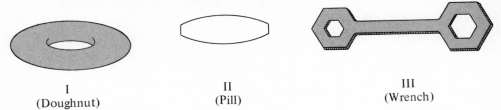

I
(Doughnut)

II
(Pill)

III
(Wrench)

Examine items (a)–(l) and determine to which item (I, II, or III) each is topologically equivalent.

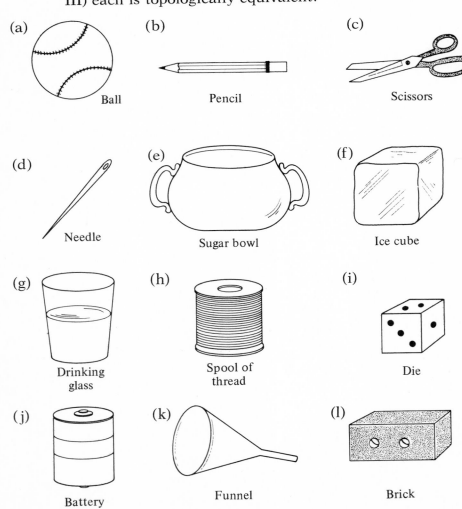

(a) Ball

(b) Pencil

(c) Scissors

(d) Needle

(e) Sugar bowl

(f) Ice cube

(g) Drinking glass

(h) Spool of thread

(i) Die

(j) Battery

(k) Funnel

(l) Brick

CLOSED CURVES

Topologists often study *closed curves*. By "closed" is meant, intuitively, "closed up," as in

rather than curves such as

which are not closed. When drawn, a closed curve finishes at the same point it starts at and there are no loose ends. A *simple closed curve* is a closed curve that does not intersect itself. This means you can start at any point on the curve and trace the entire figure without crossing the curve at any point.

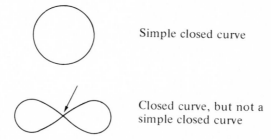

Simple closed curve

Closed curve, but not a simple closed curve

The Jordan curve theorem, named for the French mathematician Camille Jordan (1838–1922), states that every simple closed curve divides the plane into exactly two parts, an inside and an outside. Below, the 1's are inside and the 2's are outside.

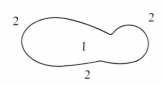

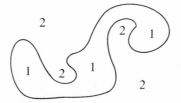

A region is *simply connected* if any closed curve lying in it can be shrunk down to a point. The region below is simply connected because there is nothing in it to prevent shrinking any closed curve in it to a point. This shrinking is shown in steps.

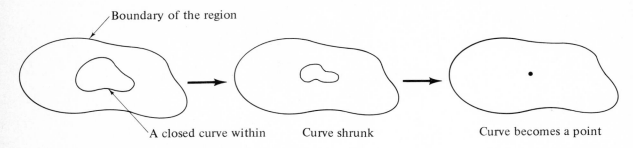

Boundary of the region

A closed curve within   Curve shrunk   Curve becomes a point

In Exercise 5, you will see at least one region in which some "obstacle" prevents the shrinking of a closed curve to a point.

APPLICATIONS AND EXERCISES

1. Determine which curves are closed curves.

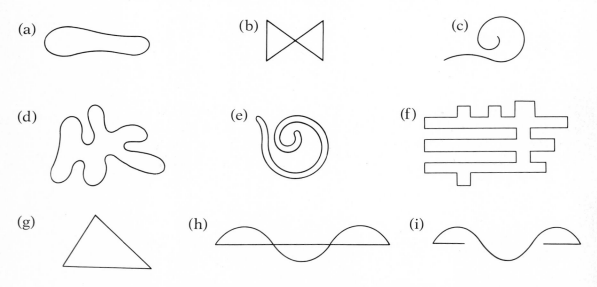

(a)   (b)   (c)

(d)   (e)   (f)

(g)   (h)   (i)

2. Determine which curves in Exercise 1 are simple closed curves.

3. Shade the inside portion of each of the following simple closed curves.

(a)

(b)

(c)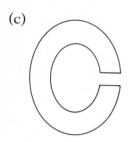

(d)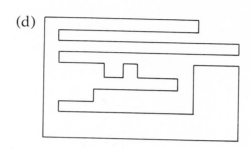

(e)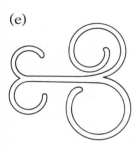

(f)

4. (a) In each of the following three illustrations, the point *p* is *inside* the simple closed curve. For each illustration, make a point that is outside the illustration and thus clearly outside the curve. Then draw a straight line from *p* to the point outside the illustration. Finally, count the number of times the line crosses the curve in each of the three illustrations.

 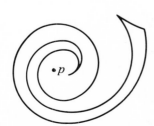 

(b)   In each of the next three illustrations, the point p is *outside* the simple closed curve. For each illustration make a point that is outside the illustration and thus clearly outside the curve. Then draw a straight line from p to the point outside the illustration. Finally, count the number of times the line crosses the curve in each of the three cases.

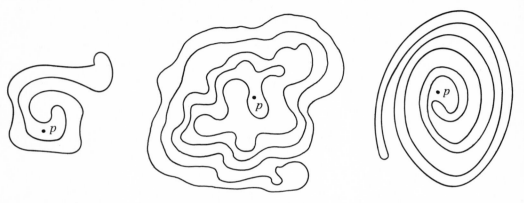

(c)   Based on the results of parts (a) and (b), state a test that can be used to determine whether a point is inside or outside a simple closed curve.

(d)   Did you arrive at your answer to part (c) by inductive or deductive reasoning?

5. Determine which of the following regions are simply connected and which are not.

(a)   (b)   (c)

(d)   (e)   (f)

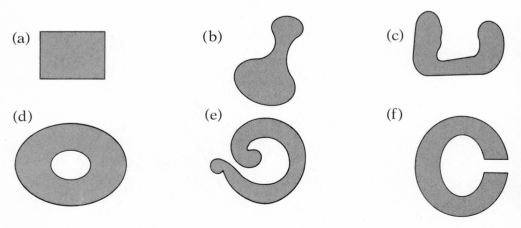

In this application you will have an opportunity to create and use a most unusual topological surface. The demonstration will require that you have three strips of paper, each about 1 inch wide and 11 inches long. You'll also need a small amount of tape and a scissors.

Möbius Strips

6. (a) Take one of the strips. How many sides does it have? Bend the strip so that it forms a ring, but keep the ends about a half inch apart, holding both ends all the while. Now turn one of the ends over and tape it to the other end. The resulting band should resemble the one drawn at the right. This band is called a *Möbius strip*, after German mathematician A. F. Möbius, who devised it in 1858.

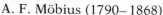

A. F. Möbius (1790–1868)

(b)   Beginning at any point halfway between the edges of the Möbius strip, draw a continuous line along the entire length of the strip. What do you notice? How many sides does the Möbius strip have?

(c)   Now use a scissors to cut all along the line you drew down the center of the Möbius strip. Describe the result.

(d)   Take another strip of paper and make another Möbius strip. Cut along the entire length of this one, too, but only about a third of the way from an edge. What is the result?

(e)   Make another Möbius strip. Suppose an ant begins at a point in the center of the Möbius strip and walks all the way around it. Relative to its position when it began, what is its position when it returns to the starting point?

Courtesy of Escher Foundation, Haags Gemeentemuseum, The Hague

Möbius Strip II by M. C. Escher

Möbius strips are not only fascinating, they are also useful. Conveyor belts made like Möbius strips last longer and wear more uniformly than conventional belts since their entire surface is used. Magnetic recording tape can record nearly twice as much when made as a Möbius strip. Some electronic resistors are made as Möbius strips to permit greater variety of performance, stability, size, and shape.

The Four-Color Problem

On maps, different countries or different states are often colored differently so that no two bordering countries or states are the same color. The problem of finding the least number of colors needed to color any possible map was originally posed by A. F. Möbius in 1840. Until very recently, proof that four colors are sufficient to color any map had remained one of the classic unsolved problems of mathematics. A proof of the four-color conjecture was suggested in 1879 by A. B. Kempe, but it required the analysis of so many maps that the approach was abandoned. However, in 1976, Kenneth Appel and Wolfgang Haken of the University of Illinois, using a computer for calculations, completed the first correct proof of the four-color conjecture. Their proof uses "networks," so additional comments on that proof will be made in the next section, where networks are explained.

7. Study each of the following maps to determine the least number of different colors that are needed to color it so that no two bordering regions have the same color.

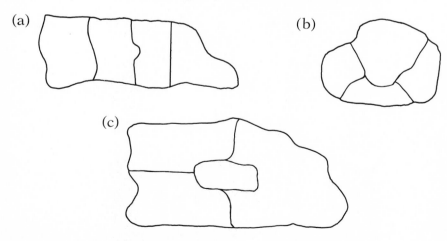

(a)

(b)

(c)

(d)   The counties of Vermont

(e)   The countries of Europe

(f)   The counties of New Mexico

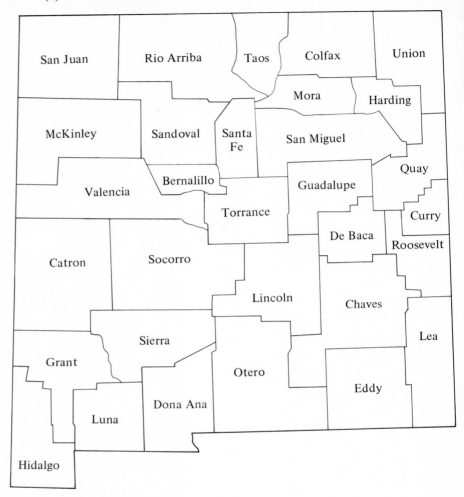

NETWORKS

The development of the branch of topology known as *network theory* began in 1735, when the great Swiss mathematician Leonhard Euler derived techniques to solve the problem of the seven bridges of Königsberg, Prussia. Let us look at the bridge problem and at Euler's approach to solving it.

A river flows through the city of Königsberg. As a result, the city exists as land on both sides of the river and two islands in the river. There are seven bridges crossing the river, as shown in the sketch. The land masses are labeled A, B, C, and D in the drawing and they are shaded.

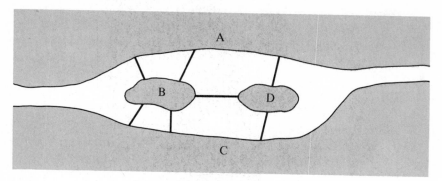

According to Euler: "The question is whether a person can plan a walk in such a way that he will cross each of these bridges once but not more than once."

Before we examine Euler's solution, spend a few minutes seeing if you can find a path that leads you across each bridge exactly once.

Many people believed there was no solution, but none could prove it. Leonhard Euler developed network theory in order to prove that indeed there is no solution. He used points (we'll call them *vertices*) to represent each land mass and lines (we'll call them *edges*) to represent each bridge. Here then is the *network* of edges and vertices that represents the Königsberg drawing.

Leonhard Euler
(1707–1783)

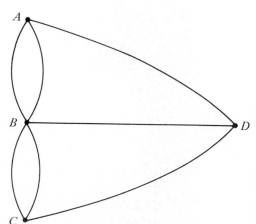

The problem is to determine whether you can begin at some vertex and draw this entire network without lifting your pencil off the paper or retracing any edge. A network that can be drawn in this way is said to be *traversable*.

If a vertex has an odd number of edges associated with it (a so-called *odd vertex*), then the number of edges entering it cannot equal the number of edges leaving it. (In drawing the network, think of the first edge drawn to a vertex as an edge which enters that vertex. Then the second edge drawn will leave the vertex. A third edge would enter, and so on.) So any odd vertex must be either the starting point or the ending point. Why? Because if the vertex has an odd number of edges, then either it has one more edge entering than leaving (which makes the vertex an ending point) or else it has one more edge leaving than entering (which makes the vertex a starting point). Furthermore, there can be only one starting point and one ending point. So if more than two of the vertices A, B, C, D are odd, then some retracing is necessary. Vertex A has three edges, vertex B has five edges, vertex C has three edges, and vertex D has three edges. Clearly, more than two of the vertices have an odd number of edges. Thus, the network cannot be drawn without retracing. This means there is no solution to the Königsberg bridge problem.

The preceding discussion leads to a more extensive theorem for networks. It is a theorem for connected networks. A network is *connected* if it is possible to get from any vertex to any other vertex by moving along the edges of the network.

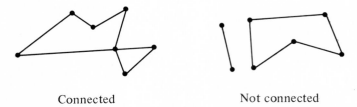

Connected   Not connected

The theorem states that *a connected network is traversable if it has exactly two odd vertices or if it has no odd vertices; otherwise it is not traversable.* You will see examples of this theorem in Exercise 1.

Today, the study of networks and related theory has been expanded, leading to many practical applications. Managers often have networks that represent both time and interrelationships of the many resources scheduled for a project; and for proper planning, organization, and optimization of resources, they need to know the longest and shortest paths through that network. In the area of communications, both the telephone company and large corporations using leased telephone lines are concerned about the shortest paths and least-cost paths from one point (city) to another. A manufacturer may want to know where to locate new plants and warehouses in order to minimize the cost of shipping raw materials to plants and finished products from plants to warehouses, wholesalers, and customers. The theory can also be applied to study processes in chemistry, electronics, and aeronautics. Most problems solved by network theory involve so many points and such volumes of data that their solution would not be practical without the use of modern computers.

As the previous section noted, the four-color problem posed in 1840 was solved only recently. In their solution, Appel and Haken converted maps to networks and determined that 1936 different networks were enough to cover all possible cases. Each case was pursued on a computer, taking a total of about 1200 hours of computer time, with the computer making more decisions and doing more calculations than any human could in a lifetime. In terms of networks, the statement that four colors are sufficient to color the regions of a map becomes "four colors are sufficient to color the vertices of any network, so that no two vertices connected by an edge are the same color." The following illustration shows how a map can be redrawn as a network. To enable you to visualize the transition from map to network, the regions (which become vertices) are numbered and the borders (which become edges) are lettered.

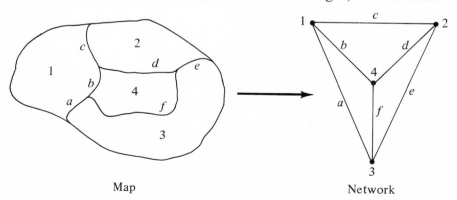

Map   Network

1. Examine each of these networks and answer the questions that follow.

(i)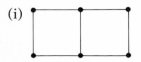

(ii)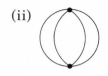

(iii)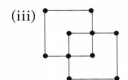

(iv)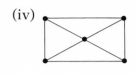

(v)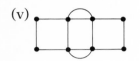

(vi)

(vii)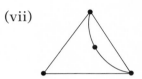

(viii)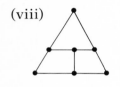

(ix)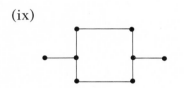

(x)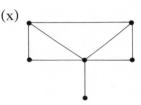

(a) Classify each network as type I, type II, or type III.

Type I: More than two vertices have an odd number of edges.

Type II: Exactly two vertices have an odd number of edges.

Type III: All vertices have an even number of edges.

(b) Which networks of type I can be drawn without retracing or lifting your pencil?

(c) Which networks of type II can be drawn without retracing or lifting your pencil? Does it matter where you begin? Explain. Can you predict where you will end based on where you begin? Explain.

(d) Which networks of type III can be drawn without retracing or lifting your pencil? Does it matter where you begin? Explain. Can you predict where you will end based on where you begin? Explain.

2. Those who feel sorry for the people of Königsberg (now named Kaliningrad) should find some consolation in knowing that an eighth bridge was built in 1935. So now we have the Kaliningrad bridge problem. Draw the network and determine whether all of the bridges can be crossed exactly once.

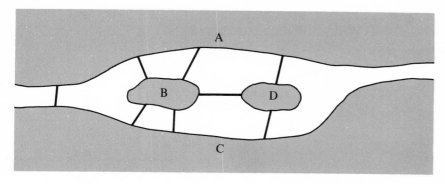

3. Early in this century, Shango children of the Congo area (now Zaire) were observed studying networks they constructed in the sand. The observer, Emil Torday, a Belgian, was asked to draw each of the figures (shown here) in the sand without lifting his finger or retracing.

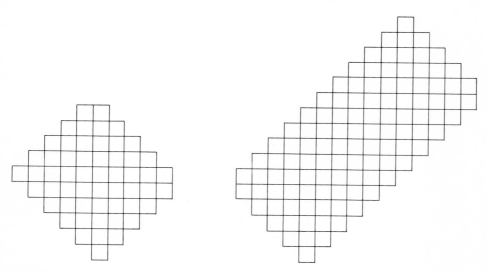

Consider each network. Determine whether or not they can be drawn without retracing, and justify your conclusion.

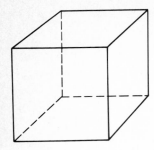

4. The cube drawn here forms a network in three dimensions. (Three-dimensional networks will be pursued in the next section.)
  (a) How many vertices does it have?
  (b) How many edges are associated with each vertex?
  (c) Can this network be drawn without retracing or lifting your pencil? Explain.

5. The following incident from the history of mathematics will seem unrelated to networks, but the formula we obtain will be applied to networks in Application 6. When the German mathematician Carl Friedrich Gauss was a young schoolchild, his teacher gave him and the rest of his class the task of adding up all of the integers from 1 to 100.

$$1 + 2 + 3 + \cdots + 98 + 99 + 100$$

Gauss noticed a shortcut; the 100 numbers could be grouped as 50 pairs of numbers, the sum of which is 101 for each pair. So the sum of all 100 numbers is $50 \cdot 101$, which is 5050.

$$
\left.
\begin{array}{r}
1 + 100 = 101 \\
2 + 99 = 101 \\
3 + 98 = 101 \\
\cdot \\
\cdot \\
\cdot \\
50 + 51 = 101
\end{array}
\right\}
\quad
\begin{array}{l}
\text{The sum of these is} \\
50 \cdot 101, \text{ which is } 5050
\end{array}
$$

  (a) Use a Gauss-type shortcut to determine the sum of the integers from 1 to 50.
  (b) Use a Gauss-type shortcut to determine the sum of the integers from 1 to 80.
  (c) There is a pattern in the products that result from finding the sum of the integers from 1 to n by Gauss's shortcut. Observe the results we have so far.

$$1 + 2 + 3 + \cdots + 100 = 50(101)$$
$$1 + 2 + 3 + \cdots + 50 = 25(51)$$
$$1 + 2 + 3 + \cdots + 80 = 40(81)$$

Now fill in the blanks below, based on the pattern.

$$1 + 2 + 3 + \cdots + 60 = \underline{\hspace{1.5cm}}$$
$$1 + 2 + 3 + \cdots + 200 = \underline{\hspace{1.5cm}}$$

(d)   Are your answers to part (c) based on inductive or deductive reasoning?

(e)   Fill in the blank with the expression representing the sum of the integers from 1 to n.

$$1 + 2 + 3 + \cdots + n = \underline{\hspace{2cm}}$$

This formula will be used in Application 6, a network application.

6.   It is impractical to have separate, direct telephone connections between all of the residents of a town. To do so it would require millions of separate lines. Instead, telephone companies use switching systems in order to reduce the number of separate phone lines needed. With a switching system, only one line per customer is required. Let's investigate why the number of separate lines would be so large.

(a)   If there are only two phones in town, how many lines are needed?

(b)   If there are three phones in town, how many lines are needed so that each phone has a separate, direct connection to each other phone?

(c)   If there are four phones, then six lines are needed in order to provide each phone with a separate, direct connection to each other phone. This can be seen in the network drawing here.

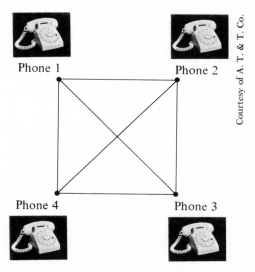

Phone 1   Phone 2

Courtesy of A. T. & T. Co.

Phone 4   Phone 3

You can count the six lines. There are three lines from

phone 1, two other lines from phone 2, and one other line from phone 3. Thus,

$$4 \text{ phones:} \quad 3 + 2 + 1 = 6 \text{ lines}$$

With five phones, the network is

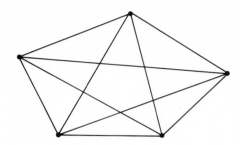

Verify that the number of lines for five phones is $4 + 3 + 2 + 1$, which adds up to 10.

(d) Draw the network for six phones. The number of lines needed is ____ + ____ + ____ + ____ + ____, which adds up to ____.

(e) Use Gauss's formula from Exercise 5, part (e), to determine (without any drawing or adding) how many lines are needed for ten phones. *Note:* based on Exercise 6, parts (a)–(d), you should use 9 for n when there are 10 phones.

(f) How many lines are needed for 1001 phones? Perhaps it is now apparent that it is impractical to have separate, direct phone connections between all residents of a town. A town of 10,000 phones would require approximately 50 million separate lines. (You might want to verify that.) With a switching system, only 10,000 lines are needed.

Note now the extension of the previous application to Exercises 7 and 8.

7. In a round-robin baseball tournament, each team plays each other team once. If 31 teams are entered, how many games will be played?

8. There are 71 people in a room. Each person shakes hands exactly once with each other person. How many handshakes occur in all?

9. Change each map to a network. The regions of each map are numbered for reference.

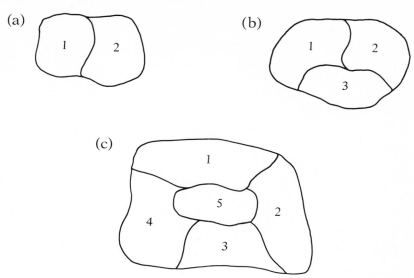

(a)

(b)

(c)

POLYHEDRA AND NETWORKS

The study of special solid figures called regular polyhedra is often included under the heading of topology. Such figures can be considered three-dimensional networks, as noted in Application 4 on page 248.

A *regular polyhedron* is a solid with faces that are all regular polygons of the same size and type. (Regular polygons were presented in Chapter 1, beginning on page 49.) A die is an example of a regular polyhedron with six faces (or sides), each of which is a square. There are five different kinds of regular polyhedra, and each is named according to the number of faces it has. The cube is called a hexahedron because it has six faces ("hexa-" means six). A tetrahedron has four faces ("tetra-" means four), each of which is an equilateral (regular) triangle. An octahedron has eight faces ("octa-" means eight), each of which is an equilateral triangle. A dodecahedron has 12 faces ("dodeca-" means 12), each of which is a regular pentagon. An icosahedron has 20 faces ("icosa-" means 20), each of which is an equilateral triangle. The Greek prefixes hexa-, tetra-, octa-, dodeca-, and icosa- are used together with the Greek stem

A die

Prefix	Faces
Tetra	4
Hexa	6
Octa	8
Dodeca	12
Icosa	20

Tetrahedron

Hexahedron

Octahedron

Dodecahedron

Icosahedron

"hedra" (meaning face) because regular polyhedra were first studied by the Greeks more than 2000 years ago. The regular polyhedra are also called *Platonic solids*, after Plato, who believed that atoms had such shapes.

In 1640, French mathematician René Descartes discovered a formula relating the number of vertices (V), faces (F), and edges (E) of a given regular polyhedron.

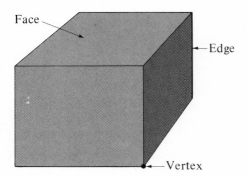

Face

Edge

Vertex

Study the following table and see if you can discover the formula.

Polyhedron	V	F	E
Tetrahedron	4	4	6
Hexahedron	8	6	12
Octahedron	6	8	12
Dodecahedron	20	12	30
Icosahedron	12	20	30

In 1757, Leonhard Euler proved the formula that shows the relationship between the vertices, faces, and edges of any polyhedron (not just regular polyhedra). That formula is $V + F = E + 2$. There are several equivalent ways of writing it (such as $V + F - E = 2$, for example). Were you able to discover this formula from the table? Euler also used the formula to prove that there are only five regular polyhedra.

The section on mineralogy graphs (pages 163–170) explained the use of equilateral triangle graphs to represent the composition of minerals consisting of three compounds. If, however, the mineral consists of four compounds, then an extra dimension must be added. The resulting graph is a tetrahedron. Illustrated next is a tetrahedron graph that can be used to represent common types of sediments, each consisting of the compounds carbonate, chert, clay, and quartz.

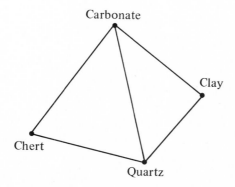

1. Here are patterns for making your own polyhedra. Trace the patterns, fold on the dotted lines, and then use tape along the edges.

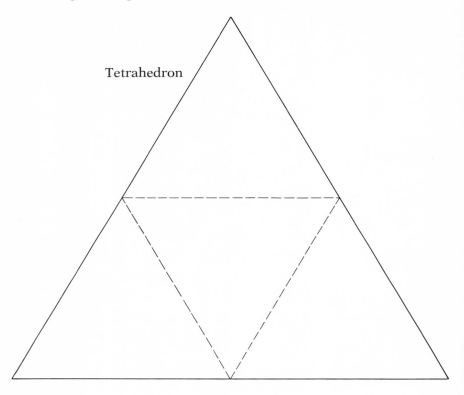

Tetrahedron

Hexahedron

Octahedron

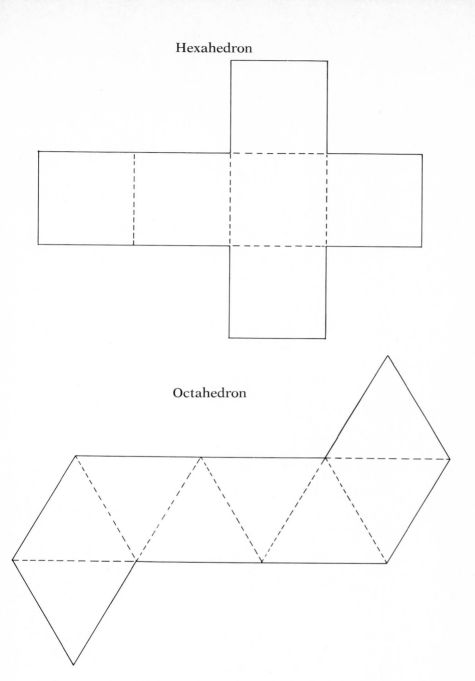

Dodecahedron

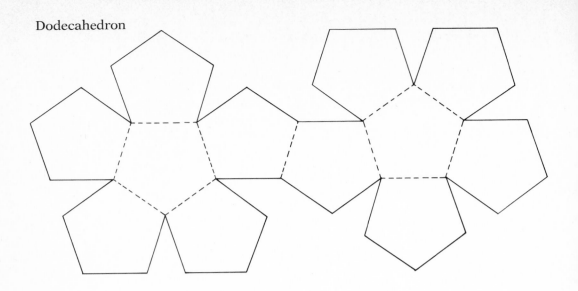

Icosahedron

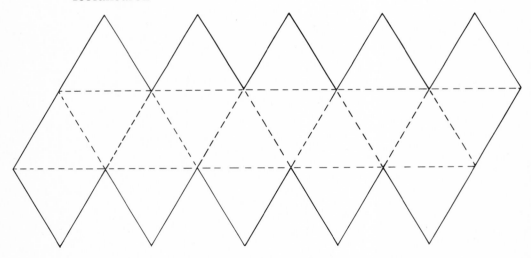

2. In the following illustration, face I can be used to represent minerals composed of carbonate, chert, and quartz. Face II can be used to represent minerals composed of carbonate, clay, and quartz. If we call the base of the tetrahedron face III and the fourth face IV, then what composition of minerals can be represented by face III and what composition can be represented by face IV?

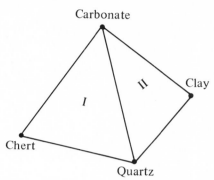

3. For each regular polyhedron, compare the number of edges with the number of sides of all faces considered as separate polygons. What is the relationship? The polyhedra you made in Exercise 1 should be useful here.

Polyhedron	Edges	Sides of all faces
Tetrahedron	6	12
Hexahedron		
Octahedron		
Dodecahedron		
Icosahedron		

4. Suppose one face is removed from any of the regular polyhedra.

(a) Does the number of edges change?
(b) Does the number of vertices change?
(c) Write a variation of Euler's polyhedra formula for all polyhedra that have had one face removed.

5. You have noticed the use of the network terms vertices and edges in this section on polyhedra. Polyhedra can be considered three-dimensional networks (see Application 4 on page 248). If one face of a hexahedron is removed, it can be displayed as a two-dimensional network. The five remaining faces are labeled 1 through 5 in the illustration here.

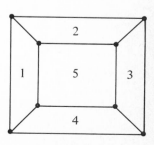

Since both two and three-dimensional figures can be displayed as networks, we can see that our definition of face does not have to be restricted to three-dimensional figures. In view of this, we might redefine the word face within a network setting, and say that a *face* is the region bounded by two or more edges.

(a) How many faces are in each of the following networks?

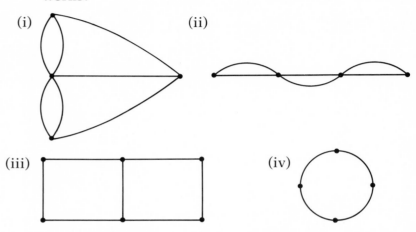

(i)   (ii)

(iii)   (iv)

(b) Complete the table and try to determine a formula that relates vertices, faces, and edges for networks.

Network	V	F	E
i		4	
ii		3	
iii		2	
iv		1	

If you have done this correctly, the formula obtained should be the same as that determined previously in Application 4, part (c).

6. Construct a network satisfying each set of conditions.
   (a) 2 vertices, 1 face, 2 edges
   (b) 2 vertices, 2 faces, 3 edges
   (c) 4 vertices, 1 face, 4 edges
   (d) 3 vertices, 2 faces, 4 edges

(e)   4 vertices, 3 faces, 6 edges
(f)   5 vertices, 4 faces, 8 edges

7. Do all the networks of Exercise 6 satisfy $V + F = E + 1$?

Topological graphs are used to represent chemical structures **Hamilton circuits**
so that the latter can be analyzed in terms of the individual
atoms that make up a molecule. The vertices of such graphs
represent atoms. The edges represent the chemical bonds
between the atoms. Such graphs are called *Hamilton circuits.*
    A *Hamilton circuit* is a graph in which it is possible to make a
round trip that crosses each vertex exactly once. Hamilton's
original circuit (shown here) was proposed as a game in which
each vertex represented a city that a round-the-world traveler
would wish to visit only once.

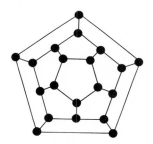

8. (a)   How many vertices does the Hamilton circuit have?
  (b)   How many edges does the Hamilton circuit have?
  (c)   How many faces does the circuit have?
  (d)   Check that this network does indeed satisfy the for-
        mula obtained in Exercise 4, part (c). (That formula is
        $V + F = E + 1$.)
  (e)   Verify that this network is indeed a Hamilton circuit
        by making an appropriate round trip.

CATASTROPHE THEORY

This chapter concludes with an excursion into a truly modern branch of topology, one that has the potential to be applied
to many areas of biological and social sciences.

René Thom

Catastrophe theory was originated in the 1960s by French mathematician René Thom. It is applied in those situations where gradually changing forces or motivations lead to abrupt changes in behavior. This is why the subject is called catastrophe theory.

We will use a model of aggression in dogs to illustrate this theory. It has been observed that agressive behavior in dogs is influenced by two conflicting drives—rage and fear. Rage can be measured by the extent to which a dog bares its teeth. Fear can be measured by the extent to which a dog's ears are flattened back.

If only one of these conflicting drives is present, the response of the dog is predictable. An enraged dog will growl, or possibly even attack. A frightened dog will be shy, or possibly even retreat or run away.

However, if the dog feels both rage and fear at the same time, it will not remain indifferent. These are conflicting rather than neutralizing factors. The chances are very good that the dog will either attack or flee. A model of aggression is used to provide a basis for predicting just which behavior the dog will choose under all possible conditions.

The following drawing is used to illustrate a model of aggression. The letter N is used to represent the original point of neutrality on the surface. This is the origin. Increase in fear is shown (see arrow) in one direction—downward and to the left—and the dog's reaction varies from avoidance to retreat. Increase in rage is shown (see arrow) in a different direction—upward and to the right—and the dog's reaction varies from growling to attacking. The gray shaded fold represents neutrality, and its position is between rage and fear in terms of the height of the illustration.

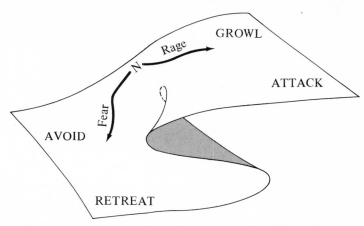

If a frightened dog is angered, its rage increases (see X in the next drawing) and its behavior follows a so-called attack catastrophe, shown next. Notice the jump or catastrophe (see Y in the diagram) in going from the lowest surface (fear) to the highest surface (rage) without ever using the smooth transition of the shaded neutral surface in between.

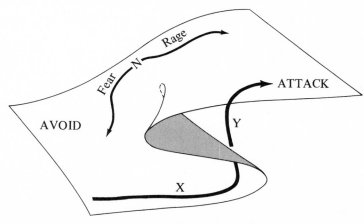

An Attack Catastrophe

If an angered dog is frightened, its fear increases (see X in the diagram) and its behavior follows a so-called flight catastrophe (that is, it flees). Note the fall or catastrophe in going directly from the highest surface (rage) to the lowest surface (fear).

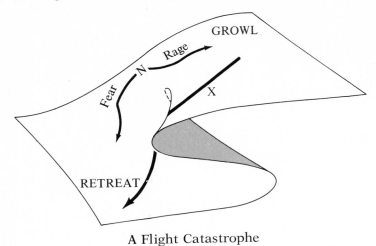

A Flight Catastrophe

A dog that is simultaneously enraged and frightened will likely either attack (see path 1 in the next diagram) or retreat (path 2), depending on the relative amounts of rage and fear it experiences.

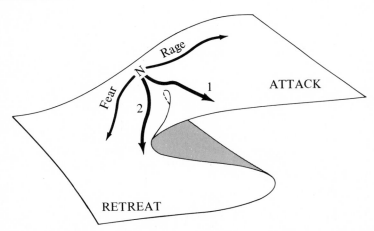

The basic illustration used throughout this section is an example of an "elementary catastrophe" classified as the *cusp catastrophe*. There are several other such elementary catastrophes, each with folds and slopes different from the cusp catastrophe. They are swallowtail, butterfly, fold, hyperbolic umbilic, elliptic umbilic, and parabolic umbilic.

Catastrophe theory can be used to explain rainbow formation, analyze bridge collapses, predict prison riots, and explain the shape development of living organisms. Each elementary catastrophe can be associated with a complex mathematical model of a situation. Statistical data, behavioral data—in fact, all factors involved in a given situation—must be considered in order to obtain a useful computerized mathematical model.

APPLICATIONS AND EXERCISES

1. Describe in words the catastrophe suggested in the following illustration.

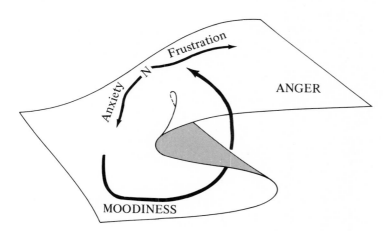

2. Suppose that the anxiety in Application 1 is caused by studying for a final exam. Which of the following are likely to cause catastrophic relief from the moodiness and thus a return to normal mood?
   (i)   Passing the exam
   (ii) Failing the exam
   (iii) Having the exam postponed
   (iv) Being excused from the exam

3. The next illustration represents the weight-loss diets many people try. Describe in words what the drawing suggests.

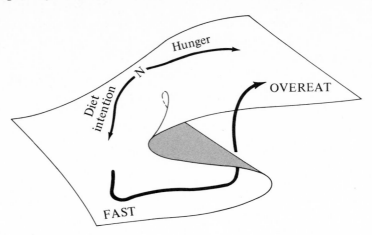

4. The following illustration shows a catastrophe commonly known as a stock market crash. Describe in words what the drawing indicates. Be sure to make reference to increase and/or decrease in demand and speculation. Include pertinent comments on price increases and decreases.

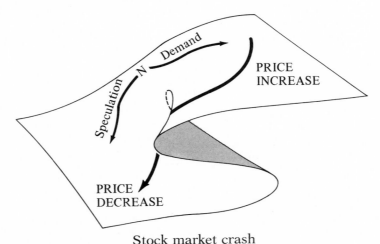

Stock market crash

5. After stock market crashes there have always been smooth recoveries, that is, price increases without any catastrophic jump. Draw such a recovery on the surface shown on the next page. Begin at X. Assume all labels are the same as in Application 4.

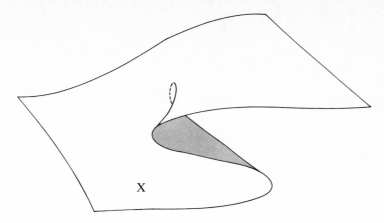

X

6. Shown here are two other forms of catastrophes—the fold and the swallowtail. Can you guess by their shape which is which?

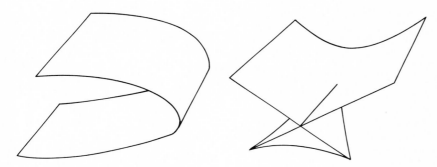

7. The hyperbolic umbilic, elliptic umbilic, and parabolic umbilic catastrophes are three-dimensional curves based roughly on some two-dimensional conic sections studied in Chapter 4 (pages 188–204). Name the conic section that corresponds to each of these three catastrophes.

Introduction to Analysis

6

Analysis is the branch of mathematics that includes calculus and its extensions. It can provide the key to understanding relationships, because analysis offers clear, concise, and quantitative means of expressing relationships and the way they change. The application of algebra and geometry to the study of analysis will become apparent as you read through this chapter. First, you'll be introduced to some of the notation of analysis and the application of that notation. Then, sections on slopes and limits will set the stage for a discussion of calculus.

NOTATION

In earlier chapters of this book we encountered relationships between two variables, such as $y = 2x + 1$. In Chapter 4 we used values for x to obtain corresponding values for y. In this way we obtained points of the form (x, y) to plot. Then we were able to pass a straight line through those points.

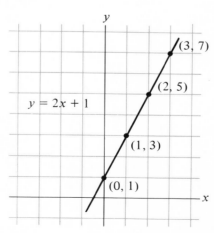

x	$y = 2x + 1$	(x, y)
0	$y = 2(0) + 1$	$(0, 1)$
1	$y = 2(1) + 1$	$(1, 3)$
2	$y = 2(2) + 1$	$(2, 5)$
3	$y = 2(3) + 1$	$(3, 7)$

Leonhard Euler suggested that some relations, such as $y = 2x + 1$, be called "functions" and be written using notation such as $f(x) = 2x + 1$ for some applications. Similarly, $y = x^2$ might be written as $f(x) = x^2$. Besides f, other letters are often used to name functions. The letters f, g, F, and G are popular. You will see the use of appropriate function names in the sections of examples that follow this introduction to function notation.

If you compare this function notation with the earlier notation, you will see that y is simply replaced by $f(x)$. This suggests that $y = f(x)$. So for graphing purposes, (x, y) becomes $(x, f(x))$, and $f(x)$ can be thought of as the second coordinate when the first coordinate is x.

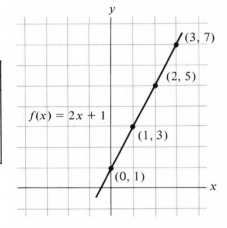

x	$f(x) = 2x + 1$	$(x, f(x))$
0	$f(x) = 2(0) + 1$	$(0, 1)$
1	$f(x) = 2(1) + 1$	$(1, 3)$
2	$f(x) = 2(2) + 1$	$(2, 5)$
3	$f(x) = 2(3) + 1$	$(3, 7)$

Function notation suggests a rule of correspondence between the two coordinates. For any first coordinate x supplied, f explains how to obtain the second coordinate $f(x)$. In $f(x) = 2x + 1$, the second coordinate $f(x)$ is obtained by multiplying the first coordinate by 2 and then adding 1. Suppose x is replaced by 5. Then

$$f(x) = 2x + 1$$

becomes

$$f(5) = 2(5) + 1$$

or

$$f(5) = 11$$

The statement "$f(5) = 11$" includes the idea that "if x is 5, then y is 11." It also expresses clearly that 11 corresponds to 5. It says that the value of the function f at 5 is 11. Here is another example. If

$$g(x) = x^2 + 3$$

then

$$g(4) = 4^2 + 3 = 19$$

and

$$g(0) = 0^2 + 3 = 3$$

Another way of visualizing $g(x) = x^2 + 3$ is

$$x \xrightarrow{\ g\ } x^2 + 3$$

which shows that the function g takes any number supplied for x and transforms it into the number $x^2 + 3$. From the examples above with $g(x) = x^2 + 3$, we see that

$$4 \xrightarrow{\ g\ } 19 \qquad \text{and} \qquad 0 \xrightarrow{\ g\ } 3$$

APPLICATIONS AND EXERCISES

1. Although f and g are the most common function names, other letters are used when appropriate. For example, the expression $5x$ represents the total *cost* in dollars of x items that cost \$5 per item. An appropriate name here for the cost function is C. We might write $C(x) = 5x$. For each of the following settings select an appropriate letter to name the function and write it using function notation.

   (a) The distance a dropped object travels in t seconds is $16t^2$.

   (b) The number of bacteria after t seconds is 2^t.

   (c) The amount of money earned in n hours is $4n$ dollars.

2. In Chapter 1 we noted that Galileo determined a formula, $d = t^2$, that gives the distance d in feet that a dropped object will fall in t *quarter seconds.*

(a) Consider $d = f(t)$ and write $d = t^2$ using function notation.

(b) What is the meaning of $f(5)$ in this physical setting?

(c) Determine the value of $f(5)$; that is, what is the value of f at 5?

(d) How far does the object travel in $2\frac{1}{2}$ *seconds?*

(e) Determine the value of $f(0)$.

(f) What is the meaning of $f(0)$ in this physical setting?

3. Write the function $x \xrightarrow{g} 5x + 1$ in function notation without using an arrow.

4. For each function obtain a few points of the form $(x, f(x))$ and sketch the graph.

(a) The line $f(x) = x - 1$

(b) The line $f(x) = 3x + 2$

(c) The line $f(x) = -2x + 3$

5. When regular polygons were illustrated in Chapter 1, you may have noticed that the more sides a polygon has, the larger are its interior angles. For example, compare interior angles θ of the polygons drawn here. The number of degrees (call it D) of each interior angle of a regular polygon of n sides is given by the function

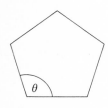

$$D(n) = \frac{n - 2}{n} \cdot 180°$$

Use this function to determine the number of degrees in each interior angle of the following regular polygons: triangle, rectangle, pentagon, hexagon, octagon.

6. All the examples and exercises thus far have dealt with functions of *one* variable. Consider the following example of a function of *two* variables. You sell m radios at \$25 each and n televisions at \$400 each. So your total revenue from these sales is $25m$ dollars plus $400n$ dollars, or $25m + 400n$ dollars. If R is used to represent total revenue, then

$$R(m, n) = 25m + 400n$$

shows revenue as a function of the two variables m and n.

(a) Determine the value of $R(10, 3)$. What does it mean in this setting?

(b) What number should be placed after the arrow below?

$$4, 7 \xrightarrow{R}$$

7. It costs a manufacturer x dollars each to produce bicycles. He sells them to stores for $x + 15$ dollars each. The store then sells them at twice what it paid, namely, $2(x + 15)$ dollars each. If m is the function that shows what the manufacturer does to the price and s is the function that shows what the store does to the price, then we have

$$x \xrightarrow{m} x + 15$$

and

$$x + 15 \xrightarrow{s} 2(x + 15)$$

This can also be stated as

$$m(x) = x + 15$$

and

$$s(x + 15) = 2(x + 15)$$

Since $x + 15$ is the same as $m(x)$, the function

$$s(x + 15) = 2(x + 15)$$

is the same as

$$s(m(x)) = 2(x + 15)$$

The function $s(m(x)) = 2(x + 15)$ is an example of a *composite function*. It shows the effect of two functions on a variable. It is a function of a function.

(a) Consider $s(m(30))$. How much does this indicate that it costs the manufacturer to produce a bicycle? How much does the store pay for it? How much does the store sell it for?

(b)   Suppose $g(x) = 2x$ and $f(x) = x + 1$. Write the composite function $f(g(x))$. Write the composite function $g(f(x))$. What is the value of $f(g(5))$? What is the value of $g(f(5))$?

MATHEMATICAL LINGUISTICS

All languages share some structural properties, and these properties can be described mathematically. The application of mathematics to the study of the structure of languages is called *mathematical linguistics*. In this section we will see functions that involve words and phrases, rather than numbers.

A language can be considered a set of elementary sentences together with a set of *transformations*, or functions. An elementary sentence is usually a combination of noun and verb, such as "Robert talks." The functions combine these elementary sentences with other elementary sentences or words to produce complex sentences. Thus functions extend the language, perhaps in the same manner in which the language developed originally.

Consider the construction of a complex sentence from two elementary sentences and a series of transformations. Let $S_1 =$ *Ken walks* and $S_2 =$ *Sue walks* be two elementary sentences. We'll construct the sentence "Ken and Sue walk to school" by using a series of transformations. First, let t_1 be the transformation in which S_1 and S_2 are combined by using the conjunction "and" to produce a new sentence S_3. Abstractly, this can be considered as

$$S_1, S_2 \xrightarrow{\ t_1\ } S_3$$

or as

$$S_3 = t_1(S_1, S_2)$$

The new sentence S_3 is "Ken walks and Sue walks." The redundant use of the word "walks" can be eliminated by another transformation, t_2. When applied to S_3, the result is a new sentence, S_4. That sentence is "Ken and Sue walks." The transformation t_2 can be considered as $S_3 \xrightarrow{t_2} S_4$ or as $S_4 = t_2(S_3)$.

The word "walks" must be changed to "walk" for plural usage here. This is accomplished by another transformation (call it t_3). The result is the new sentence S_5: "Ken and Sue walk."

One final transformation t_4 can be used to obtain the desired sentence S_6: "Ken and Sue walk to school." This final transformation adds the phrase "to school" to S_5. Thus, $S_6 = t_4(S_5)$.

This example showed the use of four different types of transformations (or functions):

t_1:   Insert conjunction between two elementary sentences.

t_2:   Eliminate redundant verb.

t_3:   Change form of verb from singular to plural.

t_4:   Add prepositional phrase.

The chain of transformations can be expressed as

$$S_1, S_2 \xrightarrow{t_1} \xrightarrow{t_2} \xrightarrow{t_3} \xrightarrow{t_4} S_6$$

or as the composite function

$$S_6 = t_4(t_3(t_2(t_1(S_1, S_2))))$$

APPLICATIONS AND EXERCISES

---

1. (a) Let S_1 = *Ellen studies* and S_2 = *Don works*. Use a transformation t_1 that will produce the sentence "Ellen studies and Don works." Call that sentence S_3.

   (b) Now use a transformation t_2 that will produce S_4 from S_3, where S_4 is the sentence "Today Ellen studies and Don works."

   (c) In part (a), $t_1(S_1, S_2)$ produces the sentence "Ellen studies and Don works." What would $t_1(S_2, S_1)$ produce?

2. Let S_1 = *Father mows* and S_2 = *Son mows* be elementary sentences.

    (a) Use a transformation t_1 that will produce the sentence "Father mows the lawn." Call that sentence S_3.

    (b) Use a transformation t_2 that will produce the sentence "The father mows the lawn" from S_3. Call this new sentence S_4.

    (c) If t_1 is applied to S_2, what sentence results; that is, what is $t_1(S_2)$? Once you obtain it, call it S_5.

    (d) Use a transformation t_3 that will produce the sentence S_6: "His son mows the lawn" from the sentence S_5: "Son mows the lawn."

    (e) Let t_4 be a transformation that inserts "or" between two sentences. Write in words the sentence S_7 created as $S_7 = t_4(S_4, S_6)$. Assume S_4 and S_6 are the sentences mentioned earlier in this exercise.

    (f) Use a transformation to change the sentence "The father mows the lawn or his son mows the lawn" to "The father or his son mows the lawn." Describe the transformation used.

    (g) Use sentences S_1 and S_2 to build the sentence "The father and his son mow the lawn." List the transformations used.

3. Use the two elementary sentences below and all of the transformations (in any order you prefer) to build a complex sentence.

S_1 = Gary must be ill.

S_2 = Gary would have missed the party.

    t_1: Insert conjunction "or" between two sentences.

    t_2: Negate a sentence by inserting the word "not."

    t_3: Change a proper noun (person's name) to a pronoun (he, she, etc.)

    t_4: Add the prepositional phrase "at Bill's house."

4. Begin with the complex sentence "Ken and Sue walk to school" and break it down into two elementary sentences by defining and then applying transformations that will reverse the process studied in this section. Such transforma-

tions are called *inverses* of the original transformations used to build the sentence.

5. Give an example of a sentence of infinite length, that is, one that continues indefinitely (having no "last" word). *Hint:* Let your sentence say something mathematical involving numbers.

TRANSFORMATIONAL GRAMMARS

The study of linguistic theory and description known as *transformational grammar* began in the 1950s and experienced a surge of interest in the 1960s. Now that computers have become a common and useful tool, interest in the transformational grammar approach to the practical problem of describing languages has been continually increasing. Many articles are published in linguistics journals and courses are offered at many universities. In this short section we cannot delve into the problems solved by the theory or into actual techniques used. However, we can present some of the basic notation and offer you a taste of this application of mathematics to the study of languages.

A *grammar* is a series of statements describing the underlying structure of a language. In this section, a grammar will consist of a set of symbols interrelated by a set of rules. Every rule is a transformation of the form

$$X \longrightarrow Y$$

which means "rewrite X as Y." The rules are applied in turn to the symbols of an *initial string* of symbols. Here is an example of a simple abstract grammar.

$$\text{Initial string:} \quad AB$$
$$\text{Rule 1:} \quad A \longrightarrow CD$$
$$\text{Rule 2:} \quad C \longrightarrow p$$
$$\text{Rule 3:} \quad D \longrightarrow q$$
$$\text{Rule 4:} \quad B \longrightarrow r$$

This grammar can be abbreviated as

$$AB$$
$$A \longrightarrow CD$$
$$C \longrightarrow p$$
$$D \longrightarrow q$$
$$B \longrightarrow r$$

When the rules of this grammar are applied to initial string AB, the resulting string produced, called a *derivation,* is pqr. How this is obtained is shown next in steps. First, *AB* becomes *CDB* (via $A \rightarrow CD$, which means A is rewritten as *CD*). Next, *CDB* becomes *pDB* (from $C \rightarrow p$), *pDB* becomes *pqB* (from $D \rightarrow q$), and *pqB* becomes *pqr* (from $B \rightarrow r$).

Perhaps you observed that there are no rules for changing p, q, and r. In other words, in this grammar the strings p, q, and r cannot appear to the left of an arrow. Appropriately then, they are called *terminal strings.*

This next example presents a simple grammar in which the resulting derivation is an ordinary English sentence rather than abstract symbols. See if you can determine the derivation produced when the following rules are applied to initial string *AB*.

$$AB$$
$$B \longrightarrow CD$$
$$A \longrightarrow \text{the}$$
$$C \longrightarrow \text{child}$$
$$D \longrightarrow \text{cries}$$

First, B becomes *CD*. So *AB* has become *ACD*. Then A becomes "the," C becomes "child," and D becomes "cries." Thus, in the end *AB* becomes "the child cries."

In practice, a grammar is not useful if only one sentence can be derived from it. Accordingly, the rewrite symbol → can suggest more than one replacement value. For example, $A →$ boy, girl, dog means that you can rewrite A as "boy" or as "girl" or as "dog." The following grammar suggests three different derivations.

$$AB$$
$$B \longrightarrow CD$$
$$A \longrightarrow \text{the}$$
$$C \longrightarrow \text{boy, girl, dog}$$
$$D \longrightarrow \text{runs}$$

Work out the derivations for each of the three possible replacement values of C in order to determine the three different terminal strings. The answers are (1) the boy runs, (2) the girl runs, (3) the dog runs.

The notation $A → B(C)$ means $A → B$ or $A → BC$, but not $A → C$. Thus, the grammar

$$DEFA$$
$$A \longrightarrow B(C)$$
$$D \longrightarrow \text{the}$$
$$E \longrightarrow \text{man, woman, cat}$$
$$F \longrightarrow \text{walks}$$
$$B \longrightarrow \text{home, away}$$
$$C \longrightarrow \text{quickly}$$

will yield derivations in which the word "quickly" is optional. Verify that among the derivations possible are (1) the man walks home, (2) the man walks home quickly, (3) the cat walks away quickly, and (4) the woman walks away. There are eight other derivations.

1. Write the derivation from each grammar.

   (a) AB
   $B \longrightarrow CD$
   $A \longrightarrow x$
   $C \longrightarrow y$
   $D \longrightarrow z$

   (b) A
   $A \longrightarrow BC$
   $B \longrightarrow DE$
   $C \longrightarrow t$
   $D \longrightarrow p$
   $E \longrightarrow m$

   (c) $ABAC$
   $A \longrightarrow DE$
   $B \longrightarrow p$
   $C \longrightarrow w$
   $D \longrightarrow x$
   $E \longrightarrow t$

   (d) $ABCD$
   $A \longrightarrow B$
   $B \longrightarrow C$
   $C \longrightarrow D$
   $D \longrightarrow x$

2. Write all possible derivations from each grammar.

   (a) ABC
   $A \longrightarrow DE$
   $B \longrightarrow F$
   $C \longrightarrow DG$
   $D \longrightarrow$ the
   $E \longrightarrow$ ant
   $F \longrightarrow$ climbs
   $G \longrightarrow$ hill

   (b) A
   $A \longrightarrow B$
   $B \longrightarrow ED$
   $D \longrightarrow CF$
   $C \longrightarrow$ is, isn't
   $E \longrightarrow$ today
   $F \longrightarrow$ warm, cold

(c) *AB*

$A \longrightarrow CD$

$C \longrightarrow EF$

$B \longrightarrow$ warm, hot, cold

$D \longrightarrow$ often, sometimes

$E \longrightarrow$ summer, winter

$F \longrightarrow$ is

3. Write all possible derivations from each grammar.

(a) *AB*

$B \longrightarrow C(D)$

$A \longrightarrow x, y, z$

$C \longrightarrow u, w$

$D \longrightarrow t$

(b) *ABC*

$A \longrightarrow F$

$B \longrightarrow GH$

$C \longrightarrow D(E)$

$H \longrightarrow$ fled, flew

$G \longrightarrow$ flea, bat

$F \longrightarrow$ a

$D \longrightarrow$ here, there

$E \longrightarrow$ yesterday

4. Write one grammar that uses only the words included in the following two derivations. The grammar will, of course, have other derivations. But no other words will appear in those derivations than the words given here.

One derivation: last night was beautiful

Another derivation: this afternoon is cold again

5. Determine the other eight derivations of the section-ending *DEFA* example.

MELODY GRAPHS

This section presents another application of the "correspondence" concept of functions. In this sense, functions can be used to describe music.

In music, the word pitch is used to mean the highness or lowness (but not the volume) of sounds. A melody is a succession of sounds, a succession of pitches. The melody occurs over a period of time. Accordingly, a graph with pitch and time as coordinates provides a visualization of music.

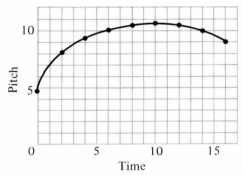

The graph of a melody

Compare this graph with the corresponding musical score, shown next, in which the large "dots" of the notes are "plotted" on the staff/measure line grid in a similar fashion.

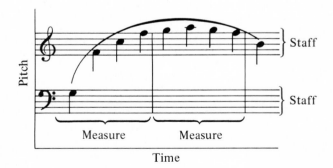

For any melody, there is a correspondence between time and pitch. At any specific time t, there is a specific pitch p.

$$t \longrightarrow p$$

Most music derives its effect from the use of simultaneous melodies that differ in pitch. In other words, more than one note (more than one pitch) is heard at a given time. For example, perhaps two pitches p_1 and p_2 correspond to a given time t.

Graphically, such music could be represented like this:

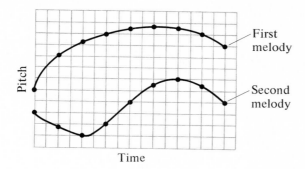

When two or more melodies occur simultaneously (as in the diagram here), the music is said to be *polyphonic*. When the melodies are similar but staggered in time, the music is called *imitative polyphonic*. Rounds of "Three Blind Mice" or "Row, Row, Row Your Boat," in which several people sing the same melody but start at staggered times, are examples of imitative polyphonic music.

APPLICATIONS AND EXERCISES

1. There is no break or gap in the smooth melody curve given at the beginning of the section. Mathematically, this suggests that there is a pitch for every time given.
   (a) Musically, what does this say about the melody?
   (b) Is this situation realistic for short intervals of time? Explain.
   (c) Is this realistic for longer intervals? Explain.

2. Make a graph showing the relationship between two imitative polyphonic melodies of your choice.

3. When two simultaneous melodies are different, the music is called *nonimitative polyphonic*. Label the music graphed here as imitative polyphonic or nonimitative polyphonic, and explain your answers.

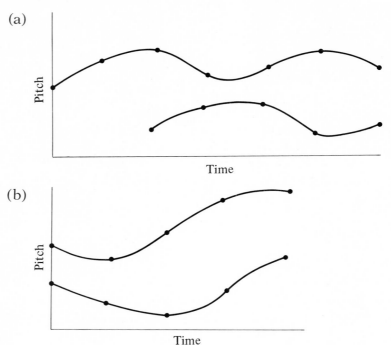

4. An acoustician uses a spectrograph to record sounds and study them. His interest is in the pitch, loudness, and duration of sounds—and these qualities cannot be determined merely by listening. The spectrogram (or graph) produced by a spectrograph is most useful in the analysis of sounds. In the following spectrogram, pitch is measured in the vertical direction, time is measured horizontally, and loudness is shown by the thickness of the lines. The music:

The corresponding spectrogram:

(a) Which sound (A, B, C, or D) has the highest pitch? Give a reason for your choice.
(b) Which sound has the longest duration? Explain your decision.
(c) Which sound is loudest? Explain your decision.

5. When two musical instruments are playing tones of different frequencies, a third tone of lower frequency may be heard. Its frequency is equal to the difference between the two frequencies being played. This phenomenon was first discovered independently by the German organist Sorge (in 1745) and the Italian violinist Tartini (1754). Suppose a flute plays F at a frequency of 1397 cycles per second (cps) and another flute plays A at a frequency of 880 cps. In this case, the third tone that results is a C. What is its frequency?

6. Experiments have shown that if two musical instruments are simultaneously playing different frequencies f_1 (the lower frequency) and f_2 (the higher frequency), some listeners may hear one or more subjective tones (tones heard by the listener but not actually played). The Tartini tones of frequency $f_2 - f_1$ were discussed in Application 5. Other, less prominent tones are those of frequency $f_1 + f_2$, $2 \cdot f_1$, and $2 \cdot f_2$. Assume f_1 is 300 cps and f_2 is 500 cps. What then are the frequencies of the four possible subjective tones?

7. The sounds of two different instruments playing the same note can be distinguished because of the difference in *tone color*. When a note is played on an instrument, our ears identify the basic note, called the *fundamental* frequency, and several additional frequencies, called *overtones*. Each instrument has its own pattern of strength and weakness among its overtones, and this pattern accounts for its distinctive tone color. A trombone may sound a tone having a fundamental frequency of $f = 220$ cps. The frequencies of the overtones are $2 \cdot f$, $3 \cdot f$, $4 \cdot f$, $5 \cdot f$, and $6 \cdot f$. Express each overtone in cycles per second.

8. Very often the frequencies of overtones are multiples of the fundamental, as they were in Application 7. In such cases, the fundamental and the overtones are together called *harmonics*. When the frequencies of the overtones are not multiples of the fundamental, the fundamental and the overtones are together called *inharmonics*. For each list of fundamental and overtones that follows, indicate whether they are harmonics or inharmonics.

(a) 315, 630, 1260, 2520, 5040
(b) 230, 345, 450, 600, 735, 860, 980
(c) 400, 500, 600, 700, 800, 900, 1000
(d) 210, 420, 840, 1680, 3360, 6720

9. Each of the next three graphs gives the "spectrum" of harmonics for a tone made by a particular instrument. Examine the graphs and then fill in the blanks in the three statements that follow.

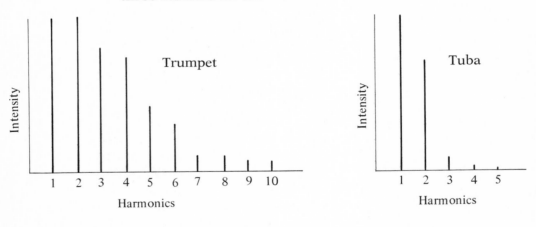

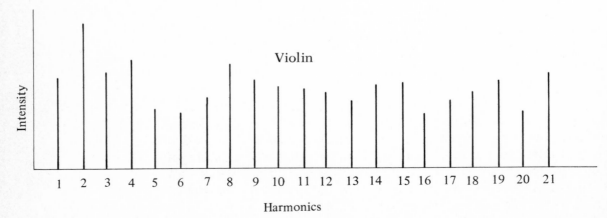

(a) The _____ has a great variety of tone color because it has so many overtones. It is not surprising, then, that this instrument is often used in solo to convey a range of emotions.

(b) The notes of the _____ have low harmonic content.

(c) Each of the first four harmonics is strong and the others gradually decrease in order. Consequently, the _____ has full and penetrating tones.

FUNCTIONS IN ECONOMICS

Basic economic theory includes relationships between supply and demand. Cost, revenue, and profit all involve supply and demand. Supply, demand, cost, revenue, and profit can all be expressed in terms of the number of units (call it x) that are produced or sold. So we are involved with supply functions, demand functions, and others.

Perhaps we should define some of these economic terms before proceeding to express them in function notation.

A *supply function* expresses an average price per unit at which x units can be supplied. We will use $S(x)$ to denote supply functions. Suppose watermelons can be supplied at an average of $1 each, regardless of how many are requested. Then $S(x) = 1$; x watermelons can be supplied at an average of $1 each. Some manufactured products, such as stereo equipment, can be supplied at a lower price if more can be made. This is due to the lower cost per unit when the product can be mass produced. The supply function $S(x) = 1000 - x$ suggests that one stereo unit can be supplied at $999, two units at an average of $998 *each*, and 100 units at an average of $900 *each*. Note

$$S(1) = 1000 - 1 = 999$$
$$S(2) = 1000 - 2 = 998$$
$$S(100) = 1000 - 100 = 900$$

This function might only be good for x up to 200 or 300. It surely isn't accurate for $x = 990$, since $S(990) = 10$ says that if 990 units can be produced, they can be supplied at $10 each. Some products are supplied at a higher price if more are made, perhaps because the resources needed are scarce or in great demand.

A *cost function* expresses the total cost at which x units can be supplied. We will use $C(x)$ to denote cost functions. What is the total cost of 5 watermelons supplied at $1 each? The answer is $5; $5 \cdot \$1 = \$5$. And what is the cost of 33 watermelons supplied at $1 each? The answer is $33; $33 \cdot \$1 = \$33$. What is the cost of x watermelons supplied at $1 each? The answer is $x; $x \cdot \$1 = \$x$. Can you see that the cost of x units is always x times the average cost per unit? This can be expressed as

$$C(x) = x \cdot S(x)$$

For the watermelon example,

$$S(x) = 1$$
$$C(x) = x \cdot 1 \quad \text{or} \quad C(x) = x$$

Recall that a supply function for stereos was given as $S(x) = 1000 - x$. Can you write the cost function? The cost of x units is x times the average cost per unit. Thus,

$$C(x) = x \cdot S(x)$$

or, specifically,

$$C(x) = x \cdot (1000 - x)$$

If you multiply out $x(1000 - x)$, the result is $1000x - x^2$. Using 10 units as an example, we find that the cost can be computed as $C(10)$.

$$C(10) = 10 \cdot (1000 - 10)$$
$$= 10 \cdot 990$$
$$= \$9900$$

A *demand function* expresses an average price per unit at which x units can be sold. The demand is, in effect, how much people are willing to pay per unit. We will use $D(x)$ to denote demand functions. If watermelons can be sold at an average of $1.50 each, regardless of how many, then $D(x) = 1.5$.

A *revenue function* expresses the total revenue received if x units are sold. We will use $R(x)$ to denote revenue functions. What is the total revenue if 5 watermelons are sold at $1.50 each? The answer is $7.50; $5 \cdot \$1.50 = \$7.50$. What is the revenue received when x watermelons are sold at $1.50 each? The answer is $1.5x$; $x \cdot \$1.50 = \$1.50x$, or $1.5x$. Can you see that the revenue from x units is always x times the average price per unit? This can be expressed as

$$R(x) = x \cdot D(x)$$

For the watermelon example,

$$D(x) = 1.5$$
$$R(x) = x \cdot 1.5 \quad \text{or} \quad R(x) = 1.5x$$

So how much *profit* is made by the dealer who buys 10 melons at $1.00 each and sells them at $1.50 each? The profit is revenue minus cost; that is, what he sells them for minus what he paid for them. The 10 melons cost $C(10) = \$10$. He sells them for $R(10) = 1.5(10) = \$15$. So his profit is $\$15 - \$10 = \$5$. In general, profit equals revenue minus cost. If $P(x)$ represents profit (that is, a *profit function*), then

$$P(x) = R(x) - C(x)$$

APPLICATIONS AND EXERCISES

---

1. Any quantity of Nadir brand radios that you (a store owner) request can be supplied to your store at $37 each. You can sell them at $52 each.

    (a) Determine the functions for supply, cost, demand, revenue, and profit.

    (b) What are the values of $S(20), C(20), D(20), R(20),$ and $P(20)$?

    (c) What is the profit on the sale of 31 radios?

2. In this section we used supply and cost functions for some stereos. Recall that $S(x) = 1000 - x$ and $C(x) = x(1000 - x)$. Suppose the dealer can sell any quantity of stereos at \$1350 each.

   (a) Write the demand function. What is the value and meaning of $D(4)$?

   (b) Write the revenue function. What is the value and meaning of $R(4)$?

   (c) Write the profit function. What is the value and meaning of $P(4)$?

3. We have seen that the cost of supplying units depends on how many units are to be supplied. There are usually, however, certain costs in a business that are not affected by the number of units that are produced. The rent on a building and the cost of machinery are two examples of such *overhead* costs. In view of this, we can define overhead as the cost of supplying zero units. In other words, overhead = $C(0)$. Use this definition to determine the overhead in each of the following cases. All costs are given in dollars.

   (a) $C(x) = 5x + 100$.

   (b) $C(x) = x^2 - 3x + 500$.

   (c) $C(x) = 2x$.

4. A product is said to reach a state of *equilibrium* when the supply equals the demand. If $S(x) = 8x - 4$ and $D(x) = 7x + 1$, for what quantity x will equilibrium exist? *Hint:* One approach is to try different values for the quantity x until you find one for which supply $(8x - 4)$ is equal to demand $(7x + 1)$.

5. The following demand curve shows that as the price of these items decreases, the number consumers will demand (that is, purchase) ———. As the price increases, quantity purchased ———.

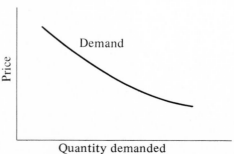

6. The supply curve below shows that as the price of items increases, the quantity that the manufacturer will supply _____. As the price decreases, the quantity supplied _____.

7. (a) Which point on the following graph (*A, B, C, D,* or *E*) represents a state of equilibrium, that is, a state where the quantity supplied is equal to the quantity demanded? What is the quantity and price at that point?

(b) What is the quantity supplied when the price is $10? What is the quantity demanded when the price is $10? Since more units are supplied than are demanded at this price, there is a *surplus* of _____ units.

(c) What is the quantity supplied when the price is $8? What is the quantity demanded when the price is $8? Since more units are demanded than are supplied at this price, there is a *shortage* of _____ units.

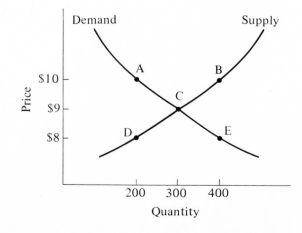

SLOPE OF A LINE

The introduction to this chapter mentioned that analysis is the branch of mathematics that includes calculus. This section on slopes and the next section on limits are intended to provide you with the background you will need to understand the section on calculus that follows them. The concepts of slope and limit are essential to the development of calculus.

The *slope* of a line is a numerical measure of its steepness. One way to compare the lines drawn next is to say that the first line (the one on the left) is steeper, or has a greater slope, than the second line.

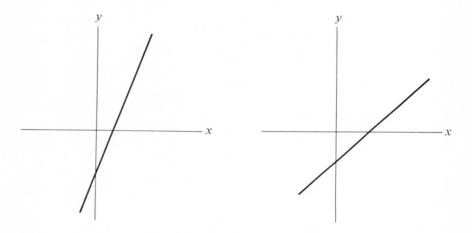

Since it is often useful to have precise definitions of words we use, the slope of a straight line is defined next. Slope is defined in terms of the change in y coordinates compared with the change in x coordinates in moving from one point of the line to another. Specifically,

$$\text{slope} = \frac{\text{change in } y}{\text{change in } x}$$

The symbol Δ (a capital Greek letter *delta*) is used to specify a change or increment. With this in mind we can rewrite the previous definition as

$$\text{slope} = \frac{\Delta y}{\Delta x}$$

Note that Δy means "change in y"; it does *not* mean Δ times y. Both Δy and Δx are numbers, so the slope $\Delta y/\Delta x$ is also a number. But what does all this mean? For example, what does a line with a slope of 3/4 look like? Let's have a look.

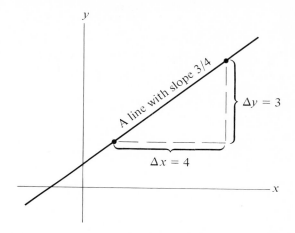

This relationship suggests that you can move from one point of this line to another point of the line by changing the x and y coordinates according to

$$\frac{\Delta y}{\Delta x} = \frac{3}{4}$$

In other words, beginning at any point of the line, change x by 4 units in the positive direction and change y by 3 units in the positive direction and you will have another point on the line.

Let's consider another example. Suppose you want to sketch the graph of the line passing through the point $(3, 2)$ and having slope 4. Your first step would be to plot the point $(3, 2)$.

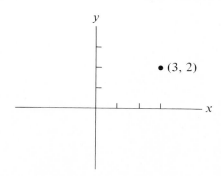

Next, you know the slope $\Delta y/\Delta x$ is 4. Expressed as a fraction, the slope is

$$\frac{\Delta y}{\Delta x} = \frac{4}{1}$$

So move from the plotted point (3, 2) as follows: change x by 1 in the positive direction and then change y by 4 in the positive direction. This will yield another point on the desired line. Now you can draw the line.

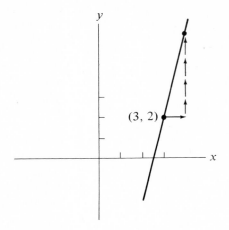

Can you determine the coordinates of the new point we have just obtained? The x coordinate of the original point is 3, and you have changed x by + 1. So the new x coordinate is 3 + 1, or 4. Similarly, the y coordinate is changed by + 4, so it becomes 2 + 4, or 6. So the new point is (4, 6). As a check, you could examine the two points (3, 2) and (4, 6) to see if indeed the slope of the line through them is 4. This can be done by using the definition to compute the slope.

$$\text{slope} = \frac{\Delta y}{\Delta x}$$

Δy, the change in y, is 6 − 2, or 4. It is the change in the y coordinate in going from (3, 2) to (4, 6). Similarly, Δx, the change in x, is 4 − 3, or 1. It is the change in the x coordinate in going from (3, 2) to (4, 6). It should be clear now that

$$\text{slope} = \frac{\Delta y}{\Delta x} = \frac{4}{1} = 4$$

This completes the check. Now let's see a few applications of slope.

Geologists who study rivers are concerned with the slope of river channels. Changes in slope—whether man-made or natural—result in changes in channel cross sections, the pattern of a meandering river, the velocity of water, and the erosion of river banks.

An engineer's drawing of the South Fork Dam of the Conemaugh River (1839) shows and states that the slope of the front of the dam should be 1/2 and that of the rear 2/3. The dam functioned well until 1889, when careless maintenance led to the collapse that produced the catastrophic Johnstown flood.

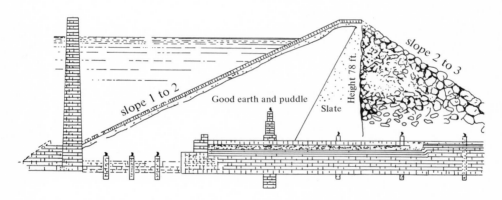

The fraction $\Delta y/\Delta x$, which is called the slope, is also called the *rate of change* of y with respect to x. This means that if $\Delta y/\Delta x = 3$, or 3/1, then the rate of change of y with respect to x is 3, or 3 to 1. In other words, y changes three times as fast as x.

In forestry, the slope is used to measure the average rate of change in organic matter per acre over a period of years.

Do you think of speed in terms of miles per hour? In general, speed is the rate of change of distance (d) with respect to time (t). This means that the average speed can be computed as the change in distance (Δd) divided by the change in time (Δt). Average speed is $\Delta d/\Delta t$. If you travel 200 miles in 4 hours, then $\Delta d = 200$ miles and $\Delta t = 4$ hours, so your average speed for that travel is 200 miles/4 hours, or 50 miles per hour.

The amount by which human lungs will expand when pressure is applied to them internally is called the *compliance* and is computed as $\Delta V / \Delta P$, where V is volume and P is pressure.

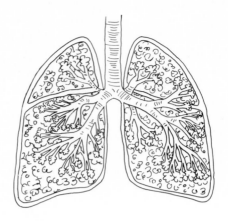

APPLICATIONS AND EXERCISES

1. Graph each line described here by plotting the point it passes through and then using the definition of slope to obtain another point.
   (a) Through (2, 1) with slope 3/4
   (b) Through (3, 2) with slope 1/2
   (c) Through (0, 4) with slope 2
   (d) Through (1, 1) with slope 5/2
   (e) Through (5, 5) with slope 1

2. Obtain two points for each line and then determine its slope. Perhaps the best way to find points is to choose values for x and calculate the corresponding y values.
   (a) $y = 2x + 1$.   (b) $y = 3x$.
   (c) $y = 5x - 1$.   (d) $y = 4x + 5$.
   (e) $y = 6x + 10$.   (f) $y = x + 2$.

3. Compare the slope of each line in Exercise 2 with the equation of the line.
   (a) What pattern do you notice?
   (b) Fill in the blank in the following sentence. If the equation of a straight line is written in the form $y = mx + b$, then _____ is the slope of the line.

4. The slope of a straight line has been defined as $\Delta y/\Delta x$. The slope can also be defined in terms of the angle of inclination θ of the line with respect to the x axis.

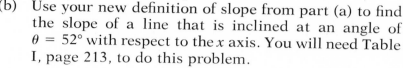

(a) Recall from Chapter 4 (page 209) the trigonometric functions sine, cosine, and tangent. Is the slope $\Delta y/\Delta x$ equal to $\sin \theta$, $\cos \theta$, or $\tan \theta$? Explain. In other words, is slope $= \sin \theta$, slope $= \cos \theta$, or slope $= \tan \theta$ another definition of slope?

(b) Use your new definition of slope from part (a) to find the slope of a line that is inclined at an angle of $\theta = 52°$ with respect to the x axis. You will need Table I, page 213, to do this problem.

5. Using the function notation $y = f(x)$, slope $= \Delta y/\Delta x$ becomes

$$\text{slope} = \frac{\Delta f(x)}{\Delta x}$$

(a) Obtain two points for the line $f(x) = 4x + 1$ and determine its slope.

(b) There is a straight line for which $f(1) = 2$ and $f(5) = 14$. Determine the slope of the line.

(c) Suppose there is a straight line for which $f(a) = b$ and $f(c) = d$. Express the slope of the line in terms of a, b, c, and d.

6. Consider these two slope-related drawings:

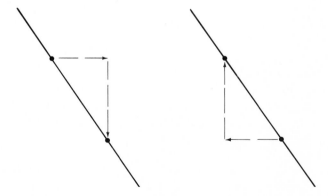

In the first drawing we move over 2 to the right and down 3. In the second, we move over 2 to the left and up 3.

(a) What is Δy in the first case? What is Δx?

(b)   What is Δy in the second case? What is Δx?
(c)   What is the slope in both cases? Is there anything significantly different about the numerical value of this slope compared with other slopes encountered in this section?
(d)   What is the difference in appearance between a line with slope 2/3 and a line with slope $-2/3$?
(e)   Sketch the line through (4, 7) with slope $-3/4$.
(f)   Sketch the line through (5, 6) with slope -2.

7. (a)   In $\Delta d/\Delta t = 20$, suppose d represents distance in miles and t represents time in hours. What then does $\Delta d/\Delta t = 20$ indicate?
(b)   A man begins at 1 P.M. and walks until 5 P.M. Overall he walks 12 miles. If d represents distance in miles and t is time in hours, determine Δd and Δt for this setting. Also, find the average speed at which the man walked.
(c)   The Smiths bought a house for $35,000 in January of 1972 and sold it for $50,000 in January of 1977. What was the average rate of change in the price of the house per year during that period?

LIMITS: AN INTUITIVE GLANCE

Several kinds of sequences were presented in Chapter 1, as you may recall. Here is a sequence that is different from any of those studied earlier.

$$1, 1/2, 1/3, 1/4, \ldots$$

What are the next two terms of the sequence? You should have determined that the next term is 1/5 and the term after that is 1/6. Furthermore, the seventh term is 1/7 and the nth term is $1/n$. What are the values of the 100th term, 1000th term, and 1,000,000th term of this sequence? The 100th term is 1/100, or .01; the 1000th term is 1/1000, or .001; the 1,000,000th term is 1/1,000,000, or .000001. Notice that the terms of the sequence get smaller and smaller as you go further in the sequence. But just how small is the smallest term of the sequence? Perhaps that's a difficult question. Although the terms get smaller and smaller, there is no last term. The sequence has an infinite number of terms, each smaller than any term that precedes it in the sequence. Since the terms get smaller and smaller without a last term, there is no smallest term. But can you see what number the terms are getting closer and closer to (that is, "approaching") as you go further and further in the sequence? Can you see that there is a number toward which the terms appear to be heading or reaching? What number is that? The number that the terms get closer and closer to is 0. We say that 0 is the *limit of the sequence*. Numbers of the form $1/n$ get closer and closer to 0 as n gets larger and larger. This can be stated symbolically as

$$\lim_{n\to\infty} \frac{1}{n} = 0$$

which says that $1/n$ gets closer and closer to 0 as n gets larger and larger. The "lim" is read as "limit." The symbols $n \to \infty$ indicate that n increases without bound (that is, approaches infinity). Thus,

$$\lim_{n\to\infty} \frac{1}{n} = 0$$

can be read as "the limit of $1/n$ as n approaches infinity is zero." Of course, $1/n$ is never equal to zero. This limit equation suggests the tendency toward zero; it suggests what would happen if n could become infinite.

Another intuitive way of thinking of zero as the limit of the sequence 1, 1/2, 1/3, 1/4, . . . is to note that if you go out far enough in the sequence, you can find terms that are as close to zero as desired. For example, terms of the form $1/n$ are within 1/100 (or .01) of zero when n is 100 or larger. So all terms beyond 1/100 are within .01 of zero. Terms of the form $1/n$ are within 1/1,000,000 (or .000001) of zero when n is 1,000,000 or larger.

Let's consider another type of limit problem, one that does not come directly from a sequence.

$$\lim_{x\to 2} (5x) = ?$$

The notation suggests we determine the limit of $5x$ as x approaches 2. The question is, to what value does $5x$ get closer and closer as x gets closer and closer to 2? Consider some x values near 2. Observe what happens to $5x$ as x gets closer and closer to 2: First, using numbers less than 2,

x	$5x$
1.5	7.5
1.6	8.0
1.7	8.5
1.8	9.0
1.9	9.5
1.95	9.75
1.99	9.95
1.999	9.995

Next, using numbers greater than 2,

x	$5x$
2.5	12.5
2.4	12.0
2.3	11.5
2.2	11.0
2.1	10.5
2.05	10.25
2.01	10.05
2.001	10.005

Do you see that as x gets closer and closer to 2, $5x$ gets closer and closer to 10. We write this observation as

$$\lim_{x \to 2} (5x) = 10$$

The French mathematician Augustin-Louis Cauchy was the first to establish formal definitions of limits. He did this to remove dependence on intuitive and geometric interpretations of limits. Intuitive notions of limit, such as we have used in this section, are useful in many settings. Unfortunately, more precision is needed to handle many limit problems that arise in modern calculus and analysis.

Augustin–Louis Cauchy (1789–1857)

In the next section we shall see some examples of how the concept of limit is used in calculus.

APPLICATIONS AND EXERCISES

1. Study each sequence to determine its limit.
   (a) 2, 1, 2/3, 2/4, 2/5, 2/6, . . .
   (b) 1/2, 2/3, 3/4, 4/5, 5/6, . . .
   (c) 7.1, 7.01, 7.001, 7.0001, . . .
   (d) 3, 3.1, 3.14, 3.141, 3.1415, . . . (*Hint:* A special number studied in Chapter 4.)

2. What is the limit of the sequence 1, 2, 3, 4, 5, . . . ? Explain.

3. Find the value of each limit by using the suggested values of x.

   (a) $\lim\limits_{x \to 3} (10x)$. Use $x = 2.9, 2.95, 2.99, 3.1, 3.05, 3.01$.

   (b) $\lim\limits_{x \to 2} (x^2)$. Use $x = 1.9, 1.95, 1.99, 2.1, 2.05, 2.01$.

4. Perhaps you noticed an easier way to determine the limit in the example $\lim_{x \to 2} (5x)$. Did you notice that $5x$ is 10 if 2 is substituted for x? In other words, why not just use 2 for x instead of values close to 2? Sometimes this "plug-in" method works and sometimes it doesn't. For example, it doesn't work for finding the limit of the sequence 1, 1/2, 1/3, 1/4, ... How does the plug-in method work for the limits of Exercise 3?

5. Study the behavior of $1/x^2$ as x approaches zero; that is, determine the value of

$$\lim_{x \to 0} \frac{1}{x^2}$$

Use the following values for x: 1, 1/10, 1/100, 1/1000. *Note:* You may prefer to offer an explanation rather than a numerical answer.

6. An insect is standing one unit away from a tree. It jumps in such a way that it lands one-half unit from the tree. It jumps again and lands one-fourth unit from the tree. It jumps still another time and lands one-eighth unit from the tree. Assuming the insect continues according to this pattern, after how many jumps will it hit the tree? Explain.

7. Imagine regular polygons having four sides, five sides, ten sides, a hundred sides, and so on. What name would you give to the figure representing the limit of a polygon of n sides as n approaches infinity?

8. Suppose you have a circle whose radius is approaching zero.

   (a)   What size is the circumference of the circle approaching?

   (b)   What size is the area of the region inside the circle approaching?

   (c)   What term from geometry describes the "circle" being created?

9. Study each graph and determine the limit that is requested.

(a)

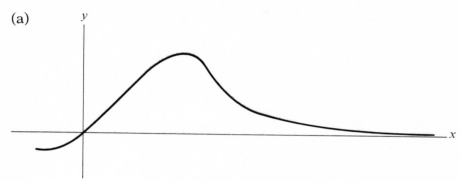

As $x \to \infty$, $y \to$? In other words, $\lim_{x \to \infty} y =$ _____ .

(b)

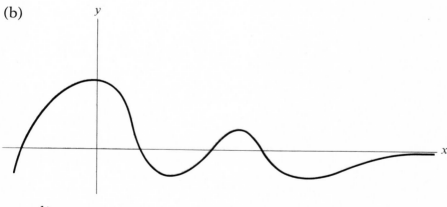

$\lim_{x \to \infty} y =$ _____ .

10. Recall the Fibonacci sequence 1, 1, 2, 3, 5, 8, 13, . . . (see page 2) and the golden ratio (see page 140)

$$\frac{1 + \sqrt{5}}{2}$$

Let us call the nth term of the Fibonacci sequence a_n and the term just before that a_{n-1}. As it happens,

$$\frac{a_n}{a_{n-1}} \longrightarrow \frac{1 + \sqrt{5}}{2} \quad \text{as} \quad n \to \infty$$

In words, the ratio of successive terms of the Fibonacci sequence approaches the golden ratio. In limit notation, this can be stated as

$$\lim_{n \to \infty} \frac{a_n}{a_{n-1}} = \frac{1 + \sqrt{5}}{2}$$

Now let's examine this limit.

(a) Use the approximation 2.236067977 for $\sqrt{5}$ to determine a good approximation for the golden ratio.

(b) Use $a_6 = 8$ and $a_5 = 5$ for a_n and a_{n-1} and compute a_n/a_{n-1}.

(c) Do the same as for part (b), except use a_7 and a_6 of the Fibonacci sequence.

(d) Same, except use a_{11} and a_{10}.

(e) Same, except use a_{14} and a_{13}.

(f) Same, except use a_{18} and a_{17}.

The answers to parts (b)–(f) should be better and better approximations to the golden ratio.

11. The number e is used as the base of natural logarithms. It was noted in the explanation of logarithms that e is approximately equal to 2.718 (see page 37). The number e arises in situations involving the expression

$$\left(1 + \frac{1}{x}\right)^x$$

In fact, e can be defined as the limit of this expression as x becomes infinite. In symbols,

$$e = \lim_{x \to \infty} \left(1 + \frac{1}{x}\right)^x$$

If you have a calculator that can raise quantities to large powers, complete the following table as a convincing argument that e is indeed the limit just given. Compare the results with the actual value of e, which to seven decimal places is 2.7182818.

x	$\dfrac{1}{x}$	$1 + \dfrac{1}{x}$	$\left(1 + \dfrac{1}{x}\right)^x$
10			
100			
1,000			
10,000			
100,000			
1,000,000			
10,000,000			

WHAT IS CALCULUS?

The English mathematician Isaac Newton and the German mathematician Gottfried Wilhelm Leibniz are credited with the nearly simultaneous (though independent) invention of calculus. Newton invented calculus in 1665, but took over 20

Isaac Newton (1642–1727)

Gottfried Wilhelm Leibniz (1646–1716)

years to publish his findings. As a result, Leibniz published his own development of calculus several years before Newton; and it was Leibniz who developed superior notation, including some that linked the differential calculus with the integral calculus.

Although Newton and Leibniz are credited with inventing calculus, many aspects of this area of mathematics were known to them because of work their predecessors had done. Archimedes (287–212 B.C.) used a "method of exhaustion" involving limits to find areas bounded by circles and parabolas. His method resembles one basic definition used for the calculus operation of integration. Simon Stevin (1548–1620) used methods resembling integral calculus to determine the force due to water pressure on a vertical dam. Johannes Kepler (1571–1630) used calculus-like applications in his investigations of the motion of planets. Others who used calculus-like methods before the calculus was formally described include Galileo (1564–1642), Cavalieri (1598–1647), Torricelli (1608–1647), Fermat (1601–1665), Huygens (1629–1662), Wallis (1616–1703), and Barrow (1630–1677). The invention of calculus had a tremendous impact on technology and on the expansion of the study of mathematics.

Historically, calculus was developed as two separate branches—integral calculus and differential calculus. The original problems that led to the invention of differential calculus did not appear to resemble the problems solved by integral calculus. Later, the two branches were linked by the *Fundamental Theorem of Calculus*. This theorem is now used by all calculus students. The operations of differential and integral calculus are in fact inverses of one another, just as addition and subtraction are inverses and multiplication and division are inverses.

The problem that eventually led to the development of integral calculus was that of finding the area of a region having a curved side. As an example, let's study the area of the shaded region shown on the next page.

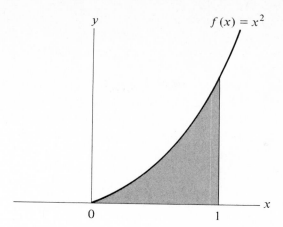

In this example we seek the "area under the curve" $f(x) = x^2$ between $x = 0$ and $x = 1$. This area can be *approximated* by using rectangles. Suppose we use three rectangles, each with width 1/4 and heights equal to the functional values at 1/4, 1/2, and 3/4.

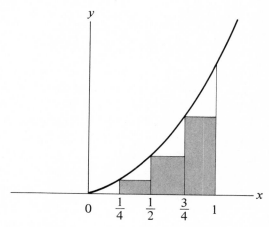

Since $f(x) = x^2$, $f(1/4) = 1/16$, $f(1/2) = 1/4$, and $f(3/4) = 9/16$ are the heights (or lengths) of the rectangles. Also, each rectangle is 1/4 unit wide. So the area of the first rectangle is $1/4 \cdot 1/16$; the second is $1/4 \cdot 1/4$; the third is $1/4 \cdot 9/16$. Each area is, of course, length times width. The approximate total area, then, is $1/4 \cdot 1/16 + 1/4 \cdot 1/4 + 1/4 \cdot 9/16$. From the unshaded space left between the rectangles and the curve, you can see that this is not a very good approximation of the area. A better approximation can be obtained by using more rectangles (that is, a greater number of smaller intervals). The next illustration demonstrates this. See how much closer the shaded rectangles are to the desired area than they were when only three larger rectangles were used.

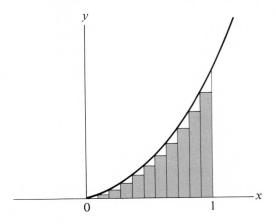

As n, the number of rectangles, approaches infinity, the approximate area approaches the desired exact area. The exact area, then, is the limit of the sum of n rectangles as $n \to \infty$. The limit of the sum is called an *integral*. The area we seek is given by the following integral.

$$\int_0^1 x^2 \, dx$$

The symbols $\int dx$ denote the limit of the sum. Here $f(x) = x^2$ is the function we are using in this example, and we seek the area from 0 to 1. Notice how x^2, 0, and 1 are used with the notation.

The process of evaluating an integral is called *integration*. Area under a curve is just one use and interpretation of integration. There are many others. Volumes of solid figures can be found by methods of integration. The center of mass of objects (that is, the point at which all the mass can be considered to be concentrated for the purpose of balancing) can be determined by integration. The entire force due to water pressure on the face of a dam can be computed using integral calculus. Finding the amount of work done in moving an object, even when its weight may change while it is being moved, is another integration problem. Differential equations are solved by techniques of integration. Some examples of differential equation applications will be given after our discussion of differential calculus, which begins next; then we will see how the techniques of integration are used.

One of the original problems that led to the development of differential calculus was that of finding the slope of the tangent line to a curve. A *tangent* line is a straight line that touches a curve at one point. Four such tangent lines are illustrated here. Observe how the slope of the tangent line varies, depending on what part of the curve you are considering. (Although no axes are drawn or labeled in these illustrations, assume as usual that the horizontal axis is the *x* axis and the vertical axis is the *y* axis.)

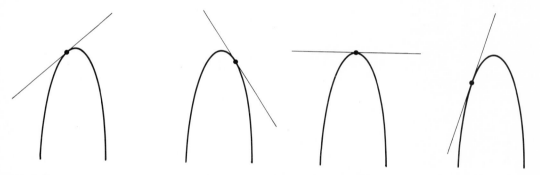

The slope of the tangent line to the graph of a function is one geometric interpretation of the *derivative* of a function. The process of determining derivatives of functions is called *differentiation*.

Recall that the slope of a line is $\Delta y/\Delta x$. We shall use the letter m to mean "slope," so that we don't have to write the word slope. So

$$m = \frac{\Delta y}{\Delta x} \quad \text{or} \quad m = \frac{\Delta f(x)}{\Delta x} \quad \text{if we use } f(x) \text{ for } y.$$

This same formula for slope will help us find the slope of a tangent line to the graph of a function. Since that slope varies, the result will be a formula for the slope of all tangent lines to the curve. The formula will depend on the point (x, y) at which you want the line to be tangent to the curve.

The formula for the slope of a straight line requires the use of two points to determine slope m. If we select two points on the curve, the line through those points might look like the one shown next.

This is not a tangent line, but rather a *secant* line. It crosses the graph in two points rather than touching at one point. This secant line can be used to obtain a tangent line, however. So let's proceed. Suppose we call the lower point $(x, f(x))$. The first coordinate of the other point is $x + \Delta x$, since it is some number of units (say Δx) to the right of x. If $x + \Delta x$ is the first coordinate, then $f(x + \Delta x)$ is the corresponding second coordinate.

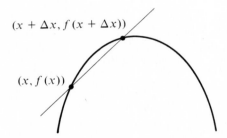

So the slope of the secant line can be determined by using $m = \Delta f(x)/\Delta x$. The result is

$$m_{\text{sec}} = \frac{f(x + \Delta x) - f(x)}{\Delta x}$$

since $\Delta f(x)$ is the difference in the second coordinates and Δx is the difference between the first coordinates.

Look at what happens as Δx gets smaller and smaller. Can you describe it in words?

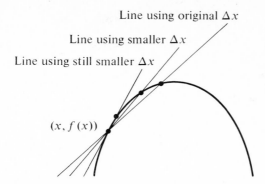

Line using original Δx

Line using smaller Δx

Line using still smaller Δx

$(x, f(x))$

As Δx gets closer to zero, the secant line begins to look more and more like a tangent line. As Δx approaches zero, the numerical slope of the secant line approaches the numerical slope of the tangent line. We say that the slope of the tangent line is the limit, as Δx approaches zero, of the slope of the secant line. This limit is called the *derivative* of $f(x)$ with respect to x.

$$\text{derivative} = m_{\text{tan}} = \lim_{\Delta x \to 0} m_{\text{sec}} = \lim_{\Delta x \to 0} \frac{f(x + \Delta x) - f(x)}{\Delta x}$$

This definition of the derivative of $y = f(x)$ is actually used to compute some derivatives and to obtain general formulas.

There are several popular ways to denote the derivative of $y = f(x)$ with respect to x, including $f'(x)$, y', dy/dx, and $D_x y$. Leibniz used dy/dx and Newton used the form $\dot{y}$. Newton's notation is not widely used outside certain areas of physics to which calculus is applied.

As an introduction to some applications of the derivative, consider the next sketch. What is the slope of the tangent line at point A? What is the slope of the tangent line at point B?

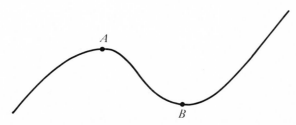

A

B

Both slopes are zero. Below, the tangent lines are actually drawn so that you can see this more clearly. The slopes are zero because $\Delta y / \Delta x = 0 / \Delta x$. The change in y is always zero for a horizontal line.

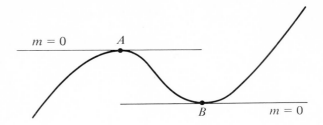

In this drawing, point A is called a *relative maximum* point of the function, because it is higher than all other points in some interval about A. Similarly, point B is called a *relative minimum* point because it is lower than all other points in some interval about B. Points A and B can be determined by using calculus. All you have to do is determine where the derivative (that is, the slope of the tangent line to the curve) is equal to zero.

Differential calculus techniques such as those just suggested can be applied to find the maximum or minimum values of functions representing a wide range of applications. If functions represent revenue, profit, and cost, then calculus techniques can be used to determine how to obtain maximum revenue and profit or minimum cost. If a container is made to hold a specific volume, you can determine the dimensions that will minimize the amount of material used. For example, the "tin can" that uses the smallest amount of metal is one in which the height is equal to the diameter. Similarly, if a given amount of material is used to make a container, you can determine the dimensions that will maximize the amount the container will hold.

Differential equations, which are equations containing derivatives, describe a variety of situations: a chemical reaction involving compounds that have different rates of reaction; rates of growth of bacteria in a culture; motion of planets and projectiles; the relationship between electric current and the rate of change of current in an electric circuit. Differential equations are solved using the techniques of integral calculus.

1. In the presentation of integral calculus, the graph of $f(x) = x^2$ is shown only for x between 0 and 1. Complete the following table and draw a more complete sketch of that parabola.

x	$f(x) = x^2$	Point: $(x, f(x))$
0	0	$(0, 0)$
1	1	$(1, 1)$
2		
3		
-1		
-2		
-3		

2. The exact area under the curve $f(x) = x^2$ between 0 and 1 is $1/3$, or $.333\overline{3}$, where the bar indicates that the 3's repeat indefinitely.

   (a) What is the sum of the areas of the three rectangles of width $1/4$ used as an approximation earlier in this section?

   (b) Obtain a better approximation by using seven rectangles, each of which is $1/8$ unit wide.

   If rectangles of width $1/16$ are used, the approximation improves to $.3027$. This process is half of Archimedes' "method of exhaustion." He also used rectangles that went over the curve, like this:

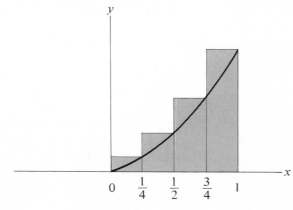

Here the approximation is larger than the actual area. Archimedes reasoned that the value of the actual area was between that of the rectangles under the curve and those over the curve. For rectangles of width 1/16, the area over the curve is .3652. So the actual area is between .3027 and .3652. You can see that the actual area, .3333, is almost exactly halfway between these two estimates.

(c) Find the value of the shaded approximation in the diagram in which the four rectangles extend over the curve.

(d) The exact area, then, lies between the two numbers obtained in parts (a) and (c) of this problem. What number is halfway in between those values? How close is it to the exact area?

3. An integral such as

$$\int_0^1 x^2 \, dx$$

is evaluated by the following mechanical procedure. No attempt will be made to explain why the process of integration is done this way for these functions.

(i) Increase the exponent by 1 to get x^3.

(ii) Divide x^3 by the new exponent, 3, to get $x^3/3$.

(iii) Determine the value of $x^3/3$ for $x = 1$. That value is 1/3.

(iv) Determine the value of $x^3/3$ for $x = 0$. That value is 0.

(v) Subtract the result of (iv) from the result of (iii). The result is 1/3, which is the value of this integral.

The process is displayed as follows.

$$\int_0^1 x^2 \, dx = [x^3/3]_0^1 = 1^3/3 - 0^3/3 = 1/3 - 0 = 1/3$$

Most integrals cannot be evaluated this simply, or by anything resembling this mechanical approach, but those given next can be. Evaluate each integral by using the five-step process just suggested.

(a) $\int_1^2 x^2 \, dx$

(b) $\displaystyle\int_1^2 x^3\, dx$

(c) $\displaystyle\int_3^5 x\, dx$

4. (a) Evaluate these two integrals by using the mechanical method suggested in Exercise 3.

$$\int_3^3 x^2\, dx \qquad \int_8^8 x\, dx$$

(b) Explain how you might justify the results of part (a) on the basis of an "area" interpretation of the integral.

(c) Apply inductive reasoning to the results of part (a) to complete the statement

$$\int_a^a f(x)\, dx = \underline{\hspace{3em}}$$

5. The derivative with respect to x of $f(x) = x^4$ is $4x^3$. The derivative with respect to x of $f(x) = x^5$ is $5x^4$. Do you see a pattern? Determine the derivative with respect to x of each of the following functions, assuming each follows this same pattern.

(a) $f(x) = x^6$.
(b) $f(x) = x^2$.
(c) $f(x) = x$. (*Note:* $x^0 = 1$.)

This mechanical process works for only a few special kinds of functions.

6. The derivative with respect to x of $f(x) = 5x^4$ is $20x^3$. The derivative with respect to x of $f(x) = 3x^5$ is $15x^4$. Note the pattern and compute the derivative of each of these functions, assuming they follow the pattern (which they do).

(a) $f(x) = 4x^6$.
(b) $f(x) = 3x^7$.
(c) $f(x) = 5x$.

7. In the process of evaluating $\displaystyle\int_0^1 x^2\, dx$, the term $x^3/3$ was obtained (and later evaluated at 1 and at 0). We say that $x^3/3$ is an integral of x^2.

(a) If $x^3/3$ is written instead as $c \cdot x^3$, what is the value of c?

(b) Following the examples of Exercise 6, what is the derivative with respect to x of $\frac{1}{3}x^3$?

(c) How does the derivative in part (b) compare with the function $f(x) = x^2$ in the original integral, $\int_0^1 x^2\, dx$?

Can you see why we say that differentiation and integration are inverse operations? Explain. You might be interested to know that addition and subtraction are inverse operations, as are multiplication and division.

8. The *derivative* of a formula for distance as a function of time is a formula for velocity as a function of time. Similarly, the derivative of a formula for velocity is a formula for acceleration.

By contrast, velocity can be determined as the *integral* of an acceleration function, and distance is the integral of a velocity function.

(a) Explain, based on these applications, why we say that differentiation and integration are inverse operations.

(b) A ball is dropped from atop a tall building. If $s = 16t^2$ indicates the distance in feet that the ball will travel in t seconds from the time it is dropped, use calculus to determine a function for the velocity of the ball at any time t.

(c) How fast is the ball traveling 3 seconds after it is dropped, that is, when t is 3?

(d) Use calculus to determine the acceleration of the ball at any time.

9. For each integral in Exercise 3, sketch enough of the function to shade the area you determined.

(a) $f(x) = x^2$ from $x = 1$ to $x = 2$.

(b) $f(x) = x^3$ from $x = 1$ to $x = 2$.

(c) $f(x) = x$ from $x = 3$ to $x = 5$.

10. The shaded area in Exercise 9, part (c), is a trapezoid. The area of a trapezoid is

$$A = \tfrac{1}{2}(b_1 + b_2)h$$

where b_1 and b_2 are the two parallel bases and h is the height. Compute the area shaded in Exercise 9, part (c), by using this trapezoid formula, and compare your answer with the answer to Exercise 3, part (c).

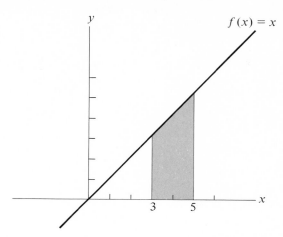

11. It was noted in this section that for a tin can to use the smallest amount of metal, it should be designed so that its height is equal to its diameter. Is this a popular shape in the supermarket? From an ecological point of view, what are the implications of your answer?

12. Logarithms with a base of e ($e \doteq 2.718$) were introduced earlier (see page 37). Such natural logarithms can also be defined by calculus. Specifically, for any positive number t, $\log_e t$ (or $\ln t$ for short) is defined as

$$\ln t = \int_1^t \frac{1}{x}\, dx$$

   (a) Write $\ln 4$ as an integral.
   (b) Since $\ln t$ is an integral, this suggests that $\ln t$ can be interpreted geometrically as the area under the curve $f(x) = 1/x$ from $x =$ _____ to $x =$ _____.
   (c) Sketch the graph of $f(x) = 1/x$ for positive values of x. Then shade the region that represents $\ln 4$.
   (d) Write $\ln 1$ as an integral. Look carefully at the integral. What is the numerical value of $\ln 1$?

Probability and Statistics

7

You have undoubtedly played a variety of games in which dice or cards are used. Perhaps you have tried your luck at a raffle. State lotteries are becoming increasingly popular as a means of raising revenue. All of these games are situations in which the laws of *probability* can be applied. Although the actual outcome of events cannot be predicted each time, the chance that any particular outcome will occur can be determined methodically by applying these laws of probability.

The formal study of probability began in 1654 when French mathematicians Blaise Pascal and Pierre de Fermat studied a gambling problem presented to them. In fact, many of the original applications of probability were to gambling problems.

Blaise Pascal
(1623–1662)

Pierre de Fermat
(1601–1665)

PROBABILITY

Let's begin by flipping a coin. A coin has two sides, heads and tails, and we'll assume that when it is flipped it lands as either heads or tails, rather than on its edge.

heads   tails

How often would you expect a coin to land heads? If we assume the coin is fair, then it should land heads half the time. So we'll say that the probability that a flipped coin will land heads is 1/2. How often should the coin land tails? Again, if the coin is fair, it should land tails half the time. So the probability that a flipped coin will land tails is also 1/2. If "$P(\ )$" is used to denote the probability of an event, then

$$P(\text{heads}) = \frac{1}{2}$$

$$P(\text{tails}) = \frac{1}{2}$$

The two events above are a flipped coin landing heads and a flipped coin landing tails.

Suppose next that we roll one die. There are six possible outcomes: 1, 2, 3, 4, 5, 6.

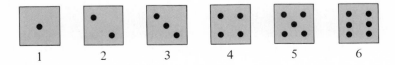

1   2   3   4   5   6

How often would you expect the die to come up 4? One sixth of the time, if the die is a "fair die." With a fair die, all faces are equally likely to come up. How often would you expect the die to come up odd (1 or 3 or 5)? Half the time. We can write these two probabilities as

$$P(\text{four}) = \frac{1}{6}$$

$$P(\text{odd}) = \frac{1}{2}$$

All of these examples lead to a natural definition of the probability that an event E will occur. If *all outcomes are equally likely*, and if you divide the number of favorable outcomes (that is, the number of ways in which E can occur) by the total number of possible outcomes, the fraction obtained is called the *probability* of E occurring. Symbolically,

$$P(E) = \frac{\text{favorable}}{\text{total}}$$

If we apply this definition to finding the probability that a flipped coin lands heads, we obtain

$$\text{favorable} = 1$$

$$\text{total} = 2$$

$$P(\text{heads}) = \frac{\text{favorable}}{\text{total}} = \frac{1}{2}$$

For the die example above,

$$P(\text{four}) = \frac{\text{favorable}}{\text{total}} = \frac{1}{6}$$

$$P(\text{odd}) = \frac{\text{favorable}}{\text{total}} = \frac{3}{6} = \frac{1}{2}$$

Now suppose a die is rolled and a coin is tossed. First of all, how many outcomes are possible? You could list all the possibilities—*one* on die and *heads* on coin, *two* on die and *heads* on coin, and so on. If you list them, you'll find there are 12 possible outcomes. There is, however, a much shorter way to determine this result. The coin can come up any of two ways and the die can come up any of six ways. For either coin outcome, there are six die outcomes: six die outcomes for heads and six die outcomes for tails. This is $6 \cdot 2$ or 12 outcomes. In general,

If one event can occur in M ways and an event following it can occur in N ways, then both events can occur in M · N ways.

Before continuing with the coin and die, let's be sure this last concept is clear. Suppose you are in a bookstore and plan to buy a book and a candy bar. Unfortunately, you're having trouble deciding which book and which candy to buy. There are 7 books that look interesting and there are 8 different candy bars that look tasty. In how many different ways can you select one book and one candy bar? Since there are 7 books, and any of 8 candy bars could be selected with whichever book is selected, there are $7 \cdot 8$ or 56 possible ways to select a book and a candy bar.

Now let's return to the coin and die. We found before that there are 12 possible outcomes. What is the probability of getting heads on the coin and an odd number on the die? From the definition of the probability of an event E,

$$P(E) = \frac{\text{favorable}}{\text{total}}$$

In this setting, the total number of outcomes possible is 12. How many are favorable? Using the notation (H, 1) to mean heads on the coin and 1 on the die, we can quickly list all of the favorable outcomes.

$$(H, 1), (H, 3), (H, 5)$$

There are three favorable outcomes. Thus,

$$P(E) = \frac{\text{favorable}}{\text{total}} = \frac{3}{12} = \frac{1}{4}$$

This problem can be solved another way. Observe that the two probabilities

$$P(\text{heads on coin}) = \frac{\text{favorable}}{\text{total}} = \frac{1}{2}$$

and

$$P(\text{odd on die}) = \frac{\text{favorable}}{\text{total}} = \frac{3}{6}$$

produce 3/12 if multiplied together. This suggests that

$$P(\text{heads and odd}) = P(\text{heads}) \cdot P(\text{odd}) = \frac{1}{2} \cdot \frac{3}{6} = \frac{3}{12} = \frac{1}{4}$$

What is suggested here is that for these two events A and B,

$$P(A \text{ and } B) = P(A) \cdot P(B)$$

As it happens, this is always true for any two independent events A and B. Two events are independent if the outcome of one event has no influence on the outcome of the other. This result can be extended to three or more events. For example, if A, B, and C are three independent events, then

$$P(A \text{ and } B \text{ and } C) = P(A) \cdot P(B) \cdot P(C)$$

APPLICATIONS AND EXERCISES

1. A die is rolled.
   (a) What is the probability that it comes up 1, 2, 3, 4, 5, or 6?
   (b) What is the probability it comes up 7?
   (c) Based on your answers to parts (a) and (b), it is apparent that all numerical values of probabilities are between _____ and _____ inclusive.

2. Two dice (one red, one white) are rolled.

(a) Using the notation (4, 3) to mean that the red die came up 4 and the white die came up 3, list all the possible outcomes.

(b) How many outcomes are there?

(c) Since the red die can come up any of six ways and for each of those ways the white die can come up any of six ways, the total number of outcomes is ____ .

(d) There are five different movies that you and your date can go see. After a movie, you might go to any of four different places for a snack. In how many different ways can this sequence of two events be accomplished?

(e) What is the probability of obtaining a sum of seven on the roll of two dice?

(f) What is the probability of obtaining a sum of eight on the roll of two dice?

3. (a) Someone who knows nothing about you tries to guess the month in which you were born. What is the probability he guesses correctly? What is the probability he guesses wrong?

(b) A standard deck of 52 cards consists of 13 hearts, 13 diamonds, 13 clubs, and 13 spades (see the illustration on the next page). Assume it is well shuffled. You draw one card. What is the probability it is a heart? What is the probability it is not a heart?

(c) Referring to part (b), hearts and diamonds are red, clubs and spades are black. You draw one card from the deck of 52. What is the probability it is black? What is the probability it is not black?

(d) If $P(E)$ represents the probability of an event E occurring and $P(\sim E)$ is the probability of event E not occurring, then what number goes in the blank in each of these statements?

$$P(E) + P(\sim E) = \underline{}$$

or

$$P(\sim E) = \underline{} - P(E)$$

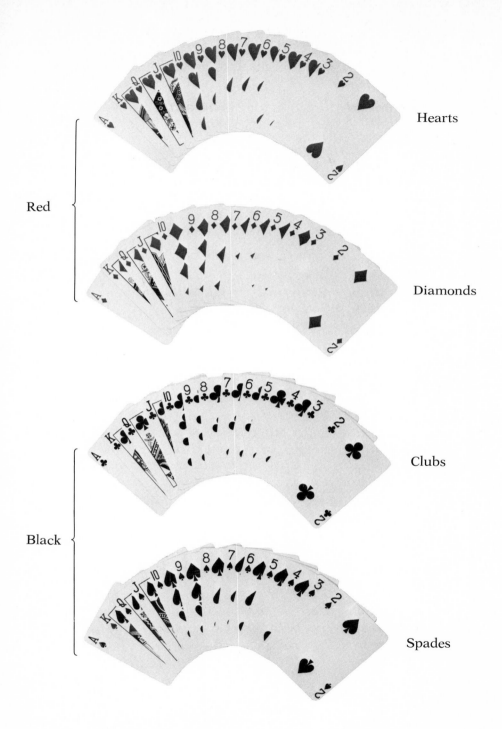

Red

Hearts

Diamonds

Black

Clubs

Spades

4. Weathermen sometimes say that the chance of rain on a particular day is 0%, sometimes even 100%. Change these numbers to probabilities and discuss the wisdom of such statements.

5. What is your reaction to being rained on when the weatherman says that the chance of rain is 10%? Should it have rained? Comment.

6. A factory operates in such a way that it pollutes the air in excess of Federal standards about 10% of the days it operates. Specifically, the chance it will pollute on any given day is 10%. What is the probability that the factory pollutes the air excessively two days in a row?

7. Each time he bats, a particular baseball player gets a hit with probability 3/10.

   (a) He bats three times. What is the probability he gets three hits? *Hint:* Each hit is an event.
   (b) He bats three times. What is the probability he gets no hit?
   (c) He bats three times. What is the probability that he gets a hit the first time and gets no hit the second and third times?

8. Two cards are selected from a standard deck of 52 cards, one right after the other. In other words, the first card is not replaced before the second card is drawn.

   (a) What is the probability that the first card drawn is a club and the second card is a heart?
   (b) What is the probability that both cards drawn are hearts?
   (c) What is the probability that both cards drawn are black?
   (d) What is the probability that neither card drawn is a diamond?

9. A coin has been flipped seven times and has come up heads each time. What is the probability that it will come up heads the next time it is flipped?

Genetics and Probability   When purebred red-flowering pea plants are crossbred with purebred white-flowering pea plants, all plants of the resulting generation (called F₁) are red. Each original red plant has two dominant genes *RR* (for red-red). Each original white plant has two recessive genes *ww* (for white-white). Both the red-flowering and the white-flowering parent plants are called *homozygous*, because both their color genes are the same. The resulting plants of generation F₁ are *heterozygous;* their color genes are different. Each plant of F₁ has one red gene and one white gene, which can be denoted as *Rw*.

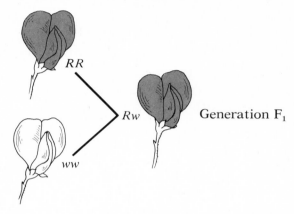

Although each plant of F₁ contains one red (*R*) gene and one white (*w*) gene (one gene from each parent), the flowers are red because the gene for red is *dominant*. The only way that a white-flowering plant can be produced is by uniting two white genes, one from each of two plants. Observe next the generation F₂ produced by two plants from F₁, both with genes *Rw*.

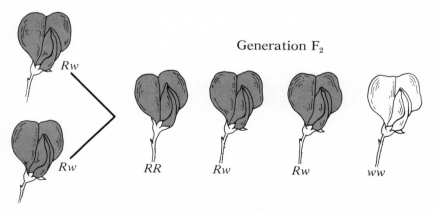

The results *RR*, *Rw*, *Rw*, and *ww* represent all four ways that genes can be combined using one gene from each plant. Four is not necessarily the number of plants produced; there may, in fact, be dozens of plants produced. Three fourths of the plants of generation F_2 are red-flowering and one fourth (*ww* only) are white-flowering plants. If a plant of F_2 is selected at random, the probability is 3/4 that it will have red flowers. Determine the probability of each event in Application 10.

10. (a) A plant of F_1 will have red flowers.
    (b) A plant of F_1 will have white flowers.
    (c) A plant of F_1 will be heterozygous.
    (d) A plant of F_2 will have white flowers.
    (e) A plant of F_2 will be homozygous.

11. When purebred red snapdragons (RR) are crossbred with purebred white snapdragons (WW), all plants of the resulting F_1 generation are pink (RW). This is an example of what is called *incomplete dominance*. Neither color dominates, they blend. When two pink members (RW and RW) of F_1 are crossbred, the results are RR, RW, RW, and WW—in equal amounts. Determine the probability of each event listed below.

    (a) A plant of F_1 will be red.
    (b) A plant of F_1 will be white.
    (c) A plant of F_1 will be pink.
    (d) A plant of F_2 will be red.
    (e) A plant of F_2 will be white.
    (f) A plant of F_2 will be pink.

12. If two events A and B are mutually exclusive (that is, A and B cannot both occur at the same time), then

$$P(A \text{ or } B) = P(A) + P(B)$$

One card is selected from a standard deck of 52 cards.

    (a) What is the probability that either a club or a diamond is selected. (Let A be the event a club is selected and B be the event a diamond is selected.)
    (b) What is the probability that the card selected is either an ace or a face card?
    (c) What is the probability it is either a red card or a seven?

Are the events in part (c) mutually exclusive, or is it possible to select a card that is both red and a seven? Did you notice that $P(A \text{ or } B) \neq P(A) + P(B)$ in this case? The rule fails because the events are not mutually exclusive, so you are counting the two red sevens twice—once as red cards and once as sevens.

13. Let $P(E)$ be the probability of an event. Suppose it is known only that $P(E)$ is greater than $1/2$. In view of this, is event E (a) unlikely to occur, (b) certain to occur, (c) very likely to occur, or (d) more likely to occur than not occur? Explain your choice.

14. A cardplayer is dealt two cards, a 7 and a 10. He asks to be dealt a third card. What is the probability that the sum of the three cards is 21 or less? Assume that a standard 52-card deck is being used and that face cards are worth ten each, aces are worth one each, and all others are worth whatever the number on them specifies.

15. Here is a situation in which all outcomes are not equally likely. A die is loaded so that 5 will come up half the time, and half the time a number other than 5 will come up. Each of the numbers 1, 2, 3, 4, and 6 is just as likely to come up as any other of these numbers. The die is rolled.
    (a) What is the probability that 5 will come up?
    (b) What is the probability that either 1, 2, 3, 4, or 6 will come up?
    (c) What is the probability that 3 will come up?
    (d) What is the probability that an even number will come up?
    (e) What is the probability that an odd number will come up?

PSYCHOLOGICAL PROBABILITY

People often make decisions based on experience and emotion rather than on the actual mathematical probabilities associated with a situation. Probabilities based on emotion are called *psychological probabilities*. Such subjective probabilities are applied, among others, by students who study until they *think* they are sufficiently prepared for a test or exam, by people who will not fly in an airplane because they *fear* that the plane will crash, and by managers who offer big raises to key employees who they *suspect* will leave unless they receive such raises. Such psychological probabilities are still numerically between 0 and 1, just like other probabilities.

APPLICATIONS AND EXERCISES

1. Psychological experiments have demonstrated a definite relationship between the length of time people take to respond to a question and their doubt about the answer to the question. What do you think this relationship would be for most people? Give a few examples to support your suspicion.

2. You are about to walk across a constantly busy intersection. There is no signal or stop sign. When you feel it is safe enough, you cross the street. What do you believe is the probability that you will get safely to the other side?

3. You are trying to make a left turn across a busy street. You've been waiting for at least two minutes and you're growing increasingly impatient. What probability of success would you assign to the most dangerous chance you would take to make a turn?

4. A psychologist interviews married couples. One question asked each couple interviewed is "What is the probability that your first child is a girl?" Explain how different couples will answer this question, and why their answers will differ. Also, comment on response time for different people. Keep in mind that some couples may not want children, may already have children, may plan to adopt children, or may not be capable of having children.

5. Parents having two children, both girls, are asked about the chances that their next child (if they were to have another) would be a boy. List and explain possible responses.

6. The following exercise was designed by a psychologist to raise questions regarding perception and the manner in which perception is influenced by past experience. Begin with the following list of numbers covered. Then reveal the numbers so that viewers can see only one number at a time: First 1000; then 1000; then 20; and so on. Ask the par-

ticipants to add the numbers out loud as they are uncovered.

$$1000$$
$$1000$$
$$20$$
$$1000$$
$$40$$
$$1000$$
$$30$$
$$1000$$
$$10$$

Invariably, more than half the participants will arrive at a total of 6000 rather than 5100.

(a)   If E is the event that a participant chosen at random will guess 6000, then is $P(E)$ (a) greater than $\frac{1}{2}$, (b) less than $\frac{1}{2}$, (c) equal to $\frac{1}{2}$, (d) equal to 1? Explain your choice.

(b)   If F is the event that a participant chosen at random will guess 5100, then is $P(F)$ (a) at least $\frac{1}{2}$, (b) less than $\frac{1}{2}$, (c) $\frac{1}{2}$, (d) 0? Explain your choice.

(c)   Can you explain why so many people will add these numbers incorrectly?

EXPECTATION

Next, we'll describe two different games of chance. Decide which game you would rather risk your money playing. In each game you pay $1 to play. In the first game a coin is flipped. If it comes up heads you win $2. If it is tails you win nothing. In the second game a die is rolled. If it comes up 4 you win $3. Otherwise, you win nothing.

Which game do you prefer? Which game is fairer to you? In which game can you *expect* to do better in the long run (that is, many plays at $1 each) or on the average? In the first game, the probability of winning $2 is $\frac{1}{2}$. So in the long run you'll win $2 half the time and $0 half the time. Can you see that on the average you'll win $1 per time you play the game? Mathematically, the idea that half the time (probability $= \frac{1}{2}$) you'll win $2 and half the time (probability $= \frac{1}{2}$) you'll win $0 can be stated as

$$\frac{1}{2} \cdot \$2 + \frac{1}{2} \cdot \$0$$

This expression is called the *expectation* or *expected value* of the game. It is the amount that you can expect to win on the average, even though in this case you can never actually win $1 on a given try. So for this coin game,

$$\text{Expectation} = \frac{1}{2} \cdot \$2 + \frac{1}{2} \cdot \$0 = \$1$$

The expectation is the fair price to pay in order to play the game; and since in this case you had to pay $1 to play, this coin-flipping game is indeed fair.

Were you able to determine intuitively that the second game is not fair, that you should expect to lose money in the long run playing that game? Recall that you win $3 if a 4 is rolled on the die, which occurs with probability $\frac{1}{6}$. On the other hand, you win nothing if a 1, 2, 3, 5, or 6 is rolled, which happens $\frac{5}{6}$ of the time. Mathematically, the expectation of this game is only 50¢, as shown next.

$$\text{Expectation} = \frac{1}{6} \cdot \$3 + \frac{5}{6} \cdot \$0 = \$.50$$

You can expect to win only 50¢ on the average, yet you pay $1 to play. Clearly, this game is not a fair one.

APPLICATIONS AND EXERCISES

1. You are asked to play a card game in which one card is dealt face up. If it is a diamond, you win $100. Otherwise you win nothing. What is the fair price to pay in order to play this game once? The deck used is a standard 52-card deck.

2. The Maryland state lottery issues one million (1,000,000) tickets. One ticket is drawn and the winner gets $50,000.

Courtesy of Maryland State Lottery Commission

(a) What is the expectation of this game?
(b) Marylanders pay 50¢ per ticket. Is this fair?
(c) Why do you think the ticket is priced to give the state such an advantage?

3. A raffle offers a first prize of $500 and a second prize of $200. If 10,000 tickets are being sold, what is the fair price to pay for a ticket, assuming the raffle is not intended to net any profit for those running it?

4. I will roll two dice. If they both come up the same, you win $30. If the sum of the dice is odd, you win $4. Otherwise you win nothing.

(a) What is the expectation of this game?
(b) I request that you pay $3 to play. Comment.
(c) I request that you pay $10 to play. Comment.

5. The probability of a businessman's making $800 in a business deal is $\frac{3}{4}$. The probability of his losing $200 on the deal is $\frac{1}{4}$. What is his expectation? Be careful on this one.

6. The person spinning the spinner shown here wins according to where the arrow stops. If it stops on A, he wins $10, if on B, $8, and if on C, $3. What is the expectation of this game? (Assume the arrow never stops on the boundary between regions.)

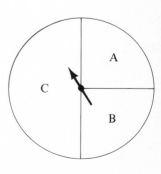

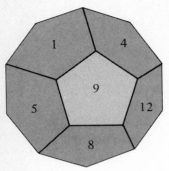

7. The sides of a dodecahedron are numbered with integers 1 through 12. When it is rolled, you win $1 if it comes up 1, $2 if 2, $3 if 3, and so on. What is the expectation of this game?

8. The dodecahedron of Exercise 7 is rolled. If it comes up a number that is a divisor of 12, you win $10. If not, you win $2. It costs $5 to play this game. Is it fair? Explain.

9. A carnival weight guesser guesses people's weights correctly about $\frac{7}{10}$ of the time. If she guesses wrong, you win a prize worth $2. How much is the fair price to pay to try to win a prize?

PERMUTATIONS AND COMBINATIONS

Sometimes probability problems have settings in which permutations and combinations are involved. This section presents basic concepts of permutations and combinations and some associated probability problems.

A *permutation* is an order or an arrangement. There are many different ways in which the letters a, b, c, d, and e can be arranged in a row. Here are three different arrangements.

a b c d e

b a e c d

e c b a d

Just how many different arrangements are there altogether? You could try listing all the different arrangements and then counting them, but that's a long process, because as it turns out there are 120 different arrangements. The number of arrangements, 120, can be determined without listing all the possibilities. To see how this is done, imagine five slots, each to be filled in with one letter.

___ ___ ___ ___ ___

Any one of the five letters can be placed in the first slot.

<u> 5 </u> ___ ___ ___ ___

Then there will be only four letters available for placement in the next slot.

$$\underline{5}\quad\underline{4}\quad\underline{}\quad\underline{}\quad\underline{}$$

Continuing, there are successively 3, 2, and 1 letters for the remaining slots.

$$\underline{5}\quad\underline{4}\quad\underline{3}\quad\underline{2}\quad\underline{1}$$

The placing of five letters has been considered five events; and all five must occur one right after the other. That is, we place any of

5 and 4 and 3 and 2 and 1

letters in succession. The number of ways this can be done is $5 \cdot 4 \cdot 3 \cdot 2 \cdot 1$, which multiplies out to be 120.

Products such as $5 \cdot 4 \cdot 3 \cdot 2 \cdot 1$ and $7 \cdot 6 \cdot 5 \cdot 4 \cdot 3 \cdot 2 \cdot 1$ occur frequently enough to be named and given a special notation. They are examples of *factorials*. Here is a table of some such products, their names, and the notation.

Product	Name	Notation	Value
$7 \cdot 6 \cdot 5 \cdot 4 \cdot 3 \cdot 2 \cdot 1$	7 factorial	7!	5040
$6 \cdot 5 \cdot 4 \cdot 3 \cdot 2 \cdot 1$	6 factorial	6!	720
$5 \cdot 4 \cdot 3 \cdot 2 \cdot 1$	5 factorial	5!	120
$4 \cdot 3 \cdot 2 \cdot 1$	4 factorial	4!	24
$3 \cdot 2 \cdot 1$	3 factorial	3!	6
$2 \cdot 1$	2 factorial	2!	2
1	1 factorial	1!	1

Suppose your club has ten members, from among whom will be elected a president, vice-president, secretary, and treasurer. In how many ways can the results of the electron turn out? There are 10 possibilities for president. After the president is elected, then there are 9 people left who could be elected vice-president. After that selection, there are 8 people who could be secretary. Finally, there will be 7 people who could be elected treasurer. The overall election can thus turn out in any of $10 \cdot 9 \cdot 8 \cdot 7$, or 5040, ways. The election of four officers was treated as four separate events, one following the other.

What is the probability that Bob is elected president, Ann vice-president, Albert secretary, and Donna treasurer? Of the 5040 possible elections, only one of them is the particular result mentioned in the question. Thus, there is only one favorable outcome. On the other hand, there are 5040 total outcomes. Thus, the probability of this particular election result is 1/5040. This assumes, of course, that each person is equally likely to be elected to any office. Is that usually the case in clubs?

If some of the elements used in permutations are the same, then there will be fewer distinguishable permutations than if all are different. For example, the letters a, b, c, and d can be arranged in 4! or 24 different ways. These permuations are listed next.

abcd	bacd	cabd	dabc
abdc	badc	cadb	dacb
acbd	bcad	cbad	dbac
acdb	bcda	cbda	dbca
adbc	bdac	cdab	dcab
adcb	bdca	cdba	dcba

If instead three of the letters are the same, as with a, b, b, and b, then there are fewer distinguishable permutations. In fact, there are only four permutations: abbb, babb, bbab, and bbba. The reason there are fewer is because there are no longer four different letters. If the three b's were different, then there would be 3! times as many permutations. Three different letters would contribute 3! permutations to the product.

$$a, \underline{b}, \underline{b}, \underline{b} \qquad 4 \text{ permutations}$$

$$a, \underline{b}, \underline{c}, \underline{d} \qquad 4(3!) \text{ permutations}$$

Note that 4(3!) is the same as 4!, since $4(3!) = 4 \cdot 3 \cdot 2 \cdot 1 = 4!$

Working backward, you should see that the number of permutations of a, b, b, and b, namely four, could have been computed by dividing 4! by 3!; that is, by dividing out the effect of the three b's being the same. In other words, divide out the 3! orders that are not present because the b's are the same. Again, the number of permutations of a, b, b, and b is 4!/3! = 4.

See if you can determine how many different permutations

are possible using the letters of the word CHEESE. If all six letters were different, there would be 6! permutations. But since there are three E's, divide out the 3! orders that are not contributed. So the number of permutations of the word CHEESE is 6!/3!, which can be simplified as

$$\frac{6!}{3!} = \frac{6 \cdot 5 \cdot 4 \cdot 3 \cdot 2 \cdot 1}{3 \cdot 2 \cdot 1} = 6 \cdot 5 \cdot 4 = 120$$

If the five letters a, b, c, d, and e are taken two at a time for different arrangements of two letters each, there will be $5 \cdot 4$ or 20 permutations (since the first of the letters can be any of five letters, and the second any of the four remaining letters). For the purpose of the development in the next few paragraphs only, we'll write $5 \cdot 4$ as 5!/3!. The following calculation shows that these two expressions are indeed equal.

$$5 \cdot 4 = \frac{5 \cdot 4}{1} \cdot \frac{3!}{3!} = \frac{5!}{3!}$$

Here are the 20 arrangements.

ab ad bc be ce ac ae bd cd de
ba da cb eb ec ca ea db dc ed

Suppose instead that we change our intention and insist that we don't care about different orders; we only want to count different *combinations* of letters. In other words, ab and ba are different permutations, but they are the same combination of letters, since both use a and b. To obtain combinations, divide out the order built into the 5!/3! permutations. In each case two letters are used, so divide by 2! to eliminate the orders. Here, permutations = 5!/3! = 20, and combinations = 5!/(3!2!) = 10. To convert from permutations to combinations, you must divide by the factorial of the number of elements selected for each combination. This will divide out the order. But to avoid relying on permutations for every problem involving combinations, a special notation is used for combinations. We write 5!/(3!2!) as

$$\binom{5}{2}$$

Thus, $\binom{5}{2}$ is the number of combinations of 5 things selected 2 at a time. Similarly, $\binom{9}{4}$ is the number of combinations of 9 things taken 4 at a time. In terms of factorials,

$$\binom{9}{4} \quad \text{is} \quad \frac{9!}{4!5!}$$

For computation,

$$\binom{5}{2} = \frac{5!}{2!3!} = \frac{5 \cdot 4 \cdot 3 \cdot 2 \cdot 1}{2 \cdot 1 \cdot 3 \cdot 2 \cdot 1} = \frac{5 \cdot 4}{2} = 10$$

$$\binom{9}{4} = \frac{9!}{4!5!} = \frac{9 \cdot 8 \cdot 7 \cdot 6 \cdot 5 \cdot 4 \cdot 3 \cdot 2 \cdot 1}{4 \cdot 3 \cdot 2 \cdot 1 \cdot 5 \cdot 4 \cdot 3 \cdot 2 \cdot 1}$$

$$= \frac{9 \cdot 8 \cdot 7 \cdot 6}{4 \cdot 3 \cdot 2} = 126$$

The 3! that appears in the calculation of $\binom{5}{2}$ is the factorial of the difference between 5 and 2. The 5! that appears in the calculation of $\binom{9}{4}$ is the factorial of the difference between 9 and 4. In general,

$$\binom{n}{r} = \frac{n!}{r!(n - r)!}$$

Committees, for example, are combinations of people rather than permutations of people. The order in which the members of a committee are selected, or seat themselves, or enter a room has nothing to do with the makeup of the committee. Suppose there are seven people from whom a committee of three people must be chosen. In how many different ways can that committee be selected? The committee can be selected in any of $\binom{7}{3}$ ways. This simplifies to 35, which you can check by evaluating $\binom{7}{3}$.

Here is a probability problem that involves the use of combinations. You are dealt five cards from a standard deck of 52. What is the probability that all five cards are spades? Recall that there are 13 spades in the deck. So the number of ways in which you could get a combination of five spades from the 13 spades in the deck is $\binom{13}{5}$. This is the number of favorable outcomes. The total number of outcomes possible is $\binom{52}{5}$, the number of ways in which any five cards can be selected from the deck of 52 cards. This means

$$P(5 \text{ spades}) = \frac{\text{favorable}}{\text{total}} = \frac{\binom{13}{5}}{\binom{52}{5}} = \frac{1287}{2,598,960} \doteq .0005$$

The symbol $\doteq$ means approximately equal to.

APPLICATIONS AND EXERCISES

1. How many different license plates can be made in the form of two letters followed by three digits: LL DDD (L = letter, D = digit)? Assume that any letter A through Z can be used and any digit 0 through 9 can be used. Letters and digits can be repeated on a given license plate.

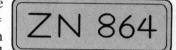

2. In how many ways can a committee of four people be selected from a group of nine people?

3. In how many ways can a committee of three faculty and two students be selected from 100 faculty and 2500 students? Do not attempt to simplify or work out the expression that represents your answer.

4. A secretary has typed five letters and addressed five envelopes.

    (a) In how many ways can the five letters be placed in the five envelopes, one per envelope?

    (b) If she places letters in envelopes at random, what is the probability that she will get all five letters in the correct envelopes?

5. Computers use binary digits—0 and 1 only. A computer word then is an ordered pattern of zeros and ones. How many different computer words having exactly eight binary digits each are possible?

Typical word: | 0 0 1 0 1 0 0 0 |

6. A crossword puzzle has space for five words. The first can be any of three possible words. The second can be any of six other words. The third can be any of four other words. The fourth can be only one word. The fifth can be any of three possible words. How many different "solutions" are possible?

7. A basketball squad has a total of 12 players, but only five of them can play at a given time, of course. How many different teams of five can be made up from the squad?

8. A basketball squad has five guards, four forwards, and two centers. How many different teams can they field? (A team consists of two guards, two forwards, and a center.)

9. You are dealt five cards from a standard deck of 52. What is the probability that all five cards are red?

10. A test has seven true–false questions. It also has five multiple-choice questions with four selections possible for each.
    (a) In how many different ways can the test questions be answered?
    (b) What is the probability that someone will answer all 12 questions correctly purely by guessing?

McAuliffe 2b
Northrup cf
Kaline rf
Horton lf
Cash 1b
Freehan c
Stanley ss
Wert 3b
Lolich p

11. A baseball team has nine players that are listed in the order they bat.
    (a) How many different batting orders are possible?
    (b) If the first four batting positions have already been determined, how many batting orders are possible?

12. In bridge, a standard deck of 52 cards is dealt to four players. In other words, each bridge hand contains 13 cards.
    (a) How many different bridge hands are possible? Do not simplify your answer.

(b) In how many ways can the 52 cards be dealt to the four players? Again, do not simplify your answer.

13. The explanation of the 15 puzzle in Chapter 1 (page 43) included a note that the number of different positions possible is more than 20 trillion. Use your knowledge of permutations to verify this. Keep in mind that the position of the blank space matters as much as the position of any number. *Use a calculator.* Note: 20 trillion = 20,000,000,000,000.

1	2	3	4
5	6	7	8
9	10	11	12
13	14	15	

14. In the hexadecimal number system, 16 different symbols are used as digits. How many different four-symbol hexadecimal numbers can be written?

15. The Greek alphabet contains 24 letters.

(a) How many different two-letter fraternity names can be composed with Greek letters?

(b) How many different three-letter fraternity names can be composed with Greek letters?

(c) How many different two- or three-letter fraternity names can be composed with Greek letters?

A	Alpha	N	Nu
B	Beta	Ξ	Xi
Γ	Gamma	O	Omicron
Δ	Delta	Π	Pi
E	Epsilon	P	Rho
Z	Zeta	Σ	Sigma
H	Eta	T	Tau
Θ	Theta	Υ	Upsilon
I	Iota	Φ	Phi
K	Kappa	X	Chi
Λ	Lambda	Ψ	Psi
M	Mu	Ω	Omega

16. A manufacturer of men's slacks decides to make plaid slacks. The company has ten different colors to choose from. It is agreed that some slacks will be made using three different colors; others will contain four different colors. How many different pairs of slacks can be made? Note that two pairs of slacks are the same only if all of their colors are the same.

17. A box contains seven yellow marbles and five blue marbles. Sally reaches in and grabs three marbles at random. What is the probability that when she opens her hand she will see three yellow marbles?

18. Explain why a combination lock should really be called a *permutation* lock.

19. Pascal's triangle was introduced in Chapter 1 (page 6). The numbers in the triangle happen to be the values of various combinations. The triangle

$$
\begin{array}{ccccccc}
 & & & 1 & & & \\
 & & 1 & & 1 & & \\
 & 1 & & 2 & & 1 & \\
1 & & 3 & & 3 & & 1 \\
\end{array}
$$

is the same as

$$
\begin{array}{cccc}
 & & \binom{0}{0} & & \\
 & \binom{1}{0} & & \binom{1}{1} & \\
\binom{2}{0} & & \binom{2}{1} & & \binom{2}{2} \\
\binom{3}{0} & \binom{3}{1} & \binom{3}{2} & \binom{3}{3} \\
\end{array}
$$

Of course, both triangles can be extended indefinitely.

(a) Generate three more rows of each triangle.

(b) By comparing the two triangles, you can see that $\binom{4}{3} = 4$, $\binom{5}{3} = 10$, and $\binom{6}{3} = 20$. Verify this by working out each of the combinations according to the meaning of the combination symbol.

(c) According to the triangles, what is the value of $\binom{3}{0}$?

(d) In terms of a combination problem, what is the meaning of $\binom{3}{0}$? Does the value of $\binom{3}{0}$ obtained in part (c) seem consistent with this meaning?

(e) From the triangle, $\binom{4}{4} = 1$. What must be the value of 0! for this to be true?

(f) From a combination problem point of view, does $\binom{4}{4} = 1$ seem reasonable? Explain.

(g)   Determine the value of $\binom{4}{3}$ and of $\binom{4}{1}$. Determine the value of $\binom{5}{2}$ and of $\binom{5}{3}$. Determine the value of $\binom{6}{2}$ and of $\binom{6}{4}$. Comment on an apparent relationship.

STATISTICS

In probability, computations are made by determining the number of favorable outcomes and the total number of outcomes. Dividing the number of favorable outcomes by the total number of outcomes produces the probability that an event will occur. The number obtained is exact, because all cases have been considered. *Statistical inference* often deals with situations in which it is impossible to obtain directly an exact value for favorable/total outcomes. Instead, a relatively small representative sample of the desired population is studied and conclusions about the whole population are made from that study. For example, political polls sample perhaps 1000 voters and then draw conclusions about the political feelings of the entire voting public. Sponsors of TV shows want an estimate of the number of people watching their show. They may be told that 20 million people watched their show. That result is a statistical conclusion based on monitoring or contacting only a few thousand viewers.

One of the statistician's problems is obtaining fair data. If the poll takers go to the college campus to interview all 1000 voters for their survey, then they will not get a fair sample of the opinions of the country. The percentage of voters in college is very small, and it is a biased group, not representative of the entire country. Similarly, a visit to Wall Street for the 1000 voters might be misleading. One thousand votes from the inner city is also a biased sample. Obtaining a truly unbiased random sample of the population is very difficult; and if such a sample is not obtained, then the conclusions drawn may not be valid.

Actual techniques of statistical inference are beyond the scope of this book. Instead, this section is devoted to a brief look at *descriptive statistics*. In descriptive statistics, averages and other numbers are computed from the data obtained in order to describe or classify that data. No conclusions or inferences are made about any larger group of data.

Specific characteristics of a set of data can be obtained through numerical computation. There are several different kinds of averages, or measures of *central tendency*. Perhaps the most popular measure of central tendency is the *arithmetic mean*, denoted by $\bar{x}$ (read as "x bar"). This is the average obtained by adding all n numbers and dividing by n. As an example, consider a student who has taken five tests in a mathematics course. Her grades are 87, 75, 78, 91, and 92. Can you determine her average, that is, the arithmetic mean of the grades? Use pencil and paper. You should find the sum of the five numbers and then divide the sum by 5. Her average is 84.6.

$$\bar{x} = \frac{87 + 75 + 78 + 91 + 92}{5} = 84.6$$

The *median* of a set of data is the middle number in the set, when the numbers are arranged in order. In other words, there are just as many numbers larger than the median as there are numbers smaller than the median. If the set of data contains an even number of numbers, then the median is the arithmetic average (mean) of the two central numbers. Average per capita income of counties and states is often given as median income. A median income of $6500 means that there are just as many incomes above $6500 as there are incomes below $6500. The median is less susceptible to distortion by extreme values than is the mean. Although an income of $2,000,000 would distort the mean, the median would essentially be unaffected by it. The median of the incomes $5000, $6000, $9000, $10,000, and $70,000 is $9000 because $9000 is in the middle when the set of data is arranged in order. The mean income is $20,000, but that does not present a really good picture of the "average" in this instance, since four out of the five incomes are far less than this "average." Here the median is more representative of the average than is the mean.

The *mode* of a set of data is the number that has the greatest frequency, that is, the number that occurs most often in the set of data. (For instance, the mode of dress is the form or style most people adopt.) If there are two such numbers of greatest frequency, then the data set has two modes and is called bimodal. An advantage of the mode over other kinds of averages is that it requires no calculations. It is used in order to answer the following types of questions: What make of car do most people drive? What disease is the leading cause of death? Which brand of toothpaste do most dentists recommend? The mode of the numbers 1, 5, 8, 4, 6, 2, 8, 5, 8, 4, 9 is 8 because 8 has the greatest frequency. The number 8 appears three times in the set of data, and that is more times than any other number.

When stating the mean $\bar{x}$ for a set of data, it is also helpful to give some indication of the variation or dispersion of the data. In other words, how much, on the average, do the data items deviate from the mean? Are the data items grouped together near the mean or are they spread out? To see this point more clearly, consider two sets of data, both of which have a mean of 7.

$$\{1, 7, 13\} \qquad \{5, 7, 9\}$$

Both sets of data have a mean of 7, but you can see that they are quite different sets. In the first set, deviation from the mean is large compared with the much smaller deviation of the data of the second set.

The *standard deviation* (SD) is one type of computed deviation from the mean. It gives the average amount by which data items deviate from their mean. The standard deviation is computed as follows.

1. Determine by how much each data item differs from the mean.
2. Square each of those deviations.
3. Add all of the squares of the deviations to form one sum.
4. Divide that sum by n, the number of numbers.
5. Take the square root of that quotient.

Now let's determine the standard deviation of the data $\{1, 7, 13\}$, whose mean is 7.

Number	Deviation	(Deviation)^2
1	6	36
7	0	0
13	6	36
		72

The sum of the squares of the deviations is 72. Following step 4 next, divide this sum by 3. The result is 24. Finally, the square root of the quotient is $\sqrt{24}$, or approximately 4.9. So the standard deviation of the data {1, 7, 13} is approximately 4.9. A calculator was used to obtain the approximation of the square root.

See if you can follow this procedure to find the standard deviation of the data set {5, 7, 9}, which also has a mean of 7. When you have finished all your step-by-step calculations, compare with the following results. The deviations are 2, 0, and 2. So the squares of the deviations are 4, 0, and 4. The sum of the squares of the deviations is $4 + 0 + 4 = 8$. The sum divided by 3 (since $n = 3$ numbers) is 8/3 or about 2.67. So the standard deviation of the data is approximately $\sqrt{2.67}$, which (by calculator) is about 1.6. Did you notice that this data set, whose items are grouped much closer together, has a smaller standard deviation than the data set {1, 7, 13}, which is more spread out?

A standard deviation of 4.9 for the data {1, 7, 13} with mean 7 indicates that the data items deviate from their mean an average of nearly five units per data item. This indicates not only that the data items are spread out, but also that the mean of 7 is questionable as a so-called average representative of the data. On the other hand, a standard deviation of 1.6 for the data {5, 7, 9} with mean 7 indicates a relatively small average deviation of the data from the mean. This means not only that the data items are closer together, but also that a mean of 7 is reasonable as an "average" representative of the data.

We might digress for a moment to note that a student's grade point average (GPA) is computed in a way that resembles the computation of the arithmetic mean. Corresponding to each letter grade is a number of quality points. In one popular system, an A is 4 quality points, B is 3, C is 2, D is 1, and F is 0. To compute the total number of quality points earned for one course, multiply the number of credits given for the course by the number of quality points corresponding to the letter grade received in the course. For example, the grade of C in a 3-credit course is worth 6 quality points ($3 \cdot 2 = 6$, 3 credits times 2 quality points per credit for a C). The grade of A in a 2-credit course is worth a total of 8 quality points ($2 \cdot 4 = 8$, 2 credits times 4 quality points per credit for an A). The grade point average is defined and computed as

$$\text{GPA} = \frac{\text{total number of quality points for all courses}}{\text{total number of credits attempted}}$$

Suppose you have the following grade report:

Grade	Credits
A	3
B	2
C	4

Let's compute your grade point average. First, an A is worth 4 quality points for each credit, and the A is in a 3-credit course. Thus, the quality points contributed by the A are $3 \cdot 4 = 12$. Similarly, 2 credits of B at 3 quality points per credit yields a total of 6 quality points: and 4 credits of C at 2 quality points per credit yields a total of 8 quality points. Thus, the total number of quality points from all courses is $12 + 6 + 8$, or 26. The total number of credits is $3 + 2 + 4$, or 9. Thus,

$$\text{GPA} = \frac{\text{total quality points}}{\text{total credits}} = \frac{26}{9} = 2.89$$

The grade point average for this report is approximately 2.89.

Speaking of grades, some teachers distribute grades according to a "normal distribution." In such a distribution of grades there will be more C's than any other grade. The number of A's and F's will be small. The number of B's and D's will be about equal, and there will be more B's than A's, but more C's than B's. Similarly, there will be more D's than F's, but more C's than D's. The next illustration is a graph, called a *histogram*, of the frequencies of letter grades in a distribution that is roughly normal. By frequency we mean "how many." The distribution is based on grades given to a class of 45 students.

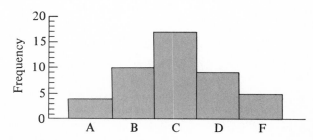

If you are able to read the histogram, then you have determined that there are 4 A's, 10 B's, 17 C's, 9 D's, and 5 F's.

Often the histogram is drawn instead as a smooth bell-shaped curve.

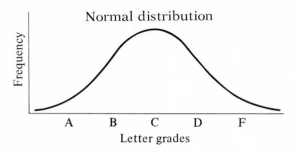

If the distribution is indeed normal, then approximately 68% of the data is distributed within 1 standard deviation of the mean; a total of about 95% is distributed within 2 standard deviations of the mean; and approximately 99% is distributed within 3 standard deviations of the mean.

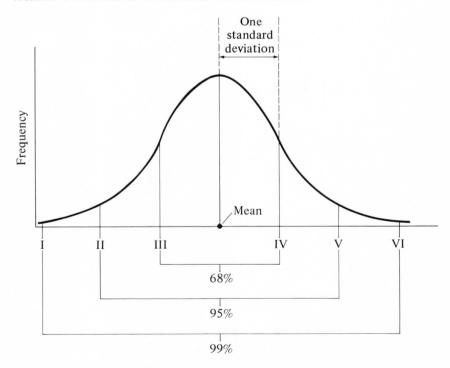

Approximately 68% of the data is distributed between III and

IV. A total of 95% is distributed between II and V, and 99% is distributed between I and VI.

A Galton board (illustrated next) is an interesting device that is used to produce a normal distribution. Balls drop from a funnel onto a board. On route to the bottom of the board they strike nails that are set in rows on the board. Compartments at the bottom of the board catch the balls. The center compartment catches the most, while the end compartments receive the fewest. The distribution of the balls is approximately a normal distribution.

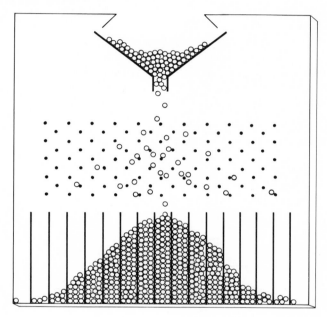

1. Find the mean, mode, and median of each set of data. Then explain which of these averages is probably the best choice to represent the average of the given set of data.

   (a) Weekly salaries in dollars: 200, 200, 210, 225, 540
   (b) Ticket prices in dollars: 1, 1, 2, 3, 4, 4, 4, 6, 6, 6, 6, 6, 20
   (c) Heights of people in inches: 65, 72, 69, 75, 75, 68, 71
   (d) Prices per pound of tomatoes: 79, 79, 69, 79, 49, 49, 49, 49, 59, 59, 69

2. Find the mean of the following numbers. One way to do this, of course, is to add up all the numbers and divide by 38. Do you see a better way, a short cut?

   5, 4, 7, 6, 4, 5, 5, 5, 4, 6, 7, 7, 6, 5, 4, 6, 6, 6, 7,
   7, 4, 4, 6, 5, 5, 6, 5, 4, 7, 7, 6, 4, 5, 5, 4, 6, 6, 7

3. Determine the mean and standard deviation of each set of data. Do not attempt to approximate the value of the square roots in sets (b) and (c) unless you have a calculator.
   (a)   4, 7, 11, 13, 15
   (b)   8, 3, 5, 6, 7, 10, 10
   (c)   6, 8, 12, 4, 2, 7, 5, 9, 10

4. Determine the grade point average (GPA) for each of the following grade reports. Assume an A is worth 4 quality points per credit; B is worth 3; C, 2; D, 1; and F, 0.

   (a)

Grade	Credits
A	3
B	3
C	3

   (b)

Grade	Credits
B	2
C	1
D	3

   (c)

Grade	Credits
A	3
B	4
C	5

   (d)

Grade	Credits
C	3
C	4
D	3
F	3

5. What is the numerical value of a perfect GPA? In other words, a straight A student has a GPA equal to ____.

6. Discuss the wisdom of automatically using a normal distribution to assign letter grades in a course. Can this work to the disadvantage of some members of the class? Explain. Can it be an advantage to some members? Explain.

7. Assume the following statement is true: The average American family includes 1.9 children.
   (a)   What does this mean, and how was this average computed?

(b) What kind of average could have been used instead in order to obtain a whole number? Do you think the whole-number average would be better in this case? Do you think the whole-number average would be better if the original average obtained had been 2.5 rather than 1.9? Explain.

8. One local newspaper claims the *average* income per household is $18,500. The other paper claims it is $15,700. Both newspapers are correct, and both used the same data. How is this possible?

9. A manufacturer of light bulbs is pleased to learn that his bulbs last an average (mean) of 200 hours.
   (a) Should the manufacturer still be pleased when he learns that the standard deviation is 10?
   (b) Should the manufacturer be pleased if he learns instead that the standard deviation is 100?
   (c) Based on your answers to parts (a) and (b), explain the importance of knowing the standard deviation as well as the average—in other words, that average alone is inadequate in many cases.

10. When Wilbur and Orville Wright wrote to the U.S. Weather Bureau, they were told that Kitty Hawk, North Carolina, offered the average wind speed they wanted for their experiments. Unfortunately, the Wright brothers wasted many days at Kitty Hawk because the winds were either too calm or too gusty. What additional statistical information probably would have been useful to the Wright brothers?

11. Explain why the mean, median, and mode of a normal distribution must all be the same number, namely, the number at the center of the distribution.

12. Suppose 200 test scores are distributed normally with mean 62 and standard deviation 9.
   (a) Based on the explanation given in our discussion of the normal distribution curve, approximately 68% of the scores are within 1 standard deviation of the mean. This means that about 68% of the scores are between ____ and ____ .

(b) Numerically, about how many scores are between 53 and 71?

(c) About how many scores are between 62 and 71?

(d) About how many scores are between 44 and 80?

(e) About 99% of the scores are between ____ and ____.

CRYPTANALYSIS AGAIN

One statistical approach to cryptanalysis is based on the relative frequencies of the letters of the alphabet as they occur in written text. To study such cryptanalysis, we shall use some of the techniques developed in Chapter 3 (see pages 128–133), although modular arithmetic itself will not be needed or used here.

Suppose a message is enciphered by using a variation of the Caesar cipher, one in which the alphabet is shifted. Suppose, too, that you don't know how many places it has been shifted. Each letter in the message may have been replaced by the letter three places beyond it in the normal alphabet (as with the Caesar cipher), or perhaps by the letter 17 places beyond it, or by . . . . There are many possibilities you could check, but you would not care to decipher the message 10 or 20 times until you find the right shift and therefore get a message that makes sense.

A better method for determining what shift has been made is based on the relative frequencies of the letters of the alphabet. In large samples of ordinary writing, the relative frequencies of the letters are always about the same. For example, about 13% of all letters are E, 6% are S, and 0% are Z. Note that these percentages are rounded off. To say that 0% are Z is misleading if the statement is not properly interpreted. Far less than 1% of letters are Z, and the percentage is so much closer to 0% than to 1%, that 0% is used in this setting. Next is a complete table of relative frequencies of letters based on large samples of ordinary text. Each number is a percentage.

A	8	J	0	S	6
B	1	K	0	T	9
C	3	L	4	U	3
D	4	M	3	V	1
E	13	N	7	W	2
F	3	O	8	X	0
G	2	P	2	Y	2
H	5	Q	0	Z	0
I	7	R	7		

If the letters A through Z are written in one horizontal line and marks are used to denote relative frequencies (one mark for 1%, two marks for 2%, and so on), we obtain the distribution pattern of letters of the alphabet. The pattern resembles a histogram.

To decipher a coded message, write down the letters A through Z of the message and mark the frequency of occurrence of each letter. Use one mark per occurrence. When all letters of the message have been noted and marked, compare the distribution obtained from the cipher message with the distribution of the normal alphabet. Determine how many places it must be shifted in order to look approximately like the distribution of the normal alphabet. As an example, suppose the cipher message yields the distribution shown next.

If you take this distribution and place it directly under the normal alphabet distribution, you can begin a comparison procedure. Move the cipher distribution to the right until the two distributions look about the same. Actually, you can only align a portion of the alphabets. In order to see all 26 letters align, you have to write the normal alphabet twice as shown next.

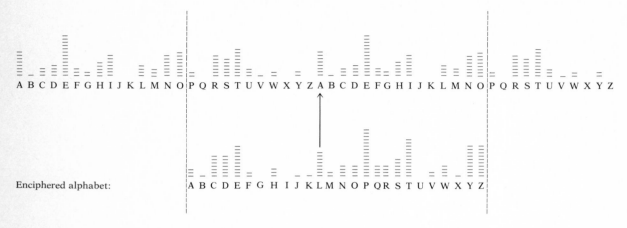

Enciphered alphabet:

Now you can see that an enciphered L is a normal A, an M is a B, and so on. Decoding the message is now a simple matter. When sliding one alphabet under the other, you may find it easier to align them if you observe that E will usually have the greatest frequency, or at least will almost always be outstanding in its region of the alphabet. The letter A comes four letters before E and has a rather high frequency. N and O are a high-frequency pair. R, S, and T are a high-frequency triple, with T almost always the highest of the three. J and K are a low-frequency pair and V, W, X, Y, and Z are five rather low ones in a row.

APPLICATIONS AND EXERCISES

1. Using a newspaper, newsmagazine, or novel, select a passage of approximately 1000 letters. Then go through the material and determine the frequency of each letter. One

way to do this is to first write all the letters of the alphabet on paper. Then go through the material once. Each time a particular letter is encountered, make a mark after that letter on the paper. When you have finished with the tally, compare your distribution with the distribution of the normal alphabet.

2. For each enciphered distribution (a)–(c), use the alignment approach to determine what cipher has been used. Then report which letter of the cipher corresponds to the letter A of the normal alphabet.

(a)   A B C D E F G H I J K L M N O P Q R S T U V W X Y Z

(b)   A B C D E F G H I J K L M N O P Q R S T U V W X Y Z

(c)   A B C D E F G H I J K L M N O P Q R S T U V W X Y Z

3. For each enciphered message (a)–(c), determine the distribution. Then determine what cipher has been used. Finally, translate the message.

(a)   BMJS FNW NX HTTQJI GJQTB NYX XFYZWFYNS UTNSY YMJ BFYJW AFUTW NS NY HTSIJSXJX YT KTWR HQTZIX. BMJS BFYJW AFUTW FY F YJFP-JYYQJ XUTZY NX HTTQJI GD YMJ FNW FWTZSI NY, F XRFQQ HQTZI KTWRX.

(b)   QTTIWDKTCH GTAPIXDC ID PGI BXVWI PABDHI QT STHRGXQTS PH ETGHDCPA. PGI LPH WXH VDSSTHH ID LWDB WT BPST ETIXIXDC, ID LWDB WT GTCSTGTS IWPCZH, LWDB WT STUTCSTS.

(c) IFHB QEB OBPQ LC XJBOFZXK XOQ, QEXQ LC QEB XJBOFZXK FKAFXK FP ZILPB QL LRO EBXOQP XKA IXKA. ZLIIBZQFKD FQ FP LKB LC QEB CBT LMMLOQRKFQFBP XJBOFZXKP EXSB LC ZLJFKD FK ZLKQXZQ TFQE X IFSFKD ZRIQROB QEXQ FP MXOQ LC QEBFO EBOFQXDB.

4. For each of the following enciphered paragraphs, determine the distribution. Then determine what cipher has been used. Finally, translate the paragraph.

(a) AOL JOPLM MHJAVYZ PUCVSCLK PU WYVKBJPUN AVVAO KLJHF HYL TVBAO IHJALYPH, MVVK, KLUAHS WSHXBL, HUK H ZBZJLWAPISL AVVAO ZBYMHJL. TVZA KLUAHS HBAOVYPAPLZ UVD JVUZPKLY HSS MVBY MHJAVYZ ULJLZZHYF AV AOL MVYTHAPVU VM KLJHF.

(b) AF LZW GDV VSQK ZW UGMDV ZSNW JWYSAFWV DWSVWJKZAH TQ YGAFY LG OSJ, TML LZW LJWSLAWK HDWVYWV ZAE FGL LG WFYSYW AF ZGKLADALAWK OALZ WALZWJ LZW OZALW EWF GJ GLZWJ LJATWK.

SERIATION

Archaeologists use a technique called *seriation* to determine relative dates of their findings. Relative dating amounts to placing the age of different findings in a chronological order without putting a specific date on any of the findings. For example, suppose an archaeologist discovers three different assemblages (call them A, B, and C) of related materials. By using seriation he may be able to deduce which assemblage came first in time, which came second, and which came last—even if he is unable to determine in what years they were made.

Seriation is based on the assumption that popularity is a fleeting thing. Styles change, usually according to the same pattern. The new style comes in slowly, being accepted at first by only a small percentage of possible users. Then, as the new style is accepted, its popularity increases. Eventually, however, people tire of the style and newer styles appear. As a result, the once-popular style decreases in popularity. The pattern of frequencies for style, then, will tend to have the following general look.

The length of each line indicates the frequency (or popularity) of the style. At first it is not too popular. This is shown by the first line. The second line shows an increase in popularity as the style begins to catch on. The third line shows the frequency of the style when it is at its peak of popularity. The next two lines show the decrease in popularity as people tire of the style or a newer style appears.

There is nothing sacred about the number of lines in the pattern. Five lines were used above, but more or fewer lines could be used to describe the same idea. Each of the following patterns conveys about the same message as the original one.

Is it apparent that each of these four patterns is essentially the same?

One style usually decreases in popularity as another style increases in popularity. See if you can observe this in the next two patterns.

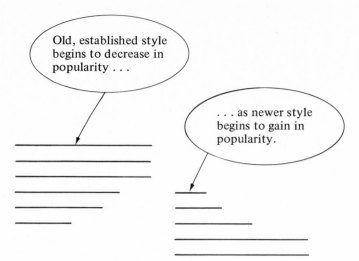

This second style will decrease in popularity when a third style catches on. This is shown next (and this process could continue indefinitely).

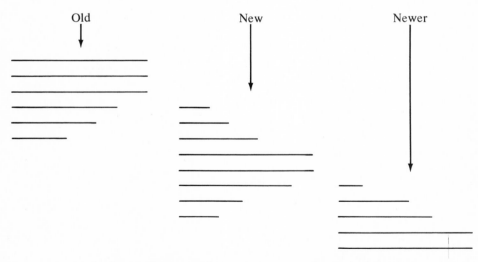

Now let's see how such patterns can be helpful in seriation, that is, arrangement of archaeological assemblages in relative chronological order. Suppose that nine sites within a region are excavated. There are similarities among the artifacts found, but there are enough differences to suggest that the sites were inhabited at different times. It is observed that the pottery is made in three different styles: plain white, white with wavy red markings, and white with straight red markings.

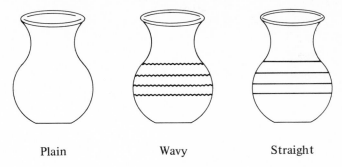

| Plain | Wavy | Straight |

The percentage of each style found varies from site to site. The findings are tabulated as

Site	Plain (P)[a] %	Wavy (W)[a] %	Straight (S)[a] %
1	100	0	0
2	0	70	30
3	50	50	0
4	0	20	80
5	0	0	100
6	70	30	0
7	0	100	0
8	30	70	0
9	0	60	40

[a]Relative frequencies expressed as percentages.

We could use lines to represent frequencies, as we did before this example. But unless we plan to place each line of information on a separate strip for rearranging, such an approach would be difficult visually.

The problem now is to arrange the nine items so that they yield a sequence showing gradual increase and decrease. Done randomly, this arranging can be quite a task, unless you are lucky enough to find the right sequence early. From your knowledge of permutations, you should realize that there are 9! (which is 362,880) different arrangements (see Exercise 3, page 361).

Looking carefully at the data can save some time. Note that site 1 shows 100% plain, site 5 shows 100% straight, and site 7 shows 100% wavy. So if the sites are to be arranged chronologically, then one of these three sites must be first, one in the middle, and one last in sequence.

Assume for the moment that site 1 is first. This means plain pottery came before the others. So plain pottery should decrease in frequency from 100% to 0% as some other kind of pottery increases in frequency. Looking at the table that displays the frequencies, we see that the order of sites must begin as 1, 6, 3, 8.

Site	P	W	S
1	100	0	0
6	70	30	0
3	50	50	0
8	30	70	0

Noting that the percentage of wavy pottery is increasing, and examining the five remaining entries in the table, we conclude that 100% wavy should come next if the pattern is to continue. Since it is at site 7 that there is 100% wavy, our table of chronological order of sites is now

Site	P	W	S
1	100	0	0
6	70	30	0
3	50	50	0
8	30	70	0
7	0	100	0

Now, of course, wavy pottery must decrease in frequency as straight pottery increases in frequency. So the next site numbers must be 2, 9, 4, and 5.

Site	P	W	S
1	100	0	0
6	70	30	0
3	50	50	0
8	30	70	0
7	0	100	0
2	0	70	30
9	0	60	40
4	0	20	80
5	0	0	100

The table seems to suggest that the chronological sequence of pottery is

plain
wavy
straight

But we could just turn the table upside down to get the sequence:

straight
wavy
plain

In other words, why must the sites be in the order

1
6
3
8
7
2
9
4
5

Why not, instead, the opposite order?

5
4
9
2
7
8
3
6
1

You might want to make the complete table of sites and frequencies that corresponds to this opposite order of sites. Doing so would enable you to see clearly that the pattern of increases and decreases in frequency is the same as in the order 1, 6, 3, 8, 7, 2, 9, 4, 5. With any luck at all, there are probably more artifacts at the sites, and they can be used to help determine whether plain or straight should come first. But it cannot be determined from just the data we now have.

It should be apparent from looking at the table that wavy cannot come first. If this is not apparent now, it will be when you do Exercise 1.

APPLICATIONS AND EXERCISES

1. Redo the pottery example by beginning with the assumption that wavy pottery came first. In other words, list site 7 as chronologically first, since it shows 100% wavy pottery. What happens when you continue this procedure, and what conclusion can you make?

2. (a) Use seriation to determine the chronological order of the following three axlike tools found at ten sites.

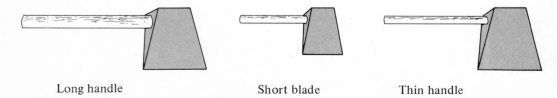

Long handle   Short blade   Thin handle

Site	Long %	Short %	Thin %
1	80	20	0
2	40	60	0
3	0	100	0
4	50	0	50
5	25	75	0
6	0	0	100
7	30	0	70
8	60	40	0
9	75	0	25
10	100	0	0

(b) Suppose that evidence at sites 2 and 8 suggests that site 2 is older than site 8. What then must be the chronological order of the three axlike tools?

3. Explain why there are 9! permutations in the P–W–S pottery example.

4. Suppose two lines with a combined length of 1 centimeter are used to represent the frequencies of plain pottery and wavy-lined pottery. If 70% is plain and 30% is wavy, then how many millimeters long should each line be? (Note that 1 centimeter is the same as 10 millimeters.)

5. Use seriation to determine the chronological order of the following four cups found at 12 sites within a region. Assume that site 1 is known to be older than site 2.

One handle

Two handles

No handle

Tall

Site	One %	Two %	No %	Tall %
1	0	0	100	0
2	0	0	0	100
3	70	0	30	0
4	0	20	0	80
5	0	100	0	0
6	0	0	80	20
7	100	0	0	0
8	0	0	50	50
9	0	40	0	60
10	10	0	90	0
11	0	70	0	30
12	40	0	60	0

Computers and Mathematics

8

We have spent seven chapters looking at patterns, logic, and various fields of mathematics. You have undoubtedly gained some insight into mathematics and perhaps some appreciation for the subject. Calculations were minimized in order to help you look beyond the numbers and arithmetic, which can obscure the mathematical principles. Mathematicians who lived before the computer age were sometimes frustrated by the incredible quantities of computations that were necessary parts of their research. The search for machines to free thinkers from tedious computations began hundreds of years ago, but not until 1937 were the first large mechanical calculators and crude computers designed and built. Improvements have continued ever since.

Photo courtesy of IBM

A modern electronic computer

In some classes it may be advantageous to cover this chapter earlier in the course. In such cases, many of the programming problems can be integrated as parts of several chapters.

As computer capabilities have improved, the number and kinds of applications of computers to mathematics have increased. You are undoubtedly aware of many uses of computers in society. Most likely, though, you are unaware of the applications of computers in mathematics.

The application of computers to solve problems in *number theory* is especially natural, since many tests and routine calculations are sometimes the method of proof. The French mathematician Pierre de Fermat (1601–1665) used a few test cases and reasoned inductively that perhaps

$$F(n) = 2^{2^n} + 1$$

produces only prime numbers for $n = 0, 1, 2, 3, \ldots$. Such numbers are now called *Fermat primes*. It can be shown that $F(0) = 3$, $F(1) = 5$, $F(2) = 17$, $F(3) = 257$, and $F(4) = 65{,}537$. All five of these numbers are prime. It was not until 1732 that Leonhard Euler showed that $F(5) = 4{,}294{,}967{,}297$ is not prime, since it is divisible by 641. But think of all the divisors that were tried and all the tiresome calculations before 641 was hit upon. The numbers $F(n)$ get large very quickly as n increases. A computer was used to show that $F(73)$ is not prime. Such a feat is admirable even for a computer and impossible for any man in his lifetime. Why? The number $F(73)$ contains approximately three sextillion *digits*. It is estimated that if the digits of $F(73)$ were typed on a tape, the tape would be long enough to wind around the equator thousands of times.

If you had a high school course in *geometry*, you may recall the proofs you studied and learned. There have been some proofs given in the earlier chapters of this book. Imagine a computer proving theorems! Yes, programs have been written that enable computers to prove some theorems of high school geometry as well as other theorems of more use to mathematicians who already know proofs of high school geometry theorems. Sometimes, the proof offered by the computer is surprisingly different from what is expected by those who programmed the computer. In one interesting case, a computer was requested to prove that if two sides of a triangle are equal, then the angles opposite those sides are equal. It proved this by first proving the triangle (call it *ABC*) was congruent to itself (but considered as *ACB*). Then the two angles in concern are corresponding parts of congruent triangles *ABC* and *ACB*, and hence they are equal. (An illustration is given with Exercise 4.)

Perhaps *numerical analysis* is the branch of mathematics in which the computer is most utilized. In numerical analysis, numerical procedures are developed for approximating processes in analysis and some other fields. In *calculus,* for example, the exact area under a curve is given by an integral. Evaluating the integrals considered in Chapter 6 is a simple matter compared with the evaluation of most other integrals that mathematicians and scientists encounter. Many require tricks, insight, tables, or various lengthy procedures to evaluate. As a result, numerical methods have been devised that approximate the value of the integral. In the development of the area under a curve in Chapter 6, we used a sum of rectangles to approximate the area. One standard numerical method uses a sum of trapezoids, another a sum of parabolas, to approximate the area under a curve. Many numerical methods have been devised to solve *differential equations.* (You recall that a differential equation is an equation containing derivatives.) Some methods of numerical analysis are designed to solve various algebraic equations and systems of equations. Still other methods yield the exact function whose graph passes through specific given points.

Curve fitting techniques such as the least squares method are still another group of numerical methods. In *statistics* the method of least squares is used to determine the equation of the line or curve that most closely fits the given data.

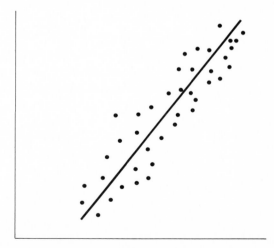

There are other applications of computers to mathematics. Entries in tables, such as the trigonometry table in Chapter 4, can be obtained quickly and to any desired degree of accuracy with the help of a computer. Approximations of numbers such as π and $\sqrt{2}$ can be obtained to any desired degree of accuracy. Students can let a computer assist them in examining limits, such as those presented in Chapter 6. Mechanical graph plotters exist that can be directed by computer instructions and data to sketch accurate graphs of desired mathematical functions.

The list of computer applications in mathematics is impressively long. This section has presented merely a glimpse of a few of them.

APPLICATIONS AND EXERCISES

1. Verify that $F(5)$ is indeed divisible by 641.

2. Using Fermat's formula $F(n) = 2^{2^n} + 1$, show that $F(3) = 257$. Then show that 257 is a prime number. (You may find it helpful to know that $\sqrt{257} \doteq 16$.)

3. $F(73)$ contains approximately 3 sextillion digits, that is, 3,000,000,000,000,000,000,000 digits. Assuming you could write the digits at the rate of one per second and without interruption, how many years would it take just to write down all of the digits of the number $F(73)$?

4. The computer showed that triangle ABC is congruent to triangle ACB by showing that two sides and the included angle of $\triangle ABC$ equal two sides and the included angle of $\triangle ACB$. All that is given is that $AB = AC$. List all the steps and reasons in the proof.

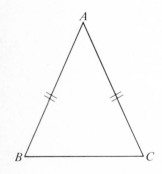

5. In 1801, Carl Friedrich Gauss proved a relationship between the Fermat primes $F(n) = 2^{2^n} + 1$ and geometry. He showed which regular polygons could be constructed by use of compass and straightedge only, and which ones could not be so constructed. In order to be constructed by compass and straightedge, the number of sides of the regular polygon must be either a Fermat prime, a product of distinct Fermat primes, or a power of 2 multiplied by a

Fermat prime or by a product of distinct Fermat primes. (The powers of 2 are $2^1 = 2$, $2^2 = 4$, $2^3 = 8$, and so on). According to Gauss's theorem, which of the following regular polygons can be constructed by compass and straightedge and which cannot? Explain your answer for each polygon. The numbers given are the number of sides of each polygon.

(a)	3	(b)	5	(c)	6	(d)	9
(e)	11	(f)	12	(g)	15	(h)	17
(i)	20	(j)	21	(k)	24	(l)	25
(m)	30	(n)	90	(o)	101	(p)	257
(q)	514						

6. Try to arrange a tour of a computer facility for yourself or perhaps even for the entire class. There is probably a computer center on campus or a company in your community that has a computer facility.

7. Read about computer applications. Many interesting applications are described from time to time in newsmagazines such as *Newsweek* and *Time* or in *Scientific American* and other magazines likely to be in your campus library. Look, too, in the journals of your major field of study.

PROGRAMMING IN BASIC

Just what is a computer? A *computer* is a machine capable of accepting instructions and data as input, automatically processing the data according to the instructions, and producing the results of processing in a usable form, called output. A main storage consisting of magnetic cores, thin film, or monolithic integrated circuits is used to hold the program of instructions while it is being executed. Instructions are decoded and executed one at a time by the central processing unit (CPU) of the computer system. The original input of instructions and data may be on punched cards (also called data processing cards), paper tape, magnetic tape, or other media. The output after processing may be on printed pages, punched cards, paper tape, magnetic tape, magnetic disk, or other media.

A *computer program* is a list of instructions for a computer to follow in order to process data. People who write computer programs are often called *programmers*. The code in which programmers write their programs is called a programming language. There are many programming languages. Among the most popular are APL, BASIC, COBOL, FORTRAN, and PL/I. In this section, you'll have a chance to learn the language called BASIC. You will also see how computers free you of the burden of tedious calculations. Furthermore, computers provide fast, accurate results, enabling you to spend your time in more creative activities.

The programming language BASIC was originally intended for use by nonprogrammers. It is a language that can be learned with no previous knowledge of computers, and it can be learned relatively quickly. Throughout this section we'll assume that all your communication with a computer will be made at a teleprinter terminal, one that resembles a typewriter. It will also be assumed that you are using a time-sharing system, one that allows you to enter programs and data and run programs with virtually no waiting.

Constants

Numbers such as 17, 183.54, 0, and −.013 are constants. Constants can be used in BASIC as long as they do not contain more digits than the computer can accept. Nearly all systems accept at least six digits. Commas must not be used in constants. For example, the number 67,456 is not allowed, but 67456 is all right. Very large and very small constants can be represented by using a variation of scientific notation. The number 76,000,000 is written in scientific notation as 7.6×10^7. In BASIC it is written 7.6E7. Similarly, the smaller number .0000000045 is 4.5×10^{-9} in scientific notation and 4.5E−9 in BASIC. Notice that the letter E is used in this setting to indicate a power of 10. As a check on your understanding of BASIC constants, complete the following table.

Arithmetic	Basic
29.6	————
12,349	————
15,000,000	————
————	2.94E4
————	8.01E−3
.00000006	————

33 ASR Teletypewriter

Selectric terminal

The answers are 29.6, 12349, 1.5E7, 29,400, .00801, and 6E−8.

Variables

In algebra we use x, y, z, a, b, c, n, and other letters for variables. You can do the same in BASIC. Thus, X, Y, Z, A, B, C, N, or any other letter is an acceptable BASIC variable. Note that only capital letters are used; there are no lowercase letters available on most terminal keyboards. You can also use a letter followed by a digit, such as X1, Y6, N3, and J8, to name a variable.

Functions

BASIC contains built-in library functions to handle computations involving square root, absolute value, trigonometric functions, logarithms, exponential functions, and others. The only function we shall use is the square root (SQR) function. In BASIC, $\sqrt{x}$ is coded as SQR(X). Note that parentheses are placed around the number whose square root is being requested.

Expressions

Constants, variables, and functions can be combined to form expressions. The operators used are + (addition), − (subtraction), * (multiplication), / (division), and ↑ (exponentiation). Here are some examples of BASIC expressions.

Algebra	BASIC
$a + b$	A+B
$2x + 3y$	2*X+3*Y
$7x^4$	7*X↑4
$\sqrt{k + 1}$	SQR(K+1) or (K+1)↑.5 or (K+1)↑(1/2)
$\dfrac{m + n}{x + 2}$	(M+N)/(X+2)

As a check of your understanding of BASIC expressions, complete the table below.

Algebra	BASIC
$x + 5$	_____
$3(y - 2)$	_____
$3x^2 + 8x$	_____
$\sqrt{1 - x^2}$	_____
$\dfrac{5}{n + 1}$	_____
_____	A/2+9
_____	3*X+2*Y
_____	X↑3−1

The answers are X+5, 3*(Y−2), 3*X↑2+8*X, SQR(1−X↑2), 5/(N+1), $\dfrac{a}{2} + 9$, $3x + 2y$, and $x^3 - 1$.

LET

Values are assigned to variables by using LET statements. The statement LET K=3 assigns a value of 3 to K, so that K has a value of 3 for future reference in that program unless and until another statement of the form LET K=··· assigns K another value later in the program. If the statement LET J=K+4 is encountered after K has been assigned a value of 3, then J will be assigned the value 7, that is, 4 more than K. The statement LET I=I+1 may look strange, but it is an important type of LET statement. When executed, it has the effect of increasing the value of I by 1. To see this, look at the right side, which is I+1. This says add 1 to I (or, increase I by 1). The left side says LET I=, which means that once the expression on the right has been computed, it becomes the new value of I. As another example, suppose the three statements LET I=5, LET I=I+1, and LET J=I+5 are encountered in sequence in a program being executed. The first statement assigns a value of 5 to I. The second statement adds 1 to the value of I and makes this the new value of I. Thus, I becomes 6. The third statement adds 5 to I in order to get a value for J. As a result, the value of J is 11.

Although the value of I was used to compute a value for J, the value of I was not replaced by any new value. So I is still 6.

Now see if you can follow the list of program statements below. Keep track of the values of A, B, and C and indicate the value of each once all of the LET statements have been executed.

```
LET A=6
LET B=A+3
LET C=2*A/6
LET A=A+2
LET B=C↑2
```

In the end, A is 8, B is 4, and C is 2. Why? First, A is assigned a value of 6. Then B is computed as 6 + 3, or 9. Next C is $2 \cdot 6/6$, which is 2. Then 2 is added to A to obtain the new value of 8 for A. Finally, the value of B is changed to C^2, which is 4.

PRINT

You can get the computer to print results of computations (and other desired output) by using the PRINT statement. PRINT T will print the numerical value that T has when this statement is executed. The statement PRINT A;B will print a value for A and then a value for B. The values printed will be the current numerical values of each variable. Consider the following small program.

```
LET X=6
LET Y=4
LET S=X+Y
PRINT X;Y;S
```

This program will cause the following information to be printed when it is executed:

6   4   10

If you prefer the output to appear as

X = 6   Y = 4   S = 10

to specify to the reader just what the numbers 6, 4, and 10 are values of, use the PRINT statement

```
PRINT  "X ="; X, "Y ="; Y, "S ="; S
```

Any messages that are desired (such as X =, Y =, S =) must be enclosed in quotation marks, so the computer does not mistake them for variables.

The computer spaces output appropriately across the line. From the example, you may have noticed that more blank space is left between printed items when a comma is used in the PRINT statement. On the other hand, less space is left when a semicolon is used. Results are printed on the next line when space runs out on a given line. Most times that the execution of a PRINT statement is begun, a new line is used. The exception is if a comma or semicolon is used after the last item in a PRINT statement, in which case the next PRINT causes printing on the same line rather than on a new line.

If you want to leave a line of blank space under some output, use PRINT alone—with no variables or message. The statements

```
PRINT
PRINT
PRINT
```

will cause three lines to be skipped before anything else is printed.

Examine the next program and indicate the appearance of the output, assuming the program is executed.

```
LET I=9
LET J=10
LET K=SQR(I)
LET J=J-3
PRINT "THE NUMBERS ARE"; I; J; K
```

If you have done this correctly, your output should look like the printing below.

```
THE NUMBERS ARE  9  7  3
```

END

The statement that is physically in the last position in the program must be an END statement. It has the simple, one-word form END.

Given next is a program that assigns values to A, B, and C, computes their sum, and prints the result. An explanation of the numbers in front of the statements follows the program.

```
10   LET A=50
20   LET B=76
30   LET C=38
40   LET S3=A+B+C
50   PRINT S3
60   END
```

What will be printed after the program has been executed? You should have determined that the sum S3 is 164, computed as 50 + 76 + 38. The number 164 is printed. Did you notice that each line of the program has a number in front of it? Every line of a BASIC program must have a line number, and statements are executed in order of ascending statement numbers. You can use consecutive line numbers, such as 1, 2, 3, 4, 5, 6. However, if you later want to insert a line in the program, you would have to renumber and retype all following lines of the program. Using line numbers such as 10, 20, 30, and so on allows for the insertion of additional program lines. For example, lines numbered 5, 11, 12, 15, 18, 23, 26, and 28 may be inserted if desired. Notice that all the statements are aligned, each beginning one space after the line number. This alignment is neat and advisable, but it is not necessary. You can leave no space or more space between line number and statement and between characters in a statement, if you like. Moreover, statements need not be aligned. For example,

```
30LETC=38
```

and

```
30 L E TC   =38
```

are understood and accepted by the computer. However, the form

```
30   LET C=38
```

is preferable, since it is more easily understood by humans.

INPUT

If you were restricted to using the LET to assign values to variables, then you would have to change your program each time you wanted to change the data values used. Instead, values for A, B, and C could be read into the computer by the preceding program, by using the statement

```
INPUT A, B, C
```

When the computer carries out this statement, it will type a question mark (?). You must then respond by typing a value for A and then a value for B and finally a value for C. The three numbers you enter should be typed on the same line and separated by commas. For example, if you want to enter a value of 7 for A, 23 for B, and 14 for C, then you would type your input as

```
7, 23, 14
```

Note that there is no comma after the last number.

This form of data entry requires you to be at the terminal during program execution. Furthermore, large volumes of input cannot be handled practically in this way. The READ and DATA statements (explained later) are better suited for large-volume users who will not be at the terminal when their programs are run.

Suppose you do decide to change the program to include input for A, B, and C rather than the specific values 50, 76, and 38 assigned. Which statements would you remove from that program? What statement would you insert in the program? Rewrite the program. To do this correctly, statements 10, 20, and 30 should be removed and replaced by a statement of the form INPUT A, B, C. This input statement can be numbered using any whole number from 1 through 39. If the INPUT statement is numbered 10, then the revised program appears as

```
10   INPUT A, B, C
40   LET S3=A+B+C
50   PRINT S3
60   END
```

To have the computer execute this program, type in the word RUN and press the RETURN key. The computer will ask for data by typing a question mark. You should respond by typing a number for A, a number for B, and a number for C. The three numbers you enter must be separated by commas, and after typing them, you must press the RETURN key. The computer will then take the values of A, B, and C, compute S3, and print its value. The complete conversation, including the original typed program, appears next. The values chosen for A, B, and C are 1, 2, and 3, respectively.

```
10   INPUT A, B, C
40   LET S3=A+B+C
50   PRINT S3
60   END
RUN
?   1, 2, 3
6
```

GO TO

The GO TO statement is used to transfer to another statement, usually out of the normal one-after-the-other sequence. For example, GO TO 150 will transfer control to line 150, so that the next statement executed is the one numbered 150. You can use a GO TO in the preceding program to enable you to calculate S3 for many different sets of A, B, C values. If a GO TO is inserted after the PRINT, we return again and again to read another set of A, B, C values, compute S3, and print the result. Here is the program:

```
10   INPUT A, B, C
40   LET S3=A+B+C
50   PRINT S3
55   GO TO 10
60   END
```

Each time a value is printed for S3, the computer will request input from you. A run of this program might appear as

```
RUN
?  1, 2, 3
6
?  10, 20, 50
80
?  15, 25, 20
60
.
.
.
```

You can quit whenever you like by hitting the appropriate "panic button" or giving the computer an appropriate command. Methods vary from system to system.

1. Write a program that will accept values for four numbers, compute their sum and arithmetic mean (average), and print the value of that sum and arithmetic mean.

2. There are approximately 2.54 centimeters in an inch. So if a quantity measured in centimeters is divided by 2.54, then the units are changed to inches.

   (a) Write a program to accept a value for a measurement in centimeters (call it C) and change it to inches (I). Print the measurement in inches.
   (b) Modify your program to keep returning to get another C to convert to inches.

3. The relationship between temperatures measured in degrees Celsius and Fahrenheit can be stated as

$$F = 1.8C + 32$$

   (a) Write a program to accept a value for degrees Celsius and change it to Fahrenheit. Print the temperature in degrees Fahrenheit.

(b)   Modify your program to keep returning to get another Celsius temperature to convert to Fahrenheit.

4.   The area of the region inside a triangle with sides a, b, and c can be computed as

$$A = \sqrt{s(s - a)(s - b)(s - c)}$$

where s is the semiperimeter, that is, half the distance around the triangle. Write a program to accept values for a, b, and c and compute and print the value of the area of the triangular region. Watch your parentheses!

5.   Refer to Application 2 on page 176. Write a program that will accept any two counting numbers m and n and compute the corresponding Pythagorean triple $a-b-c$. Print the values of a, b, and c. Run the program for several choices of m and n. In each case verify by hand calculation that the a, b, and c produced do indeed satisfy the Pythagorean theorem.

6.   Write a program that will accept two points of a line and compute and print the slope of the line. Call the coordinates of the first point $X1$ and $Y1$. Call the coordinates of the second point $X2$ and $Y2$. Refer to page 290 for a discussion of slope, if necessary. Be sure to run the program with a few sample sets of data, check the slopes by hand calculation, and compare.

7.   Write a program to do the following. Input four grades called G_1, G_2, G_3, and G_4 (if the grade is A, use the number 4 as input, for B use 3, and so on). Then input the corresponding number of semester hours S_1, S_2, S_3, and S_4. Compute the grade point average and print it. If necessary, refer to the discussion of grade point average on page 344. Run several test cases and check the computations by hand.

8.   Input a value for I (the initial odometer reading), F (the final odometer reading), and G (the number of gallons of gas used). Compute and print M (the number of miles per gallon), where

$$M = \frac{F - I}{G}$$

Run the program with several sets of data.

BRANCHES AND LOOPS

The last section ended with the use of a GO TO statement to transfer control back to the beginning of a program. The GO TO is one type of statement used to transfer out of the ordinary sequence in which statements are numbered. There is another type of transfer or branch statement—the IF. We shall examine its use next.

IF

The IF statement provides the ability to transfer out of sequence if a condition has been satisfied. The statement IF S>0 THEN 180 means that if S is greater than zero, transfer is made (backward or forward) to line 180 in order to execute the statement there. However, if S is not greater than zero, then the next statement in sequence is executed. Besides the greater than symbol >, other symbols can be used with the IF statement. They are < (less than), = (equal to), > = (greater than or equal to), < = (less than or equal to), < > (not equal to).

Given next is a partial program showing how you might direct a computer to determine which of two numbers is larger. The numbers are the values of M and N. It is assumed that M and N are not equal.

```
50   IF M>N THEN 80
60   PRINT "THE LARGER NUMBER IS"; N
70   GO TO 90
80   PRINT "THE LARGER NUMBER IS"; M
90   END
```

Can you explain why the GO TO statement is in the program? In other words, what would happen if it were not there? The answer is that the GO TO statement is used to avoid execution of the second PRINT in the case that N is the larger number and is printed. The statement GO TO 90 could instead have been a STOP statement. The STOP statement is used to stop program execution before the physical end of the program. Line 70 would then read

```
70   STOP
```

Suppose you want to write a program to form the sum of the integers from 1 to 12. A statement such as

```
LET  S=1+2+3+4+5+6+7+8+9+10+11+12
```

seems sufficient. But what if you wanted the sum of the integers from 1 to 100 or from 1 to 1500? Certainly you don't want to write a statement with 1500 numbers in it. Instead, you can have the computer add the numbers by using a *loop*, or cycle. Start the sum S at 1 and add one of the numbers each time that you go through the cycle. In this way, the sum is gradually accumulated as the program is executed. Consider, for example, the sum $1 + 2 + 3 + 4 + \cdots + 100$ of all the integers from 1 to 100. Begin the sum at 1. Next let 2 be added to the sum. Next let 3 be added to the sum. Then let 4 be added to the sum. Continue the process until 100 has been added to the sum. The sum is formed in steps by adding the value of a *counter* (say K) to the sum S to form the new sum, which is also called S. But only when the process is complete will S represent the entire sum of all the integers from 1 to 100. The key BASIC statement used is

```
LET S=S+K
```

The value of K begins at 2 and proceeds $2, 3, 4, 5, 6, \ldots, 100$. It is increased by 1 each time through the cycle, so that the next integer K can be added to the sum S to form the new sum S.

After K is added to the sum—that is, after the statement LET S=S+K is executed—and after K is increased by 1 via LET K=K+1, the K value should be tested. The process should continue only as long as K does not exceed 100. Once a K value of 100 has been added to the sum, the sum is completely formed. Here is the program.

```
10   LET S=1
20   LET K=2
30   LET S=S+K
40   LET K=K+1
50   IF K<=100 THEN 30
60   PRINT S
70   END
```

Did you notice that there is no input? Here is a computer run.

```
RUN
5050
```

The result, 5050, is the sum of the integers from 1 to 100.

How can you change this program to accept any value for N and form the sum of the integers from 1 to N? The answer is given in the program below. The two changes needed are underlined.

```
5    INPUT N
10   LET S=1
20   LET K=2
30   LET S=S+K
40   LET K=K+1
50   IF K<=N THEN 30
60   PRINT S
70   END
```

This program can be modified by inserting the statement GO TO 5 after the PRINT. In this way, each time the sum of integers from 1 to a specified N is computed and printed, another value for N will automatically be requested. So with this modified program you can sit at the terminal and enter different N values and instantly get the corresponding sums printed. The modified program is shown next.

```
5    INPUT N
10   LET S=1
20   LET K=2
30   LET S=S+K
40   LET K=K+1
50   IF K<=N THEN 30
60   PRINT S
65   GO TO 5
70   END
```

Here is a computer run using 100, 200, and 400 for N.

```
RUN
?  100
5050
?  200
20100
?  400
80200
   .
   .
   .
```

Note that statements such as 5 and 65 are shown placed in the desired position in the program. Certainly you cannot type them into those positions once the program has already been typed without them. On many systems there is a special command to the terminal that permits you to add new statements to a program. When you add them, you give each statement a line number that will locate it in the desired portion of the program. The computer does the rest, and if you request it specifically, the terminal will even list the modified program with the new statements (such as 5 and 65 above) located in sequence within the program. The exact mechanics of carrying out this procedure vary from system to system.

FOR **and** NEXT

The FOR and NEXT statements are designed for use in loop construction. The program for computing and printing the sum of the integers from 1 to 100 can be coded as

```
10   LET S=1
20   FOR K=2 TO 100
30   LET S=S+K
40   NEXT K
50   PRINT S
60   END
```

All statements between the FOR and NEXT (in this case just statement 30) are executed first with K=2, then with K=3, . . . , and finally with K=100. When the FOR statement is used, the counter K for the loop changes by 1 each time the loop statements are executed, unless you specify otherwise. The sum of the odd integers from 1 to 99 is computed by executing the statements of the following loop.

```
10   LET S=1
20   FOR K=3 TO 99 STEP 2
30   LET S=S+K
40   NEXT K
```

The STEP 2 specifies that the counter will be increased by 2 each time, but only as long as it does not exceed 99. Please keep in mind that there is nothing special about using the variable K in these examples. Other variables could have been used. Variables such as I, J, N, and X are popular choices.

Subscripts and DIM

You really cannot use the full power of loop construction until you use subscripted variables. In algebra, if you have 50 numbers that are related, you could indicate this by using subscripts. You might represent the numbers as $x_1, x_2, x_3, x_4, \ldots,$ x_{50} rather than use 50 completely different letters and other names for them. This is called an *array* of 50 x's. In BASIC, x_1 is coded as X(1). Similarly, x_2 is X(2) and x_n is X(N). The name of an array can only be a single letter, any letter from A through Z.

A DIM statement, which can be placed anywhere in the program, must be used to indicate the dimension, or size, of an array of more than ten elements. Arrays of ten or fewer elements are dimensioned automatically by the computer. For the array of 50 elements $x_1, x_2, \ldots, x_{50}$, you need the statement

```
DIM X(50)
```

As an example of the use of subscripted variables in a program, here is a program that computes the arithmetic mean (or average) of 25 numbers. The numbers are called $a_1, a_2, a_3, \ldots,$ a_{25}. Recall that the mean of 25 numbers is computed by adding the 25 numbers and then dividing by 25, as explained in Chapter 7 (page 342).

```
10    DIM A(25)
20    FOR I=1 TO 25        ⎧ This loop takes care of
30    INPUT A(I)          ⎨ inputting the $a_i$'s one at
40    NEXT I              ⎩ a time.
50    LET S=A(1)
60    FOR J=2 TO 25        ⎧ This loop adds all 25 of
70    LET S=S+A(J)        ⎨ the $a_i$'s.
80    NEXT J              ⎩
90    LET M=S/25           ⎧ Divide the total (sum) by
100   PRINT M             ⎨ 25 to get the mean.
110   END
```

The two loops in this program can be combined into one loop, if preferred.

READA **and** DATA

Perhaps you realize that the computer will ask 25 times for numbers as it goes through the first loop of the preceding program. This means that as you sit at the terminal you will be asked to type in one number first. Then you will be asked to type in another number, and so on. Wouldn't it be better if you could just type all 25 numbers in advance and let the computer read them all at once? To do this, use a statement that begins with the word DATA and continues with all 25 numbers, one right after the other, separated by commas. Now, instead of the INPUT A(I), use READ A(I). The READ statement should appear where the INPUT statement was before. The DATA statement can be placed anywhere in the program before the END statement. It is traditional to place the DATA statement either near the beginning or near the end, that is, out of the way.

Here then is the previous program, rewritten using READ and DATA statements instead of an INPUT statement. Selection of the specific data for inclusion in the program was arbitrary.

```
10    DIM A(25)
20    FOR I=1 TO 25
30    READ A(I)
40    NEXT I
50    LET S=A(1)
60    FOR J=2 TO 25
70    LET S=S+A(J)
80    NEXT J
90    LET M=S/25
100   PRINT M
105   DATA 8,12,19,6,4,7,13,12,10,9,4,11
108   DATA 9,8,16,15,17,12,7,4,11,10,6,14,3
110   END
```

When the quantity of data is too great for one DATA statement, additional statements can be used as above.

APPLICATIONS AND EXERCISES

NOTE. Many of these programming problems are difficult without some programming experience or familiarity with the nature of solving such problems. In view of this, various hints, comments, and suggestions are given.

1. Earlier in this section we examined a program for computing the sum of the integers from 1 to N. Another way to do this is to use a known formula for such a sum. The sum of the integers from 1 through N can be computed as

    $$\frac{N(N + 1)}{2}$$

    Write a program that uses this formula to compute the sum of the integers from 1 to N. Print N and the sum. Be sure to include a way for the value of N to be accepted by the computer. Then run the program using the values 10, 20, 50, and 100 for N. Also run the program given in the section for this sum. Use the same values for N and compare the results.

2. The expression $n^2 - n + 41$ generates prime numbers for any integer n between 1 and 40. Write a computer program that will generate the 40 primes suggested. Print all 40 numbers. Your program should include a loop with a counter that goes from 1 to 40. Calculation and printing should be done within the loop. There is no input.

3. Write a program to evaluate the revenue function $R(x) = 30x - x^2$ for $x = 0, 1, 2, 3, 4, 5, \ldots, 40$. Print all x values and the corresponding function values. Examine the output to determine how many units should be produced and sold to obtain the maximum amount of revenue. You may wish to refer to the explanation of functions in economics beginning on page 285.

4. Write a program to evaluate the profit function $P(x) = (40x - x^2) - 6x$ for $x = 0, 1, 2, 3, 4, 5, \ldots, 25$. Print all x values and the corresponding function values. Examine the output to determine how many units should be produced and sold to obtain the maximum amount of profit. Again, you may wish to refer to the explanation of functions in economics beginning on page 285.

5. A brief explanation of compound interest was given in Application 17 on page 16. Review that explanation and then write one program that will do all of the following:
   (i) Accept values for the amount invested (P), annual interest rate (I), and number of years invested (N).
   (ii) Compute the amount accumulated.
   (iii) Print the amount accumulated.
   Be sure to run the program using several different values for amount, interest rate, and number of years invested.

6. Print a table of the integers from 1 through 100 and their square roots. Your program should include a loop with the counter going from 1 to 100. The square root calculation and output should be done within the loop. There is no input.

7. According to the Pythagorean theorem, if $a^2 + b^2 = c^2$, then the triangle with sides $a, b,$ and c is a right triangle. Here c is the hypotenuse and a and b are the other two sides. Write a computer program that will accept values

for a, b, and c as input and test them by means of the Pythagorean theorem to see if such sides can compose a right triangle. If they do, print the values of a, b, and c and the message "right triangle." If not, print the values of a, b, and c and the message "not a right triangle." Test the program with the following triplets.

(a) 3–4–5   (b) 5–12–13   (c) 2–3–4
(d) 7–24–25   (e) 10–12–16   (f) 3–7–11
(g) 5–10–15   (h) 8–40–41   (i) 11–60–61

8. Write a program to help you determine the value of

$$\lim_{x \to \infty} \frac{2x - 5}{3x + 9}$$

Set up your program to accept a value for x, compute the value of the expression, print that result, and then return to request another value of x from you. You might want to use values such as 100, 300, 1000, and still larger for x. As you obtain results, study them to decide the value of the limit. You might want to refer to page 296 for a discussion of limits.

9. Write a program to help you determine the value of

$$\lim_{x \to 4} \frac{x^2 - 5x + 4}{x - 4}$$

Use values of x between 3 and 4, such as 3.5, 3.8, 3.9, 3.99, and so forth. Also, use values of x between 4 and 5, such as 4.5, 4.3, 4.2, 4.1, 4.09, 4.01, ... Print the results of each computation. Then study the output to determine if there is a number that the fraction approaches as x approaches 4. You might want to refer to page 296 for a discussion of limits.

10. For each of the following sequences write a program to print the first 50 terms. These sequences were introduced at the beginning of Chapter 1. In order to compute the terms you will need to recognize the pattern, express it as a formula, and put that formula in a loop.

(a) 1, 2, 3, 4, 5, . . .
(b) 2, 4, 6, 8, 10, . . .
(c) 1, 4, 9, 16, 25, . . .

11. Write a program to accept the first two numbers, call them A(1) and A(2), of any *arithmetic* sequence and then generate the next eight members of the sequence. Call those eight members A(3) through A(10). As output, print all ten numbers of each sequence. Use as data the arithmetic sequences (a)–(h). The nature of arithmetic sequences is explained on page 10.

   (a) 1, 2, . . .   (b) 1, 3, . . .
   (c) 3, 6, . . .   (d) 5, 10, . . .
   (e) 36, 40, . . .   (f) 64, 58, . . .
   (g) 0, 7, . . .   (h) 0, − 7, . . .

12. Write a program to accept the first two numbers of any *geometric* sequence and then generate the next eight members of the sequence. As output, print all ten numbers of each sequence. Use as data the geometric sequences suggested here. The nature of geometric sequences is explained on page 10.

   (a) 1, 2, . . .   (b) 1, 3, . . .
   (c) 3, 9, . . .   (d) 4, 16, . . .
   (e) 64, 32, . . .   (f) 3, − 6, . . .

13. Write a program to compute and print the first 50 Fibonacci numbers. Include the first two numbers F(1) = 1 and F(2) = 1 in LET statements. You may wish to refer to page 2 for information on the Fibonacci sequence and to Exercise 3 on page 5 for the desired relationship among terms.

14. Write a program that will read three numbers, determine the largest, and print it. Assume all three numbers are different. Run the program with a few test cases.

15. Write a program to accept a value for n and compute and print the product of the integers from 1 to n. This is called n factorial and denoted $n!$. For example, if n is 5, then the value of $1 \cdot 2 \cdot 3 \cdot 4 \cdot 5$ should be computed. Such products can be computed in a loop that resembles the loop used to form sums by adding one term at a time.

16. Write a program to accept as input a natural number (positive integer) n and convert it to a number modulo m, where m is a natural number that is also read in. For example, if the input is 53 for n and 7 for m, then your pro-

gram should convert 53 to a number (it happens to be 4) modulo 7. The printed output would then appear something like

```
53  IS  CONGRUENT  TO  4  MODULO  7
```

When the computer divides by seven, the remainder is not conveniently available afterward. So you'll have to subtract 7's from the original until the result is eventually less than seven. Be sure you write a general program, not just one for modulo 7, as used in the example here. Modular arithmetic is explained in Chapter 3, beginning on page 118.

17. A salesman's weekly salary is $175 plus commission. His commission is 5% of the first $400 he sells and 8% of all sales beyond that per week. Write a program to read a value for dollars of sales and print the amount he will be paid accordingly. Run the program for several values of sales, including some that are less than $400 and some that are more than $400.

18. In Maryland, state income tax is charged on taxable income according to the following schedule: 2% on the amount between $0 and $1000, 3% on the amount between $1000 and $2000, 4% on the amount between $2000 and $3000, and 5% on everything over $3000. Most counties within the state levy a 50% surcharge (that is, 50% of the Maryland state tax) on top of this tax. Write a program to read a value for taxable income and print the corresponding Maryland tax. Note that the Maryland tax is the sum of the tax computed from the tax schedule plus the county surcharge. Run your program for several values of taxable income, including one value between $0 and $1000, one between $1000 and $2000, one between $2000 and $3000, and one value greater than $3000.

19. Write a program that will read a list of ages of 35 people. Consider the ages to be the values of $a_1, a_2, a_3, \ldots, a_{35}$. Count the number of people who are under 21 years of age, and print that total with an appropriate corresponding message. Use the READ and DATA statements.

Answers to Selected Exercises

Page 4

232 less 1 !

1. At the end of 12 months there will be 233 pairs of rabbits.

2. (a) 2, 6, 8, 14, 22, 36, 58, 94
    (c) 12, 19, 31, 50, 81, 131, 212
    (d) 3, 10, 13, 23, 36, 59, 95

3. $a_{n+1} = a_{n-1} + a_n$

4. (a) The fourth term is the sum of the second term (y) and the third term ($x + y$), so it is $y + x + y$, which is $x + 2y$.

6. (a) The increase is 1¢. The original cost was 4¢. So the relative increase is 1¢/4¢, which is 1/4, or 25%.
    (c) Largest is from 3¢ to 4¢ and from 6¢ to 8¢. Both are approximately 33% increases.

7. (a) When you *add* two adjacent numbers of a row, you get the element that will appear between them in the next row down.
    (b) 1   5   10   10   5   1
    (d) One such pattern is that the second last number in each row is always the row number.

8. (a) A is 12-1, B is 12-2, C is 12-3, . . . , I is 12-9.
    (d) For this code the alphabet is divided into three groups of letters: A through I, J through R, and S through Z. JR symbolizes the letters in the second group and therefore tells you indirectly which letters must be in the other two groups.

Page 8

1. Bode's distance is 196, which compares well with the actual distance of 192.

3. Bode's distance is 772, which compares poorly with the actual distance of 396.

5. (a) Mercury is .39 astronomical units (AU), Venus is .72 AU, Mars 1.52 AU, Jupiter 5.20 AU, and Saturn 9.53 AU.

7. There is a suggestion that planets closer to the asteroid belt have more moons and that the relative number of moons decreases as you go farther away from the asteroid belt.

Page 11

1. (a) 12, 19, and 26
   (b) arithmetic sequence

2. (a) 10; arithmetic
   (b) 32; not arithmetic
   (c) 17; arithmetic

3. (a) 81; geometric
   (b) 160; geometric
   (c) 25; not geometric

4. (a) geometric
   (b) 216
   (c) $46,656

5. (a) arithmetic

6. (a) $31
   (b) He wins $32, but he is only $1 ahead because he lost $31 on the five previous bets.
   (c) In the long run you cannot lose, *if* you have enough money to keep you going during the times you are losing money. On the other hand, you may not win much when you do win, as suggested by the second answer to part (b).
   (d) geometric

9. (a) arithmetic
   (b) geometric
   (c) 1000

10. (a) 128

12. The only person clearly going to Saint Ives is the person telling the rhyme. There is no indication that the man with seven wives, etc., is going anywhere. Even if that man is going to Saint Ives, that still makes a total of only two people.

13. 2802 things. Did you notice the hint of a geometric sequence in this exercise?

15. (a) approximately $6\frac{1}{4}$

17. (a) $(1.05)^4\$3000$ (b) geometric
    (c) $(1.06)^3\$5000$ (d) $(1.05)^n\$8000$

18. (a) millionth, billionth, trillionth
    (b) 1000
    (c) geometric
    (d) femto = 1/1,000,000,000,000,000
       atto = 1/1,000,000,000,000,000,000
    (e) 1 billion

Page 20

1. (a) thousandth
    (b) hundredth
    (c) ten

2. (a) 18 mm

3. (a) thousandth   (b) 1000

4. (b) 1000   (d) 1000

6. (a) Each fraction is equal to 1.
    (b) 4.24 quarts
    (c) approximately 8.49 liters
    (d) 3 pounds = 1362 grams
       950 grams = about 2.09 pounds
    (g) approximately .20 meter
    (h) 39,370 in.
    (j) 15 cm = approximately 5.90 in.
       15 in. = approximately 38.10 cm

Page 27

1. (a) $2 \cdot 2 \cdot 2$, which is 8.
    (b) Place values are 1, 10, 100, 1000, etc., all of which can be written with 10 as the base; that is, all the numbers are powers of ten.

3. (a) 1/10, 1/100, 1/1000
    (b) *decimal* point

4. (a) 13   (c) 21
    (e) 31   (g) 64

5. (a) 1100   (c) 100011
    (e) 1001001   (g) 1100100

6. 0, 1, 10, 11, 100, 101, 110, 111, 1000

7. Here's a partial check. The first two numbers are 1001 and 1010. The last two numbers are 10010 and 10011.

8. Notice that the first three digits of each binary number are 101. The distinction between the numbers is in the number of zeros following the 101. The decimal number equivalents are 5, 10, 20, and 40. So, . . . what is the effect of attaching a zero to the right end of a binary number?

Page 30

1. (a) 4, 8, 16, 32   (b) $n = 2^t$
   (c) geometric   (d) 200

3. (a) top row: 140, 180;   bottom row: 44, 60, 62
   (b) $63\frac{1}{2}$ degrees   (c) 164 times   (d) 50 degrees

4. (a) 25 feet   (b) $d = t^2$ (c) $t = \sqrt{d}$

5. (a) 164 feet, which is considerably more than the dropped object of Application 4.

   (b) Zero feet. Note that t is zero at the instant the object is released.

   (c) Think! First, how far does the object travel in 3 seconds? Second, where does the object begin and where does it end? The answers to these questions should lead you to conclude that the building is 294 feet high.

7. (a) 1000   (b) -20

8. (a) 161 yards
   (b) The formula should not be applied in this case. However, if you do use it with 70 for velocity, then the carry is only 2 yards, a result that seems unlikely in reality.
   (d) 44 feet per second

9. (a) 10, 12   (b) $a_n = 3n$
   (c) $a_n = n^2$ (e) $a_n = 1/n$

11. (a) bottom: 32, 16;   top: 17,190

12. (a) bottom: 25, 81, 64;   top: 2, 2, 2, 4, 3, 4
    (b) (i) $\log_2 32 = 5$ (c) (i) $4^3 = 64$
        (ii) $\log_7 49 = 2$ (ii) $2^{10} = 1024$

Page 39

1. (a) If you use 3 for n, s will be 15.

3. (a) 25   (b) n^2

7. (b) Yes. One of the diagonals contains all 1's.
            Yes. One of the diagonals contains all 1's.

     (c) One such square:

```
A  B  C  D
B  A  D  C
C  D  A  B
D  C  B  A
```

10. (a) 260   (b) 130   (c) 130

11. One such square:

```
9  8  7
2  1  6
3  4  5
```

Page 45

1. (a) 12; possible   (b) 36; possible
     (c) 31; impossible   (d) 28; possible
     (e) 48; possible   (f) 105; impossible

Page 48

2. (a) yes   (b) yes   (c) no

4. (a) yes
    (b) yes
    (c) No—7201 is not a multiple of 9.
    (d) yes

Page 55

2. octagon   **3.** pentagon

4. snow   **5.** starfish

6. pentagram   **7.** hexagram (six-pointed star)

Page 64

1. (a) 32   (b) Who knows?
    (c) 2/6, or 1/3 if you reduce it.
    (d) Expect the ninth, but it's the eighth.
    (e) Objects fall at the same rate regardless of size or weight.

2. (a) $x = 6$ (b) Rockefeller
    (c) Mark got his answers from someone else's paper.
    (d) 3   (e) 11
    (f) Yes, the more popular candidate can lose if the other candidate manages to narrowly win key (large electoral vote) states and lose all or most of the other states. In fact, it happened in 1888. Grover Cleveland received 5,538,233 votes

and Benjamin Harrison received only 5,440,216. Yet Harrison won the electoral vote and hence the election.

(g) Yes, if there are more than two candidates receiving electoral votes.

(h) Electoral votes are based on the population of states. The greater the population, the greater the number of electoral votes.

3. (a) deductive   (b) inductive
    (c) inductive   (d) deductive

5. (a) top of cube   (c) left side of cube
    (e) back of cube

8. (b) 31

9. Made 1 or 0, whichever will result in an odd number of 1 bits in the character. The computer then checks each character whenever it is used or moved. If the number of 1 bits ever becomes even, a "parity error" is indicated to the computer operator.

10. (a) 100   (b) (i) 70

11. (a) All cats are warm-blooded animals.
    (b) All books are magazines.
    (c) All teachers are on welfare.

Page 76

1. (a) valid argument   (b) fallacy
    (c) fallacy   (d) valid argument
    (e) valid argument   (f) fallacy

3. (a) All lawyers are wealthy.   (b) All birds have feathers.

5. (a) fallacy   (b) fallacy

Page 83

1. (a) $A \cdot B \cdot C \cdot D$ (c) $(A) + (B \cdot C)$
    (d) $(A + B) \cdot (C)$, or $(A \cdot C) + (B \cdot C)$ (f) $(A \cdot C \cdot E) + (B \cdot D)$

2. (a)

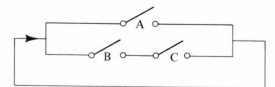

(b)

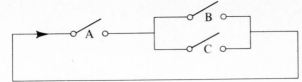

(d)

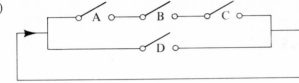

(g)

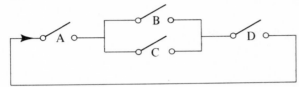

Page 88

2. (a) {1, 3, 5} (b) {5, 7, 9}
(c) { }, or ∅ (d) {13}
(e) {1, 2, 3, 4} (f) {1, 2, 3, 4, 5, 6, 7, 8, 9, 10}
(g) {4, 9, 12, 16, 23, 35, 67} (h) {1, 2, 3}

5. (a) intersection, series

6. (a)

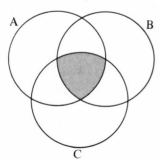

7. (a) $A' = \{2, 3, 5, 6\}$, $B' = \{1, 2, 3, 4\}$.

Page 94

1. (a) $C_1 = d$, $V_3 = u$ (b) $C_3 = r$, $V_1 = a$
(c) ru (f) $C_2V_1 = ka$, $C_1V_1 = da$

4. (a)   −: 1,   =: 2,   ☰: 3,   ☰: 4,

☰: 5,   ⊢: 6,   ⊨: 7,   ⊫: 8,

○: 10,   ‖‖‖: 15,   ⊥: 21,   ⊥‖‖: 28,

‖‖‖‖: 35,   ⊢‖‖‖: 56,   ⊣○: 70

Page 99

1. (a) 1, 2, 5, 10
    (c) 1, 2, 4, 8, 16
    (e) 1, 2, 5, 10, 25, 50
    (g) 1, 2, 3, 4, 6, 8, 12, 16, 24, 48
    (i) 1, 3, 9, 27, 81

2. (a) 1, 2, 3, 4, 5, 6, 8, 10, 12, 15, 20, 24, 30, 40, 60, 120

4. 4, 6, 8, 9, 10, 12, 14, 15, 16, 18, 20, 21, 22, 24, 25, 26, 27, 28, 30, 32

5. No, 9 and 15 (for example) are not prime numbers.

6. Every even number *except* 2.

8. (a) 12 = 5 + 7   (b) 32 = 13 + 19

10. The results are 3, 7, 11, 15, 19, 23, 27. Only 3, 7, 11, 19, and 23 are primes.

13. An even number is a number that is divisible by 2.

15. 4 is deficient, 18 is abundant.

16. (b) $53 = 7^2 + 2^2$ (c) $91 = 9^2 + 3^2 + 1^2$
    (d) *Hint:* Not necessarily three *different* squares.

Page 102

1. (a) $2 \cdot 3 \cdot 5$ (c) $3^2 \cdot 7$
    (d) $2^3 \cdot 3^2$ (e) $2 \cdot 3 \cdot 5^2$
    (h) $3^2 \cdot 7^2$

2. (a) $2^2 \cdot 3 \cdot 5 = 60$ (c) $2^4 \cdot 3 \cdot 7 = 336$
    (d) $2^3 \cdot 5^2 = 200$ (g) $2 \cdot 5 \cdot 7^2 = 490$

3. (a) 12
    (b) $10 = 2 \cdot 5$; $15 = 3 \cdot 5$; $20 = 2^2 \cdot 5$. So the LCM is $2^2 \cdot 3 \cdot 5 = 60$.
    (c) 288   (d) 840

4. (a) 78   (b) 108
   (c) 40   (d) 715
   (e) 5040

5. (a) 75/78

   (c) 49/40, or $1\frac{9}{40}$

   (e) 2411/5040

6. (b) 1/5

Page 108

1. (a) $+1$ (b) $+2$
   (c) -2 (d) -1
   (e) $+3$ (f) $+5$
   (g) $+4$ (h) $+6$

2. (a) $3O_2 \rightarrow 2O_3$
   (b) $2Na + Cl_2 \rightarrow 2NaCl$
   (c) $6Ag + O_3 \rightarrow 3Ag_2O$
   (f) $4Al + 3O_2 \rightarrow 2Al_2O_3$
   (h) $2CO + 2NO \rightarrow 2CO_2 + N_2$
   (i) $3Ca + 2PO_4 \rightarrow Ca_3(PO_4)_2$

Page 115

1. (a) 2 and 4   (b) 2, 3, and 9
   (c) 2, 3, 4, 5, 8, and 9   (g) 2, 4, and 8
   (i) 2, 3, 4, 5, and 8   (k) 2, 3, 5, and 9

2. (a) 6   (c) 6 and 12
   (e) none of them

3. Since $30 = 2 \cdot 3 \cdot 5$, a number is divisible by 30 if it is divisible by 2 and 3 and 5. Of those listed, only 660 and 540 are divisible by 30.

4. Divide the number by 14. If the remainder is zero, the number is indeed divisible by 14. Of those listed, only 6496 and 7770 are divisible by 14. On the other hand, you may find the following test quicker (you be the judge): A number is divisible by 14 if it is divisible by 2 and by 7. So, if the number in question is even (that is, divisible by 2) and you get no remainder when it is divided by 7, then the number is divisible by 14.

8. $15,344 = 15 \cdot 1000 + 344$. Since 1000 is divisible by 8, the number $15 \cdot 1000$ is divisible by 8. Now the entire number $15 \cdot 1000 + 344$ is divisible by 8 because 344 is divisible by 8.

11. A number is divisible by 10 if its last digit is zero. This follows from combining the test for divisibility by 5 (last digit 0 or 5) and for divisibility by 2 (last digit even). To be divisible by both 2 and 5 (and thus by 10), the last digit must be zero.

12. (a) $10n + m$
(b) $10m + n - (10n + m)$
(c) $9m - 9n$, or $9(m - n)$

13. This is essentially the *definition* of divisibility given at the beginning of the chapter.

16. (a) $2 \cdot 10 + 4$ (b) $15 \cdot 10 + 9$
(c) $783 \cdot 10 + 6$ (d) $0 \cdot 10 + 9$

17. (a) Yes. There is an integer r such that $p = qr$.
(c) No. There is no guarantee that there is an integer such that $q = p$ times that integer.

18. (a) 13/15   (b) 4/7
(c) 12/13   (e) 9/14
(f) 5/7   (j) 21/26

19. (a) yes
(b) yes (Zero is a multiple of 11, namely, zero times 11.)
(d) no
(h) yes
(i) no

20. (a) The place value of the digit a is 1000, of b is 100, of c is 10, and of d is 1.
(b) $1001a + 99b + 11c$
(c) Yes, $11 = 11 \cdot 1$.
Yes, $99 = 11 \cdot 9$.
Yes, $1001 = 11 \cdot 91$.

Since 11, 99, and 1001 are each divisible by 11, so are multiples of 11, 99, and 1001 also divisible by 11. This means that $1001a$, $99b$, and $11c$ are each divisible by 11. Also, the sum of these three numbers is divisible by 11. Why? This means that $1001a + 99b + 11c$ is divisible by 11.
(d) We have that $(1000a + 100b + 10c + d) + (a - b + c - d)$ is divisible by 11 and that $a - b + c - d$ is divisible by 11. Thus, the original number $1000a + 100b + 10c + d$ must be divisible by 11.

Page 121

1. (a) true   (b) true   (c) false
(d) true   (e) true   (f) false

2. (a) 7   (b) 1   (c) 11
     (d) 4   (e) 0   (f) 2

3. (a) $a \equiv b$ (mod 7) if $a - b$ is divisible by 7.
     (b) No. $31 - 5 = 26$ and is not divisible by 7.
     (c) Yes. $51 - 2 = 49$, which is divisible by 7.
     (d) 6, since $69 - 6 = 63$ is divisible by 7.

5. (a) 1   (b) 5   (c) 6

7. (a) yes (b) yes
     (c) Not necessarily. For example, $7 \equiv 2$ (mod 5) and $12 \equiv 2$ (mod 5), yet $7 \neq 12$.

8. (a) $x = 6, 13, 20, 27, 34, \ldots$.

9. (a) seven

10. (c) No, their difference (31) is not divisible by 12.

11. (a) 4
     (b) Group the beans into fours and look at the remainder. Then add the difference between 4 and this remainder. Apparently the Mbuti usually won because they were skilled at grouping beans into fours very quickly.
     (c) If they were just guessing, they would lose three fourths of the time and win only one fourth of the time. The reason: of the four possible guesses (0, 1, 2, 3), only one number can be correct and three numbers are wrong guesses. This application hints at *probability*, the main topic of Chapter 7.

12. (a) 6   (b) 0   (c) 8
     (d) 2   (e) 2   (f) 7

13. (a) 1247. In the check, each sum is congruent to 5 modulo 9.
     (c) 1383. In the check, each sum is congruent to 6 modulo 9.

14. (a) 8091. Both results are congruent to 0 modulo 9.
     (c) 544,790. Both results are congruent to 2 modulo 9.

Page 127

1. Tuesday

3. (a) Thursday   (b) 1983, 1988, 1994

4. 1984 is a leap year. Since February 5 comes before February 29, it is unaffected by the extra day. On the other hand, June 11 comes after February 29 and is affected by the extra day.

5. Sunday

6. 1971

Page 131

1. (a) KHOS
   (b) JRRG PRUQLQJ
   (c) L FDPH L VDZ L FRQTXHUHG
   (d) FDOO WKH SROLFH

2. (a) HAIL CAESAR
   (b) IT IS SNOWING
   (c) I HAVE A HEADACHE

3. (a) S KW MYXPECON
   (b) GROX SC DRO MVKCC YFOB

4. (a) NUMBER THEORY
   (b) ONE MORE DAY

5. (a) LQ FKDSWHU
   (b) WZR ZH

6. (a) THE PROOF
   (b) KNOW NOT I

7. (a) BHV L VDZ DQ RA DW WKH CRR

8. (a) INTRODUCTION TO MATHEMATICS

9. (a) Yes
   (b) 27 → 1 (A)
       28 → 2 (B)
       29 → 3 (C)
       30 → 4 (D)
       31 → 5 (E)
       32 → 6 (F)
       33 → 7 (G)
   (c) − 1 → Y
       − 2 → X
       − 3 → W
       − 4 → V
       − 5 → U
       − 6 → T

11. (a) GSDR WKVSMO DYGKBN XYXO
    (b) CZOKU PYB IYEBCOVP TYRX

12. (a) PHYSICIAN HEAL THYSELF
    (b) GREAT MEN ARE NOT ALWAYS WISE

2. (a)   (b)

3. (a) 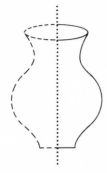   (c)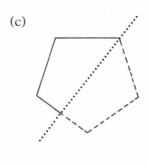

4. (a) 100   (b) 90, 96

Page 150

3. First, mark a point C on line l. Then measure AB with a compass (by putting the point on A and opening it till it reaches B). With the compass open to this measure, put the point on C and draw an arc across line l. Call the point of intersection D. This makes CD the desired segment. No straightedge is needed for this.

4.

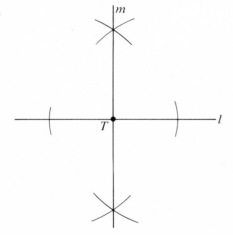

5. This is the same construction as Exercise 4.

6.

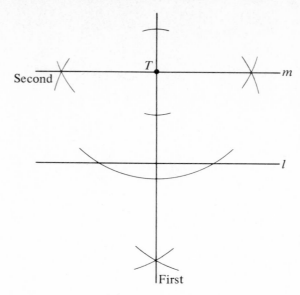

7. Construct a right angle and bisect it.

8.

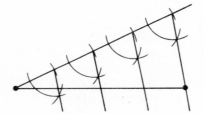

11. regular hexagon

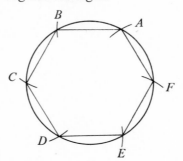

13.

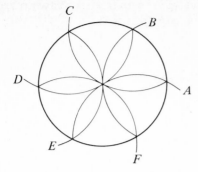

15. Draw two arcs: one from A and one from B, both equal to AB in length.

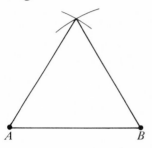

16. square

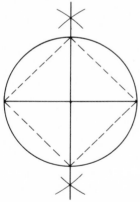

19. Construct the perpendicular bisector of each chord. Those two perpendicular bisectors will meet at a point, and since each one must pass through the center of the circle, the circle must be at the intersection of the two perpendicular bisectors. Why?

21. The solution requires some thought, but very little construction.

22. All such points are on the perpendicular bisector of the line segment AB.

23. First, mark off side III (segment *AB*). Then from *A* draw an arc of radius I and from *B* draw an arc of radius II.

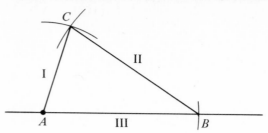

24. Copy the angle first.

Page 160

1. (a) +1 (b) +3
   (c) +3 (d) −3

6. Same as Application 15 of the preceding section.

Page 166

1. *w*: 40% A, 30% B, 30% C
   x: 70% A, 0% B, 30% C
   y: 0% A, 100% B, 0% C
   z: 20% A, 55% B, 25% C

2.

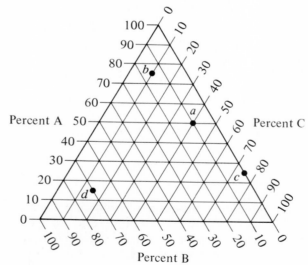

4. Only (b) and (e)

6. Inductive

Page 176

1. (a) yes
   (b) no
   (c) yes
   (d) no
   (e) no

2. (a) $a = 3, b = 4, c = 5$

3. (a) right, right
   (b) 500

4. $\sqrt{16,200}$ feet, or about 127 feet

6. (a) The integers are 1 and 2.
   (b) Let AB be 1 unit. Then mark off AC on the perpendicular, making sure that AC is twice AB. The hypotenuse BC is then $\sqrt{5}$ units in length.
   (c) $\sqrt{2}$

Page 182

1. (a) $C = \pi d$
   (b) $C = 2\pi r$

2. (a) π
   (b) 3.14
   (e) 9π, yes

5. (a) Radius is 1, since diameter is 2.
   (b) 2π
   (c) $\frac{1}{2}\pi$, 90°
   (d) π, 180°
   (e) 45°, $\frac{1}{4}\pi$
   (f) 60°, $\frac{1}{3}\pi$

1. (a) Note that the line begins at the origin, since the number of hours (x) cannot be less than zero.

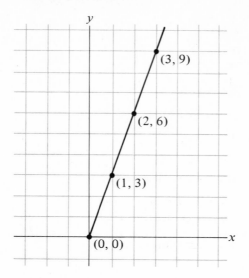

(b) (0, 0), (1, 8), (2, 16), (3, 24). Again x cannot be negative.

2. (a) He has moved neither horizontally nor vertically at the beginning.
   (b) $1\frac{3}{4}$, 3, $3\frac{3}{4}$, 4, $3\frac{3}{4}$, 3, $1\frac{3}{4}$, 0

5. (1, 2), (2, 1), (3, 2/3), (4, 1/2), (5, 2/5), (6, 1/3), (8, 1/4), (20, 1/10), (1/2, 4), (1/4, 8), (1/8, 16)

14. circle, center, radius

17. Release the most farthest from the center and the least near the center, because the area to be watered gets larger as you go farther from the center.

18. (a) (6, 1)   (b) 4
    (c) 3   (d) 5

1. (a) (0, 2)   (b) (−3, 0)
   (c) (5, 0)   (d) (0, 0)
   (f) (0, −4)

2. (a) 15°   (b) 1 hour
   (c) 8 A.M.

1. If two angles add up to 90°, then the sine of one of the angles is equal to the cosine of the other angle.

$$\sin \theta = \cos(90° - \theta) \quad or \quad \cos \theta = \sin(90° - \theta)$$

3. The larger the triangle, the better the approximation.

4. (a) 90°   (b) 50°

5. sine, 1062 miles

7. (a) about 10 feet

8. (a) tangent

9. approximately 180 feet

12. (a) 61 meters

13. (a) 1   (b) 1
    (c) inductive; 3 examples

14. (a) They are reciprocals.
    (b) They are reciprocals.
    (c) 1/3

Page 225

2. (a) The rabbit population increases. This causes the lynx population to increase. The increase in lynxes then causes the rabbit population to decrease. The decrease in rabbits causes a decline in the lynx population. The decreasing lynx population causes the rabbit population to increase.

Page 231

1. (a) I   (b) II   (c) III
   (d) I   (e) I   (f) II
   (g) I   (h) II   (i) III

2. (a) II   (b) II   (c) III
   (d) I   (f) II

Page 234

1. Closed curves: (a), (b), (d), (e), (f), (g), (h)

2. Simple closed curves: (a), (d), (e), (f), (g)

3. (c)   (e)

4. (a)   The line crosses the curve in 1 place for the first simple closed curve, 3 or 5 places for the second, and 5 or 7 places for the third.

    (b)   The line crosses the curve in 2 or 4 places for the first simple closed curve, 4 or 6 places for the second, and 6 places for the third.

5. Simply connected: (a), (b), (c), (e), (f)

7. (a) 2   (b) 3   (c) 4

Page 246

1. (a)   I: (iv), (viii), (ix), (x)   (b)   none
           II: (i), (vii)
           III: (ii), (iii), (v), (vi)

4. (a) 8   (b) 3
    (c) No, it has more than two odd vertices.

5. (a) $25 \cdot 51 = 1275$ (b) $40 \cdot 81 = 3240$
    (c) $30 \cdot 61$, $100 \cdot 201$ (d) inductive

    (e) $(\frac{1}{2}n)(n + 1)$, or $\dfrac{n(n + 1)}{2}$

6. (a) 1
    (b) 3

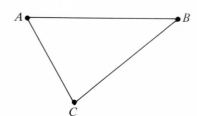

    (e) 45
    (f) Use 1000 for n. The number of lines is $1000 + 999 + 998 + \cdots + 3 + 2 + 1$, which is $500 (1001)$ by Gauss's formula. When multiplied out it is 500,500.

7. You should see that this problem is the same as Exercise 6, which deals with telephone lines. There are 15(31) = 465 games.

Page 254

3. Hexahedron: 12, 24
Octahedron: 12, 24
Dodecahedron: 30, 60
Icosahedron: 30, 60
The number of sides of all faces is twice the number of edges.

6. (a)   (b)

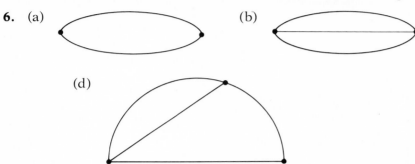

(d)

Page 263

1. Anxiety may create a feeling of moodiness. As the anxiety increases, moodiness increases. If the anxiety and resulting moodiness continue, there may eventually be an increase in frustration (perhaps the result of a nasty remark or some other "last straw"). The frustration increases to the point where it will suddenly turn to anger. The anger will release tension and may help produce a more neutral mood.

3. The dieter will fast until he or she reaches a point at which hunger is felt. The person will get hungrier and hungrier until he or she overeats in response to the unbearable hunger.

4. As the demand by investors for stocks increases, so does the price. Eventually the price gets high enough so that the number of speculators begins to increase. Increasing speculation can reduce demand and thus price. If that goes too far, a market crash results.

6. The fold is on the left.

Page 269

1. (a) $D(t) = 16t^2$
(b) $B(t) = 2^t$
(c) $E(n) = 4n$

2. (a) $f(t) = t^2$.

(b) $f(5)$ is the distance an object will fall in 5 quarter seconds.

(c) $f(5) = 5^2 = 25$ feet.

(d) $2\frac{1}{2}$ seconds = 10 quarter seconds. So we want $f(10)$, which is 100 feet.

(e) $f(0) = 0$.

(f) The distance the object has fallen at the instant it is released.

4. (a)

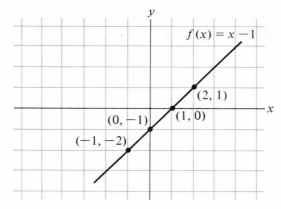

5. Triangle. $n = 3$. $D(3)$ h $\dfrac{3 - 2}{3} \cdot 180° = \dfrac{1}{3} \cdot 180° = 60°$. There are 60° in each interior angle of an equilateral triangle.

7. (a) $30, $45, $90

(b) $f(g(x)) = 2x + 1$
$g(f(x)) = 2x + 2$
$f(g(5)) = 11$
$g(f(5)) = 12$

Page 273

1. (a) t_1: Insert "and" between the first sentence listed and the second sentence listed. $S_3 = t_1(S_1, S_2)$.

(b) t_2: Add "Today" to the beginning.

(c) Don works and Ellen studies.

2. (a) t_1: Add "the lawn" to the end. $S_3 = t_1(S_1)$.

(b) t_2: Add "the" to the beginning. $S_4 = t_2(S_3)$.

(c) $S_5 = t_1(S_2) =$ Son mows the lawn.

(d) t_3: Add "His" to the beginning. $S_6 = t_3(S_5)$.

(e) $S_7 =$ The father mows the lawn or his son mows the lawn.

(f) The transformation eliminates the words "mows the lawn" from the first half of the sentence.

(g) Use $S_3 = t_1(S_1)$, $S_4 = t_2(S_3)$, $S_5 = t_1(S_2)$, and $S_6 = t_3(S_5)$ as in the earlier part of this exercise. Then use a new t_4, a transformation that inserts "and" between two sentences. Specifically, $S_7 = t_4(S_4, S_6)$. Next use the transformation used in part (f) to delete the words "mows the lawn" from the first half of the sentence. Finally, use a transformation that will change "mows" to "mow."

4. t_1: delete the phrase "to school."
t_2: change "walk" to "walks."
t_3: insert "walks" after "Ken."
t_4: remove "and."
Begin: Ken and Sue walk to school.
After t_1: Ken and Sue walk.
After t_2: Ken and Sue walks.
After t_3: Ken walks and Sue walks.
After t_4: Ken walks, Sue walks.

Page 278

1. (a) *xyz*   (b) *pmt*

2. (a) The ant climbs the hill.
   (b) Today is warm.
   Today isn't warm.
   Today is cold.
   Today isn't cold.

3. (a) *xu, xut, xw, xwt, yu, yut, yw, ywt, zu, zut, zw, zwt*

Page 281

1. (a) There is no break in the melody.
   (b) Yes, a musician might play a short tune without any interruption in his melody.
   (c) No, eventually the musician must take a break, if only for a second or two.

2.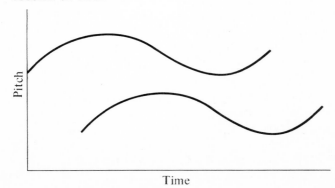

4. (a) C has the highest pitch, because the line representing C is the highest.

(b) B is the sound of longest duration, because B is the longest line.

(c) D is the loudest, because line D is the thickest line.

5. 517 cps

8. (a) harmonics   (b) inharmonics

Page 287

1. (a) $S(x) = 37$
$C(x) = 37x$
$D(x) = 52$
$R(x) = 52x$
$P(x) = 52x - 37x = 15x$

(b) $S(20) = \$37$
$C(20) = \$740$
$D(20) = \$52$
$R(20) = \$1040$
$P(20) = \$300$

(c) $465

3. (a) Overhead $= C(0) = \$100$

(b) Overhead $= C(0) = \$500$

(c) Overhead $= C(0) = \$0$ (no overhead)

5. Increases. Decreases.

7. (a) C. Quantity $= 300$, price $= \$9$.

Page 294

1. (a)

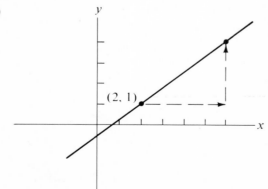

(c)

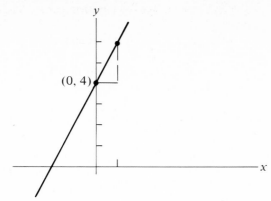

2. (a) $(0, 1)$, $(1, 3)$, slope $= 2$
   (b) $(0, 0)$, $(1, 3)$, slope $= 3$
   (c) $(0, -1)$, $(1, 4)$, slope $= 5$

5. (a) Slope $= 4$
   (b) Slope $= 3$

6. (a) $\Delta y = -3$, $\Delta x = +2$
   (b) $\Delta y = +3$, $\Delta x = -2$

   (c) Slope $= -\dfrac{3}{2}$

   (d) Both lines have the "same" steepness. However, a line with slope 2/3 rises as it goes from left to right, and a line with slope $-2/3$ falls as it goes from left to right.

   (e)

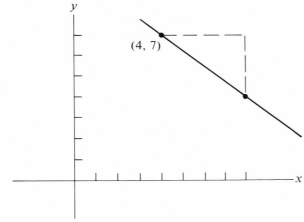

7. (a) The average speed is 20 miles per hour.

(b) $\Delta d = 12$ miles, $\Delta t = 4$ hours, average speed $= \Delta d / \Delta t = 3$ miles per hour.

Page 299

1. (a) 0   (b) 1
   (c) 7   (d) π

2. There is no limit. The terms are getting larger and larger without bound.

6. *In theory* the insect will never hit the tree. The sequence of distances from the tree is $1, \frac{1}{2}, \frac{1}{4}, \frac{1}{8}, \ldots$. Although the terms of this sequence get closer and closer to zero, no term of the sequence is zero.

8. (a) zero   (b) zero   (c) point

9. (a) 0

10. (a) 1.618033989   (b) 1.6   (f) 1.618033813

Page 311

1. The points are $(0, 0), (1, 1), (2, 4), (3, 9), (-1, 1), (-2, 4), (-3, 9)$.

2. (a) .21875   (b) .2734   (c) .46875

3. (a) 7/3, or $2\frac{1}{3}$ (c) 8

5. (a) $6x^5$

6. (a) $24x^5$

7. (a) $\frac{1}{3}$ (b) x^2
   (c) They are the same. The integral of $f(x) = x^2$ is $x^3/3$. The derivative of $x^3/3$ is x^2. In general, the derivative of the integral of a function is the original function.

8. (c) 96 feet per second

10. Both areas are 8 square units.

12. (a) $\ln 4 = \int_1^4 \frac{1}{x}\, dx$ (b) From $x = 1$ to $x = t$

Page 321

1. (a) $\frac{6}{6}$, or 1   (b) $\frac{0}{6}$, or 0

   (c) 0 and 1. If $P(E) = 0$, then E is said to be an *impossible* event, one that *cannot* occur. If $P(E) = 1$, then E is said to be a *certain* event, one that *must* occur.

2. (b) 36　　(c) 36 (from $6 \cdot 6$)　　(e) $\dfrac{6}{36}$

3. (a) $\dfrac{1}{12}, \dfrac{11}{12}$　　(b) $\dfrac{13}{52}, \dfrac{39}{52}$　　(c) $\dfrac{26}{52}, \dfrac{26}{52}$

　　(d) 1, 1

4. 0% = 0
100% = 1
It seems absurd to say that the probability of rain is zero (or 0%), since this means that it is *impossible* for it to rain. Unless it is indeed raining, to say that the probability of rain is 1 (or 100%) is absurd, since this means that it is certain that it will rain.

6. $\dfrac{1}{10} \cdot \dfrac{1}{10} = \dfrac{1}{100}$

7. (a) $\dfrac{3}{10} \cdot \dfrac{3}{10} \cdot \dfrac{3}{10} = \dfrac{27}{1000}$

　　(b) *Hint: P*(no hit the first time at bat) is $\dfrac{7}{10}$.

8. (a) $\dfrac{13}{52} \cdot \dfrac{13}{51}$. There are only 51 cards left for the second draw.

　　(b) $\dfrac{13}{52} \cdot \dfrac{12}{51}$. There are only 12 hearts left for the second draw.

10. (a) 1　　(b) 0　　(c) 1
　　(d) $\frac{1}{4}$　　(e) $\frac{1}{2}$

12. (a) $\dfrac{13}{52} + \dfrac{13}{52} = \dfrac{26}{52}$, or $\dfrac{1}{2}$.

　　(b) $\dfrac{4}{52} + \dfrac{12}{52} = \dfrac{16}{52}$, or $\dfrac{4}{13}$.

　　(c) $\dfrac{28}{52}$, or $\dfrac{7}{13}$. Be sure to read the explanation that follows this question in the text.

Page 330

1. $25.00

3. 7¢

6. $6.00

8. The expectation is $6.00, so $5.00 is a bargain. As a player you would have an advantage and should win money *in the long run* by playing this game.

1. 676,000

2. $\binom{9}{4}$

3. $\binom{100}{3} \cdot \binom{2500}{2}$

5. 256

10. (a) 131,072   (b) 1/131,072

15. (a) 576   (b) 13,824
    (c) 14,400

18. Order matters. 16–3–21 will not open a lock that has a combination of 3–21–16.

Page 347

1. (a) Mean = 275,   mode = 200,   median = 210.
       The median is best, since the mean is higher than four of the five data items and the mode is the smallest data item.
   (c) Mean $\doteq$ 70.7,   mode = 75,   median = 71.
       Both the mean and median are good choices. Perhaps the median is better because it is an integer. The mode is too extreme to be representative.

3. (a) Mean = 10, standard deviation = 4.
   (b) Mean = 7, standard deviation $\doteq \sqrt{5.7} \doteq 2.4$.
   (c) Mean = 7, standard deviation $\doteq \sqrt{8.7} \doteq 2.9$.

4. (a) 3.0
   (b) 1.83 (approximately)

6. The class may not be a normally distributed class. If the class has many smart students, then some will suffer by being graded according to a normal distribution. On the other hand, if the class has many less capable students and very few smart students, then some students will benefit from grading according to a normal distribution.

9. (a) Yes. Note that 10 is not a large standard deviation if the mean is 200.
   (b) No. A standard deviation of 100 is incredibly large for this situation.
   (c) The standard deviation indicates the average amount by which data items deviate from the mean. Consider the case of light bulbs with a mean life of 200 hours. If the

standard deviation is small (say 10), then bulbs may last, say, 190 hours or 210 hours. But on the average, their life will be within 10 hours of 200 hours. On the other hand, a standard deviation of 100 suggests that some bulbs may last 300 hours and others only 100 hours, and that on the average they tend to last either much longer than 200 hours or much less than 200 hours.

12. (a) 53 and 71   (b) 136

Page 352

2. (a) Z of the cipher corresponds to A of the normal alphabet.

3. (a) An enciphered F is a normal A.

4. (a) An enciphered H is a normal A.

Page 360

1. If wavy is assumed to come first, then the first site is 7. Then, either plain or straight could come next. You can't tell. Either way, the percentage of wavy decreases, and when the percentage of wavy gets down to zero, the newer pottery is up to 100% but has no chance of gradually decreasing to zero.

2. (a) Either short blade, long handle, thin handle *or* thin handle, long handle, short blade.

4. Plain: 7mm
Wavy: 3mm

Page 366

1. If you divide $F(5)$ by 641, the result is the integer 6,700,417.

4. First, side AB of $\triangle ABC$ is equal to side AC of $\triangle ACB$ because it is given. Second, side AC of $\triangle ABC$ is equal to side AB of $\triangle ACB$ because it is given. Finally, angle A of $\triangle ABC$ is equal to angle A of $\triangle ACB$ because it is an angle they share in common. This means that $\triangle ABC$ and $\triangle ACB$ are congruent.

5. (a) yes
(b) yes
(c) yes
(d) no
(e) no
(f) yes
(g) yes
(h) yes

1.
```
10   INPUT A, B, C, D
20   LET S=A+B+C+D
30   LET M=S/4
40   PRINT S; M
50   END
```

2. (a)
```
10   INPUT C
20   LET I=C/2.54
30   PRINT I
40   END
```

(b) Insert: 35   GO TO 10

6.
```
10   INPUT X1, Y1, X2, Y2
20   LET M=(Y2-Y1)/(X2-X1)
30   PRINT "THE SLOPE IS"; M
40   GO TO 10
50   END
```

8.
```
10   INPUT I, F, G
20   LET M=(F-I)/G
30   PRINT M
40   GO TO 10
50   END
```

2.
```
10   FOR N=1 TO 40
20   LET P=N↑2-N+41
30   PRINT P
40   NEXT N
50   END
```

3.
```
10   FOR X=0 TO 40
20   LET R=30*X-X↑2
30   PRINT "X="; X, "REVENUE="; R
40   NEXT X
50   END
```

5.
```
10   INPUT P, I, N
20   LET A=P*(1+I/100)↑N
30   PRINT A
40   GO TO 10
50   END
```

8. 10   INPUT X
    20   LET Y=(2*X−5)/(3*X+9)
    30   PRINT Y
    40   GO TO 10
    50   END

10. (a)   10   FOR I=1 TO 50
          20   LET A=I
          30   PRINT A
          40   NEXT I
          50   END

11. 10   INPUT A(1), A(2)
    20   LET D=A(2)−A(1)
    30   FOR I=3 TO 10
    40   LET A(I)=A(1)+(I−1)*D
    50   NEXT I
    60   FOR I=1 TO 10
    70   PRINT A(I)
    80   NEXT I
    90   END

17. 10   INPUT S
    20   IF S>400 THEN 50
    30   LET P=175+.05*S
    40   GO TO 60
    50   LET P=175+20+.08*(S−400)
    60   PRINT "PAY="; P
    70   GO TO 10
    80   END

Index

D

Dali, 136
Data processing card, 6–7
DATA statement, 384–385
Da Vinci, 136
Day of the week, 126
Decagon, 56
Deci-, 21
Decimal number, 23
Deciphering, 128
Deck of cards, 323
Deductive reasoning, 61
Deficient number, 100
Deka-, 21
Demand curve, 288
Demand function, 286
Derivation of a grammar, 276
Derivative, 307, 309, 313, 314
Descartes, 186, 252
Descriptive statistics, 341–342
Deterioration of buildings, 110
Dice, 318
Dieting, 264
Differential calculus, 307–310
Differential equations, 310,
    365
Differentiation, 307
DIM statement, 383–384
Distance between points, 204
Distance from Earth to Moon,
    210–212
Distribution of letters of
    alphabet, 350–351
Distributive property, 82
Divide a line segment, 148–150
Divisibility tests, 110–114, 118
Divisor, 97
Dodecagon, 56, 152
Dodecahedron, 251–252, 256
Drama and symmetry, 137–138
Duplicate a line segment, 151
Duplicate an angle, 146–147
Dürer, 38

E

e, 37, 302–303, 315
Earthquakes, 13–14
Eclipses, 3
Ecology, 37, 169, 222, 315
Economics, 285–289
Edges, 243, 252
Egyptian architects, 143–144
Einthoven's triangle, 154–163
EKG, 154
Elections, 15, 65
Electrical axis, 159–160
Electric generator, 223
Electrocardiogram, 154
Elementary sentences, 272
Elements of a set, 86
Ellipse, 194–196
Elliptic umbilic catastrophe, 265
Empty set, 86
Enciphering, 128
END statement, 374
English System, 18
Equilateral triangle, 49, 152,
    154, 164
Equilibrium, 288
Equivalence classes, 123
Eratosthenes, 98
Escher, 136–137, 238
Euclidean geometry, 136, 140
Euler, 41, 70, 242–243, 253, 268,
    364
Euler circles, 70
Exhaustion, 304–306, 311–312
Expectation, 329–332
Expected value, 329–332
Exponential decay, 35
Exponential growth, 35
Expressions in BASIC, 370–371
Eye, 52

F

Face, 252, 258
Factor, 97